Classic Northeastern Whitewater Guide

3d Edition

The Best Whitewater Runs in
New England and New York–Novice to Expert

Bruce Lessels

D1616997

APPALACHIAN MOUNTAIN CLUB BOOKS
BOSTON, MASSACHUSETTS

Cover Photograph: Scott Underhill
Back Cover Photograph: James Swedberg
All photographs by the author unless otherwise noted
Cover Design: Alicia Ozyjowski
Book Design: Carol Bast Tyler

Distributed by The Globe Pequot Press, Inc., Old Saybrook, CT

Library of Congress Cataloging-in-Publication Data
Lessels, Bruce.
Classic northeastern whitewater guide: the best whitewater runs in
New England and New York—novice to expert / Bruce Lessels. —3rd ed.
p. cm.
Based on: New England white water river guide / by Ray Gabler.
Includes index.
ISBN 1-878239-63-5 (alk. paper)
1. White-water canoeing—Northeastern States—Guidebooks.
2. Northeastern States—Guidebooks. 3. Rivers—Northeastern States.
I. Gabler, Ray. New England white water river guide.
II. Appalachian Mountain Club. III. Title.
IV. Title: Classic northeastern white water.
GV776.N75L47 1998
797.1'22"0974—DC21   98-13403
                                                        CIP

The paper used in this publication meets the minimum requirements of
the American National Standard for Information Sciences—Permanence
of Paper for Printed Library Materials, ANSI Z39.48–1984.∞

**Due to changes in conditions, use of the information in this book
is at the sole risk of the user.**
Printed on recycled paper using soy-based inks.
Printed in the United States of America.

10 9 8 7 6 5 4 3 2 1   98 99 00 01 02 03

Contents

Part Two: River Descriptions

VT/NH/Maine	Trip/Rating

Acknowledgments

This book was far from a one-man project. Thanks first and foremost to Ray Gabler, who is the original author of much of the information contained here. His meticulous research and clear, concise writing style made the first two editions classics. Thanks to the many people who checked river descriptions, provided level information, and confirmed the existence of gauges: Steve Brownlee and Heidi Krantz of Umiak Outfitters; Chris Koll, Janet Burnett, Tom Stevens, Mike Feldman, Mike Hornbach, Skip Morris, Bob Jackson, Jamie McEwan, Mark Ciborowski, Ed Chase, Jennifer and Mark Clarke, Doug Gordon, E. J. McCarthy, Tim Vogel, Matt Polstein, Charlie Walbridge, Dave Rose, Brenda Kennedy, Doug Azaert, and Bruce Weik. Henry Dandeneau from New England Power Company provided information about runoff patterns in different seasons. Thanks also to the many people who provided the photos that accompany the descriptions. Each photographer's name is indicated below the photos they contributed. Gordon Hardy and Mark Russell at the AMC were encouraging and understanding editors who helped me see this project to completion. Finally, thanks to my family for putting up with a year's worth of river-scouting vacations where five-hour drives were the main event on many days.

Foreword

This is the third edition of a book that I grew up calling "the bible." I read it in classes in high school, memorized river descriptions at night, and dreamed of paddling the tougher runs described in it. The quirky sense of humor that spiced up the river descriptions has endeared the original editions to boaters in the New England area, and the accurate, thoroughly researched information they contained made it the most respected whitewater guide to the Northeast.

Now, twenty-two years after I first bought a copy of "Gabler's Guide," I am honored to have a chance to add my mark to it. I have made changes that reflect the differences between paddling in 1981 and paddling in 1997. I have included new rivers to reflect boaters' changing tastes and the shifting patterns of whitewater boating in the Northeast. I have also reclassified some rivers according to the revised river-classification system.

It would take many years to run each of the rivers described within these pages at each of the levels described. Gabler's original text was very well researched and written, so rather than try to improve on it, I have simply modified it where necessary and added 42 descriptions. Readers of the previous edition will recognize many of the descriptions with slight modifications. I checked most of the rivers previously described by Gabler in the period from 1994 to 1997. To check some of the rivers I could not run, I have relied on other paddlers who know them well. Still other rivers I have scouted from the road. All the new descriptions were written from my personal experience on the rivers described, or from descriptions given to me by paddlers who know them well.

Limitations

The best-researched guidebook is bound to become inaccurate within months of publication due to the changing nature of rivers. For this reason, this book should be used only as a general guide. Be sure to confirm lines down rapids, the presence or absence of obstacles, and water levels before proceeding down any river. Whitewater canoeing and kayaking have inherent risks. If you are new to the sport, be sure to seek expert instruction from your local club or outfitter.

Several rivers described in this book are class V and above. These are runs for true experts only and should be attempted only by those with years of experience and at optimal water levels. If you need a book to show you where to go on this kind of water, you don't belong there.

Paddling Whitewater
in the Northeast

Of the three main regions of the eastern U.S., the Northeast has been the slowest to develop as a whitewater center. While West Virginia and the North Carolina/Tennessee/Georgia area have many rivers that are known nationally, such as the Gauley, Chatooga, Nantahala, and New, with a few exceptions the Northeast's rivers are not generally famous outside the region. Aside from the Kennebec, Hudson, and Penobscot, Northeast classics such as the West, Swift, Dead, and Deerfield are clearly as scenic and as challenging as runs in other parts of the East Coast, but they remain relatively obscure to all but residents of the region and surrounding states.

The reasons for this are many. First, and perhaps foremost, is weather. The season for boating in the Northeast is shorter than in the Southeast. Even dry-suit-clad paddlers rarely venture onto the rivers of the Northeast in the winter months, while from West Virginia southward it is not unreasonable to expect to be able to paddle twelve months of the year. Along with this is the generally lower rate of precipitation in the Northeast compared to the Southeast, and the paucity of large watersheds with free-flowing whitewater runs. Of the larger rivers in the Northeast, only the Hudson, Kennebec, and Penobscot provide any sort of regularly boatable water, and the Hudson is usually dry by the end of May. This situation has improved since the mid-1970s when the Kennebec and Penobscot Rivers began to be developed for commercial rafting with the emergence of The Forks in Maine as a major northeastern whitewater center.

The Androscoggin and Rapid Rivers have always had water releases through the summer, but the inaccessibility of the Rapid and the lack of challenging whitewater on the Androscoggin kept them from becoming major draws. In the late 1980s several groups of boaters independently "found" the Deerfield River in northwestern Massachusetts and southern Vermont. Of course, it had been discovered by hydro developers more than a hundred years earlier, but due to the irregular release schedule and the lack of water in the Monroe Bridge Dryway, it had remained a secret among the few local boaters who paddled it. When New England Power Company's (NEPCo) federal operating license came up for renewal in the early 1990s, a coalition of whitewater groups known as New England FLOW successfully lobbied NEPCo to set up a regular schedule of releases on the Fife Brook and Monroe Bridge sections.

Another trend that has driven the popularity of paddling (or been driven by it) in the Northeast is the increase in the use of such single-rapid sites as Cohasset, Blue Hill Falls, and Hartland Rapid. The popularity of rodeo paddling, where a boater extracts every ounce of acrobatic potential from a wave or a hole has been paralleled by the development of ultrashort rodeo boats that can make surfing even small waves and holes a challenge. By spending time at single-rapid play sites, boaters are perfecting maneuvers and challenging themselves more than ever before.

One result of this explosion in the popularity of whitewater boating has been that paddlers these days are more highly skilled than at any time in the past. It is not unusual for a motivated, somewhat athletic individual to start paddling in April and be running class III–IV water by September. Likewise, experienced paddlers are pushing the limits as never before. Such runs as the West Branch of the Penobscot, the West Branch of the Deerfield, and the Bottom Moose, which a decade ago represented the upper limit of the sport, are now being eclipsed by steeper, more technical and more dangerous rivers as equipment and skill improve by leaps and bounds. Paralleling this trend in recent years has been an increase in the number of deaths among top paddlers running cutting-edge rivers. Clearly the limits are being pushed harder than ever before.

The rivers described in this book represent most of the frequently paddled stretches in the Northeast. They range in difficulty from some that contain very little whitewater to experts-only runs that drop as much as 400 feet per mile. Obviously not all these rivers are suitable for all boaters. The selections are admittedly biased toward New England, since that is where the author's experience is most broad. Rivers from New York are also included to broaden the geographic scope of the book and to fill in where existing guides leave off.

For paddlers who are new to the region, a few Northeast superlatives:

The biggest water is found on the Kennebec, Penobscot, Dead, Hudson, Moose, Contoocook, and Lower Ashuelot.

The most-technical runs are the Boreas, Big Branch, Hubbard, West Branch of the Deerfield, Dunbar Brook, Cold River (Mass.), Pelham Brook, Roaring Branch (Arlington, Vt.), Pond Brook, Ellis, and Swift.

Rivers that usually run during the summer include the Kennebec, Penobscot, Dead, Deerfield, Hudson, Merrimack (in Manchester, N.H.), Sumner Falls on the Connecticut, Bristol Gorge on the Pemigewasset, Blue Hill Falls, Cohasset, Magalloway, Rapid, Androscoggin, Black (N.Y.), and the Falls Village–to–Cornwall section of the Housatonic.

Among the Northeast's classic runs are the Kennebec, Penobscot, Deerfield, Hudson, Swift, Pemigewasset, Rapid, and West.

The most-scenic runs are the Hudson, Kennebec, Penobscot, East Branch of the Deerfield, Saco, Gale, Rapid, Boreas, Dead, White, and West Branch of the Westfield.

Organization of This Book

This guide is essentially organized in two parts, and although the book is not intended to be a teaching manual, the first section is somewhat instructional. It consists of definitions and descriptions of terms that are used throughout the rest of the book and sets the stage for the river descriptions themselves. It is the place where explanations are given for precise meanings of particular words or conventions. Degree of difficulty, river level, average gradient, maximum gradient, and the use of gauges are among the topics presented. Without a clear understanding of these concepts, the river descriptions later in the book cannot be fully utilized. Discussions on safety, life jackets, hypothermia, and scouting, along with river hand signals, are also included, as is a chart that condenses the key characteristics of every river, so the reader may have easy access to a plethora of information. The chart is also useful for comparisons.

The second part of the book is the river descriptions themselves; included are explanations of starting and stopping points, specific difficulties to be found, gauge locations, and a paragraph or two giving an overall feeling for a river's character. A map accompanies each river trip so the reader has a pictorial as well as a verbal representation. Rivers are list-ed alphabetically by sub-region. The sub-regions are New York, Ver-mont/New Hampshire/Maine, and Massachusetts/Connecticut/Rhode Island. If there is more than one trip per river, trips are labeled A, B, and C, with the A trip being the closest to the headwaters. These descriptions are usually based on notes taken while the river actually was being pad-dled, although a few write-ups are the result of a scouting trip only. Descriptions are usually sequential and are presented just as a paddler would encounter the various rapids and obstacles. The directions left and right are always with respect to a boater facing downstream.

The descriptions are as accurate as possible, although the reader should be aware that nature changes with time and that these accounts should not be taken as absolute. Where deviations from the descriptions are found, use your own skills and judgment. No guidebook can substitute for these.

RIVER CHART

River	Trip	Difficulty	Driving Distance: Boston	Driving Distance: New York	In	Out	Trip Distance	Shuttle Distance	Avg. Gradient	Max. Gradient	Scenery
Ammonoosuc (NH)	A	II–III	160	330	River Bend	Pierce Bridge	3	3	43	50	Good
Ammonoosuc (NH)	B	I–IV	160	330	Pierce Bridge	Route 116	7	7	35	55	Fair
Androscoggin (NH)		I–II	225	380	Errol Bridge	Pontook Rapid	20	20	4	14	Good
Ashuelot (NH)	A	III–IV	100	205	Lower Stillwater	Gilsum Gorge	5	5	63	80	Good
Ashuelot (NH)	B	II	95	200	Gilsum Gorge	Shaws Corner	4	4	30	50	Good
Ashuelot (NH)	C	III–IV	85	190	Ashuelot	Hinsdale	3.5	3.5	52	80	Poor
Ashuelot— S. Branch (NH)		III–IV	75	225	Troy	Route 12	2.5	2.5	80	100+	Fair
Ball Mtn. Brook (VT)		III–IV	135	205	Metcalf Rd.	Jamaica S.P.	3.5	3.5	120	130	Good
Bantam (CT)		I–II	130	83	Stoddard Rd.	Shepaug River	5.4	5	25	32	Good
Bearcamp (NH)		II–III (IV)	130	325	Bennett Corner	Whittier	3.5	3.5	32		Good
Beaver (NY)	A	IV–V	330	310	Moshier Pond	Moshier Powerhouse	1.5	1.5	50		Exc.
Beaver (NY)	B	V	340	320	Eagle Pond	Soft Maple Reservoir	0.75	0.75	219		Exc.
Beaver (NY)	C	IV	350	330	Taylorville Dam	Belfort Pond	0.75	0.75			Exc.
Big Branch (VT)		V+	155	200	Big Branch Trail	Tabor Mtn. Rd. Bridge	1.3	1.7	400		Exc.
Black (NY)		III–IV	355	340	Watertown	Brownville	7	7.5	28		Good
Black (VT)		II+	160	240	Whitesville	Perkinsville	5.5	5.5	27	40	Fair
Blackledge (CT)		II	105	115	Route 66	Salmon River	5.9	5	20	30	Good
Blackwater (NH)		I–IV	85	260	Route 127	Snyder's Mill	2.5	2.5	24	50	Fair
Blue Hill Falls (ME)		II–III	230	450	Blue Hill Falls	Blue Hill Falls	100 yds.	n/a	n/a	n/a	Good

River Levels

Too Low	Low	Medium	High	Too High	Flood	Gauge/Dam Location	Level Info	Runoff Pattern	Date Checked	Page
	3.6		5.1		10	Bath		n/f	1997	44
	3.6	5	5			Bethlehem	USGS Web pg			
		5			10	Bath		n/f	1981	48
		4.5	4.5			Bethlehem	USGS Web pg			
	1500 cfs					Errol Dam	USGS Web pg	d/l	1997	52
3.6	4.1	5.5	7.5			Gilsum Gorge		n	1997	56
	4.6	5.7	6.5	7.5		Gilsum Gorge		n	1981	60
	2	4	6	7		Paper Mill		n/l	1997	63
0.5		1.5	3			Route 12		n/f	1997	67
	6	5	4	3		Rte. 30 Bridge		n/f	1997	71
	0.5					Rte. 47 Bridge		n/f	1997	248
0.5	1					Whittier		n/l	1997	74
		400 cfs				Moshier Dam	AWA Journal	d/r	1997	2
		200 cfs				Eagle Dam	AWA Journal	d/r	1997	4
		400 cfs				Taylorville Dam	AWA Journal	d/r	1997	6
						none		n/f	1997	77
	1500 cfs	2500 cfs	4000 cfs			Glen Park Hydro	518-465-2016	n/d/r/l	1997	8
0.5	1.5					Covered Bridge		n/d/l	1997	80
1.4	3					Comstock Bridge		n/f	1981	251
	3.8	4.7	6			Webster		d/r	1997	83
n/a	n/a	n/a	n/a	n/a	n/a	none	tide tables	t	1997	87

RIVER CHART

River	Trip	Difficulty	Driving Distance: Boston	Driving Distance: New York	In	Out	Trip Distance	Shuttle Distance	Avg. Gradient	Max. Gradient	Scenery
Boreas (NY)		IV–V	222	250	Route 28N	Minerva Bridge	7	11	45	100	Exc.
Chickley (MA)		II–III	108	170	Route 8A	Deerfield River	4.4	4	77	100	Good
Clear-Branch (RI)		I–II	60	170	Harrisville	Glendale	4.8	3.5	8	90	
Cohasset (MA)		II	30	220	Border St.	Border St.	100 yds	n/a	n/a	n/a	Fair
Cold (MA)		IV	110	185	Dead Man's Curve	Deerfield River	4.25	4.25	125	135	Exc.
Cold (NH)	A	II	110	225	S. Acworth	Vilas Pool	5.5	5.5	43	53	Good
Cold (NH)	B	II	115	220	Alstead	Drewsville	2	2	40	40	Good
Concord (MA)		III–IV	25	210	Bradford Industries	Merrimack River	1.5	1.5	35	44	Poor
Connecticut—Sumner Fls (VT)		III	135	240	Sumner Falls	Sumner Falls	0.25	n/a			Good
Contoocook (NH)		III–IV	90	240	Hillsboro	Henniker	6.2	6	23	60	Good
Contoocook—N. Branch (NH)		IV–V	90	225	Route 9	Steels Pond	9.5	6.5	42	250	Good
Dead (ME)		II–III / IV	260	450	Spencer Stream	The Forks	15	20	28	50	Exc.
Deerfield — East Br. (VT)	A	I–II	135	195	Somerset Reservoir	Searsburg Reservoir	6	7	40		Exc.
Deerfield—Searsburg (VT)	B	III	125	190	Searsburg Dam	Harriman Reservoir	4.5	4.5	50		Good
Deerfield—West Br. (VT)	C	V	135	210	Readsboro Falls	Readsboro	3	3	190	200	Fair
Deerfield—Dryway (MA)	D	III–IV	125	205	Monroe Bridge	Dunbar Brook Picnic Area	3	3	60	80	Good
Deerfield—Fife Brook (MA)	E	II–III	115	195	Fife Brook Dam	Zoar Gap	5	5	25		Exc.
Deerfield—#2 (MA)	F	I–II	100	185	Wilcox Hollow	Stillwater Bridge	7		17		Exc.
Dunbar Brook (MA)		IV–V	130	210	South Rd.	Dunbar Brook Trailhead	3	5	223	354	Exc.

RIVER CHART

River	Trip	Difficulty	Driving Distance: Boston	Driving Distance: New York	In	Out	Trip Distance	Shuttle Distance	Avg. Gradient	Max. Gradient	Scenery
Ellis (NH)		IV	165	345	Route 16	Harvard Cabin	3	3	87	100+	Good
Esopus (NY)		II–III	210	125	Rte 28	Phoenicia	3				Good
Farmington (MA)	A	II	110	155	Otis Bridge	Route 8	2.4	2.4	27	50	Good
Farmington (MA)	B	III–IV	110	160	Route 8	New Boston	3	3	75	100	Fair
Farmington (CT)	C	II–III	100	120	Route 189	Route 187	1.5	2	15	40	Fair
Gale (NH)		I–IV	155	310	Franconia	Ammonoosuc River	7.5	5.5	25	80	Exc.
Green (VT/MA)	A	II–III	110	200	Green River	West Leyden	6.5	6.2	30	50	Exc.
Green (MA)	B	II	105	205	West Leyden	Eunice Williams Road	5	5	31	40	Good
Housatonic (CT)	A	I–II	145	110	Falls Village	Housatonic Meadows S. F.	11	13	12		Good
Housatonic— Bulls Br. (CT)	B	IV (V)	160	85	Bulls Bridge	Route 7	2.5	2.5	45	100	Good
Hubbard Brook (MA/CT)		IV–V	115	130	Granville S. F.	Barkhamsted Reservoir	2.75	6	153	160	Exc.
Hudson/Indian (NY)		IV	220	250	Indian River	Route 28	12.5	14	29	80	Exc.
Kennebec (ME)		IV	260	480	Harris Stn. Dam	The Forks (Route 201)	11	11	23	53	Exc.
Lamoille (VT)		I–II	205	330	Slide Falls	Jeffersonville	11.5	11			Good
Mad (NH)		III–IV	135	325	Waterville Valley	Goose Hollow	6.3	6.3	85	100+	Exc.
Magalloway (ME)		III	240	395	Aziscohos Hydro	Wilson Mills	1.75	1.75	91		Good
Mascoma (NH)		II–III (IV)	125	265	Mascoma Lake	Lebanon	4	3.5	38	80	Fair
Mattawamkeag (ME)		III–IV	290	510	Mattawam- keag W. P.	Lower Gordon Falls	3.5	3.5			Exc.

River Levels

Too Low	Low	Medium	High	Too High	Flood	Gauge/Dam Location	Level Info	Runoff Pattern	Date Checked	Page
1.3	2.1	2.9				Route 16		n/f	1997	123
	4.3	5.6				Schoharie Res.	914-657-2388	d/r	1997	18
	4	5				New Boston		d/r/f	1997	288
3.6	4	4.5				New Boston		d/r/f	1997	291
	1.9	3.2				Tariffville	NE Riv. Forecast Ctr web page	d/l	1997	296
	0.5	1	2			Streeter Pond Br.		n	1997	127
						none		n/f	1997	300
						none		n/f	1997	304
	500 cfs	1500 cfs	2000 cfs	3500 cfs		Falls Village Hydro	860-824-7861	n/d/l	1997	306
	1	3	6 / 7			Bulls Bridge Gaylordsville	Waterline	n/d/l	1997	310
	3.9	4.5				Barkhamsted Res.		n/f	1997	315
2.8		5.5	6.3	7	10	North Creek	518-465-2016	n/d/r/l	1997	21
	1500 cfs	4800 cfs	7000 cfs			Harris Station	800-557-3569	d/r/l	1997	131
							Umiak Outfitters 802-253-2317	d/l	1997	137
	1.5	2.5				Upper Mad R. Rd.		n/f	1997	139
	640					Aziscohos Hydro	800-557-3569	d/r/l	1997	142
	340 cfs / 2.3	1000 cfs / 3.5		2600 cfs / 8		Route 4A/ Mascoma	USGS web pg	d/l	1997	145
	2000 cfs	6000 cfs		12000 cfs		Mattawamkeag	USGS web pg	n/l	1997	149

RIVER CHART

River	Trip	Difficulty	Driving Distance: Boston	Driving Distance: New York	In	Out	Trip Distance	Shuttle Distance	Avg. Gradient	Max. Gradient	Scenery
Millers (MA)	A	II–III	65	215	S. Royalston	Athol	7		32	60	Fair
Millers (MA)	B	III	70	190	Erving	Millers Falls	6.5	6	29	64	Fair
Moose— Lower (NY)	A	III–IV	300	280	Moose River Road	Fowlersville Road	8.2	11	40	90	Exc.
Moose— Bottom (NY)	B	IV–V	310	280	Fowlers- ville Road	Lyonsdale Road	3.5	3.75	80	120	Good
North—Halifax Gorge (VT/MA)	A	IV (V)	115	195	Route 112	Route 112	3	3	100	125	Exc.
North (MA)	B	II	105	185	Veratec Dam	Deerfield River	3	3	32	50	Good
Otter Brook (NH)		III–IV	85	210	East Sullivan	Otter Brook Park	3.3	3.3	80	100	Fair
Pelham Brook (MA)	V		115	195	Rowe Center	Deerfield River	3.25	3.25	188	315	Good
Pemigewasset— East Br. (NH)	A	IV	140	265	Kancamagus Hwy.	Loon Mtn.	2.5	2.5	72	80	Good
Pemigewasset— East Br. (NH)	B	IV	135	260	Loon Mtn.	Route 93	3.4	3.4	65	100	Fair
Pemigewasset— Bristol (NH)	C	II–III	105	300	Ayers Island Dam	Coolidge Woods Road	1	1	25		Good
Penobscot— West Br. (ME)	A	III	305	515	Seboomook Dam	Roll Dam Cmpgrnd.	2.5	2.5	15	70	Exc.
Penobscot— West Br. (ME)	B	IV–V	285	495	McKay Station	Pockwoc- kamus Falls	11	11	22	80	Exc.
Pond Brook (NH)		IV–V	155	280	Baker Pond	Wentworth	3	3	117	200	Good
Quaboag (MA)		II–IV	80	170	Warren	Route 67	5.5	6	31	85	Poor
Rapid (ME)		IV	235	370	Middle Dam	Cedar Stump	4.5	4.5	40	80	Exc.
Roaring Branch— Arlington (VT)		V	160	185	Kelly Stand Rd.	East Kansas	3.5	3.5	230		Good
Rock (VT)		III–IV	120	190	Williams- ville	Route 30	3.5	3.5	66		Good

River Levels

Too Low	Low	Medium	High	Too High	Flood	Gauge/Dam Location	Level Info	Runoff Pattern	Date Checked	Page
4.4	6	7				South Royalston		d/r/l	1997	319
2.9	3.5	4.8	5.5			Farley		d/r/l	1997	323
	3.5	4	6	9		McKeever	USGS web pg/ 518-465-2016	d/r/l	1997	25
	2.8		4	5		McKeever	USGS web pg/ 518-465-2016	d/r/l	1997	28
	3.4	3.8				Shattuckville	USGS web pg	n/f	1997	152
	3.6					Shattuckville	USGS web pg	n/f	1997	328
	1.5	350 cfs	3			East Sullivan Otter Brook Dam	USGS web pg	d/f	1997	155
						none		n/f	1996	331
0.2	1	1.5	2			Kancamagus Br.		n/l/f	1997	158
	1	1.5	2			Kancamagus Br.		n/l/f	1997	163
	500 cfs	1500 cfs				Ayers Island Dam	603-634-FLOW	d/r/l	1997	167
	400 cfs	1000 cfs	1500 cfs			Seboomook Dam	207-723-2328	d/r/l	1997	170
	1800 cfs	2400 cfs	3000 cfs			McKay Station	207-723-2328	d/r/l	1997	173
						none		n/f	1997	178
	3.9	4.4	5.5	6		West Brimfield	USGS web pg	n/l	1997	335
		1400 cfs				Middle Dam	800-557-3569	d/r/l	1997	182
						none		n/f	1995	187
						none		n	1997	189

RIVER CHART

River	Trip	Difficulty	Driving Distance: Boston	Driving Distance: New York	In	Out	Trip Distance	Shuttle Distance	Avg. Gradient	Max. Gradient	Scenery
Sacandaga— West Branch (NY)	A	II–III+	195	230	White House	Campground	8.5	12	36	70	Good
Sacandaga— Middle Branch (NY)	B	IV–V	205	240	Old Rte. 30	Old Rte. 30 Bridge	3.2	3.2	250		Exc.
Sacandaga— Middle Branch (NY)	C	III	195	230	Route 8/30	Route 30	2.7	3	43	50	Good
Sacandaga— East Branch (NY)	D	III–IV	195	230	Route 8/30	Route 30	2	2	55	80	Good
Sacandaga (NY)	E	II–III	225	215	Stewarts Br. Reservoir	Hudson River	2.8	3	15		Good
Saco (NH)		III–IV	170	335	Crawford Notch	Bartlett	6.5	6.5	40	60	Exc.
Salmon (CT)		II	110	120	Jeremy River	Route 16	3		27	50	Good
Sandy Brook (CT)		III–IV	125	125	Sandy Brook Rd.	Route 8 Bridge	3.3	3.3	80	100	Good
Shepaug (CT)		II–III	135	90	Route 341	Route 47	7	7	40	50	Good
Smith River (NH)		IV	115	310	Route 104	Old Rte. 104	2	2	90	100	Good
Souhegan (NH)		II–III	60	235	Greenville	Wilton	3.5	4	50	65	Good
Sugar (NH)		II–III	120	240	Newport	Route 103	2.5		34	40	Good
Swift (NH)	A	I–III	155	310	Bear Notch Road	Rocky Gorge	4	4	22		Exc.
Swift (NH)	B	III–IV	150	315	Rocky Gorge	Gorge	3.5	3.5	40		Good
Swift (NH)	C	IV	145	320	Gorge	Kanca-magus Hwy.	3	3	80	100	Good
Waits (VT)		II–III	205	285	Waits River	Route 25B	10	10	38	50	Good
Wardsboro Brook (VT)		III–IV	135	215	Wardsboro	West River	4.5	4.5	90	160	Good
Warner (NH)		IV	90	250	Melvin Mills	Warner	2.5	2.5			Fair
West (VT)	A	III	133	210	Ball Mtn. Dam	Jamaica S. P.	2.5	3.8	40	50	Exc.
West (VT)	B	II–II+	130	205	Jamaica S. P.	Townshend Reservoir	5.5	6	30	40	Fair

River Levels

Too Low	Low	Medium	High	Too High	Flood	Gauge/Dam Location	Level Info	Runoff Pattern	Date Checked	Page
	3.3	5			6.5	Hope	USGS web pg/ 518-465-2016	n	1997	31
								n/l	1997	34
3.3		5.5			6.5	Hope	USGS web pg/ 518-465-2016		1997	37
3.3		5	5.5		6.5	Hope	USGS web pg/ 518-465-2016		1997	39
						none		d/r/l	1997	42
0.5	1		4			Bartlett		n	1997	192
	1.4		3			Comstock Bridge		n	1981	339
2.1	2.6	3.3				Route 8 Bridge		n/f	1997	342
	0.5	1	2			Route 47 Bridge		d	1997	345
-0.5	0.5		1.5			Cass Mill Bridge		n/l	1997	196
0.5	1	2.5				Old Powerhouse		n	1981	200
1.8	2	4	4.5	5	10	W. Claremont	USGS web pg	n	1997	204
2.4		3.1				Bear Notch Rd.		n	1997	209
0.5	1.3	2	3			Gorge		n	1997	212
0.5	1.3	2	3			Gorge		n	1997	216
0.4		2				Route 25B Bridge		n	1997	220
						Route 100 Bridge		n/f	1997	223
						Laing Bridge Ln.		n	1997	227
	1000 cfs 6.3	1600 cfs/ 7.0	2500 cfs/ 7.7			Jamaica S. P.		d/r/l	1997	230
	1000 cfs/ 6.3		1600 cfs/ 7.0			Jamaica S. P.		d/r/l	1997	235

RIVER CHART

River	Trip	Difficulty	Driving Distance: Boston	Driving Distance: New York	In	Out	Trip Distance	Shuttle Distance	Avg. Gradient	Max. Gradient	Scenery
Westfield—Middle Branch (MA)		II–III	115	155	River Road	Littleville Dam	7	7	43	50	Good
Westfield— N. Branch (MA)	A	I–III	120	170	Cummington	Chesterfield Gorge	7.2	5.4	36	60	Good
Westfield— N. Branch (MA)	B	I–III	125	170	Chesterfield Gorge	Knightville Dam	9.2	16	12	40	Good
Westfield— N. Branch (MA)	C	III	105	160	Knightville Dam	Huntington	5.2	5.5	17	45	Fair
Westfield—West Branch (MA)	A	III–IV	110	145	Bancroft	Chester	6	6.3	50	100	Exc.
Westfield—West Branch (MA)	B	II–III	105	145	Chester	Huntington	7.5	7.5	30	40	Fair
White (VT)		I–II	145	255	North Royalton	Sharon	7.5	7.5			Exc.
Wild Ammonoosuc (NH)		II–III	155	300	Swiftwater	Route 302	2	2	90	100	Good
Winhall River (VT)		III–III+	140	220	Grahamville School	Londonderry Road	4.5	4.5	62	100	Fair
Winooski River (VT)		I–II	180	310	Dam	Waterbury	5.5	6			Good

River Levels

Too Low	Low	Medium	High	Too High	Flood	Gauge/Dam Location	Level Info	Runoff Pattern	Date Checked	Page
0	2.2 6.7	3				N. Chester Huntington	USGS web pg	n	1997	348
0 4.9	1	2 6.9				Route 9 Br. Huntington	USGS web pg	n	1997	351
0	1	2 6.9				Route 9 Br. Huntington	USGS web pg	n	1997	355
	4.5	5				Knightville Dam	USGS web pg	d/r	1997	358
5.1	5.9	6.9				Huntington	USGS web pg	n/f	1997	362
4.9	5.9	6.9				Huntington	USGS web pg	n/f	1997	365
			6			W. Hartford	USGS web pg	n	1997	238
1						Covered Bridge		n/f	1997	240
						Route 30 Bridge		n/f	1997	242
						none		n/l	1997	246

For more information on river levels, refer to the following web sites:
Northeast River Forecast Center: http://www.nws.noaa.gov
USGS web page: http://water.usgs.gov

PART ONE
River Characteristics

The terms described here are used in the River Chart on pages xvi–xxvii and in the specific river descriptions in Part II.

River

The rivers covered here are listed alphabetically. The name(s) of a river is that in common usage and the one(s) found on maps. The state(s) in which the river is located is indicated in parentheses.

Trip

If there is more than one trip reported for a given river, the trip closest to the headwaters is designated A; the next one downstream, B; etc. In cases where there are trips on different branches of the same river, the branches are listed separately and the trips are listed under the respective branches, e.g., the Westfield. Where only one trip on a river is described, no designation is given in the Trip column.

Difficulty/Class Descriptions

As one might expect, the difficulty of a particular trip is dependent upon many factors: discharge rate, gradient, complexity of rapids, and kinds of obstacles are among the more obvious. Any one of these factors could dominate and make a tough trip tougher. It is necessary to consider them all. How, then, does one objectively make a quantitative rating of difficulty? The answer is, it's not easy. However, over the years an international system of grading rivers or individual rapids, on a scale of I to VI, has evolved to be probably the most frequently encountered rating scale, and it is the one used in this guide. (There is also a rating system used by western guides using a scale from 1 to 10 that is usually reserved for large rivers having very heavy water, like the Colorado.)

An unofficial description of the six classes of rapids follows. It is a hybrid of many descriptions found in various publications. Although differing in words and some detail, most of them are quite similar overall. The following descriptions are intended to capture the spirit of the system.

Class I (easy). Fast-moving water with riffles and small waves. The current is usually smooth and can be easily neutralized by back-paddling. Passages are clear and the best course is obvious if obstacles are present. Risk to swimmers is slight; self-rescue is easy. Ledges and abrupt drops are less than six inches. Whitewater is not always visible.

Class II (moderate). Straightforward rapids with wide, clear channels that are evident without scouting. The rapids are moderately spaced, well defined, and may have numerous rocks and medium-sized waves. The current still can be neutralized by back-paddling and the crosscurrents are not strong. There are abrupt drops in straightforward chutes and over easy ledges. Swimmers are seldom injured and group assistance, while helpful, is seldom needed. The boater must think a little about the best route, which is easily discovered. Whitewater is usually visible.

Class III (moderately difficult). Rapids with moderate, irregular waves that may be difficult to avoid and can swamp an open canoe. The rapids are well defined, occurring frequently and often blending together. Passages can be narrow, and obstacles can necessitate frequent maneuvering; large waves or strainers may be present but are easily avoided. Strong eddies and powerful crosscurrents are often found, particularly on large-volume rivers. The best path is not necessarily obvious at first. Scouting is advisable for inexperienced parties. Abrupt drops are common. Moderate boat control is necessary and the boater must exert effort, both physical and mental. Injuries while swimming are rare; self-rescue is usually easy, but group assistance may be required to avoid long swims. Open boats may need to bail frequently.

Class IV (difficult). Class IV rapids are long and involved, requiring precise boat control. Channels can be very narrow and twisted, demanding fast maneuvering under pressure. Waves are large, irregular, and powerful. Hydraulics can be strong enough to hold a boat, and crosscurrents can overturn a boat. Abrupt drops over ledges can be large. Eddies have strong current differentials. Many times, only one route is practical and difficulties cannot be avoided. Rapids may require "must" moves above dangerous hazards. Class IV rapids should be scouted the first time. Instant, often irreversible, decisions are necessary. The paddler cannot see rapids fully from the boat, and the full current cannot be neutralized by back-paddling. Eddy turns become very important, as does a strong, aggressive attitude. Boaters are continuously working and planning ahead. The ability to perform an Eskimo roll is very desirable. Risk of injury to swimmers is moderate to high, and water conditions may make self-rescue difficult. Group assistance for rescue is often essential but requires practiced skills.

Class V (very difficult). Extremely long, obstructed, or very violent rapids that expose a paddler to above-average danger. Passages are very complex, with difficulty followed immediately by difficulty. Drops may be abrupt and very high, and may contain large, unavoidable waves and holes or steep, congested chutes with complex, demanding routes. Rapids may continue for long distances between pools, demanding a high level of fitness. What eddies exist may be small, turbulent, or difficult to reach. Visibility is usually severely limited by river obstructions, the extreme gradient, or large waves. At the high end of the scale, several of these factors may be combined. Scouting is mandatory but often difficult and the best passage is not obvious. Water level is critical. The utmost in skill and performance is required from the boater. Swims are dangerous, and rescue is difficult even for experts. A very reliable Eskimo roll, proper equipment, extensive experience, and practiced rescue skills are essential for survival.

Class VI (extraordinarily difficult). These runs exemplify the extremes of difficulty, unpredictability, and danger. The consequences of errors are very severe and rescue may be impossible. For teams of experts only, at favorable water levels, after close personal inspection, and taking all precautions. Even the expert paddler's life is at risk. This class does not represent drops thought to be unrunnable but may include rapids that are only occasionally run.

Much has been made in the past decade of the wholesale downgrading of rivers nationwide. What used to be a class III has become a class II, and yesterday's class V is today's class IV. The American Whitewater Affiliation (AWA) has led the charge to standardize rapid rating so that a boater traveling to another region can be confident that the class II he is used to running at home is similar to the class II rapids described in a guidebook to a new region.

Unfortunately, no consensus has yet been reached on rating rapids, although several points of agreement are clear. First, it is generally agreed that rapid rating systems should be as consistent as possible from region to region. Secondly, most paddlers seem to feel that rapid ratings should remain consistent over time—i.e., as the skill level of the general boating population improves, rapids should not be downgraded because they feel easier to the new and improved paddlers. Rather, those new and improved paddlers should acknowledge that they are now running more difficult rapids with relative ease. In addition, since the existing rapid rating system attempts to capture several parameters, including difficulty, danger, accessibility, and length, in a single number, many ratings will need further explanation to be truly meaningful to a paddler who is unfamiliar with a given rapid. Finally, at the top of the scale (class V and VI), there are not enough numbers to describe the range of difficulty now being run. As people run rapids previously considered unrunnable and reclassify them as class V, the gap between the most difficult class IV rapids and the most difficult class V rapids has expanded to the point where it is now much larger than the similar gaps between any other two consecutive ratings.

Given these concerns, I have tried to follow a few general guidelines in rating the rivers described in this guidebook.

1. I have chosen bench-mark rapids and rivers for each level of difficulty and have rated others by comparing them to these bench marks.

   Some examples are:

   Class II—Pontook Rapid at medium water, the Fife Brook section of the Deerfield except Zoar Gap at 700 to 1,000 cfs (cubic feet per second)

   Class III—Upper West River at 1,500 cfs, Zoar Gap at 700 to 1,000 cfs, Tariffville Gorge at 3.5, Poplar Hill Falls at 1,500 cfs

   Class IV—Lower Swift at 2.0, East Branch of the Pemi at 1.5, Kennebec Gorge at 6,000 cfs

   Class V—Penobscot Gorge and Cribworks below 3,000 cfs, Stairway to Hell, West Branch of the Deerfield except Tunnel Vision at 3.0 to 5.0

   Class VI—Tunnel Vision, Dead Horse Falls

2. I have kept the ratings consistent through time. I have tried to respect the ratings of the 1981 revision of Gabler and base ratings for any previously undescribed rapids on comparison with them.

3. I have decided to rate class V and VI rapids by comparing them to class IV drops and trying to maintain the same gap between IV, V, and VI as there is between II, III, and IV.

Since many rivers hold rapids of varying difficulty in a single section, I have used composite ratings as well. There are two types of composite ratings used in the descriptions. The first describes rivers that fall between two ratings. Thus, rivers such as the Esopus (II–III), the Rock (III–IV), and the West Branch of the Penobscot (IV–V) are too difficult for the lower rating but not difficult enough to warrant the higher rating. The other type of rating used here is one that describes a river that is primarily of a certain difficulty, but has a few rapids that are more difficult. The Bearcamp River (II–III (IV)) and Bulls Bridge (III–IV (V)) are examples. These rivers are commonly run by paddlers able to handle water of the first rating who walk around the few more-difficult rapids indicated by the rating in parentheses.

It is necessary to point out that not every individual characterization has to be present for a river, or rapid, to have a particular rating. The descriptions given by each classification merely indicate what might be present. Also, two rivers or rapids may be rated identically, yet be totally different in character. For example, there are rapids that involve a great deal of maneuvering—as on the Swift or West Branch of the Deerfield—but the water is not necessarily heavy. On the other hand, there are rapids where not many solid objects are visible, such as the Kennebec, yet the water formations could stop a train. Finally, combinations of these two types can be blended together to form what is usually encountered.

The ratings given assume the rivers are running at normal levels. As water levels increase, existing difficulties can be compounded, and new ones, such as strainers and floating debris, can be added, giving the river a much higher rating than what is stated here.

Driving Distance

These columns state the approximate one-way driving distance in miles to the general area of the put-in. Mileage is measured from the centers of Boston and New York. Distances were obtained using a computer mapping program or measuring road maps and following the most direct route using main roads where possible. When figuring driving times, consider the types of roads you will be traveling and your own individual driving style.

In

This column lists the name of a geographic location associated with the start, or put-in spot, of the trip. In most cases it is a town or community that may be quite unrecognizable as such from the road, such as Green River, Vermont, which consists of several houses and a covered bridge. Most of the smaller settlements do, however, show up on topographic maps. Some entries are route numbers; the specific starting spot can be found in the detailed description in part II. A good road map is of invaluable aid in finding the small, out-of-the-mainstream towns that defy detection or prompt the last-minute question, "Where the heck is...?"

Out

This column lists the name of a geographic location associated with the takeout spot.

Trip Distance

This column lists the trip length in river miles. For the descriptions in the 1981 edition, distances were obtained by measuring the lengths of the trips on a topographic map and using the scale factor to convert the measured distance to miles. For rivers that are new in this edition, distances were obtained by measuring the lengths of the trips on a computer mapping program. The trip lengths are down the middle of the river and do not take into account the distance paddled in maneuvering. These figures represent the minimum distance a boater must travel on the trip. If a river is particularly rocky, it is conceivable that the actual distance traveled could be significantly increased from the given value. Values for the shorter trips probably have a higher range of error than those for longer trips because of the method of measurement.

In determining how long your group will need to run a particular section, take into account the difficulty of the river and the number of portages (if any) that will be necessary. On most fast-moving rivers, you can count on moving at between 2 and 5 miles per hour. On very difficult class V runs, and on rivers that are very low or require frequent portages, however, it is not unusual to move at less than 1 mile per hour. All other factors being equal, trips of 2 to 4 miles are considered short, whereas 12 to 13 miles is a long voyage for a single day's outing.

Shuttle

This column gives the approximate one-way driving distance by a reasonable route from put-in to takeout. The routes are designed so that hard-surfaced roads can be used to a maximum. Those shuttle routes that are not obvious are easily found with the aid of a good road map. In several cases shuttle routes are detailed in part II.

Average Gradient

This column gives figures for the average gradient of the river in feet per mile over the total length of the trip. These values were determined by counting the number of contour intervals that cross the river on a topographic map in its path from start to finish, subtracting one, multiplying the result by the contour interval distance stated in the map key, and then dividing this product by the trip length. For example, on the 6.8 miles of the Upper Millers trip from South Royalston to Athol there are twenty-three contour intervals crossing the river, one interval for every 10-foot change in elevation for these particular topo maps. The river then drops a total of 220 feet in this distance, so the average gradient is 32 feet per mile.

Interpreting values of average gradient can be somewhat tricky. In general, the faster a river drops, the harder will be its rapids. However, there are enough exceptions to this rule almost to invalidate it. Not only must one consider how fast a river drops, but also, more important, how it drops. If the decrease in elevation is gradual, it is quite possible there will be only a fast current with no meaningful rapids, e.g., trip A on the North Branch of the Westfield. If the riverbed drops abruptly in discrete spots, waterfalls result, or, more commonly, ledges. Streams of the same average gradient can be completely dissimilar in character, depending on discharge rate, number of rocks, riverbed characteristics, etc. The Snake River through Hell's Canyon in Idaho forms, in one place, standing waves measuring 15 feet from trough to crest, yet the average gradient is only about 9 feet per mile for this section ending at Lewiston. Even with this relatively low drop, the Snake (a very large river) is constantly boiling and churning as if hydraulic engineers were busily heating selected columns of water. To give an example somewhat closer to home, the Housatonic between the mouth of the Ten Mile and Gaylordsville has an average gradient of about 16 feet per mile, yet there are two very heavy rapids in this section. The Snake and Housatonic are excellent examples that illustrate how a low average gradient can be deceiving. This type of deception, however, usually occurs only on large rivers.

Most rivers covered in this guide have a gradient that averages more than 30 feet per mile. This corresponds to a gradient of 0.57 percent or greater, whereas a drop of 100 feet per mile corresponds to a gradient of slightly less than 2 percent. To get a feeling for the magnitude of these numbers, consider Route 16 in the White Mountains as it comes south from Pinkham Notch. This road has a 9 percent gradient, as does the road that descends westward from the top of the Kancamagus Highway.

Maximum Gradient

This column gives values for the maximum gradient in feet per mile encountered in a particular trip over a distance of 0.25 to 0.5 mile or greater. These numbers were obtained by locating the section on a topographic map where the contour intervals crossing the river were judged to be the most closely spaced and then measuring the average gradient over this region in the manner already described. It is by no means the absolute maximum gradient to be encountered, since individual rapids will produce much larger drops. These larger gradients, however, are usually short-lived. In most cases, the maximum-gradient values were not obtained for sections containing unrunnable rapids.

The figure for maximum gradient, when used with the corresponding value for average gradient, can give a much better picture of the trip than either does alone. For instance, the trip from West Cummington to Cummington on the North Branch of the Westfield has a maximum gradient that is not so much higher than the average gradient, indicating a fairly uniform descent, which is the actual case. In the case of the Quaboag, the maximum gradient is almost three times that of the average, and one should expect a little excitement on some sections. Again, how the drop occurs is extremely important, and no figures will tell the whole story as well as a personal visit.

Scenery

Scenery is generally rated according to the amount of civilization visible from the river. Rivers surrounded by an untouched wilderness are rated excellent, and ones with increasing amounts of visible civilization are rated good, fair, or poor. A fair or poor rating usually represents an undesirable stream in respect to scenery and can indicate pollution in an otherwise scenic river valley, e.g., the Upper and Lower Millers. A few exceptions to this rating occur with such sections as Blue Hill Falls, which is very scenic because it is on the Maine coast, but is clearly also very civilized, earning it a good rating. The Hudson, Gale, Rapid, Kennebec, Penobscot, Green, White, Dead, Big Branch, East Branch of the Deerfield, Mattawamkeag, and Boreas are judged to have excellent scenery.

River Level

In this column an attempt is made to indicate how various water levels relate to a river's canoeability. Using the existing U.S. Geological Survey (USGS) gauges present on many Northeast rivers and a collection of hand-painted ones, along with flow levels provided by certain utility companies that operate dams on area rivers, a correlation has been made between a specific gauge reading or flow and the corresponding level of the respective river as it pertains to canoeing. Gauge readings are grouped according to six different classifications: TOO LOW, LOW, MEDIUM, HIGH, VERY HIGH, and FLOOD.

A gauge reading in the TOO LOW column corresponds to a level at which a significant number of rapids on the trip do not have enough water in them for comfortable canoeing. This means that boating such a river would result in a substantial amount of bottom scraping, canoe tugging, and cursing. At this level, the main skill required is to figure out where most of the water is and to try to follow it. Proper paddle strokes are difficult to execute, and the boat is many times propelled by pushing off the bottom or off the rocks. In rocky streams, this level is to be avoided. Since most paddlers don't care for this sort of exercise, TOO LOW has been rated rather conservatively. Some trips are passable at this TOO LOW level, but they are not enjoyable.

The TOO HIGH rating indicates a level that should not be run by the average boater; even the experts will have difficulty, and it is questionable whether the risks are worth the thrills. Make even a small mistake and the consequences could be serious. If you consistently paddle this level, either you are used to it and are very good, or your wrappings are coming loose. Only a few rivers have a TOO HIGH rating. Class II and sometimes class III rivers are occasionally washed out at this level. Rivers in flood stage are TOO HIGH.

The preferred levels are marked LOW, MEDIUM, or HIGH. LOW denotes a level that is pleasant but not challenging for a competent boater. On a class II or II+ river, LOW is a good level for beginner's instruction. The current is usually mild and the difficulties can be handled by a moderate amount of thought and action. Wider sections of river may be shallow at this level. MEDIUM levels are those where an experienced boater will find a very smooth and challenging run. The dangers involved are not great, but they exist. Currents can be pushy and disorienting. Playing and practice are frequently done at this level. Intermediate and advanced instruction can also be carried out at this level.

HIGH levels are the precursors of TOO HIGH. The banks are not well defined at this level; trees and brush are knee-deep in water, making eddying out difficult. Many eddies are washed out and those few remaining are difficult to negotiate. The current is frequently cluttered with such floating debris as trees, logs, bottles, ice (in season), and broken boats. In general, HIGH is a level only for those who know what they are doing. A mistake isn't necessarily disastrous, although good boat control is needed. Rescues at this level are very tough, and the normal difficulty rating is usually increased. A HIGH level on a class IV river can be dangerous, while on a class II river, it can be just a flush with many fewer resting or rescue spots than at lower flows. At HIGH levels, the river is definitely the master, and the boater is just trying to stay even.

In the previous edition of this guidebook, levels were rated on some rivers for open and closed boats separately. With recent advances in designs, technology, and skills of open boaters, this is no longer necessary; therefore, where earlier descriptions rated levels separately for the two boat classes, the levels in this edition are based on the old closed-boat levels.

The level ratings are designed for the competent paddler in a particular difficulty class. For instance, while a class II run at a HIGH level may be easy for a boater competent on class III rivers, to a boater used to class II water it will create a significant challenge and may be beyond their abilities. To be absolutely correct, a series, or range, of gauge readings would be appropriate for every level rating. In this book, only the highest reading observed or reported for that hypothetical range is listed for the TOO LOW, LOW, MEDIUM, and HIGH levels; for the TOO HIGH level, the lowest value is given.

As a practical example of the above convention, consider the Contoocook River trip from Hillsboro to Henniker. The ratings are as follows:

TOO LOW	LOW	MEDIUM	HIGH	TOO HIGH
5.6	7.4	9.0	10.0	10.0

At any gauge reading below 5.6, the river is too low for comfortable paddling. At readings between 5.6 and 7.4, the level will be in the low range; at readings between 7.4 and 9.0, the level will be in the medium range. Gauge readings between 9.0 and 10.0 represent a high level for the river. A level above 10.0 represents a run that's probably too difficult for all but the best boaters, since the river is in flood. Not all rivers have a complete set of canoeability or level ratings. Where there exists a void, the reader must use his best judgment.

Some runs described in part II have no gauges at all. On these runs, it is up to the individuals paddling the rivers to determine their runnability.

As with difficulty, level assignments are somewhat arbitrary and subjective. The basis for classifications made here is the author's personal experience on these rivers or the advice of competent paddlers. An effort has been made to exclude personal prejudice and to represent things as they are. Not everyone will agree with these ratings, but they can at least serve as guidelines. Considerable care has been taken to make the ratings consistent from one river to another. If you find the level ratings to be too high or too low on several rivers, then take that into account when using the ratings on another river.

Flood

This column gives the minimum gauge reading at which the river, or section of river, is officially considered to be in a state of flood. These values were obtained from the River Forecast Center in Hartford, Connecticut, which is a part of the National Weather Service. Flood stages are determined by on-site surveys in conjunction with local officials. Flood stage is that stage at which the overflow of the natural banks of the river begins to cause damage to any portion of the reach for which the gauge is used as an index. Not all gauges have been calibrated for flood. This level is to be avoided, since a boater will encounter difficulties not normally seen or previously experienced. Paddling rivers in flood is a matter of survival, not sport.

The readings for the Sacandaga River were obtained from the USGS office in Albany and are values at which they consider the river to be very high, although not necessarily at a level the Weather Service would consider flood.

Gauge/Dam Location

This column gives the locations for the various gauges or, where flow is measured at a dam, the dam locations. Locations usually are listed as the name of the nearest town or the name of the dam. Detailed descriptions of gauge locations are found in part II at the end of every trip description.

Level Information

With the advent of the Internet, the explosion in telecommunication technology in the last decade, and the relicensing of several hydroelectric dams causing utilities to do more for recreational river users, river levels are now available for many runs on a recorded phone message or a World Wide Web site. There is also at least one commercial service that offers river-level information. The beauty of this technology is that now you can plan a paddling trip from home with a degree of certainty never before possible.

Many of the rivers listed are controlled by privately operated dams. Where these offer river-information phones, the numbers are listed. Most of these are menu-driven systems that allow you to fine-tune your choices until you have found the information you seek.

The two web sites I have listed are the U.S. Geological Survey's Water Resources Information page, and the National Oceanic and Atmospheric Administration's Northeast River Forecast Center site. The USGS address-—http://water.usgs.gov/public/realtime.html—takes you to a home page that allows you to choose a state and check all the gauges reporting for that state. Most of those listed give not only gauge readings, but the corresponding flow in cubic feet per second as well. The Northeast River Forecast Center's site—http://www.nws.noaa.gov/er/nerfc/products/BOS-WRKFIA.TXT—gives only the gauge reading, making it necessary to know how this corresponds to runnability.

Waterline is a fully automated, national river-information hotline that reports more than a thousand different river levels and/or flows. Most Waterline reports are updated six to twenty-four times per day directly from the gauges via satellite. Readings are generally available on Waterline within two minutes from the time they are transmitted from the gauges.

To use Waterline you need to know the six-digit code for each site you want. These codes are available by mail, fax, or Internet. For codes by mail or fax, call Waterline's customer service number at 800-945-3376 and follow the instructions. Waterline staff is available 9:00 A.M. to 5:00 P.M. weekdays eastern time. To get the codes by fax, use the fax-back option to fax yourself a state code list. Once you have the state code list, call back and get any individual states you want. The fax system responds within two minutes of your request. The site codes and more information are available on the Internet at http://www.h2oline.com.

Once you have the site codes call either of Waterline's 800 or 900 hotline numbers from a touch-tone phone. Waterline will speak the current readings for the codes you enter. Waterline's 800 line, 800-297-4243, bills your credit card once you have set up an account. The 900 line, 900-726-4243, bills you on your phone bill.

Gauge Readings

The New England area is quite fortunate in having U.S. Geological Survey gauging stations on so many canoeable streams and rivers. Nearly every stream of medium size has a gauge on it, and only the smaller, more obscure streams lack any such measuring devices. Although these gauges were not placed for the purpose of helping itinerant canoeists and kayakers, they certainly can be of help in determining the level of a river if the trouble is taken to use them. In Massachusetts, Vermont, and New Hampshire alone, there are more than 200 of these gauges. Sometimes jointly owned and maintained with the U.S. Army Corps of Engineers, the Weather Service, or a utility company, these gauges often are located where only a minimum effort is needed to find and read them. Recognizable as tall, narrow, concrete structures by the riverbed itself, many of the gauging stations also have external staffs that are calibrated in tenths and sometimes hundredths of feet. These external staffs are quite rigid and extend into the water regardless of the level to allow a reading of the river's height to be taken. A completely automatic and separate measuring device inside the little blockhouse permits permanent record keeping. This permanent record is either punched out onto paper tape at regular intervals (digital recorder) or plotted continuously on a graph (analog recorder).

In some instances, the external staffs are not continuous, but instead are made up of several separate staffs situated in the general area. As the water level changes, one staff section may become completely submerged; it then becomes necessary to find the next-highest section.

Two types of external staffs are in use today. The newest model has an enameled section with a white background upon which the calibrations are printed in black. Older gauges, constructed from staffs of wood, have the calibrations in tenths marked by large metal staples. Both types can be mounted either vertically or on a slant. Some external staffs are attached directly to the gauging station itself; many can be found a short distance away attached to concrete walls, a tree, or a bridge. During snow and ice cover, some external gauges are quite difficult to locate even if their general area is known.

In recent years, the USGS has stopped maintaining several gauges, causing a loss of information for boaters. A group in the AMC has established the Gauge Restoration Project to replace these gauges where possible or install new ones. Some of the gauges indicated in this book were in bad shape at the time of this writing. Without maintenance, they may not last many more years.

With the application of new communication technology to gauging stations, often it is not necessary to visit the gauge site to obtain a reading. The USGS has automated many gauges so they can be read remotely. This information is available on their web site and is noted in the River Characteristics table. The name of this monitoring system is Telemark. This system was constructed to enable various government agencies to maintain constant and immediate contact with river discharge conditions, as is necessary in cases of flood, hurricane, or spring runoff. The network of gauging stations provides data that, when interpreted, allow the agencies to determine proper usage of existing flood-control facilities. The system can also be used for an additional purpose: to help boaters locate the best water.

On many rivers where official gauges do not exist, such as the Mad, the West Branch of the Deerfield, and the Wardsboro, local paddling groups have painted or installed gauges for their own reference. These are useful if you know how to correlate levels on the gauge to runnability. Obviously, these gauges do not report data remotely.

Runoff Pattern

This column gives a general idea of when you should expect a given river to run. Six categories are used to describe the rivers. They are: natural (n), dam controlled (d), scheduled releases (r), large drainage (l), flashy (f), and tidal (t). More than one designation is used for many rivers, such as n/l to indicate a river with a natural runoff pattern and a large drainage area, or d/r to indicate a river that is controlled by a dam and has scheduled releases.

The meaning of each category is as follows:

Natural (n): These are rivers with runoff patterns that are not significantly affected by reservoir storage. Many of these rivers have dams, but the dams are operated as run-of-river facilities, so they pass any water that comes downstream within a day or so. Few, if any, of these rivers run according to their "natural" runoff patterns due to the impact of development in their watersheds, which generally speeds runoff by creating fields, roads, and parking lots in the place of wetlands and forests.

Dam controlled (d): Dam-controlled rivers, for the purpose of this designation, are rivers that have significant storage capacity in reservoirs upstream of the given run or that have dams that create bypasses that are dry, or nearly so, under normal operations. While there are dams on nearly all the rivers described in this guidebook, many of them operate as run-of-river facilities, or are abandoned. Not all dam-controlled rivers have regularly scheduled releases, which leads to the next designation.

Scheduled releases (r): Rivers with scheduled releases must be dam controlled. Release schedules vary from a couple of days a year (the Millers and West Rivers) to 100 or more days throughout the boating season (the Kennebec, Penobscot, and Deerfield). Schedules can generally be obtained by calling the agency or company that operates the dam.

Large drainage (l): This indicates a river that holds its water well. Generally, large drainage areas contain enough marshes and wetlands to buffer seasonal variations in precipitation to a greater or lesser degree. A good example of this is the Mattawamkeag in Maine. The longest free-flowing river in the state, it has such a large area of marshes upstream of the section described in this book that it is usually runnable throughout the summer. On a smaller scale, the lower Ashuelot tends to hold water longer than other area rivers, but within a week or so of a heavy summer rain, it will be back down to an unrunnable level.

Flashy (f): Flashy rivers respond quickly to precipitation or melting snow. They may rise several feet or more in as little as a couple of hours and drop as quickly. Rivers with this designation tend to have small, steep watersheds that are characterized by a thin layer of topsoil on bedrock. To run some of these rivers, you must be on the river within a couple of hours of a heavy rain before the river returns to a trickle. Be especially cautious on these rivers; while you're paddling they can rise from a manageable level to a level that is out of control.

Tidal (t): Tidal rivers don't depend on precipitation for their water. They have a much larger reservoir from which to draw (the Atlantic Ocean in the case of East Coast rivers). These runs follow the schedules of the tides, which are generally available in local newspapers. These are the places to go for a whitewater fix in the driest of dry spells.

A few sections of rivers are designated as both natural (n) and dam controlled (d), which may seem to be a contradiction in terms. On these sections, some of the run is dam controlled (in most cases, diverted), and some of it is not affected by the dam, but the overall runoff pattern is not significantly affected by a dam. One example of this is the Concord River in Lowell. The amount of water feeding this section overall is determined by natural runoff and is not affected by any dams, but one rapid (Wamesit Falls) is bypassed under normal operations, making it unrunnable except when there is too much water for the hydro station to divert or when the station is turned off for a scheduled release or for maintenance.

Date Checked

This column indicates the year in which the river description was last confirmed—either by running the river, driving the river, or having a paddler who had recently run the river review and update the description.

Rating Tables

One of the most important characteristics of a gauging station is the rating table that relates the actual flow discharge to the gauge reading. Rating tables for rivers with USGS gauges are available from the USGS. They allow one to determine the actual (or approximate) amount of water flowing in a particular section of river if the gauge reading is known. It is the amount of water flowing in a river that is the important factor here, not the arbitrary scale reading of the gauge. It is best to think in terms of cubic feet per second (cfs) if possible, as this is the most widely used scale for measuring flow. Since gauges are on all sorts of rivers with different riverbed characteristics, the same readings on different gauges are completely independent of one another. Each river needs its own rating table, and, as riverbeds change, so must the rating tables if they are to be current. All rating tables are provisional and may change as riverbeds shift or gauges move. Always rely on your judgment when considering a given level's runnability.

A second reason for consulting rating tables is to allow a boater to compare a familiar river with a less familiar one. Knowing the average sizes or cross-sectional areas of two rivers, it is possible to determine a necessary gauge reading on the unfamiliar river for a particular type of boating. An example should make this clear. Let us assume that the West Branch of the Westfield and the Saxtons River are roughly the same size and have the same gradient. Let us assume also that 800 cfs makes the Westfield an enjoyable run. A similar amount of water in the Saxtons should then produce a similar type of trip. By using the Saxtons River rating table to match discharges, one finds that a gauge reading of 5.7 is needed on the Saxtons.

The discharge rate is roughly proportional to the square or cube of the gauge reading. This is due to two closely related facts. First, the velocity of water in a river increases rapidly as the gauge reading, or depth, increases. Second, it takes more water to add one inch of depth to a river when that river is at a high level than when it is at a low level, because the banks slope outward and do not go straight up. The reader should realize that at higher levels, a small increase of 0.1 or 0.2 feet in a gauge reading means considerably more water than the same increase at low river levels. To illustrate, let us consider the Contoocook River as a specific example. The difference in discharge rates between levels of 6.5 feet and 7.0 feet is 228 cfs, whereas it is 736 cfs between 9.5 feet and 10.0 feet. Even though the change in gauge levels is 0.5 feet in both cases, there is much more water involved when the river is high compared to when it is low.

Variation of Flow with Season

Discharge rates vary with season and the location of the river. As expected, the largest flow is during the spring runoff, and the peak discharges of rivers will vary from one another because of their different locations. Southernmost rivers have high water prior to northern rivers, which makes sense because the north stays colder longer, delaying the spring thaw. The next period of highest flow occurs in the late fall when the discharges are maybe one-fourth to one-third of the spring peaks. Late fall is not only a period of generally moderate to high rainfall, but also the leaves are gone from the trees and grasses and weeds are dormant, leaving any rainfall that does occur to go straight into the rivers without being sucked up by the vegetation. This effect is significant enough that a small stream such as the Cold River in Massachusetts often will rise to a runnable level with a 2-inch rainstorm in the late fall, winter, or early spring, but the same rain event in the summer will cause a barely noticeable rise in its level, since most of the water is intercepted by the tree roots before it gets to the river.

Late fall can be one of the nicest seasons for whitewater boating in the Northeast. The days can still be mild, the rivers at runnable levels, and the crowds gone from the more popular runs. Also, the water will be warmer in the fall than in the spring because rain rather than cold snow runoff brings the rivers up.

One last point to make is that it is possible to create a paddling schedule where the probability of catching a seasonal river at its peak flow can be maximized. Each river has at least a two- or three-week period where the probability (based on historical data) of finding good water is high, and that's when those canoeing trips can be scheduled with a reasonable chance of success. Of course, there are several rivers in the Northeast where dams even out the natural flow curves, making paddling possible at times of year when the rivers otherwise would be dry. On these rivers, trips can be scheduled with a high degree of certainty, although even on dam-controlled runs, drought or mechanical failure at the dam can cause the releases to be canceled.

PART TWO
Paddling Safety

Although it appears nearly last in this discussion, safety should be prac- ticed first on river trips. There is little doubt that whitewater boating can be dangerous. The only reason more individuals don't sustain serious injury is due to education by organized boating groups, outfitters, and clubs. Most tragic accidents on whitewater involve the violation of a major safety rule—paddling without a life jacket, in flood stage, above one's ability, in cold water, etc.

Through many years of experience, boaters of the American White-water Affiliation (AWA) have developed a formal safety code, which covers the points of safety to be observed. It was first adopted in 1959 and most recently revised in 1989. Boaters should become familiar with the AWA Safety Code. Obtain a copy of the AWA Safety Code by writing to the AWA at PO Box 636, Margaretville, N.Y., 12455 or by visiting their web page at http://www.awa.org.

Cold Water

A swim that would be routine in the summer can be very serious in the fall, winter, or early spring when the temperatures of both water and air are much lower. The effect of sudden immersion in water even as warm as 60° F can be temporary paralysis and gasping for air that can hamper your ability to deal with the other hazards encountered in whitewater. Your body loses heat 240 times faster in water than in air and several times faster in wind than in calm air. Cold water can lower your core tempera- ture in a matter of minutes, making you unable to help yourself or others. Your body reacts to cold by shutting off circulation to the least-needed parts first and concentrating circulation in the core where the vital organs are located. Thus, your fingers and toes get cold first, then your legs and arms, and finally, your torso and head. This condition is called hypothermia and can occur not only in obviously extreme weather, but also in remarkably warm weather as well.

The body's normal temperature is 98.6ºF. Above about 95ºF, a mildly hypothermic victim will shiver. This is the body's natural attempt to warm itself through muscle contractions. At this stage, victims may slur their speech and lose manual dexterity. Below about 95ºF shivering stops, and the victim's mental state starts to decrease. Confusion sets in and coordination will be impaired. When the core temperature drops below 90ºF muscle rigidity replaces shivering. Movements become erratic or jerky. Mental state is severely impaired. From about 86ºF to 80ºF, hypothermia victims become unresponsive or unconscious. Their muscles remain rigid. Cardiac arrhythmias may develop. At 80ºF and below, unconsciousness sets in. The heartbeat becomes erratic; pupils dilate and don't respond to light. Death is imminent.

Despite the very grim progression of hypothermia, it manifests itself subtly at first. Everyone has experienced shivering either on a river or on a ski slope, waiting for a bus, or shoveling snow. On a river trip, however, since you are often far from a heated space like a car or a house, special caution must be used to prevent hypothermia from developing, and once the early warning signs become apparent, it must be treated aggressively.

Preventing hypothermia is not difficult in principle. It involves simply dressing properly for the conditions, eating enough calories to keep your body fueled, and drinking enough liquids to keep your body hydrated.

Some basic principles of dressing for paddling are:

1. Don't wear cotton. Cotton fibers absorb water and keep it next to your skin, making you colder rather than warmer. Polypropylene, wool, Lycra, neoprene, and nylon pile make effective nonabsorbent insulating layers.

2. Dress in layers. Start with a wicking layer next to your skin to draw perspiration away from your body. Your second layer should be an insulating layer. A pile sweater or an old wool sweater works well here. Pile union suits are available for wear under a dry suit and are excellent as a first or second layer. The top layer should provide wind and water protection. A waterproof paddling jacket and/or pants or a dry suit works well as a top layer.

3. Wear a wetsuit or dry suit when conditions warrant. When there is a possibility of swimming in cold water and/or the air is cold or the day is windy, nothing beats a wetsuit or drysuit for adding an

extra layer of warmth. A wetsuit provides not only insulation, but also wind resistance. A dry suit does not provide much in the way of insulation itself, but by keeping your insulating layers dry, it adds significantly to your body's ability to tolerate cold weather and water conditions.

4. Keep your head warm. You lose 70 percent of your heat through your head. Simply wearing a hat can contribute significantly to your ability to stay warm. Pile or neoprene helmet liners are excellent head warmers. Helmets also provide significant warmth—those without drain holes and with a continuous foam lining are the warmest. For the budget-conscious paddler, a swimmer's bathing cap will do a tremendous amount to help keep your head warm.

5. Wear wind protection. Wind draws heat away from your body at an amazing rate. A simple paddle jacket or other type of nylon shell often can mean the difference between a comfortable paddle and a miserable survival experience.

6. Bring extra dry layers in a dry bag. Since there's always the possibility of getting wet, get in the habit of bringing a spare dry layer of fleece or polypropylene on the river. At the first sign that a paddler is getting cold, have him change into these dry clothes to prevent him from progressing further into hypothermia.

7. To keep your body fueled, bring along plenty of such high-energy foods as energy bars, gorp, or other carbohydrates that are quickly digested. Hydration is the easiest of all: drink plenty of water, juice, or other nonalcoholic liquid. This may not be obvious when the air temperature is low, but drinking liquids is important in any weather conditions to prevent dehydration, which can contribute to hypothermia. Note that drinking alcohol actually can exacerbate dehydration and hypothermia, since your body uses up water to metabolize the alcohol and alcohol causes your surface blood vessels to dilate. Needless to say, alcohol and paddling are a dangerous combination.

Treating hypothermia in the field is difficult, since ultimately you must remove the victim from the environment that is cooling his core temperature. With mild hypothermia victims, treatment involves replacing wet layers with dry layers. For this reason, always bring along a spare layer of fleece, wool, or synthetic clothing in a dry bag. If this doesn't warm the victim, you must actively rewarm them by involving them in physical activity or putting them in a car with the heat turned on, near a fire, or using heat packs placed around the head and neck, under the arms, and in the crotch area to gradually rewarm their core. Remember, the goal is to rewarm the core first and the extremities last.

In cases of moderate hypothermia, handle the victim gently. Any rough handling can cause ventricular fibrillation. At core temperatures below 95°F the body cannot generate enough heat to rewarm itself. These victims must be rewarmed slowly to prevent cold blood in the extremities, which has become more acidic, from being introduced too quickly into the core where it can both cool the core and cause cardiac arrest. Physical activity may not be tolerated by a moderately hypothermic victim, so rewarming must be done by using such external sources of heat as a campfire, car heater, or other bodies wrapped together in a sleeping bag. More so than with the mildly hypothermic victim, it is important to rewarm the core before the extremities.

Severely hypothermic victims with core temperatures below 90°F may appear dead. Their skin may feel cold to the touch and no heart beat may be discernible, even after feeling for a pulse for a minute or more. These victims need to be stabilized and transported to a medical facility as quickly as possible. Steps should be taken to minimize further heat loss, but field rewarming will not be successful. If the victim's heart has stopped (remember that it may be especially difficult to feel a pulse in a severely hypothermic victim), CPR should be started.

Paddling in cold conditions puts more pressure on boaters in many ways. Rescues become complicated by the shortened window of time you may have before both victims and rescuers succumb to the progressively more debilitating stages of hypothermia. It may be prudent to abandon a pinned boat rather than taking the extra half-hour needed to pull it off the rock if a paddler is showing signs of hypothermia. A single swim during an early-season trip may be enough for an individual or the entire group to call it a day, whereas the same swim, taken during the warmer summer boating season would require a mere five-minute delay for the swimmer to gather his equipment and get back in his boat and on the way.

PFDs

Anyone who has been thrown suddenly and unexpectedly from a boat into the water knows what a shock it can be—complete disorientation, momentary paralysis due to an instantaneous change in temperature, and realization that you must now think actively about how and when to breathe. The first few seconds in the water are panic as you try to reorient and to fight your way back to the surface. Occasionally the direction of the surface is none too clear, and, since you haven't prepared for this dunking, your air supply seems to be used up at an unusually rapid rate, causing even deeper panic. This picture is true for all sorts of boaters, from those who chase the America's Cup to those who go out on a lake for a Sunday paddle to whitewater canoeists. Whitewater paddlers, however, have a problem that is somewhat peculiar to their sport: Once you manage to resurface, the current thrashes you about like a toy; you may be bashed against rocks, tree branches, your own boat, floating debris, and perhaps even some ice. In addition, if the current has any force to it, you'll be intermittently submerged as standing waves wash over your head and holes rotate you around and around like a washing machine. Now, this is all aggravation you don't really need, and the point is a rather obvious one. Since you have a whole host of problems to contend with while in the water, you don't want to exacerbate the situation by having to worry about your natural buoyancy or lack of it. This is the single best argument for wearing life jackets when paddling whitewater. Among all your other problems, you don't have to worry about buoyancy or your ability to resurface if circumstances permit.

Competent whitewater paddlers have a simple rule about life jackets—they don't paddle without them. No exceptions. Jackets should always be used, especially on class I and II water, even though it doesn't look menacing. People who boat class III and IV water are usually well aware of potential dangers, but easier water can lull you into a false sense of security—that is, until you go in and get swept downstream. Nobody is immune to problems in the water; adults and children alike have the same basic obstacles to contend with, so everybody should be properly equipped. A life jacket does not guarantee your safety, but it will help. If you have ever been underwater and felt the tug of your jacket pulling you to the surface, you'll never again question its usefulness, even though it sometimes seems a nuisance and a bother.

There are two other important aspects about life jackets that are seldom emphasized. The first is their ability to keep you warm, and the second is their capacity to cushion collisions. If you have a vest-type jacket with flotation on both front and back, you have another layer of insulation between you and the environment, whether it be gaseous or liquid. The vest models surround the core part of your body, acting as a kind of sleeveless wetsuit top that gives added protection against hypothermia or plain old chills. Some jackets are comfortable enough to be worn around camp or even while sleeping on a particularly cold night. Depending on the fit and style of your jacket, it can add measurably to your warmth.

If you make the transition from boater to river swimmer, life jackets also provide extra padding when you come into contact with rocks, ledges, trees, etc. These contacts are frequently forceful, made without reference to proper etiquette, and broken ribs and bruises result. With a jacket on, the impact doesn't hurt as much, and again, if there's padding on the back, you're protected all around while being dragged over a boulder garden.

In 1973 Congress passed the Boating Safety Act, which gave the Coast Guard jurisdiction over recreational boaters on all navigable inland waterways. One of the results is that the Coast Guard now publishes and enforces regulations concerning life jackets. These include the construction of jacket materials, the jacket's performance, and the carrying of jackets while boaters are on the water. The Coast Guard's jurisdiction encompasses boaters of all types, not just whitewater paddlers. In fact, whitewater paddlers represent a rather small and specialized subgroup of boaters. The Coast Guard has classified life jackets into five groups, which are described in their publication "Federal Requirements for Recreational Boaters" (CG-290), and they now use the term personal flotation device (PFD) to describe not just life jackets but other devices not designed to be worn by the user as well.

The Coast Guard publication continues: "All PFDs that are presently acceptable on recreational boats fall into one of these designations. All PFDs shall be U.S. Coast Guard approved, in good and serviceable condition, and of an appropriate size for the persons who intend to wear them.

"All recreational boats less than 16 feet in length and all canoes and kayaks of any length must have one Type I, II, III, or IV PFD aboard for each person. Type I, II, and III devices must be readily accessible to all persons on board. The Type IV device shall be immediately available for use. PFDs must be Coast Guard approved."

The Coast Guard, therefore, is the dominant influence on the manufacturing quality of PFDs in the United States. For instance, the Coast Guard must approve not only the finished product, but also the basic raw materials, to ensure they will withstand rough use. As a rule, this is something the actual user cannot or will not do. A whitewater paddler is usually very critical in choosing a life jacket. Most people are not.

Boaters should not take these regulations lightly. First, they make overall sense. There are situations peculiar to individual sports, such as whitewater boating, where the definitions of the PFDs don't work or don't seem logical, but in general the right idea is there. Second, people in the Northeast have been stopped and fined for not having Coast Guard–approved jackets even though they were wearing life jackets. With several high-quality jackets now made overseas and approved by foreign equivalents of the Coast Guard, such as the British Canoe Union, this has been an issue on some rivers where enforcement of Coast Guard regulations is strict. Use your best judgment, and no matter what, don't get on the river without an appropriate life jacket.

Helmets

Helmets used to be worn only by closed-boaters, and before that only by boaters considered "safety freaks," but it is now well-accepted wisdom that not wearing a helmet on whitewater of class II or greater difficulty in a closed or open boat is an indication of how little there is to protect. Helmets cushion a paddler's head against bumps with rocks, trees, parts of the boat or paddle, and other paddlers. The few instances of boaters flipping and being knocked unconscious justify wearing a helmet, despite any discomfort they may cause.

There are several styles on the market today, ranging from lightweight models with cage-style suspension to heavy-duty brainbuckets that resemble motorcycle helmets. Choose yours based on the water you'll be running and the probability of close encounters with rocks—but wear one!

Dams and Other Man-Made Hazards

Although dams aren't as plentiful as rocks on northeastern rivers, if you paddle here for any length of time you'll soon find yourself approaching one. Many dams have been built for the power or processing needs of local industry. You'll find dams on all sorts of rivers and in various stages of function and repair. There are basically two types of dams; each has its own peculiarities and dangers. The first type has water going under the dam, the second has water going over the top. The latter dams are more numerous and more dangerous.

Dams that can regulate the flow of water usually present relatively few problems. They are often quite large and easily visible at a distance. The water may flow over the top or be released from the bottom through a tube. In addition, the pools behind them are frequently marked somehow, as required by federal licensing, to indicate how close you can approach without risk of being sucked in and run through a turbine. If nothing else, the maintenance personnel may spot you and invite you to get off their artificial lake. On the downstream side, the outflow can emerge with tremendous force, so it is best to put your boat in the water well downstream. Also, portaging one of these monsters can turn out to be a major project.

The type of dam where the water flows over the top in an unregulated fashion can present several subtle dangers. First, these dams are not always easy to spot since the current can continue right up to the edge of the dam itself. If you don't see it in time, over you go, or at least you may have a few frantic moments paddling your way back upstream. There are three clues that may indicate an upcoming dam: slack or dead water where you don't really expect it, a regular line across the river ahead, and the abrupt disappearance of the river. Although it may seem obvious that you should be careful of going over a dam by accident and that you should be observant, people do manage to fall over them anyhow.

Frequently dams are run on purpose, and in this instance you can encounter a second danger—hydraulics. When water recirculates at the base of a dam it is called a hydraulic. The current is actually moving upstream on the surface. A hydraulic is what keeps logs rolling around and around at the base of some large dams; it can do the same thing to you and your boat. The height or steepness of a dam does not always indicate how strong a hydraulic will be. The shape of the dam's base and of the river bottom, along with the amount of water going over the dam, all contribute to make a strong or weak hydraulic. It is often impossible to tell how strong a hydraulic is just by looking at it, a fact new boaters should keep in mind. Some relatively low dams have vicious hydraulics, while taller ones have innocuous ones. There are no hard and fast rules for predicting how a hydraulic will behave. Each must be considered separately. If you have any doubts at all, don't run the dam.

Many dams in the Northeast were built long enough ago that they have been breached by high water and are no longer in use. These dams, along with such other man-made structures as mill buildings and bridges that may have collapsed into the river, can leave sharp and often dangerous debris in rapids. While natural rocks have usually, over time, become rounded and settled into regular patterns on the river bottom, man-made debris is sometimes present where an experienced boater looking downstream would otherwise expect smooth sailing. For this reason, if you even suspect that there may be man-made debris in a rapid, the best strategy is to play it safe until you can confirm or rule out its presence.

Scouting

Scouting is examining rapids from shore prior to running or portaging them to note the best route and potential hazards. Although it sounds rather easy, good scouting actually can be quite tricky, due to the fact that, while paddling the rapids, you have a different view than you did on shore. So, once you have determined a route from the sidelines, walk upstream and squat down to river level to see how things will look when you're in the boat. If the route is still obvious, you are ready to run. If the route is no longer clear, re-evaluate the whole situation. Also, be aware that rapids frequently can paddle harder than they look, especially if you are scouting from well above them.

Scout all rapids or blind curves that you are unsure of, even if others in the group don't. Make sure you look at the whole rapids, not just the start. A channel that's clear at the beginning occasionally can end up going under an impassable ice shelf. Rivers with snow and ice cover on the banks deserve very special attention, even from experts. Stay away from people who boast, "I never scout anything." They can get both of you killed. Scouting rapids from your boat by moving from one eddy to another, known as eddy hopping, is a common practice among experienced boaters, but one not recommended for beginners. Last, don't become complacent or forgetful about scouting as you gain skill; you are probably tackling more-difficult water and the rapids may tend to become people-eaters.

River Descriptions

Interpreting the Information

The descriptions in this section give the paddler reasonably detailed accounts of particular trips. In most cases, descriptions are based on notes taken while paddling the trips, although a few are based on scouting notes only. The rivers themselves receive primary attention rather than the surrounding countryside. The descriptions all follow the same basic format. Key facts associated with the trip appear at the top of the page for easy reference. Key facts are also listed in the river chart on pages xvi–xxvii.

The first paragraph of each description gives an overview of the river and sets the character of the run. Subsequent material details the joys and difficulties to be encountered. Events are usually described sequentially.

Distances from one spot to the next are not always given. It may be necessary to paddle some distance before the next significant location comes into view, even though it is the next sentence or paragraph in the text. The final paragraph discusses the gauge situation for a river and gives the exact location of the appropriate gauge if it exists. The last paragraph also lists names of other nearby rivers that have a similar difficulty rating to the one described, and which could provide some variety for a second trip of the day or weekend.

As a rule, each description is based on a single river level. This level is usually indicated. There are also frequent comments about the river at other levels. If a river is described at a low level and you find it at a high level, its character can be completely different. The converse is also true: even the most pugnacious rivers look like pussycats when they are void of water.

Distances, when used to described rapids, are approximate, not exact. For instance, the real business part of Staircase rapid on the Swift River is roughly 20 yards long, as opposed to 50 yards. Most measurements are the result of eyeballing. Landmarks are noted, sometimes when no difficulties are near, so that boaters may have a fair idea where they are. Usually only those landmarks that seem permanent are listed: houses, concrete walls, etc. Downed trees are not considered permanent, and therefore are not noted except in rapids where they frequently occur.

The directions left and right are always with respect to a paddler facing downstream—that is, as paddlers say, "river left" and "river right."

The reader should realize that a river and its surroundings will change with time due to natural or artificial causes, so do not take the following descriptions as gospel. Think and observe on your own. Great effort has been made to ensure accuracy, but it cannot be guaranteed.

Remember—for the level ratings, only the highest reading in an interval is given for the TOO LOW, LOW, MEDIUM, and HIGH levels. For the TOO HIGH level, the lowest reported value is given.

Finally, it bears repeating that this is a guidebook, not a ticket to enjoyable and safe boating. Your success and pleasure on a trip depend primarily on you, the boater, on your paddling skills, your ability to cope with unexpected problems, and your judgment. No guidebook can ever hope to substitute for these. Guidebooks can only take away a little of the uncertainty.

SEE YOU ON THE RIVER!

Wild and Scenic Rivers

In 1968 Congress passed the National Wild and Scenic Rivers Act. Its purpose was to preserve certain rivers and sections of rivers in their natural free-flowing state and to offer protection to some of the country's most outstanding waterways. The Act was also intended to complement the established policy of building dams and other construction on rivers so every river would not be covered with concrete. The scope of the Act is rather far-reaching in that it affects not only the river itself but also its shoreline. The Act was intended not to restore rivers to their previous wilderness state but to merely protect them as they exist now.

The rivers covered under this Act should meet some or all of the following criteria:

1. Be a free-flowing river or stream;

2. Be free of certain types of alterations like dikes, levees, channelizations, dams, etc., etc.;

3. Have a largely undeveloped shoreline;

4. Be at least 25 miles in length; and,

5. Have outstanding scenic, recreational, geological, historical, or cultural value.

Under this system, rivers are placed into one of three categories:

Wild River —Rivers that are free of impoundments and whose shores are inaccessible except by trail, and whose watersheds are unspoiled and primitive.

Scenic River—Rivers that are free of impoundments and whose shores are largely primitive and undeveloped but accessible by road in a few places.

Recreational River—Rivers that are easily accessible by road, whose shorelines are somewhat developed, and whose waters may be impounded in places.

The rivers that attain the status of one of these designations are managed either by the Department of Agriculture, by the Department of the Interior, or by a comparable state agency if the river is in a state protection plan. A river can be placed into the system either by an act of Congress or by designation of the secretary of the interior if the river is already in a state system. In almost any case, a detailed study of the river and its watershed must be made prior to a river's introduction or enactment as a Wild or Scenic River. When Congress first passed this legislation in 1968, it designated eight rivers for immediate inclusion and provided for a ninth shortly thereafter. Twenty-seven rivers originally were designated for study. Since then, a number of additional rivers have been pinpointed for study.

The reader should note that several rivers that have been designated or considered for designation are whitewater streams covered in this book. This legislation preserves these streams in the present natural state, and so ensures their availability for future recreational activity. Citizens and lobbying groups can influence a river's gaining Wild or Scenic status; every boater may participate or not, depending on individual inclination. River runners at least should be aware that this legislation exists and that it can help to curtail future development and exploitation of rivers. One lobbying group keenly interested in keeping our rivers free and flowing is American Rivers, 1025 Vermont Avenue NW, Suite 720, Washington, DC 20005. If you are interested in this aspect of river work, give them a call.

Paddling on Dam-Controlled Rivers and Ensuring Future Access

One of the major factors responsible for the boom in popularity of white-water boating over the last decade has been increased access to runnable whitewater. It used to be that the boating season in the Northeast began in early March and ended in late April or early May, but with more and more dam operators making whitewater releases available on a regular basis when other rivers are dry, the peak boating season has lengthened considerably, and opportunities for high-quality whitewater runs exist every weekend and many weekdays throughout the spring, summer, and fall.

This new spirit of cooperation on the part of such dam operators as utilities, paper companies, and municipalities has not been driven entirely by altruism. In 1986, Congress passed a law known as the Electric Consumer Protection Act (ECPA), which said that when the Federal Energy Regulatory Commission (FERC) issues new licenses for dams or reviews applications for license renewals, it must give equal consideration to power generation, environmental concerns, and recreational access. This was a new concept, since previous dam licenses had been reviewed based strictly on the need for the power to be produced.

The effect of ECPA has been to give such river-conservation groups as American Rivers, the American Whitewater Affiliation, the Appalachian Mountain Club, and New England FLOW a lever with which they could negotiate mitigation measures for the damage done to a river by building a dam. This mitigation has come in the form of minimum releases of water for protection of fish habitat, improved recreational facilities and access, land-preservation agreements, and regularly scheduled white-water releases.

In order to secure these measures, countless volunteer hours have been spent by grassroots activists collecting data, meeting with company and agency officials, and getting the word out. Each boater has a responsibility to the paddling community in general to treat both company personnel and local residents with respect in order to preserve the opportunity for the next boater that comes down the river.

If you're interested in working on dam-relicensing or access issues, contact one of the groups mentioned above. They are truly grassroots organizations and welcome enthusiastic volunteers.

Maps

Maps accompany the trip descriptions to help orient the paddler and complement the written descriptions. They were prepared by tracing USGS topographic maps in some cases, and in other cases by inserting labels in a computer mapping program. A glance at one of these maps will show immediately if a trip is north-south, east-west, or something in between, and should also provide an overview of the trip. The maps also indicate the highlights of the trip—for example, starting and stopping points, rapids, dams, waterfalls, gauge locations, and other points of interest. Nearby roads are indicated to help in planning shuttles and in getting to and from the river. Not all existing roads are shown, although the majority are. A good road map along with these maps should be all that you need to get there and back.

A map key follows in which all map symbols used are explained. It should be noted also that the north arrow indicates magnetic north. Rivers and water in general are shaded for easy viewing and, where appropriate, an arrow shows the direction of the trip. A scale is also included on each map to help you judge distance.

Map Key

⋈	picnic area
★	river locator
▲	mountain
P	parking
⬧	camping
➤	river direction
─┼─┼─┼─	railroad
── · ──	boundary

Locator Map: New Hampshire and Vermont

Bennington

ROARING BR.

Arlington

ROARING BR.

Danby

BIG BR.

DEERFIELD R.

W. BR.

N.W. BR.

E. BR.

N.W. BR.

WINHALL

Bondville

HARRIMAN RES.

NORTH R.

BALL MTN.

WARDSBORO

Williamsville

ROCK R.

Jamaica

Brattleboro

GREEN R.

WEST RIVER

Grafton

SAXTONS R.

Chester

Proctorsville

OTTAUQUECHEE R.

Gaysville

WHITE RIVER

Quechee

S.

Stratford

Sharon

S. W. BR.

Ompompanoosuc

WILLIAMS R.

Perkinsville

BLACK R.

Ashuelot

ASHUELOT

COLD RIVER

South Acworth

SUGAR R.

Claremont

Newport

Hartland

Lebanon

MASCOMA RIVER

CONNECTICUT RIVER

S. BR.

OTTER

Gilsum

E. Sullivan

Troy

N. BR.

CONTOOCOOK R.

Hillsborough

HARNER R.

BLACKWATER R.

Webster

SMITH R.

NEWFOUND R.

Bristol

POND BR.

Wentworth

BASSET

MAD RIV.

SQUHEGAN R.

Wilton

S. BR.

PISCATAQUOG

New Boston

Concord

Loudon

MERRIMACK

Manchester

SUNCOOK R.

Pittsfield

LAKE WINNIPESAUKEE

BEARCAMP R.

Whittier

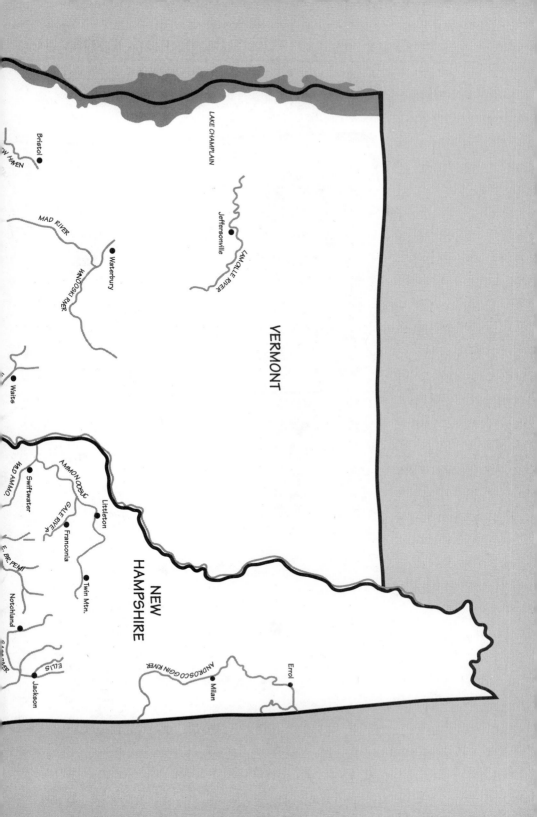

Locator Map: Massachusetts, Connecticut, and Rhode Island

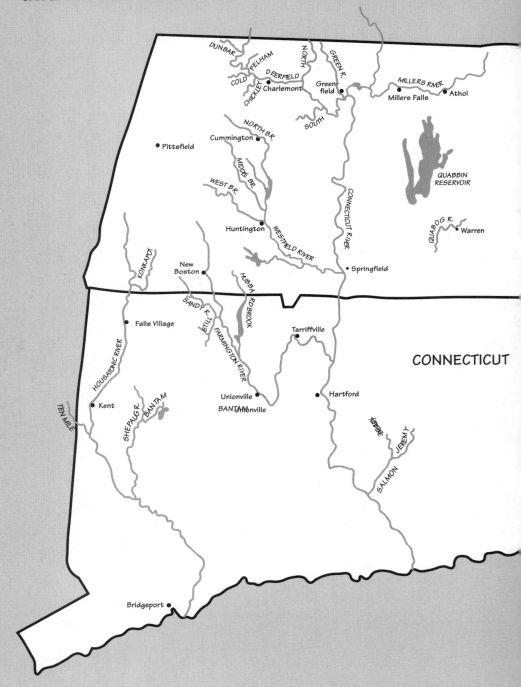

DUNBAR
COLD
PELHAM
DEERFIELD
CHICKLEY
NORTH
GREEN R.
Charlemont
MILLERS RIVER
Green-
field
Athol
● Millers Falls
● Athol

SOUTH

NORTH BR.
● Cummington
● Pittsfield

MIDDLE BR.

QUABBIN
RESERVOIR

WEST BR.

CONNECTICUT RIVER

QUABOG R.
● Warren

Huntington ●
WESTFIELD RIVER

KONKAPOT
New
Boston ●
● Springfield

HUBBARD BROOK

SANDY R.
STILL

Falls Village ●
Tarriffville ●

HOUSATONIC RIVER
CONNECTICUT

FARMINGTON RIVER

TEN MILE
SHEPAUG R.
BANTAM
● Kent
Unionville ●
BANTAM Unionville
Hartford ●

BROOK
JEREMY
SALMON

Bridgeport ●

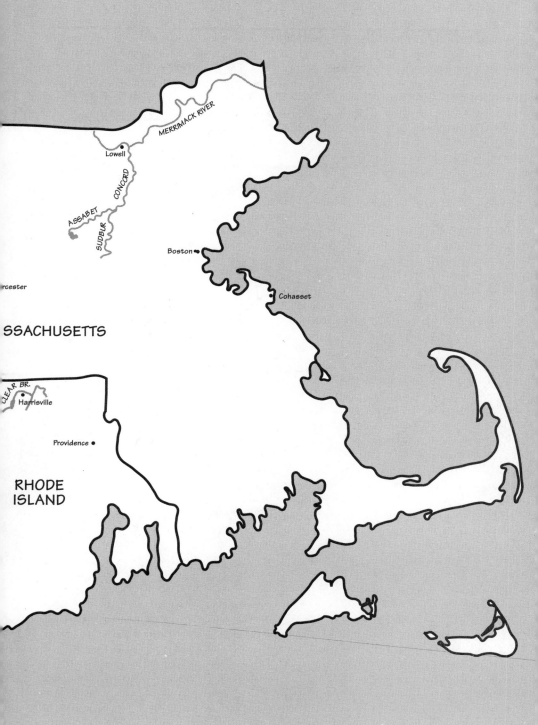

MERRIMACK RIVER

Lowell

ASSABET

CONCORD

SUDBUR

Boston

rcester

Cohasset

SSACHUSETTS

CLEAR BR.

Harrisville

Providence

RHODE
ISLAND

Locator Map: Maine

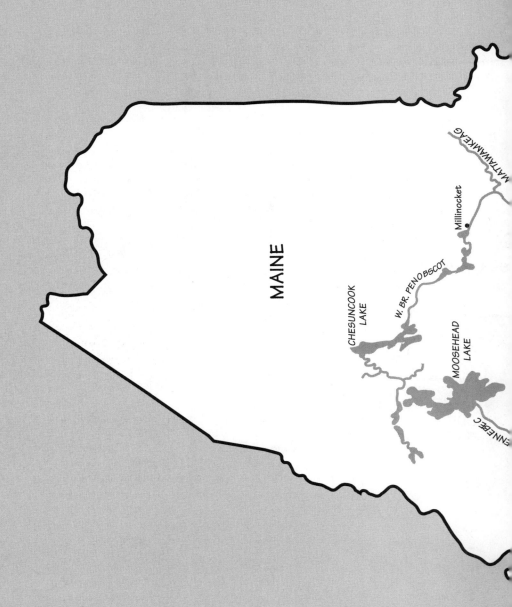

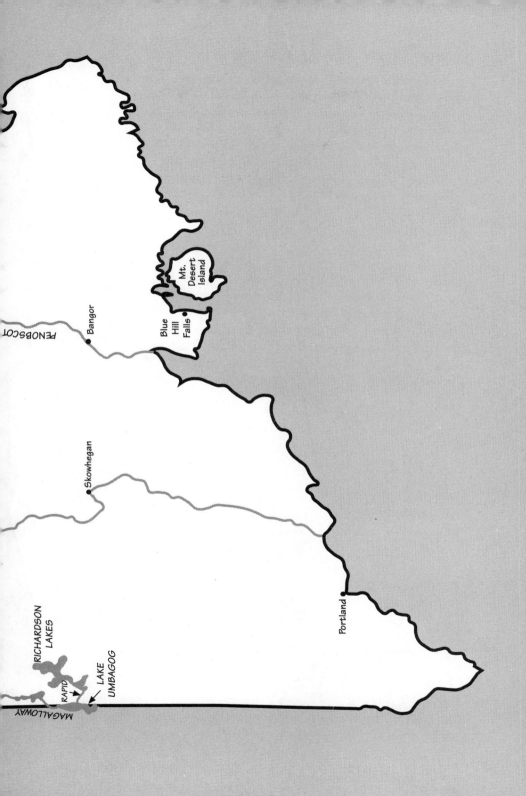

Locator Map: New York

Lake Placid

BLACK RIVER

Watertown

BEAVER RIVER

Belfort

STILLWATER
RESERVOIR

CEDAR RIVER

INDIAN RIV.

BOREAS

McKeever

MOOSE RIVER

North
Creek

HUDSON RIVER

Speculator

E. BR.

Whitehouse

W. BR.

LAKE ONTARIO

SACANDAGA

Hadley

Utica

MOHAWK RIVER

GREAT
SACANDAGA
LAKE

NEW YORK

Albany

HUDSON RIVER

ESOPUS CREEK

Phoenicia

ASHOKAN
RESERVOIR

Pough-
keepsie

TEN MILE

Webatuck

NEW YORK

Beaver River (N.Y.)

General

Thanks to negotiations conducted by the American Whitewater Affiliation, three sections of New York's Beaver River, previously dewatered by Niagara-Mohawk hydroelectric projects, now feature annual water releases during September weekends.

At one time, the Beaver might have been the most fabulous whitewater river in the eastern United States. Originating from the Stillwater Reservoir in New York's central Adirondacks, the Beaver drops 1,400 vertical feet in its 40-mile length before emptying into the Black River near Lowville, New York. Unfortunately the Beaver's spectacular gradient also attracted the attention of the Niagara Mohawk Power Corporation, which erected seven power projects during the 1950s, transforming the Beaver into a string of impoundments separated by dewatered sections where steep rapids once thundered. However, thanks to the American Whitewater Affiliation, starting in 1997 Ni-Mo agreed to release water back into three of those sections during September weekends. The three sections are short and range in difficulty from solid class IV to difficult class V.

Beaver River (N.Y.)

Moshier Pond to Moshier Powerhouse
Trip A

DISTANCE (MILES)	1.5	TOO LOW	
SHUTTLE (MILES)	1.5	LOW	
AVG. DROP (FEET/MILE)	50	MED.	400 cfs
MAX. DROP (FEET/MILE)		HIGH	
DIFFICULTY	IV–V	TOO HIGH	
SCENERY	Excellent	GAUGE LOCATION	Moshier Dam
DATE LAST CHECKED	1997	WATER LEVEL INFO.	*AWA Journal*
RUNOFF PATTERN	d/r		

The Moshier section of the Beaver is a step up in difficulty from Taylorville. Located off of Stillwater Road just 7.0 miles downstream from Stillwater Reservoir, Moshier provides a run with large vertical drops and narrow sluices, separated by quiet pools.

The overall gradient of the Moshier run is only 50 feet per mile (fpm), but most of the rapids come in the form of sheer, runnable waterfalls ranging from 5 to 15 feet in height. The drops range in difficulty from hard class IV to easy class V making the run approachable by experts and very experienced intermediates.

To reach this section, turn north off of Stillwater Road onto Moshier Road, approximately 7.0 miles west of the Stillwater Reservoir. The road is marked with a "Beaver River Canoe Route" sign. Take the road approximately 1.0 mile until you reach the Moshier powerhouse, which doubles as the takeout. To reach the put-in, follow the road from the powerhouse that parallels the river up to the dam that creates Moshier Pond.

As it does with the Taylorville section, Niagara Mohawk releases a consistent flow of 400 cfs into this stretch several times a year in the fall. The 2.0 mile Moshier shuttle encourages multiple runs during a release.

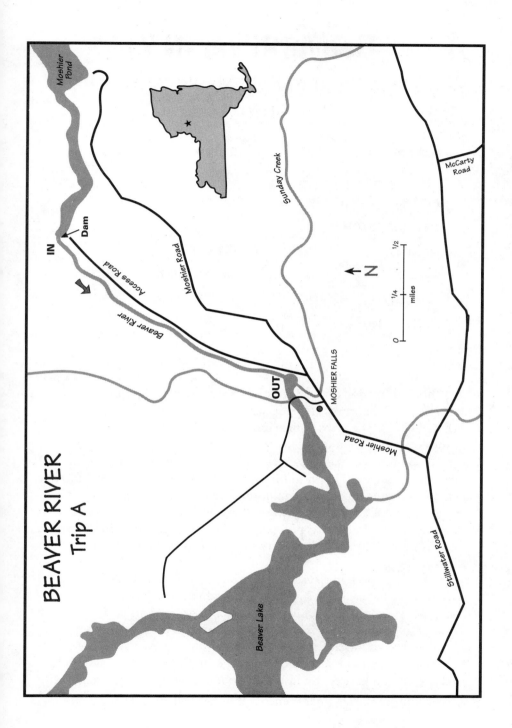

BEAVER RIVER
Trip A

Moshier Pond

Dam

IN

Access Road

Beaver River

Moshier Road

Sunday Creek

McCarty Road

N

1/2   1/4   0
miles

OUT

MOSHIER FALLS

Moshier Road

Beaver Lake

Stillwater Road

Beaver River (N.Y.)
Eagle Pond to Soft Maple Reservoir
Trip B

DISTANCE (MILES)	0.75	TOO LOW	
SHUTTLE (MILES)	0.75	LOW	
AVG. DROP (FEET/MILE)	219	MED.	200 cfs.
MAX. DROP (FEET/MILE)	n/a	HIGH	
DIFFICULTY	V	TOO HIGH	
SCENERY	Excellent	GAUGE LOCATION	Eagle Dam
DATE LAST CHECKED	1997	WATER LEVEL INFO.	*AWA Journal*
RUNOFF PATTERN	d/r		

The Eagle section of the Beaver is less than a mile in length but features some of the most dramatic whitewater to be found in the eastern United States. The crux of the run is a 0.15-mile stretch where the river drops over four separate rapids at a gradient of 475 fpm.

Eagle is more of a steep creek than a river, as Ni-Mo releases only 200 cfs into the section. However, 200 cfs is more than enough water. The river cascades through a narrow chasm bordered by 500-foot granite cliffs on one side and a sloped rock shelf on the other. The rapids consist of steep class V sluices, sheer falls, and sticky hydraulics. While short in length, the run is more intimidating than recognized expert runs like the Bottom Moose.

The Eagle section is reached by turning north off Soft Maple Road 100 yards above the Eagle powerhouse. The road will parallel a six-foot diameter pipe (which carries the river during power generation) upstream to the base of the dam that forms Eagle Pond. Take out at the powerhouse.

Because of the close proximity of the runs, the AWA generally schedules a release on one section of the Beaver in the morning followed by a release on another section in the afternoon. Annual releases include five days at Taylorville, five at Eagle, and one at Moshier.

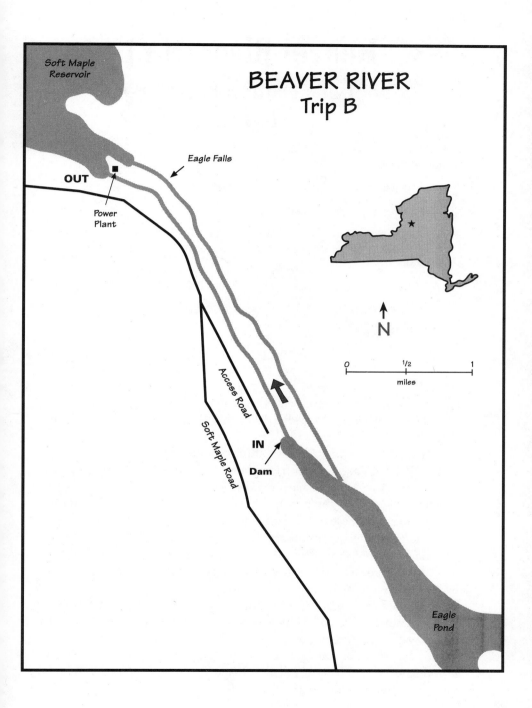

BEAVER RIVER
Trip B

Soft Maple Reservoir

Eagle Falls

OUT

Power Plant

N

0   ½   1
miles

Access Road

Soft Maple Road

IN

Dam

Eagle Pond

Beaver River (N.Y.)

Taylorville Dam to Belfort Pond
Trip C

DISTANCE (MILES)	0.75		**TOO LOW**	
SHUTTLE (MILES)	0.75		**LOW**	
AVG. DROP (FEET/MILE)			**MED.**	400 cfs.
MAX. DROP (FEET/MILE)			**HIGH**	
DIFFICULTY	IV		**TOO HIGH**	
SCENERY	Excellent		**GAUGE LOCATION**	Taylorville Dam
DATE LAST CHECKED	1997		**WATER LEVEL INFO.**	*AWA Journal*
RUNOFF PATTERN	d/r			

The Taylorville section, located just upstream of Belfort, New York, features six class IV rapids and an easy shuttle that encourages multiple runs.

To reach this section, turn right (east) onto Old State Road in the village of Belfort. Take a quick right onto Taylorville Road (marked by a Beaver River Canoe Route sign) that leads to the takeout at the Taylorville powerplant. To reach the put-in, follow the dirt road that leads from the powerplant to the base of the dam that creates the Taylorville Pond.

The action begins immediately at the base of the Taylorville dam, where a gate pours 400 cfs of water back into the narrow riverbed. It funnels through a narrow class III sluice before dropping over a class IV ledge backed by a nasty hydraulic in the middle.

After a short pool, the river pours over an impressive 30-foot-high slide that dumps into an intimidating hole at the bottom. The action continues as the river tumbles over 4-foot ledges and through narrow slots.

Appropriate for strong intermediates, Taylorville provides a perfect introduction for aspiring steep-creek boaters looking for a run to prepare them for more challenging tests like the Bottom Moose or the upper Cedar.

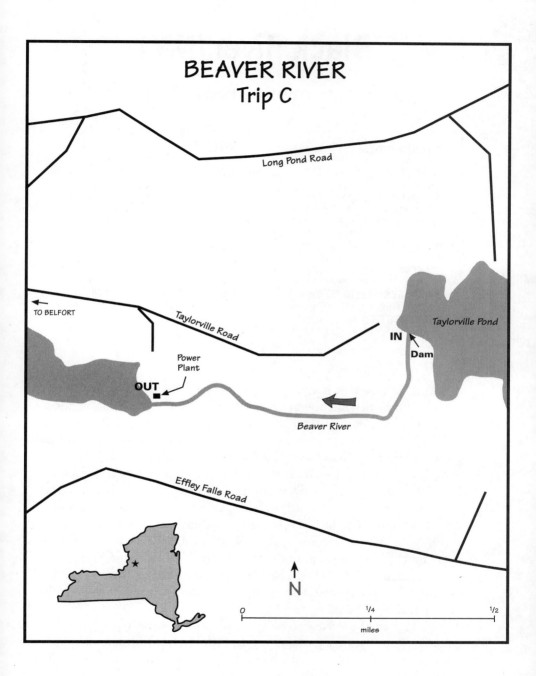

BEAVER RIVER
Trip C

Long Pond Road

← TO BELFORT

Taylorville Road

Taylorville Pond

IN ↑
Dam

Power
Plant

OUT ■

Beaver River

Effley Falls Road

↑
N

0   1/4   1/2
miles

Black River (N.Y.)

Watertown to Brownville

DISTANCE (MILES)	7		TOO LOW	
SHUTTLE (MILES)	7.5		LOW	1,500 cfs
AVG. DROP (FEET/MILE)	28		MED.	2,500 cfs
MAX. DROP (FEET/MILE)			HIGH	4,000 cfs
DIFFICULTY	III–IV		TOO HIGH	
SCENERY	Good		GAUGE LOCATION	Glen Park Hydro
DATE LAST CHECKED	1997		WATER LEVEL INFO.	518-465-2016
RUNOFF PATTERN	n/d/r/l			

Set in the midst of a dying mill town only a few miles from Lake Ontario, at first glance the Black seems an unlikely location for a whitewater run. But less than 100 yards from the put-in you'll become a believer, as you shred the silky-smooth waves and catch the well-defined, powerful eddies of Club House Turn and Burns Wall. Carved out of flat-lying limestone, the Black River drains a large area of the western Adirondacks. Its character is very different from most other northeastern rivers, which are low volume and littered with glacier-worn boulders. You won't see many boulders in the Black, but ledges are plentiful, undercut walls are everywhere, and the volume is high (1,000 to 8,000 cfs). Because of its many undercuts, you should take special care in running the Black. One rapid in particular, Knife Edge, has claimed several boaters' lives where the current slams up against a seemingly innocuous ledge that is actually undercut about 20 feet.

But despite the terrible scenery for the first mile or two and the many undercuts, the Black is a tremendous class III–IV river with several opportunities for surfing waves and holes, running big drops, and generally "messing about" in kayaks, canoes, and rafts.

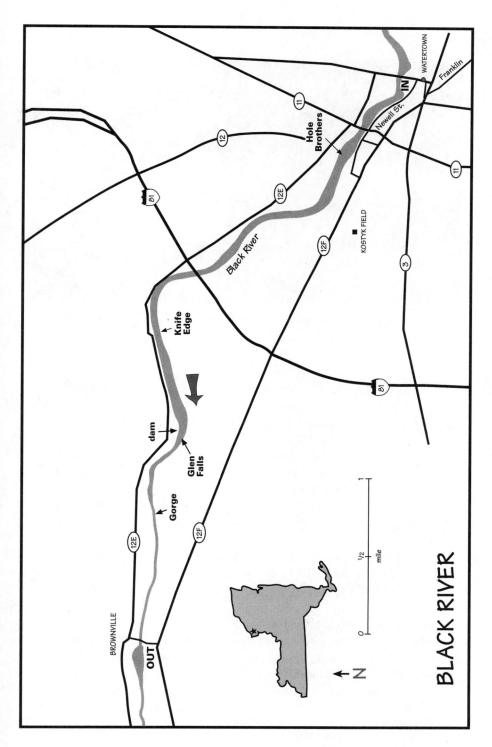

BLACK RIVER

Playing at the first broken dam on the lower Ashuelot. Photo by Bruce Lessels

The put-in is in back of and below an old city warehouse that now houses Adirondack River Outfitters at 140 Newell Street in Watertown (315-788-2297). Check in with the rafters—they won't bite—and be careful carrying boats down the long, winding stair to the river.

The first rapid, Club House Turn, is a short wave train that bends slightly to the right. This is followed by an easy class III (Burns Wall) with silky-smooth surfing waves all the way down and easy access eddies on the sides. After passing under the Court Street bridge the scenery deteriorates (if it can get any worse), but a fairly large, soft play hole known as Hole Brothers appears river center at the site of a breached low-head dam. When surfing, be careful of man-made debris. There are great access eddies on both sides of this hole, and it's well suited to learning spins, retendos, and other rodeo moves, since it has a powerful but short backwash.

Below the hole the river is flat for less than a mile before passing under a double bridge where Interstate 81 crosses. Beware as you pass under the second bridge, since Knife Edge lies a few hundred yards downstream. The best scouting takeout is on river left, although there is not a very strong eddy here; if in doubt, take out higher up and put up with a little-longer walk. Follow the trail down river left to see the three ledges that comprise Knife Edge. The first is simple, with a strong hole on river right that weakens as you move left. The second ledge is shallow on the right at lower levels, but as the water rises, the right forms a hole. River left is a clear shot with a large, but narrow, hole just left of center that's easily avoided to the left. Beware of the tempting eddy on river right below this second ledge at medium and low levels. It is about 6 inches deep and the bottom of it moves inexorably downstream, drawing an unwary boater into the third ledge out of position.

The third ledge is what makes this rapid a challenge and a hazard. The right side is a steep vertical drop of 3 to 4 feet into a horseshoe-shaped hole with a flat recycle. Just left of center is a narrow rib that offers a tempting launch into the pool at the bottom. This move requires careful water reading, but is an option at most levels. Moving left, the third ledge becomes nearly parallel to the flow, forming a nasty-looking curler with a couple of breaks in it. All the way against the shore, another trashy hole threatens the boater who tries to sneak along the left bank.

Below this third ledge the bank juts out somewhat in what appears to be simply a point of rock only a few feet above river level. What is not apparent is that, just below water level, this point is undercut to form a deadly cave. Avoid this left bank at all costs. If forced to swim this rapid, swim right at the bottom.

The standard run of Knife Edge starts left to negotiate the first two ledges, then moves center just before the final ledge. After passing the diagonal hole on river left just upstream of the third ledge, cut left at a break in the hole, and then cut immediately back right to avoid the under-cut bank at the bottom. The hardest part of Knife Edge is reading the water, since landmarks are not plentiful. Knife Edge is a solid class IV at low and medium levels, and becomes class V at high water. It warrants a look at any level, since the line is not obvious from the river, and the haz-ards are hidden as well.

Below Knife Edge and the ruins of an old factory on river right, a short flatwater section leads to the Glen Park Hydro dam run by Mercer Management. Call ahead (315-788-9121) to let them know when you're coming and they'll release for your group as you arrive at the dam. This sort of service is an outgrowth of recent efforts on the part of river-advo-cacy groups to work with hydro dam operators to make them more aware of their interdependent relationship with other river users. Remember to thank them and cooperate.

You can put in either above or below Glen Park Falls. The water usu-ally takes about fifteen minutes to start flowing over the dam after you arrive. Running the falls is not recommended above 1,500 cfs, as the hydraulic gets grabby at these flows. At runnable levels, however, the falls is a fairly straight shot down the middle and over the 12-foot plunge into the pool below. Immediately below this, Three Rocks Rapid is a technical class III that marks the beginning of the Black River Gorge, where the whitewater is superb, and the scenery takes a turn for the better as 60-foot limestone cliffs line the river, with occasional streams cascading from the top of the gorge.

The gorge is fairly continuous at low and medium levels, and is one long rapid at flows over 3,000 cfs. Most rapids are class III and IV, with two requiring special care. The first of these two is Panic Rock, where the river flows directly into a large undercut boulder on river left, then turns sharply left and runs up against an undercut wall. The move is simple— stay right and cut left just above the wall at the bottom—but the consequences of ending up in the wrong place could be severe. Following Panic Rock, a large midriver hole called the Cruncher is just above a broken dam that presents either a shallow 6-foot slide on river left over the remains of the dam, known as Rocket Ride, or a sharp, nasty dogleg on river right into a gnarly hole appropriately named the Poop Chute. The right side doesn't have much to recommend it as anything but a stunt, but make your own choice when you get there.

The last mile and a half of the gorge is full of surfing opportunities and more beautiful scenery, until the whitewater and the scenery both degrade suddenly as you approach the bridge in Brownsville, where large factories replace the gorge walls on both sides of the river and the rapids become shallow riffles.

Take out just below the Brownsville Bridge at Rexum Paper on river right. Be discreet changing and parking here, since the takeout is in the middle of a suburban neighborhood.

Call Glen Park Hydro (315-788-9121) to schedule releases and to find water-level information.

Boreas River (N.Y.)

Route 28N to Minerva Bridge

DISTANCE (MILES)	7		TOO LOW	4.8
SHUTTLE (MILES)	11		LOW	
AVG. DROP (FEET/MILE)	45		MED.	5.5
MAX. DROP (FEET/MILE)	100		HIGH	7
DIFFICULTY	IV–V		TOO HIGH	7
SCENERY	Excellent		GAUGE LOCATION	North Creek
DATE LAST CHECKED	1997		WATER LEVEL INFO.	518-465-2016
RUNOFF PATTERN	n			

There are only a few rivers whose reputations do not overshadow actual fact. Most paddlers commonly exaggerate the difficulty of rivers and rapids to the point that the unsuspecting listener really doesn't know what to expect. There are, however, a few waterways in which the horror stories, the tall tales, and the descriptions are not quite so padded with campfire chatter. These are a special breed of classic rivers that live up to the tough reputations they have. The Boreas is one of these.

Born in Boreas Pond somewhat northeast of Newcomb, New York, the Boreas flows through Cheney Pond and then generally southward to rendezvous with the Hudson. For most of its length, the watershed valley is extremely attractive, resembling paintings from the Hudson River School. Towering conifers line the banks, and, since the valley is mildly inaccessible, the scenery is generally unpierced by civilization. Through the middle part of the run, the Boreas is absolutely flat, reflecting the blue sky and white powder-puff clouds as if they were originating somehow beneath the water surface itself. The rapids are something else again. Two sections are noteworthy: the upper part has several good sets of rapids, terminating in a runnable waterfall, and the lower stretch has a long, continuous stretch of difficult rapids.

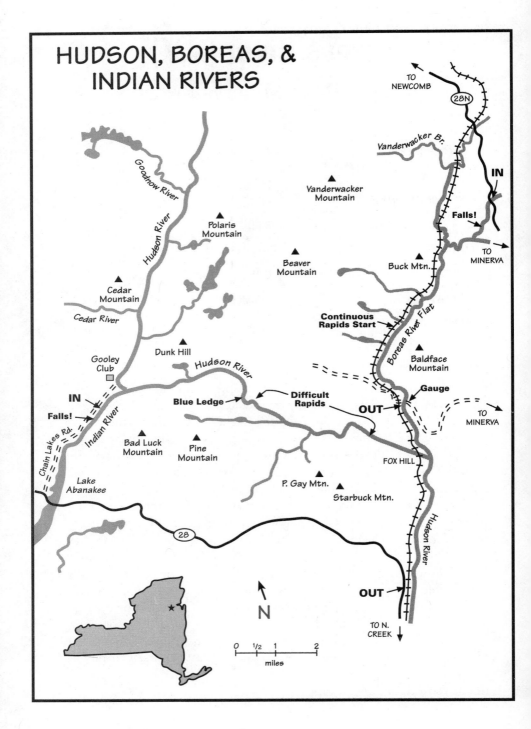

HUDSON, BOREAS, & INDIAN RIVERS

TO
NEWCOMB

28N

Vanderwacker Br.

IN

Falls!

TO
MINERVA

Goodnow River

Hudson River

▲ Vanderwacker
Mountain

▲ Polaris
Mountain

▲ Beaver
Mountain

▲ Buck Mtn.

▲ Cedar
Mountain

Cedar River

**Continuous
Rapids Start**

Boreas River Flat

Dunk Hill ▲

Hudson River

▲ Baldface
Mountain

Gooley
Club

Gauge

IN

Blue Ledge

**Difficult
Rapids**

OUT

TO
MINERVA

Falls!

Chain Lakes Rd.

Indian River

▲ Bad Luck
Mountain

▲ Pine
Mountain

FOX HILL

Lake
Abanakee

P. Gay Mtn. ▲

▲ Starbuck Mtn.

Hudson River

28

OUT

N

0   1/2   1   2
miles

TO N.
CREEK

The usual starting point for a trip, or what is more correct, a "happening" on the Boreas, is the Route 28N bridge, which crosses the river northwest of Minerva. Here the Boreas is some 50 feet wide, and, although it is flowing at a fair clip, it presents a rather mild-mannered facade. To the east of the bridge a dirt road pushes its way upstream into the woods, leading to a campsite area and a convenient launching spot. An island splits the stream here, giving the impression that one could spit across the whole river. Downstream, beyond the bridge, the Boreas turns right where a few rocks and ripples appear. The quiet water continues long enough for the paddler to limber up muscles and get comfortable in a favorite position. The first real rapids begin in a very sharp left turn where, at the start, rocks leapfrog out from the left bank, narrowing the channel. This stretch lasts about 100 yards. It is Z-shaped and tight, with numerous small drops throughout. This natural slalom's lower part is a sharp right turn where the main current is on the outside against some rocks. Immediately following is a short (15 yards), narrow (15–20 feet) chute that terminates in another abrupt drop, with a smoother tongue located on the extreme right side (low water only). If this rapid seems tough, the paddler may be well advised to shore the boat and carry it back to Route 28N, since those below are much more severe.

Shortly downstream are several more small drops over rock ledges, and then there's a waterfall. Dropping precipitously on either extreme (8 feet), the falls have a smoother, two-stage descent in the middle; the first stage is more abrupt than the second. These falls have been run in both high and low water, but boaters should judge for themselves. The portage is easiest on the right. Below the falls, in a sharp left turn, there is another chute with a stern kicker at the bottom. At low levels, the outflow is rocky but easy. An island forces the current 90° to the right or left, after which there is smoother water.

Class II water continues until the railroad makes its initial approach on the right shore. Here Vanderwhacker Brook enters from the right, and the Boreas turns 90° left. For about the next 3.0 miles, the course is smooth and mostly flat, past several islands and some small overhead cables. In this section the Boreas is at its widest, being 50 to 75 feet. The sleepy peacefulness and quiet tranquility of the scenery will impress even the most ardent city dweller. However, as always, there is calm before the storm.

Just when you're tired of paddling flatwater, notice a faster current as the river turns gently right. This is the only warning before all hell breaks loose. What follows is 2.5 miles of violent and absolutely uninterrupted difficult rapids, too complex to describe in detail. Beyond that right turn the banks crowd together, creating a natural sluiceway, and the whole riverbed tilts downward as if trying to throw the paddler off its back. This 2.5-mile stretch has an average gradient of about 90 feet per mile and achieves a maximum of more than 100 feet per mile. At first rocks are just numerous, but soon they line every conceivable space as the current stampedes uncontrolled over and around them, causing countless haystacks, hydraulics, and dizzying crosscurrents. Needless to say, the turbulence is something other than placid. This mayhem continues for a long time—at least the paddler will think so. In one spot, where the railroad is close by on the right, a series of rocks thrusts out from the left bank, squeezing the already narrow channel to that of only a boat's length. Just upstream and lasting perhaps 5 to 10 yards, is a small, quiet pool. On its left is one of the few usable eddies to be found on the trip. In high water forget about the pool—it's gone. If you can get into the eddy, however, it's a good place to rest and survey what's below.

What follows is more of the same, only harder—another long section of continuous, extremely difficult technical maneuverings. In this section, as in the one above, the current can change direction without notice, forcing the boater to make instantaneous decisions time after time. Downstream there are two boulders, one in the left and one in the right center. Between them is an abrupt 3-foot drop. Immediately below, the Boreas turns sharply left and forms a small eddy on the outside bank among some rocks. This introduces the famous Z-turns. Superimposed on the other difficulties are several very sharp turns, each choked with rocks. If you get by these goodies without broaching or bouncing down on your head, consider yourself a respectable boater.

The river continues to dish out abuse, although it diminishes somewhat just above the Minerva bridge. Along the way you'll pass an island, where there's a strong hydraulic on the left side. Once you spot the bridge, the hardest is over. If you choose to continue to the Hudson (2.0 miles from the bridge), the trip gradually will wind down. After 3.5 miles on the Hudson, Route 28 appears on the right.

Alternatively, cars can park by the Minerva bridge, reached by driving 1.8 miles north on Route 28N past the general store in Minerva, then taking a dirt road that slants off to the left just past a rustic lodge on the right. After only 4.0 miles on this class II–III (class IV if it's wet) road, the Boreas bridge is reached. In spring this road most probably will be blocked by snow or mud.

There are two gauges that indicate the canoeability of the Boreas. The easier to read, since it is in the Telemark system, is the one in North Creek on the Hudson. Unfortunately, this gauge is on the Hudson, not the Boreas, and the correlation is only a very general one—if the Hudson is up, the Boreas is likely to be up also. The other gauge is on the Minerva bridge; it is hard to read because of its location. If it reads 1.0, you should have an exciting run.

Some additional comments should be made concerning this run. Once started, the last rapids must be completed one way or another. More than one unlucky paddler has used the railroad that follows the river to walk out after losing a boat. If by chance you are forced to leave your boat, the swim could be awesome; it could be your last if the water is high. In high water people have reported being swept downstream for what they estimated to be a half-mile or more before getting out. High levels are rated at least class V, and, although the rocks are mostly covered, the pace is amazingly fast and turbulent. In low or medium water, the Boreas is rated class IV. For those who can handle it, this run is excellent sport, but it should not be taken lightly.

Esopus Creek (N.Y.)

Route 28 to Phoenicia

DISTANCE (MILES)	3	TOO LOW	
SHUTTLE (MILES)		LOW	4.3
AVG. DROP (FEET/MILE)		MED.	5.6
MAX. DROP (FEET/MILE)		HIGH	
DIFFICULTY	II–III	TOO HIGH	
SCENERY	Good	GAUGE LOCATION	Schoharie Res.
DATE LAST CHECKED	1997	WATER LEVEL INFO.	914-657-2388
RUNOFF PATTERN	d/r		

The Esopus Creek is located in the heart of New York's Catskill Mountains. Its moderate rapids, generally good scenery, and reliable release schedule make it a favorite of both open- and closed-boaters in the New York/New Jersey/eastern Pennsylvania area. It is also the site of an annual race held each June by the American Whitewater Affiliation.

The source of water for the Esopus is the Schoharie Reservoir, more than 18 miles from the put-in. Water is piped this entire distance under the mountains and emerges from beneath Route 28 north of Phoenicia, New York, at Loretta Charlie's Grill. The put-in is at the point where the tube (the Shandaken Tunnel) emerges from the mountain—a most improbable source for a river. From here the run is approximately 3.0 miles long, with mostly class II rapids until the final drop, which is a technical class III.

The floods of 1996 changed the river considerably, and many narrow channels became choked with strainers. The Esopus is especially susceptible to high water, which changes the rapids considerably, so always go with what you see on the river rather than what you read in this description. While in any river of this character strainers are a potential hazard, the Esopus seems especially prone to downed trees due to its sometimes steep earthen banks, which erode easily. Be especially careful when the river splits around islands where the channels narrow.

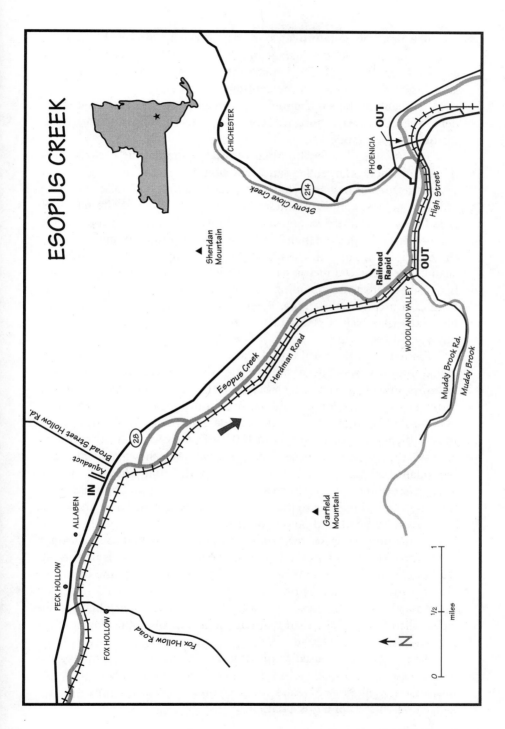

ESOPUS CREEK

CHICHESTER

Stony Clove Creek

214

PHOENICIA

OUT

High Street

Sheridan
Mountain

Railroad
Rapid

OUT

WOODLAND VALLEY

Esopus Creek

Herdman Road

Muddy Brook Rd.

Muddy Brook

28

Broad Street Hollow Rd.

Aqueduct

IN

ALLABEN

Garfield
Mountain

PECK HOLLOW

FOX HOLLOW

Fox Hollow Road

N

1

1/2
miles

0

Esopus Creek   19

The first half-mile provides an easy warm-up in class I riffles, but soon an island divides the current and the rapids become faster and steeper—a moderate class II. The left channel here may hold several strainers and the current is quick, so be cautious as you enter the rapid. On the river-left bank of the left channel, the damage from the 1996 flood is evident in several new retaining walls built to protect the houses that are precariously close to the river.

This rapid ends a few hundred yards after the channels rejoin below the island where a large, flat, sandstone boulder sits on river right. From where the current first splits to this boulder is about 0.75 mile.

For the next couple of miles, more easy class II rapids alternate with class I pools until the river approaches Route 28 in a right turn just above a large culvert under the highway. From here the difficulty increases over the next mile or so, with class II–II+ rapids leading to the second large island. The right channel is wider. The left channel slams into a gravel bank that seems to be shedding trees into the river, so be especially cautious if you choose this route. Be sure to stop after the channels rejoin below the island, since Railroad Rapid—the most difficult on the run—lurks just downstream.

Railroad is a technical class III at low to medium levels (500–1,000 cfs). At higher flows, most of the medium-size boulders are covered and it becomes a flush with irregular waves and few eddies. The rocks are sharp at any level, and the entire rapid has been transformed by heavy machinery and floods, so the location of hazards may change frequently. In the most difficult stretch, lasting about 100 yards, the river narrows considerably and the gradient steepens. Even at regular levels the infrequent eddies are small, making scouting from the boat difficult. There is an easy portage/scouting trail on river right starting at the gravel bar just above the old bridge piling that marks the lead-in to Railroad. There are several lines down Railroad, and no obvious sneak route.

At the bottom of Railroad on river right is a good takeout, although the best parking spot is at the top of the rapid, but the road is not heavily trafficked and the walk up is easy. For a slightly longer run and one more class II+ rapid, you can continue into Phoenicia and take out on river left immediately below the next rapid after Phoenicia in a sharp bend to the right called Elmer's. The road is about 100 feet through the woods. Parking is along the narrow road.

The Esopus is released frequently during the spring, summer, and fall. Releases are normally scheduled once a month throughout the boating season. Call 914-657-2388 for a recorded message telling you the gauge level in feet for a given day.

Hudson/Indian Rivers (N.Y.)

Indian River to Route 28
NOTE: Refer to map on page 14

DISTANCE (MILES)	12.5		TOO LOW	2.8
SHUTTLE (MILES)	14		LOW	
AVG. DROP (FEET/MILE)	29		MED.	5.5
MAX. DROP (FEET/MILE)	80		HIGH	6.3
DIFFICULTY	IV		TOO HIGH	7
SCENERY	Excellent		GAUGE LOCATION	North Creek
DATE LAST CHECKED	1997		WATER LEVEL INFO.	518-465-2016
RUNOFF PATTERN	n/d/r/l			

The Hudson River Gorge is certainly one of the finest runs in the East. Utterly majestic scenery, complete isolation from the daily routine, and challenging rapids all make this trip unforgettable. This part of the Hudson is one of the largest rivers described in this guide, and that means a great deal of powerful water. Once you've started the Hudson trip, it is very difficult to pull out. The course wanders through a river valley that is miles from the nearest road, so you're on your own with any problems that occur. A lost or broken paddle means a long walk—especially tough if there's still snow on the ground. The Hudson's rapids have heavy waves, big holes, and some rocks, depending on the water level. Pools are usually at the end of rapids, but rescues can be difficult due to the river's width and current. Drops are usually discrete, although in several places they blend together to form extended rapids. The Hudson is a difficult and demanding run. It is also magnificent.

A trip in the gorge section usually starts on the Indian River, which joins with the Hudson. To launch on the Indian, turn off Route 28 onto Chain Lakes Road (class II, dirt) and go for about 2.8 miles. Along the way you should pass a beach area, a dam at the end of the lake, and eventually a waterfall. Pick a good spot to turn around and change into paddling gear.

The Indian River itself is fairly narrow, with a good distribution of rocks and a discharge that depends on the level of Lake Abanakee above. It is class III under most conditions, a good warm-up for the more difficult water to come. The waterfall (class V) just above the put-in has been run, but the hole at its base has caused more than a few paddlers' days to get off to a bad start. After 1.0 to 1.5 miles, you reach the Hudson, which is twice or three times as wide as the Indian. A scattering of large boulders and some easy standing-wave rapids greet the paddler. Downstream, note that the side lines are either solid rock face or steep, tree-lined slopes. Where there is rock, it would be absolutely impossible to beach a boat or to effect an exit. Low water reveals gnarled waterline deformities that are superb examples of the water's erosive power. As with some modern-day sculptures, it is best not to stray too close: numerous undercut rocks in this first rapid will pass water, but not a boat or a boater. After more heavy class II water, a small stream enters from the left and the pace slackens as the riverbed widens. Large rocks start to appear in a slight right turn. In a wide right turn, the pace moves up to a respectable class III as the river falls over small ledges and around rocks. At the end of these rapids, Blue Ledge looms high overhead. Rising precipitously from water level, this bare rock face towers 200 feet upward. Blue Ledge is the stoic sentinel that guards the entrance to more-difficult rapids ahead. It's time to empty your boat, rest, and make a quick trip into the woods.

From Blue Ledge to about 4.0 miles downriver, the Hudson is a panorama of difficult water. At lower levels, most rapids are technical and demand maneuvering around rocks and holes in fast, heavy water. Rapids usually last for less than 100 yards, although two continue for a quarter-mile or more. Most rapids have a pool or some quieter water before the next drop. You may end up swimming, however, to reach the pool. As the water level rises, forget about the rocks. Worry about waves, souse holes, and vicious crosscurrents.

Below Blue Ledge, the Hudson bends left into a standing-wave rapid, then a pool. The river turns again after the pool into perhaps the heaviest drop on the trip, plunging downward among standing waves and souse holes, with large boulders on the sides and smaller ones in the middle. The crosscurrents are turbulent and powerful. The whole thing deserves a look if you haven't seen it previously. It is rated class IV at a gauge of 5.0. There is a pool below, a left turn into an easier class III rapid, another pool, then another class IV rapid that lasts 25 yards. Again, crosscurrents and turbulence deserve respect. After a right turn comes a long, continuous class III–IV stretch that lasts about a quarter-mile. In medium water this one is easy for competent boaters, though rocks, holes, and hydraulics gnaw constantly at the boat. Following calm water at the end is an easier class III drop, a right turn, then more rocks and turbulence. Downstream, the Hudson turns left where a stream enters from the right; then come some short, good rapids, another pool, a left turn, and an easy class III rapid.

Shortly after a right turn is the Soup Strainer. One of the trickier rapids on the trip, it has a large boulder in the center followed by a boiling eddy. The right and right center are strewn with large rocks and abrupt drops of 2 to 3 feet. The left is clearer but turbulent. If you choose right, start out very far right, then thread a "crooked needle" for 25 yards. Try to stay clear of the boiling eddy in the center—if it catches you it could mash you against the upstream rock as flavoring for the soup. After a few more turns, a right bend starts the longest rapids, which last for about a half-mile. At a gauge of 5.0, these are class III–III+ over rocks and hydraulics. The pool at the end marks the last of the major rapids, although there are still some intermediates to punctuate the otherwise calm water that follows.

Below a railroad bridge, the only structure to cross this part of the Hudson, the Boreas River enters from the left. A bit downstream, past where the railroad comes close on the right, the Hudson turns left. On the outside of this turn, extending from the right side, is a 2-to-3-foot drop followed by a large hole. Unless you want to tangle with this tiger, pass on the extreme left. Riding the hole here is like being a surfer on the Big Kahuna. Water from here to the takeout, about 3.0 miles downstream, is relatively slow flowing (at a gauge of 5.0), and paddling is a chore. Past a factory on your right, Route 28 comes close to the river, a good spot to leave cars for the shuttle. Farther down is the section where a yearly slalom and downriver race take place.

At a gauge of 5.0, this section is no place for intermediate paddlers. As the gauge edges toward 6.0 and 7.0, the Hudson changes from a friendly bear to an angry grizzly that clobbers trees in his path. At these higher levels, some people will find real sport, but most people will find huge waves, powerful currents, few rocks, cavernous souse holes, and many opportunities to break the world's record for holding their breath while upside down in a boat. At high levels, the onslaught of water seems to contain enough energy to create a local seismic event.

At a gauge reading of around 6.0, the rapids blend together so that you really cannot tell one from another. The whole run is one of unremitting difficulty; it should not be undertaken by the inexperienced. Long swims are possible at these higher levels, and you will undoubtedly wish that you had stayed home with a good book if you get separated from your boat. Also, if the Indian is high, the run down it can be as difficult as the Hudson itself. Be sure to check the level before you start. There are scheduled releases from the Indian frequently throughout the spring and less frequently through the summer and fall. These releases have aminor effect on the level of the Hudson, raising it les than half a foot, but make the Indian a fluid run.

If the weather is cold, this trip can be downright dangerous for those who don't do everything just right. The Hudson is one of the few rivers where the author has seen pieces of aluminum canoes.

The USGS gauge is in Warren County, on the left bank, 125 feet upstream from the bridge on Highway 28 in North Creek, N.Y. (about 26 miles downstream from Indian Lake). The gauge is in the Telemark system. You can obtain the latest reading by calling the Black River Regualting District's recorded message at 518-465-2016. The recording is changed each weekday and gives both river and lake stages for the Hudson at North Creek, The Sacandaga at Hope, and the Moose River at McKeever.

If you would like to try another calss IV river in the area try the Boreas, Black, or Lower Moose.

Moose River–Lower Moose (N.Y.)

Moose River Road to Fowlersville Road
Trip A

DISTANCE (MILES)	8.2	TOO LOW	
SHUTTLE (MILES)	11	LOW	3.5
AVG. DROP (FEET/MILE)	40	MED.	4
MAX. DROP (FEET/MILE)	90	HIGH	6
DIFFICULTY	III–IV	TOO HIGH	9
SCENERY	Excellent	GAUGE LOCATION	McKeever
DATE LAST CHECKED	1997	WATER LEVEL INFO.	518-465-2016
RUNOFF PATTERN	d/r/l		http://water.usgs.gov/public/realtime.html

The Lower Moose provides a challenging run appropriate for strong intermediate to advanced paddlers. The drops are steep and, depending on the flows, can be more or less pushy. Water is generally reliable from April through mid-June and again from Columbus Day weekend through the end of October. The annual fall drawdown from the Fulton Chain of Lakes augments natural flow starting on Columbus Day weekend. The Lower is remote, running mostly away from roads, and the scenery is excellent.

Put in for the Lower about 4.0 miles downstream of McKeever, New York, on Moose River Road where the road descends a hill to river level. The first rapid, Iron Bridge, is recognizable by a private steel bridge spanning the river. The river tumbles over a 200-yard lead-in before dropping over a 4-foot ledge. After a brief pool, the rapid finishes with a long runout of small ledges.

A quarter-mile below Iron Bridge the river tumbles over a long, technical rapid with three holes lurking down the middle right. At the bottom, the flow necks to the right and drops over a 4-foot ledge. After another half-mile of fast-moving water, the river enters a long rapid known as

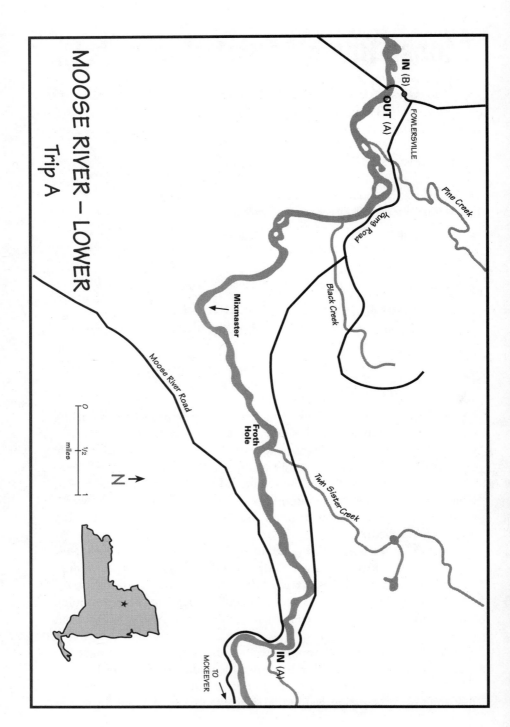

MOOSE RIVER – LOWER

Trip A

IN (B)

OUT (A)

FOWLERSVILLE

Pine Creek

Young Road

Black Creek

Mixmaster

Moose River Road

Froth Hole

Twin Sister Creek

0

½

miles

1

N →

IN (A)

TO
MCKEEVER

Rooster Tail, where the paddler crashes through a funky diagonal hole on the left, moves center through a series of ledges, then aims for the middle of a large breaking wave at the bottom.

Two miles of fastwater and a pair of class II rapids precede Froth Hole. This drop is long and difficult to scout, but the trickiest part is at the top where you must maneuver around a pair of holes. This can be avoided by scraping down the far right or carrying around the top drop on the right bank. At Froth Hole the river plunges over an abrupt 8-foot ledge. A rock in the center of the drop produces pinning possibilities at certain levels, and first-time boaters should scout from either shore.

Another 2.0-mile paddle leads to the section's most prominent rapid. At MixMaster the river flows down an 8-foot drop in a narrow diagonal tongue feeding a pair of ravenous holes. Many first-time paddlers end up in the hole, although it generally keeps a boat only temporarily. It is easy to portage or scout on the right shore.

A mile after MixMaster, a series of low ledges forms mellow surfing hydraulics. Immediately after this, the river is divided by a rocky island and drops 8 feet in a rapid called Elevator Shaft. Take the right channel and hold on.

Take out at the Fowlersville Road bridge, which is also the put-in for the Bottom Moose.

The gauge is located in McKeever, about 4.0 miles upstream from the put-in. Levels are available on the USGS web page at http://water.usgs.gov/public/realtime.html.

Although the Lower Moose is an intermediate run at low to medium water, the difficulty increases significantly at higher flows. At levels over 6 feet on the McKeever gauge, the run is appropriate for advanced paddlers, and when the river passes 8.0 on the gauge, it should be considered an experts-only run.

Moose River–Bottom (N.Y.)

Fowlersville Road to Lyonsdale Road
Trip B

DISTANCE (MILES)	3.5		TOO LOW	
SHUTTLE (MILES)	3.75		LOW	2.8
AVG. DROP (FEET/MILE)	80		MED.	
MAX. DROP (FEET/MILE)	120		HIGH	4
DIFFICULTY	IV–V		TOO HIGH	5
SCENERY	Good		GAUGE LOCATION	McKeever
DATE LAST CHECKED	1997		WATER LEVEL INFO.	518-465-2016
RUNOFF PATTERN	d/r/l			http://water.usgs.gov/public/realtime.html

The Bottom Moose is a hair-boater's dream, with several drops of more than 20 feet and a couple that are easily 40 feet plus.

Start the run at the Fowlersville Road bridge just east of Lyons Falls, New York. After a short flatwater pool, pull out on either side to scout the first of the big drops: Fowlersville Falls. This 40-foot slide is a sign of things to come, so if you're having second thoughts at this point, put back in and return to the put-in, because it doesn't get any easier. The left line is the most straightforward here. The right side has a beefy hole at the base. There's also a crossover line that starts right and cuts left halfway down. Either way, at low flows the shallowness creates the real possibility of bouncing down on valuable body parts, and at higher levels the hole at the base becomes a monster.

Below the slide, Funnel and Knife Edge present class IV challenges. On Knife Edge, where the river is contained between sheer rock walls, be especially careful in the center, since a paddler died here in 1985 when his boat pinned. There is a sneak on the left. Next comes Double Drop, where the line is generally right on the first 8-footer and all the way back to river left on the second one.

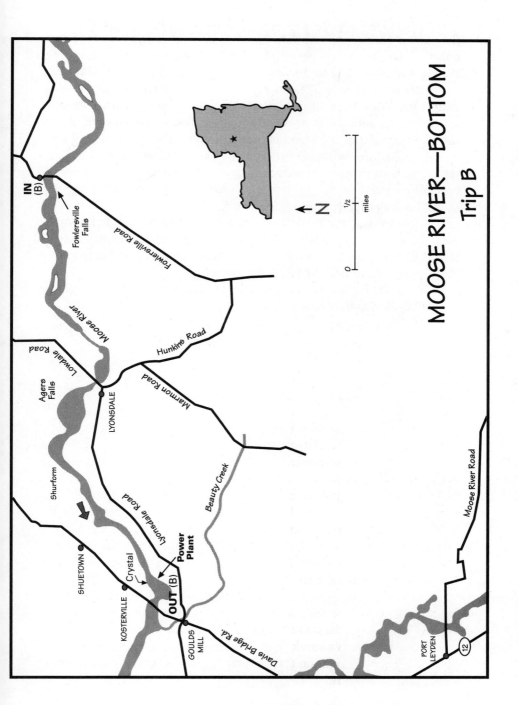

MOOSE RIVER—BOTTOM

Trip B

IN (B)

Fowlersville Falls

Fowlersville Road

Moose River

Lowdale Road

Agers Falls

Hunkins Road

Marmon Road

LYONSDALE

Shurform

Beauty Creek

Lyonsdale Road

Power Plant

SHUETOWN

Crystal

OUT (B)

KOSTERVILLE

Davis Bridge Rd.

GOULDS MILL

Moose River Road

PORT LEYDEN

12

← N

0   ½   miles

Moose River–Bottom   29

A short pool leads to a hydroelectric dam that must be carried. After the dam, a quarter-mile of flatwater ends in Ager Falls, an 18-foot sheer falls followed by a steep, powerful rapid. This one is more of a gut check than it is difficult. The lead-in drop to the falls is a 6-foot sigmoid dam.

After another mile of easier rapids comes Surform, one of the more dangerous drops. Here the river slides down rough Adirondack bedrock at a steep angle, with rocks strewn throughout and an island dividing the flow. Left or right of the island is runnable, but the whole rapid is gnarly.

After Surform, a double hydraulic known as Powerline leads to Crystal, 0.1 mile of progressively larger ledges culminating in a 12-footer. Be especially careful of the horseshoe-shaped ledge two-thirds of the way down. Getting caught here wouldn't be fun.

Below Crystal, the final dam is runnable for those who have not yet been scared out of their spray skirts. This one is perhaps the hairiest and largest drop on the river. Most boaters take out above Crystal on river left at the power-plant parking lot.

The gauge for the Moose is located in McKeever. Levels are reported on the USGS web page at http://water.usgs.gov/public/realtime.html.

Sacandaga River— West Branch (N.Y.)

White House to Campground
Trip A

DISTANCE (MILES)	8.5	TOO LOW	
SHUTTLE (MILES)	12	LOW	3.3
AVG. DROP (FEET/MILE)	36	MED.	5
MAX. DROP (FEET/MILE)	70	HIGH	
DIFFICULTY	II–III+	TOO HIGH	
SCENERY	Good	GAUGE LOCATION	Hope
DATE LAST CHECKED	1997	WATER LEVEL INFO.	http://water. - usgs.gov/public/realtime.html
RUNOFF PATTERN	n		

The longest and heaviest water in the Sacandaga is to be found on this branch. Large standing waves try to overpower any canoe, and even the smaller waves pack tremendous force that the canoeist can't really appreciate until he has had a rather brusque introduction. Superimposed on this is a current that is amazingly fast paced for the river's size, especially in high water, so your reaction time is cut down slightly. Fortunately very little maneuvering is required unless you attempt to avoid the bigger waves or souse holes that populate the run.

To start the trip on the West Branch, proceed from the campsite north on Route 30 toward Wells and turn left just before the town, near the outlet of Lake Algonquin. Continue until the road forks. Follow the left fork and go about 8.0 miles to Whitehouse over a road that could be snow blocked, depending on the time of the year. If you can't reach Whitehouse, put in by the area where the road leaves the river for the last time near Jimmy Creek. Probably the heaviest rapid on the trip is immediately

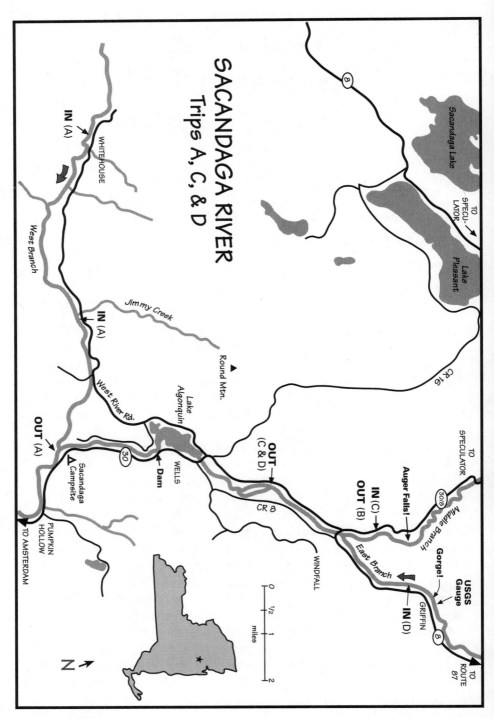

SACANDAGA RIVER
Trips A, C, & D

IN (A)
WHITEHOUSE

West Branch

Jimmy Creek
IN (A)

West River Rd.

Round Mtn.

Lake Algonquin

OUT (A)
▲ Sacandaga Campsite

WELLS

Dam

30

CR 8

PUMPKIN HOLLOW
TO AMSTERDAM

WINDFALL

OUT (C & D)

IN (C)
OUT (B)

Auger Falls!

Gorge!

East Branch

Middle Branch

30/8

USGS Gauge

GRIFFIN

IN (D)

8

TO ROUTE 87

TO SPECULATOR

CR 16

8

Sacandaga Lake

TO SPECU-LATOR

Lake Pleasant

N →

0
1/2
1
miles
2

32   New York

downstream. This rapid is large, with powerful standing waves all across the river; it can be run almost anywhere, although the waves become much bigger in high water. If you run this rapid successfully, the rest should be easy—remaining rapids are similar, although not so heavy, with an occasional hole thrown in for good measure. You can avoid most big waves if you want to, and the run is otherwise straightforward.

When the West Branch joins the outflow from Lake Algonquin, the campsite is on the immediate left bank, so a quick ferry is all you need for an afternoon's nap or another run. In low water, this entire section probably can be handled by an advanced beginner. Difficulty will be in the Class II–III range.

There is a class V–VI section upstream of Whitehouse that is the most remote and spectacular section of the Sacandaga River. A 300-foot-high gorge there contains four major drops, the first three of which are runnable. The put-in for this section is on Route 10 in the town of Arietta. There are several miles of flatwater before the gorge. Take out for this section at Whitehouse. Optimal levels for the gorge section are too low to run from Whitehouse down. This is experts-only water.

The Sacandaga has two gauges. One is on the East Branch near Griffin in Hamilton County, on the left bank 300 feet upstream from the highway bridge at Griffin, 2.0 miles downstream from Georgia Creek and 3.0 miles upstream from the mouth. It is just above the spectacular Griffin Gorge. The other gauge is on the main river near Hope, on the left bank 1.5 miles downstream from the West Branch and 4.5 miles upstream from Hope. An observer relays daily Hope readings to the Hudson River–Black River Regulating District in Albany, which you can contact at 518-465-2016.

Sacandaga River— Middle Branch (N.Y.)

Old Route 30 to Old Route 30 Bridge
Trip B

DISTANCE (MILES)	3.2	TOO LOW	
SHUTTLE (MILES)	3.2	LOW	
AVG. DROP (FEET/MILE)	250	MED.	
MAX. DROP (FEET/MILE)		HIGH	
DIFFICULTY	IV–V	TOO HIGH	
SCENERY	Excellent	GAUGE LOCATION	none
DATE LAST CHECKED	1997	WATER LEVEL INFO.	
RUNOFF PATTERN	n/l		

This section contains several waterfalls and long slides, and is an excellent advanced run that is easily accessible by road. Put in on Route 8/30 just south of Speculator where the road starts to head down a steep hill and old Route 30 bears off to the left. There is a parking area by the road here. It is also possible to put in just downstream from here and avoid carrying around a dam. For this put-in follow old Route 30 about three-quarters of a mile farther downstream to where it comes close to the river.

From the upper put-in, a quarter-mile of class II paddling leads to a hydroelectric dam that must be portaged. This is easiest on river left. Christine Falls (class V) is immediately below the dam. Scout from either side to decide whether to run it.

A mile of class III rapids interspersed with flatwater leads to the next big drop and the beginning of a section that contains several difficult rapids in a row. Scout the first 10-footer from river right. This drop can be

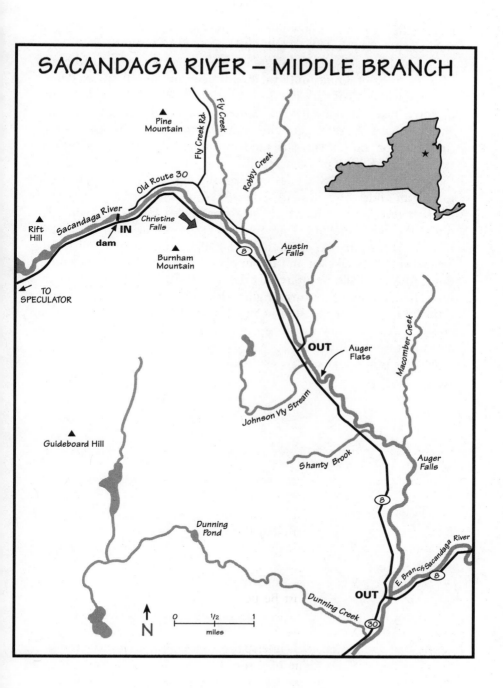

SACANDAGA RIVER – MIDDLE BRANCH

Pine
Mountain

Fly Creek Rd.

Fly Creek

Robby Creek

Old Route 30

Sacandaga River

Rift
Hill

Christine
Falls

IN

dam

8

Austin
Falls

Macomber Creek

TO
SPECULATOR

Burnham
Mountain

OUT

Auger
Flats

Johnson Vly Stream

Guideboard Hill

Shanty Brook

Auger
Falls

8

Dunning
Pond

E. Branch Sacandaga River

8

OUT

N

0   1/2   1
miles

Dunning Creek

30

run on the right at low flows, but the line changes to river left at higher water, as the right develops a large hole at the base of the drop.

Class IV slides with a few small ledge drops continue for the next three-quarters of a mile, until the rapids peter out into flatwater. After a mile and half or so of flatwater the gradient increases slightly and the river narrows. Take out along the left shore as soon as a horizon line appears ahead. Be careful not to get pulled into the next drop without scouting, since the horizon line appears suddenly and the last-chance eddy is on river left at the brink of the next falls.

Austin Falls (class V+) is a steep, sloping ledge that angles right toward an undercut rock wall. It is easily scouted or carried on river left. Below here a class IV boulder garden about 100 feet long leads to the take-out at the old Route 30 bridge. You also can continue downstream and take out at the junction of Routes 8 and 30, but unrunnable Auger Falls lies between this takeout and the upper one. If you decide to continue down to Auger Falls, be aware that the class II–III lead-in can be deceiving. The river suddenly turns right below and drops over Auger Falls. Scout partway down the lead-in rapid on river right. There is no pool above the drop. Below the drop is a class V boulder garden with sharp rocks that can be run.

There is no gauge on this section.

Sacandaga River—
Middle Branch Lower Section
(N.Y.)
Route 8/30 to Route 30
Trip C

DISTANCE (MILES)	2.7		TOO LOW	3.3
SHUTTLE (MILES)	3		LOW	.
AVG. DROP (FEET/MILE)	43		MED.	5.5
MAX. DROP (FEET/MILE)	50		HIGH	
DIFFICULTY	III		TOO HIGH	
SCENERY	Good		GAUGE LOCATION	Hope
DATE LAST CHECKED	1997		WATER LEVEL INFO.	518-465-2016
RUNOFF PATTERN			http://water.usgs.gov/public/realtime.html	

To reach the lower Middle Branch, go north through Wells on Route 30 and then onto Route 8/30. A short way past the Route 8 bridge, a small road angles off to the right, leading to the river. The river here is perhaps 50 to 60 feet wide, flowing swiftly among a wide scattering of rocks. The rapids start shortly downstream. In high water they are very closely spaced, choppy standing waves. The pace is not quite so fast as it is on the East Branch, but it is fast nonetheless. Just before the approach to the Route 8 bridge, a large island divides the river. Narrow channels exist on both sides. The excitement increases as the current accelerates.

After it joins the East Branch, the river widens considerably and speed diminishes, although there are still standing waves if the water is high. In that circumstance, one could enjoyably continue, taking out where Route 30 approaches the right bank.

It is also possible to make a longer run on the Middle Branch by starting higher up, since Route 8/30 stays close to the river for many miles. If you decide to do this, be prepared for at least one dam and several waterfalls.

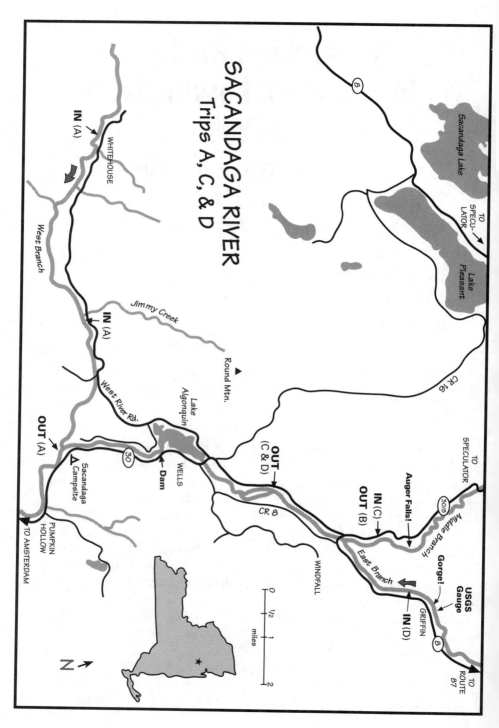

SACANDAGA RIVER
Trips A, C, & D

IN (A)

WHITEHOUSE

West Branch

IN (A)

Jimmy Creek

West River Rd.

Round Mtn.

Lake Algonquin

OUT (A)

Sacandaga Campsite

30

WELLS

Dam

OUT (C & D)

CR 8

TO AMSTERDAM

PUMPKIN HOLLOW

WINDFALL

Sacandaga Lake

TO SPECU-LATOR

Lake Pleasant

CR 16

TO SPECULATOR

Auger Falls!

IN (C)
OUT (B)

Middle Branch

30/8

Gorge!

USGS Gauge

East Branch

IN (D)

GRIFFIN

8

TO ROUTE 87

0   ½   1   2
miles

N

38   *New York*

Sacandaga River— East Branch (N.Y.)

Route 8/30 to Route 30
Trip D

DISTANCE (MILES)	2		**TOO LOW**	3.3
SHUTTLE (MILES)	2		**LOW**	
AVG. DROP (FEET/MILE)	55		**MED.**	5
MAX. DROP (FEET/MILE)	80		**HIGH**	5.5
DIFFICULTY	III–IV		**TOO HIGH**	
SCENERY	Good		**GAUGE LOCATION**	Hope
DATE LAST CHECKED	1997		**WATER LEVEL INFO.**	518-465-2016
RUNOFF PATTERN			http://water.usgs.gov/public/realtime.html	

The East Branch may be reached by proceeding north from Wells on Route 30 to Route 8, turning right, crossing the bridge over the combined Middle and East Branches, and continuing on until you find a desirable starting point. This section is fairly short and can easily be run several times in a day. Route 8 parallels the river for the entire length, which is handy for the initial scouting. Put in above the rapids section, where the river is just a small stream meandering through a marshy terrain. The current is swift but nothing like it is lower down, where an entrance would be somewhat less graceful. Be sure to put in below Griffin Gorge, since this marginally runnable cataract is great to look at but suitable only for expert boaters at ideal flows. The river then widens a bit and begins to pick up speed like a runaway truck gathering momentum. Standing waves are short and choppy at first, graduating to big and choppy. The speed with which the boat is stampeded downward is impressive. If the water is high, eddies are scarce.

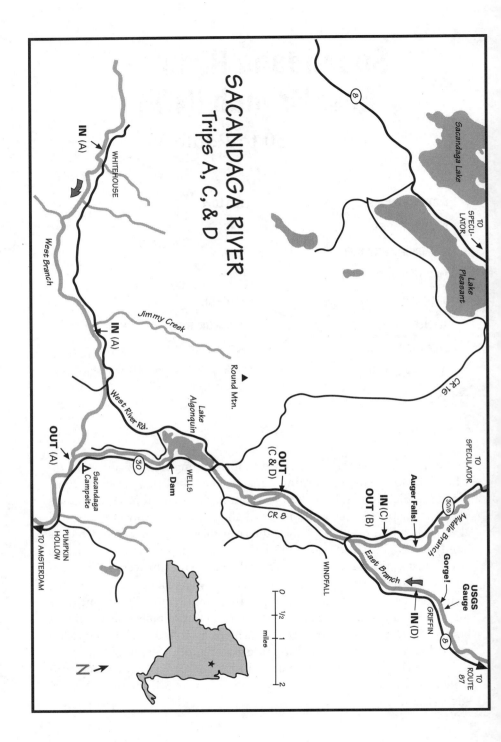

SACANDAGA RIVER
Trips A, C, & D

IN (A)

WHITEHOUSE

West Branch

Jimmy Creek

IN (A)

West River Rd.

Round Mtn.

Lake Algonquin

OUT (A)

30

WELLS

Dam

Sacandaga Campsite

PUMPKIN HOLLOW

TO AMSTERDAM

TO SPECU-LATOR

Sacandaga Lake

Lake Pleasant

CR 16

TO SPECULATOR

OUT (C & D)

CR 8

WINDFALL

Auger Falls!

IN (C)

OUT (B)

East Branch

Middle Branch

30/8

Gorge!

GRIFFIN

IN (D)

USGS Gauge

8

TO ROUTE 87

0   ½   1   2
miles

N

About halfway down, a group of rocks gathered in the center and right requires a bit of negotiation to avoid. In high water they form a nice, abrupt drop in the center, with an upsetting hydraulic immediately following. Lying in a left turn, they are most easily passed on the left. In lower water more rocks are exposed, demanding a much trickier maneuver. These rapids are easy to spot from the road—there is a little turnoff there—so look them over. The East Branch then continues on in its typical hurricane fashion, with waves and souse holes, to the Route 8 bridge where the worst, or best, is over.

In high water, the whole run is one where you'll stay upright if you can keep your bow pointed generally downstream. Easier said than done. Fierce waves and strong crosscurrents constantly divert the boat. Any maneuvering must be planned and executed well in advance, lest the extremely swift current rush the paddler headlong into trouble. In lower water, rocks naturally appear and the river becomes more technical. Any separation of a paddler from his boat in the upper stretches may result in a long swim, since other boaters probably could not give much aid. In the spring the Sacandaga can rise a foot quite easily in one day.

There are two gauges on the Sacandaga. One is on the East Branch near Griffin in Hamilton County, on the left bank 300 feet upstream from the highway bridge at Griffin where the river pulls away from the road, 2.0 miles downstream from Georgia Creek and 3.0 miles upstream from the mouth. It is just above the spectacular Griffin Gorge. Lasting only a hundred yards, the walls of the gorge rise precipitously and the water plunges violently down a series of cascades laden with huge boulders. It is certainly worth a visit. The other gauge is on the main river near Hope, on the left bank 1.5 miles downstream from the West Branch and 4.5 miles upstream from Hope. Neither gauge is in the Telemark system, but an observer relays Hope gauge readings to the Hudson River–Black River Regulating District in Albany. The latest reading may be obtained by calling 518-465-2016.

Sacandaga River (N.Y.)

Stewarts Bridge Reservoir to Hudson River

Trip E

DISTANCE (MILES)	2.8	TOO LOW	
SHUTTLE (MILES)	3	LOW	
AVG. DROP (FEET/MILE)	15	MED.	
MAX. DROP (FEET/MILE)		HIGH	
DIFFICULTY	II–III	TOO HIGH	
SCENERY	Good	GAUGE LOCATION	None
DATE LAST CHECKED	1997	WATER LEVEL INFO.	
RUNOFF PATTERN	d/r/l		

The main Sacandaga from Stewarts Bridge Reservoir to the Hudson River is notable mostly for its reliable flow pattern. The rapids are wide, with few features except waves, an occasional hole, and an even less occasional rock. The scenery is pleasant but nothing to write home about. Nevertheless, because it runs throughout the summer, the Sacandaga is a popular play spot for New York boaters who need a whitewater fix when most other rivers are dry.

The dam is owned by the Niagara Mohawk Power Company, and the river is managed by a local outfitter who provides shuttles and operates a shop at the base of the run. The shuttles are a nice feature, since for a minimal fee you can avoid the hassle of setting up your own.

There are two class III rapids in the section. The first is immediately below the dam, and the second is just above the confluence with the Hudson where a high stone bridge spans the river.

Take out on the left side at the base of this last rapid and walk to the parking area.

There is no gauge for this section, but water levels are normally runnable all summer long. Call a local outfitter for more information.

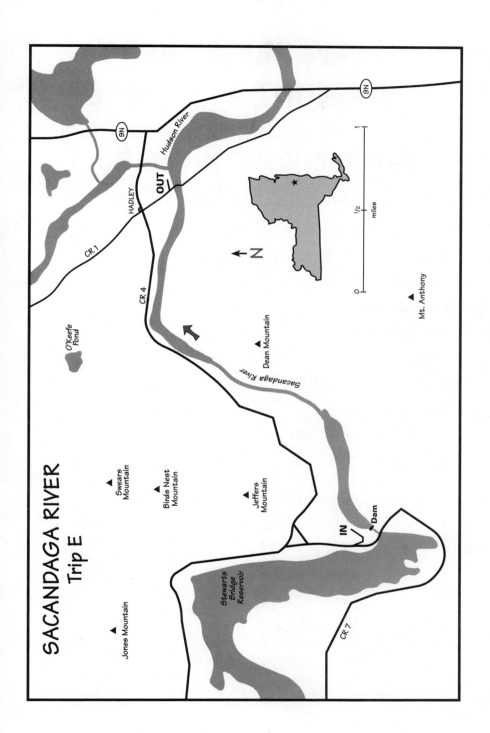

SACANDAGA RIVER
Trip E

N

Jones Mountain

Swears Mountain

Birds Nest Mountain

Jeffers Mountain

Stewarts Bridge Reservoir

IN

Dam

CR 7

O'Keefe Pond

CR 4

Sacandaga River

Dean Mountain

Mt. Anthony

CR 1

HADLEY

OUT

Hudson River

9N

9N

1

½
miles

0

NEW HAMPSHIRE, VERMONT, and MAINE

Ammonoosuc River (N.H.)

River Bend to Pierce Bridge
Trip A

DISTANCE (MILES)	3		TOO LOW	n/a
SHUTTLE (MILES)	3		LOW	3.6 / 3.6
AVG. DROP (FEET/MILE)	43		MED.	n/a / 5
MAX. DROP (FEET/MILE)	50		HIGH	5.1 / 5
DIFFICULTY	II–III		TOO HIGH	n/a
SCENERY	Good		GAGE LOCATION	Bath/Bethlehem
DATE LAST CHECKED	1997		WATER LEVEL INFO.	
RUNOFF PATTERN	n/f		http://water.usgs.gov/public/realtime.html	

Born in the Lakes of the Clouds in the heart of the Presidential Range, the Ammo enjoys a relatively long season and an attractive river valley, and it presents an excellent course for training intermediate-level canoeists. In this upper section (trip A), the rapids are closely spaced and class I–II in difficulty depending on the water level. Only one may require scouting, and then only at higher levels. The pools behind the many rocks are just waiting for eddy turns. In comparison, the lower section (trip B) has much class I–II water, but it is also laced with several class IV rapids. The lower half is the less attractive of the two. As with the other White Mountain rivers, the Ammonoosuc can rise rapidly by a foot or more in an hour. Both the upper and lower trips can be covered in a day's time.

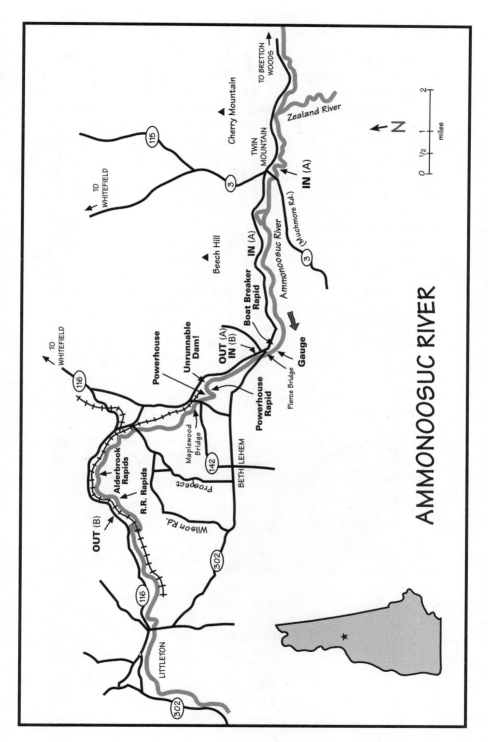

AMMONOOSUC RIVER

To start trip A, put in at Twin Mountain where Route 3 crosses the river or, as is usually done, some 2.2 miles downstream where the Ammonoosuc comes close to the road. Put in behind the stone church. The 2.0 miles down from Twin Mountain are mostly class I–II and they are good as a warm-up or to lengthen the trip. At River Bend, the river is some 50 to 75 feet wide, with a sprinkling of small rocks that are mostly covered in medium water. Below River Bend, the Ammo turns left and flows away from the road, and the rapids begin. At first there is 75 to 100 yards of easy class III water pouring over and around rocks. A sharp right turn with a boulder on the outside follows. Another playful class III rapid comes shortly, then there's a chute where rocks extend out from the left bank at the top. Here some waves are 2 to 3 feet high at gauge readings of 3.6 to 4.8 (Bethlehem). These rapids typify the rest of the run, although the pace will soon let up slightly. Except for very high water, there are always rocks, making the path somewhat less than straight. Up until the end of the trip, there should be no special difficulties.

Boat Breaker Rapid is the last and the hardest rapid on this trip. Near the end of the trip, notice a small island on the left, and below, a slight right turn with some houses on the left bank. Boat Breaker Rapid is 50 to

Canoeist approaching Ithiel Falls on the Lamoille River. Photo by Bruce Lessels

75 yards in length. It starts with a series of small, abrupt drops among large boulders; moves into a fast channel of turbulent water; and finally finishes with another small, abrupt drop with a covered, or partially covered, rock directly in the middle. The main channel starts center, shifts slightly left, then splits around that rock in the middle. In low or medium water, it is a straight run and there is plenty of room. At a gauge reading of 4.5, or higher, Boat Breaker Rapid will swamp most doubly paddled open boats if tackled directly. Closed boats should have no trouble at these levels. If the river is high, and you are in doubt, look these rapids over. At a gauge reading of 3.6 (Bethlehem), Boat Breaker is rated class III; at 4.5, it's a III+; at a reading of 5.0, it is a class IV. Below, on the left bank, is the government gauge. Following the gate there is an easier rocky rapid leading to Pierce Bridge, where the takeout is on the left up a steep, sandy bank. Muchmore Road forks off Route 302 and parallels the river up to Boat Breaker Rapid on the left side. The high rating for open boats is mainly for Boat Breaker Rapid, since the rest are not so heavy, although they do deserve respect. When paddling the Ammonoosuc, or any other New Hampshire river, be aware that state law requires cars to be parked entirely off the road. For this area, groups can usually camp at Zealand Campsite, which is upstream from Twin Mountain.

There are two gauges on the Ammonoosuc. The upstream Bethlehem gauge is in Grafton County, on the left bank 0.2 mile upstream from Pierce Bridge on Muchmore Road. The other gauge is also in Grafton County on the left bank, 0.4 mile downstream from the Wild Ammonoosuc River and 1.5 miles downstream from Bath, New Hampshire. Both gauges have outside markers, although the Bethlehem gauge is sometimes hard to read. The Bath gauge can be read remotely by the USGS. Another river of similar difficulty in the area is the Wild Ammonoosuc.

Ammonoosuc River (N.H.)
Pierce Bridge to Route 116
Trip B

DISTANCE (MILES)	7		TOO LOW	
SHUTTLE (MILES)	7		LOW	
AVG. DROP (FEET/MILE)	35		MED.	5 / 4.5
MAX. DROP (FEET/MILE)	55		HIGH	4.5
DIFFICULTY	II–IV		TOO HIGH	
SCENERY	Fair		GAUGE LOCATION	Bath / Bethlehem
DATE LAST CHECKED	1981		WATER LEVEL INFO.	
RUNOFF PATTERN	n/f		http://water.usgs.gov/public/realtime.html	

The lower Ammonoosuc (trip B) offers a longer run than the upper (trip A). It has two class IV rapids, much easy water, and a portage around a 20-foot dam. The scenery is not so attractive as that in trip A because of the signs of encroaching civilization that mark the banks. The first mile below the dam usually can be run even when other nearby streams are dry—it may be only class II, but at least it's wet.

Putting in at Pierce Bridge, or continuing down from the upper run on the Ammo, it is slightly less than 2.0 miles to an abandoned 20-foot dam and powerhouse. For most of the way there is a current with some easy class II rapids. The backwater from the dam starts just upstream before a left turn that brings the paddler to the dam itself. The portage is best on the right, over a concrete wall and down a short hill. This carry is a real pain in the keel, but it is absolutely necessary. You can look at it as good portage practice. Below the dam is approximately 1.0 mile of continuous rapids. The initial 100 to 150 yards below the dam are class II–III. The Ammo then turns right and in a short distance turns left, entering Powerhouse Rapids (class IV at a medium or high level). At this spot is a large island on the right side with a very narrow channel to its right that

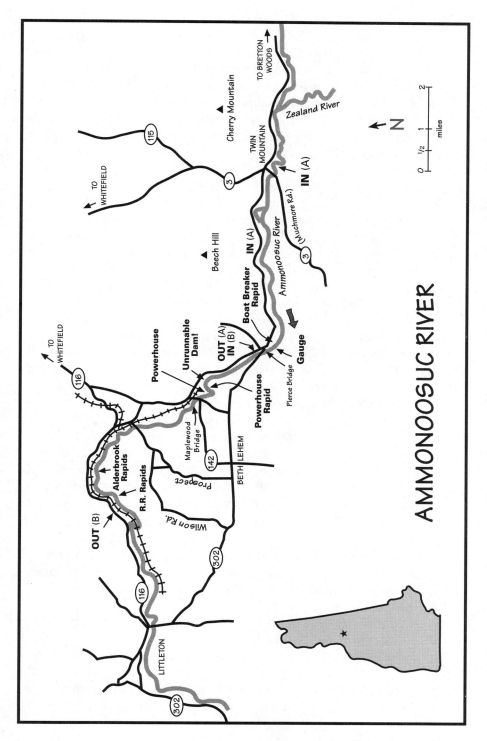

AMMONOOSUC RIVER

exists only in high water. Narrowed by the island, the Ammo races down a 100-yard chute on the left side. Halfway down is a collection of rocks in the middle and on the left. At a gauge reading of 4.5 (Bethlehem), these rocks are mostly covered and the entire course is an angry, churning broth, full of holes and hydraulics hidden by haystacks. The right center channel is usually taken at this level. Once it's set up, it's a straight shot. In lower water, more maneuvering is required to avoid the menagerie of rocks that appears. To scout, land at the upstream end of the island or walk down from the dam. Just before the left-turn entrance into Powerhouse Rapids, there are some boulders on the left. After Powerhouse Rapids, fast, calmer water rushes the paddler to a sharp right turn where there's an abrupt river-wide drop extending from the left shore. Most severe on the left and in the center (a 2-foot drop in high water), it can be skirted on the extreme right, but it's difficult to get there because the current pushes you constantly to the outside left. The associated hydraulic is a honey—get too close and it's sticky. The river then continues class II–III past another old powerhouse on the right shore, pauses long enough to catch a breath, then drops into another good rapid rated class III or III+ in high water. At low levels, be careful of the many sharp rocks here. After another left turn, there are easier rapids leading to the Maplewood Bridge.

Below the Maplewood Bridge some class III rapids start out easy, but three-quarters of the way down a rock ledge pushes out from the left (a 1.5-foot drop), as does a smaller one near the end, from the right. Several easier class II–III rapids follow. For the next eventful one, notice several large rocks, especially one on the right. In high water there is a chute here, another of those stair-step descents on the left, tapering down a bit on the right. A stretch of class I–II water follows as you pass a dead-end road on the left and an iron bridge. Below this bridge are two islands with runnable channels on either side. On the right, Route 116 approaches close for the first time, as the Ammo continues on with more class I–II water. This section of calmer water ends with a 1.5-foot drop over a rock ledge, just upstream from a pink, boxlike house on the right bank. For several hundred yards afterward, nothing much happens; then one enters Alder Brook Rapid.

Lying in wait just around a slight left turn, Alder Brook Rapid is class IV—heavy, fast, and rocky. It is sometimes recognized at its start by a rock on the left whose top contour resembles a camel, but by the time you spot this figment of someone's imagination, you're into it, so just listen for the sound of rushing water. Since a line of rocks extends out from the right side, the paddler is forced to begin left or left center. From here, one usually proceeds down the center with the main current, and then either left or right around a boulder in the middle three-quarters of the way down. This boulder usually supports a strong upstream pillow, and most paddlers choose left. Alder Brook lasts 25–50 yards and has some nice holes and haystacks measuring 2 to 3 feet in high water; it can also be run straight on the left side.

Ten minutes' paddle from Alder Brook brings you to Railroad Rapids and the trip's end. Starting in a right turn as the current picks up, rocks flash by like railroad ties. Shortly the Ammo turns sharply left, falling over more rocks with the turbulence prominent but less than at Alder Brook. Near the bottom is a 1.5-foot drop over a rock ledge on the left and center. In general, the whole left side is cluttered with rocks. The right side is a series of small drops and is the preferred route. The takeout is on the right bank where the rocks are extremely sharp and the bank is steep. A short walk up the embankment leads to a railroad track and an old dirt road where the drivers were supposed to meet you.

There are two government gauges on the Ammonoosuc. Closest to the mouth, the gauge near Bath is in Grafton County on the left bank, 0.4 mile downstream from the Wild Ammonoosuc River and 1.5 miles downstream from Bath, New Hampshire. The concrete gauge house is clearly visible from the road (Route 302). The Bath gauge is in the Telemark system. The Bethlehem gauge is also in Grafton County on the left bank, 0.2 mile upstream from Pierce Bridge on Muchmore Road and 3.0 miles east of Bethlehem.

Androscoggin River (N.H.)

Errol Bridge to Pontook Rapid

DISTANCE (MILES)	20		TOO LOW	1,500 cfss
SHUTTLE (MILES)	20		LOW	
AVG. DROP (FEET/MILE)	4		MED.	
MAX. DROP (FEET/MILE)	14		HIGH	
DIFFICULTY	I–II		TOO HIGH	
SCENERY	Good		GAUGE LOCATION	Errol Dam
DATE LAST CHECKED	1997		WATER LEVEL INFO.	
RUNOFF PATTERN	d/l		http://water.usgs.gov/public/realtime.html	

The Androscoggin is not a whitewater river in the classic sense, yet it does have one characteristic that makes it worthy of description: it runs in the summer. When most other rivers are dry, the Androscoggin keeps chugging away, even into August and September. The rapids are not noteworthy, but there are some to be found; the scenery isn't super, but it's certainly enjoyable; the drive to the river isn't short, but it's bearable. For beginning open boaters who need a river fix and are sick of dodging crowds on the Zoar Gap section of the Deerfield, the Androscoggin is one of the best opportunities around when the sun is high and the snow is long gone. The rapids are clustered into just two or three spots, and the remaining part of the river moves about as fast as the federal bureaucracy.

Passage to the Androscoggin usually goes through Berlin, New Hampshire, which is dominated by the Bowater Paper Company. The smell from the factory is evident 10 miles downwind, and the city is under a blanket of belching factory exhaust. Without the paper company, however, you probably would not have a summer run on the Androscoggin, or on the Rapid or Magalloway, for that matter. The dam at Errol, which controls the river flow, does so in response to factories in Berlin. At any rate,

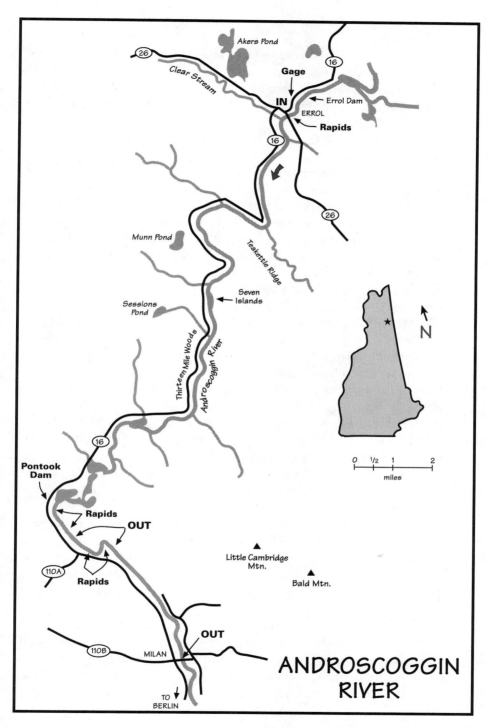

the Androscoggin is there, so why not use it? The upper parts described here are pretty and the water quality appears good, with no hint of the industrial mess that lies downstream.

The dam at Errol has been rebuilt since the mid-1980s and no longer has a rapid directly below it. Located about 0.8 mile north of Errol, it is reached via a small dirt road off Route 126. Below the sluiceways the river is fairly calm and in about 200 yards widens into a small pond. This pond, visible from Route 16, is one spot from which a trip may be started. A USGS gauge is on river right at the base of the pond. The staff is just below the gauging station, and readings are also available on the USGS web page (http://water.usgs.gov/public/realtime.html). An alternate starting point is on the right side, upstream from the Route 26 bridge in Errol. Here there is a small road that runs parallel to the river and alongside the heaviest rapids of the trip. Northern Waters—a small paddling shop and canoe outfitter—has a shop at the entrance to this road. At typical summer levels, the dam releases about 1,500 cfs.

The rapids under the Route 26 bridge in Errol are the heaviest of the trip. They begin just after a slight right turn from the pool above and proceed for several hundred yards, ending in a large pool. At 1,500 cfs, standing waves measuring up to 2 feet (trough to crest) are the biggest obstacle; the rapids are rated class II+. A line of rocks extends from the right bank at the start, and the current is quite swift. A run down the middle should be straightforward. The river is more than 100 feet wide here.

Thirteen Mile Woods begins just outside of Errol on Route 16. The river here is flat and continues to be so for about 3.5 to 4.0 miles. After this distance there is a series of small rapids interspersed with calmer water. These rapids continue for about 1.0 to 1.5 miles. All are easy, class I–II in difficulty; waves may be as high as a foot, and there are numerous very small drops over ledges and rocks.

A small bridge, known as the Brown Company Bridge, is the next landmark. The current speeds up under the bridge, and a chain of small regular waves creates several easy surfing opportunities as well as an excellent site for rapid swimming. Downstream of the Brown Company Bridge, seven islands are located on the right. Thirteen Mile Woods ends in another 2.0 miles.

When the landscape becomes marshy, you are approaching Pontook Dam. Another signal is the appearance of a small artificial stone island once used to connect log booms when the Androscoggin was a major route for transporting raw logs to the mills downstream. Pontook Dam was rebuilt in the 1980s when the timber crib and stone dam was repaired and a pipe was installed to divert water. There has been at least one death from canoeists getting too close to the recirculation below the dam, and despite the temptation to run the low-head drop, it should be avoided. The portage trail is on river right and is short. There is a large public put-in area with parking and bathrooms off Route 16 just below the dam. This is where Pontook Rapid begins.

Pontook Rapid is class II at normal summer flows (1,500 cfs). It is rocky with lots of shallow eddies and a few wave trains that reach 1 to 2 feet in height. When Route 16 comes close to the river, be prepared for the best rapids of the lower half of the trip. There's lots of whitewater caused by 1.5-foot drops over ledges and rocks. The paddler is forced to plan and choose a route for several hundred yards, but the current is not so powerful as it is in Errol. These interspersed rapids continue for some 2.0 miles from Pontook Dam. The best takeout is just at the bottom of the rapids where a small private road cuts through a hayfield. Be sure to respect the landowner.

If you want an extended trip, there are several roadside turnoffs after the river again comes close to Route 16. After the rapids the river meanders lazily through pasturelands to Milan (4.0 miles). Although this portion is flat, the distant scenery—the White Mountains—is rather pleasant.

There is no convenient gauge for the Androscoggin. For river information, check the USGS web page. Regular releases from Pontook Dam are scheduled throughout the boating season. To find out the level or to receive a copy of the schedule, call Pontook Hydro at 603-449-2903 Monday through Friday during regular business hours. Be aware that the local residents are somewhat skeptical of outsiders, so don't give them any reason to restrict river access and travel. Note also that permits are required for camping in the area.

Ashuelot River (N.H.)

Lower Stillwater to Gilsum Gorge
Trip A

DISTANCE (MILES)	5	TOO LOW	3.6
SHUTTLE (MILES)	5	LOW	4.1
AVG. DROP (FEET/MILE)	63	MED.	5.5
MAX. DROP (FEET/MILE)	80	HIGH	7.5
DIFFICULTY	III–IV	TOO HIGH	
SCENERY	Good	GAUGE LOCATION	Gilsum Gorge
DATE LAST CHECKED	1997	WATER LEVEL INFO.	
RUNOFF PATTERN	n		

The Ashuelot has its origin in several lakes to the north of Marlow, New Hampshire; it flows generally southeastward to meet the Connecticut below Hinsdale. Along most of its course the Ashuelot is flat, although two sections do offer good whitewater challenges and another is an appropriate training ground for beginners. The upper Ashuelot (trip A) is small and requires precise boat control in maneuvering through the many rock patterns. There are at least a half-dozen of these goodies, plus one that is substantially harder. In low water the passages are tight. Higher water opens new routes, but packs them with lots of turbulence. If the gauge reading is greater than 5.0, the rapids tend to blend together forming one long, difficult class IV rapid. At the trip's end, there is an impressive gorge. Trip A is short and easily can be repeated in a day. A road follows the river closely, which greatly facilitates the shuttle.

There is no single spot to start the upper Ashuelot, although one recommended put-in is by an old section of Route 10 some 3.0 miles north of Gilsum. A quarter-mile above there is a small bridge crossing the river. Immediately above the bridge the water is flat for a short distance as the river meanders through a small marsh. More-adventuresome boaters, who like a challenge without a warm-up, can put in below an 8-foot dam on a side road

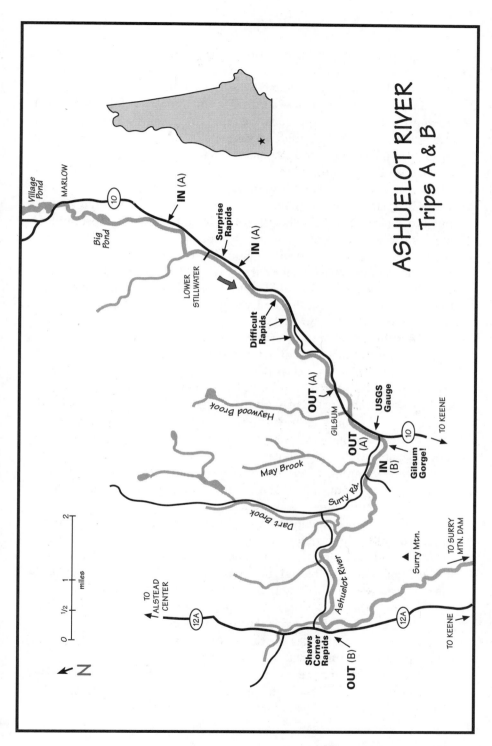

ASHUELOT RIVER
Trips A & B

just a half-mile above the small bridge. This upper put-in gives access to a couple of hundred yards of steep, ledgy class IV water before entering the marsh that leads to Surprise Rapid (class IV) and the lower put-in.

Surprise starts just below the bridge and appears as follows at low to medium water. As you approach the rapid the current speeds up and the left side is choked by a boulder, forming a chute in the right center that drops 1 to 2 feet into some haystacks. After a short stretch of fast, calmer water, several rocks sitting in the middle funnel the current to either side. The left side has an abrupt drop into a hydraulic and a series of standing waves in a narrow, but straight, outrun. The right side has a gradual drop, but a rock in the middle makes things difficult. Following almost immediately are several more drops, lots of turbulence, and finally a 2-to 3-foot drop at the end, with a strong hydraulic afterward. The entire length of Surprise is about 100 yards; the current is very fast and the channel is narrow. Surprise is the hardest rapid on the run and many people elect to start below it. It is visible from the road, though the large rocks lining the banks make scouting access a bit tricky.

After this initial outburst, the Ashuelot quickly composes itself with a steady current, a sprinkling of rocks, and an easy stone's-throw width. The rapids in this section are class II–III depending on water level. Where an island divides the river, the right side is sportier than the left. There are several rocks on the outside of the turn at the downstream end, just as the other channel returns its water to create a crisscross of currents. As the road comes close on the left side, the water becomes calm, forming a small pool-like area as the river prepares for a 50-yard narrow chute. This rapid marks the beginning of the more difficult water. From here to Gilsum, rapids are fairly continuous. At a gauge reading of 4.1, they are technical class III; at a gauge of 5.5, they are strong class IV.

In the rapids last mentioned above, the current speeds up and standing waves sprout as the paddler races toward several rocks at the end. Placed inconveniently in the middle, these rocks force the boater to go to either side. If these rapids give trouble, it is best to pull out, as the rest are harder. Below there is a chance for a brief rest, then the discharge filters between two large boulders on either side as the river prepares for a short S-turn with a small drop at its end. In a short while the current picks up again, the river turns left, and larger rocks clutter the turn, while rocks below generally clog the river's path. In the turn itself, there is an abrupt drop.

After a right turn there is a very fast chute with extremely turbulent water at high levels. The chute lasts down to and around the next left. Rocks in the center halfway down the chute force a large portion of the current to the left, then sharply right in a tight S. In medium or high water, it is possible to go through the rocks, although there are souse holes on the downstream side. This is probably the hardest rapid normally run, except for Surprise. Following the next left turn are more large rocks, with an abrupt drop near a flat rock in the center. Left center is clearest, but drops the paddler into a good hydraulic. More haystacks follow.

After another left turn another chute begins with several drops and more rocks. There is a house on the left bank slightly downstream from the start.

The Ashuelot then turns left again into two more drops that are easier than those above. The remains of an old bridge can be seen on either bank, and a small dirt road on the left goes up a hill to meet Route 10. This marks the end of the most difficult rapids, although plenty of class II–III water remains before Gilsum.

Houses soon appear on the left bank, and an island divides the river. The left channel is blocked by the more resilient remains of a dam, while the right side can be run almost anywhere over the 1-to 2-foot drop. From here it is only a short distance to the bridge at Gilsum, where one can take out by a lumberyard on the left.

It is possible to extend this trip to the next bridge (1.0 mile), where the rapids, although still class II–III, are not so difficult as above. In high water, these rapids shouldn't be underestimated, as they are tough. There is one particularly deceitful rapid just upstream of and under the bridge. The takeout for this extension is below the bridge, around a left turn. There is a roadside turnoff near this exit. Extreme care should be taken in exiting the river, especially in high water or with a weak group, because Gilsum Gorge is several hundred yards downstream. A swim started at the takeout could sweep a person through the gorge—definitely not recommended.

Gilsum Gorge is fast, narrow, and steep for several hundred yards as the river is squeezed between vertical rock walls. There are two particularly nasty looking boulder sieves—one on river left at the top and one on river right at the bottom—so swimming here is not a reasonable option. It is class V at most any level, and deserves careful scouting.

At a gauge reading of 7.5 the Ashuelot is runnable, but the water is big and continuous, with large, powerful holes and few eddies. The difficulty is solid class IV with a couple of rapids (Surprise and the rapid upstream of the put-in bridge) that may be class V. A mistake means a long, difficult swim.

The gauge is located on the right bank, 60 feet upstream from the impressive stone arch bridge guarding the entrance to Gilsum Gorge. This bridge is just off Keene-Newport Road (Route 10).

Other nearby rivers similar in character and difficulty are the Otter Brook and the South Branch of the Ashuelot.

Ashuelot River (N.H.)

Gilsum Gorge to Shaws Corner
Trip B

DISTANCE (MILES)	4		TOO LOW	0
SHUTTLE (MILES)	4		LOW	n/a
AVG. DROP (FEET/MILE)	30		MED.	5.7
MAX. DROP (FEET/MILE)	50		HIGH	6.5
DIFFICULTY	II		TOO HIGH	7.5
SCENERY	Good		GAUGE LOCATION	Gilsum Gorge
DATE LAST CHECKED	1981		WATER LEVEL INFO.	
RUNOFF PATTERN	n			

The middle Ashuelot (trip B) is a fine class II run for instructing begin-ners. The rapids consist mainly of small haystacks; the curves are gen-tle, yet it takes some skill to negotiate them; and there is a tough class III rapid to end the trip. A road follows alongside most of the way, although for the majority of the trip the paddler is unaware of it. The unfortunate aspect of this trip is that it seldom has enough water for an enjoyable run. It should be mentioned also that this trip seems straightforward even when the water is high, but coping with the strong current may be too much for people with only class II ability. Neophytes should be aware that rescues under these conditions are extremely demanding and difficult, and that boat and boater can be at the mercy of the river.

Start the trip downstream of Gilsum Gorge either where the Surry Mountain Dam Road first comes close to the river or by a small bridge a little farther downstream. The river is fairly wide here, with class II water and a scattering of small rocks. These rapids are typical of what lies ahead. The Ashuelot continues in this way, alternating between class I and class II in difficulty, reaching class III if the gauge is above 6.5.

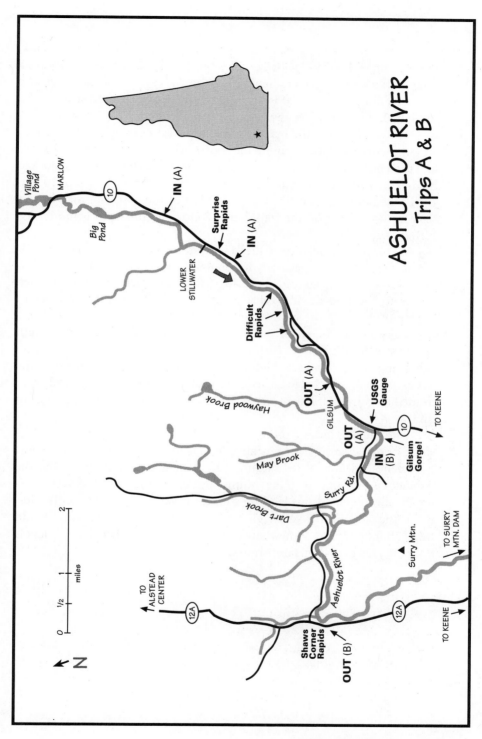

ASHUELOT RIVER
Trips A & B

At one spot, just as the river approaches the road on the right bank, there's a little chute and shortly thereafter the Ashuelot turns right into a long section of steeper gradient. Here the waves can rise to 2 feet at a gauge reading of 5.5, and it is necessary to maneuver around small rocks. Little hydraulics also give the beginner a challenge.

At a point below, the main channel funnels to the right side and into a tight S curve with rocks lining the course. The boater must turn first left and then quickly right again as the channel widens. The left side is blocked by rocks, and the current in the S is faster than normal. This rapid, rated II+ in medium water, is the second hardest of the trip. The road can be seen from the river on the right bank. Following this rapid is more class I–II water.

When you see a left turn ahead with stone blocks from an old building on the right bank, get ready for Shaws Corner Rapid (class III). Starting with a small ledge on the inside left of the turn, the current then moves to the outside and subsequently speeds up to form a series of haystacks that line the main channel on the right after the turn. These haystacks end as the water drops over two ledges about a boat's length apart. A hydraulic follows each ledge, with the wave on the downstream side being some 2 to 3 feet high in medium water. A path to the extreme left easily avoids the ledges. The normal takeout spot is a small footbridge immediately below. Shaws Corner Rapid lasts about 50 yards from start to finish.

The gauge is located on the right bank, 60 feet upstream from a large stone bridge guarding the entrance to Gilsum Gorge. This bridge is just off Keene-Newport Road (Route 10). At a gauge reading of 7.5, the Ashuelot is blowing down the mountainside, and the run looks very inviting. Be aware that at this level the current is very strong and continuous; this is the basis for the very high rating. Those with class II ability should think about paddling somewhere else. If you want another river of class II difficulty, try the New Hampshire Cold.

Lower Ashuelot (N.H.)

Ashuelot to Hinsdale
Trip C

DISTANCE (MILES)	3.5		**TOO LOW**	
SHUTTLE (MILES)	3.5		**LOW**	2
AVG. DROP (FEET/MILE)	52		**MED.**	4
MAX. DROP (FEET/MILE)	80		**HIGH**	6
DIFFICULTY	III–IV		**TOO HIGH**	7
SCENERY	Poor		**GAUGE LOCATION**	Paper Mill
DATE LAST CHECKED	1997		**WATER LEVEL INFO.**	
RUNOFF PATTERN	n/l			

The lower Ashuelot is quite different from the upper sections. This lower section is much wider, has a larger discharge, and is polluted, although the water quality has improved in recent years. Though the scenery is not great, the big-water playing opportunities are, and the river has been rediscovered in recent years by boaters who are bored with the Millers or the Contoocook. It also shares runoff patterns with the Millers and the Contoocook and is generally runnable when the Millers is above 4 feet or the Contoocook is above 7 feet.

In between dams the water can be powerful, with one set of especially heavy rapids. Even with its scenic drawbacks, this section of the Ashuelot offers good practice on one of New England's larger whitewater river sections.

When paddling this or any other river with heavy industrial activity on the banks and/or broken dams, be particularly careful of such man-made debris as spikes, timbers, and stray pieces of metal that can cause serious pinning or impalement injuries.

Put in at a covered bridge in Ashuelot, New Hampshire, where the river is wide (it would be hard to throw a stone across) and there are rocks

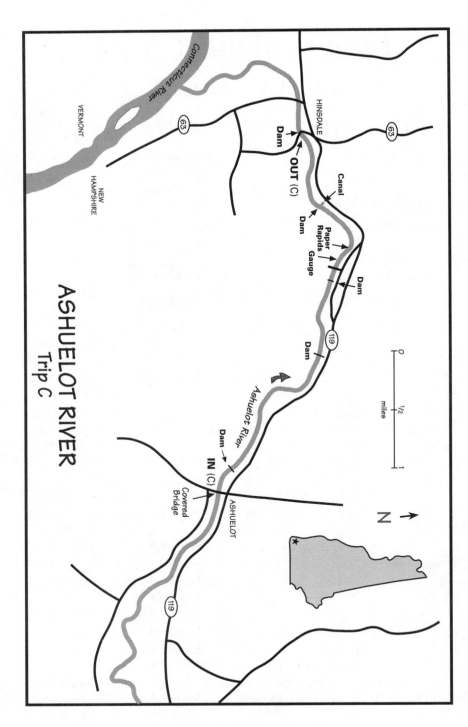

ASHUELOT RIVER
Trip C

sparsely scattered about. Below, the Ashuelot turns right where easy rapids are characteristic for a while. Within a half-mile the river enters a large pool; the first dam follows after a class III warm-up rapid.

Where the dam is breached on the left, the channel is about 100 feet wide. The wave formed at the bottom is smooth and excellent for surfing by paddlers who are very confident of their rolls. The left side is a large, fluffy hole at most levels, fed by a powerful eddy on river left. On the right side the water coming over the dam is shallow—not a good place to be upside down with the likely presence of debris on the bottom.

Just below the wave a large bridge abutment splits the current somewhat right of center. The left side is bigger water with a couple of pourovers that often catch large trees and other debris floating down the river. River right is easier and somewhat shallow. Avoid the abutment at all costs—a pin could be very serious.

This rapid continues for about 200 yards below the dam and then comes to another pool. The second dam follows. Portage easily on the right and put in just below in the tailrace of the dam. Below, the river picks up speed in some class III rapids, then turns right, where you'll encounter a good series of bumps, some clear water, and another set of waves at the bottom. Here, a large boulder sits in the middle. After a right turn, there's a long set of standing waves—straightforward, but, since the river is large, waves with a lot of power. They continue for several hundred yards. Then comes a large pool; the third dam follows. Carry on river left and put in carefully below the tailrace.

Ashuelot Paper Company is on the left bank throughout the next rapid, the heaviest of the trip. Paper Rapid moves quickly from just below the dam, so be sure your spray skirt and thigh straps are tight before letting go of shore. The river gradually picks up more speed and turbulence as it approaches a right turn below the paper company. Here there is very turbulent water with numerous pourovers and large haystacks measuring up to 4 feet at medium levels. The river drops about 5 feet over a distance of 150 yards. The main current funnels into the center, where the heaviest water contorts. Strong hydraulics and 1- to 1.5-foot drops are common. With all the aquatic gymnastics, the whitewater almost appears to be a snow-covered river. A turnoff from Route 119 that passes alongside Paper Rapid provides a good vantage point for scouting. At a gauge reading of 5.0, Paper is rated class IV; at 4.0 it is a long, tough class III.

After a left turn the river straightens out in a long, rock-studded rapid where a center route is fine. Rocks reach out from the right side. This set of rapids is class III, mainly because of its length. Below are some strong rapids where the water funnels to the center with 2-foot waves at a gauge reading of 5.0. Then the river gets quiet once again, and the fourth dam follows. This dam is rounded and the drop is short—about 5 feet. It is runnable, although the hydraulic below is weird and could be very difficult to escape. In the places where the hydraulic is weakest it intermittently becomes a small wave, then turns back into a hole again. Definitely scout this one from river right if you've never run it before, and be careful of the intake to the shoreline canal on the extreme right upstream side of the dam.

Directly below the dam, an island divides the channel and either way is fine. The ensuing rapids continue for an extended distance and stop just as the outskirts of Hinsdale come into view. The fifth dam is just below the next bridge (Depot Street), although most people take out at the bridge to avoid the difficult portage.

There is a USGS gauge on the left bank, 40 feet upstream of the downstream bridge in Hinsdale. It does not have an outside staff, but the reading is available on the USGS Water Resources Information web page (http://water.usgs.gov/public/realtime.html). The web page gives the levels in both feet and cfs. The correlation between feet on this gauge and runnability is not clear, but 1,000 cfs is thought to be a medium level and 1,400 a high level. There is also a paddlers' gauge on the left wall just downstream of the bridge in Paper Rapid. This is the gauge referred to in this description.

If you want another river that is similar in size to the lower Ashuelot, try the Contoocook. If you want another class IV run, try the upper Ashuelot.

South Branch of the Ashuelot (N.H.)

Troy to Route 12

DISTANCE (MILES)	2.5		TOO LOW	0.5
SHUTTLE (MILES)	2.5		LOW	n/a
AVG. DROP (FEET/MILE)	80		MED.	1.5
MAX. DROP (FEET/MILE)	100+		HIGH	3
DIFFICULTY	III–IV		TOO HIGH	
SCENERY	Fair		GAUGE LOCATION	Route 12
DATE LAST CHECKED	1997		WATER LEVEL INFO.	
RUNOFF PATTERN	n/f			

The South Branch of the Ashuelot typifies a small New Hampshire stream. It is steeply pitched and rocky, it flows only in early to mid-spring, and when it is runnable, it is cold. The South Branch is a good complement to and is near both the main Ashuelot and Otter Brook. The South Branch is best run when the water is up. In very high water, however, it is a river to be respected. The gradient is steep, especially in the upper portion of the run. At low water levels, rocks will annoy the boater who can paddle only in a straight line. In high water, rescues will be very difficult due to the powerful current. Route 12, which follows the river for the entire trip, is convenient for scouting and shuttle.

The South Branch gets its water from several ponds scattered around Troy, New Hampshire. As it flows through Troy, it is very narrow and relatively unexplored, and downed trees could be a big problem. A trip can be started almost anywhere along Route 12 where the river is close. Most people start near a bridge that is about a quarter- to a half-mile north of Bowers (a local store). Driving north from Troy, you will approach this bridge while going downhill. The upper portion of the trip is the most dif-

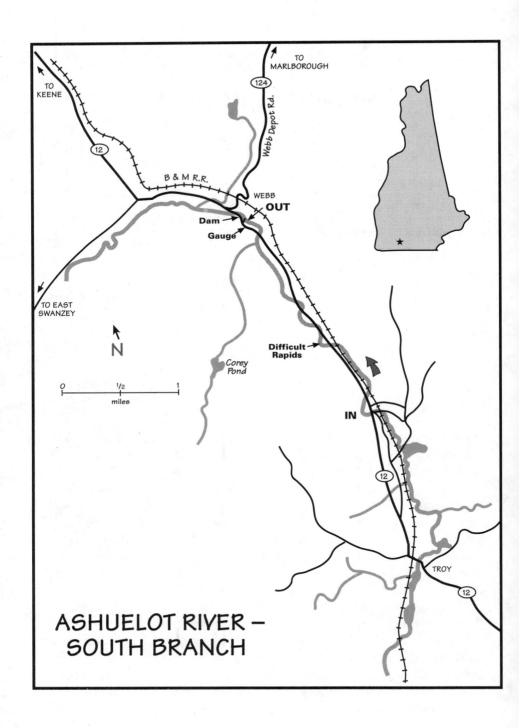

ASHUELOT RIVER –
SOUTH BRANCH

TO
MARLBOROUGH

124

Webb Depot Rd.

TO
KEENE

12

B & M R.R.

WEBB

OUT

Dam

Gauge

TO EAST
SWANZEY

N

Corey
Pond

**Difficult
Rapids**

IN

12

0   ½   1
miles

TROY

12

12

ficult, and it allows the paddler little time to warm up. The single hardest section lies in the vicinity of two closely spaced bridges: first a railroad bridge, then shortly downstream a Route 12 bridge. The river makes a sharp left turn here, banking off the right railroad bridge abutment in the process, which creates some complex currents and standing waves. The highway bridge, which is really a huge culvert, holds a surprise river-wide hole that is formed where the riverbed suddenly flattens out. Punch it head-on and with speed.

Once past the highway bridge, the South Branch starts a long, sweeping right turn that lasts down to the next Route 12 bridge. This turn has a stone wall on the outside left bank, part of which has fallen into the river along with the re-bar it contained, creating a very hazardous drop. In low to medium levels, this whole section calls for some fine maneuvering among holes and rocks. It should be scouted first and portaged if you are not sure of staying upright. In high water (5.5) this stretch is class V, not due to the difficulty of any particular section, but because the current is very fast and unbroken. It is difficult to measure the gradient here, but it must be well over 100 feet per mile. With a swollen riverbed, this part of

Surfing at Hole Brothers on the Black in Watertown, New York.
Photo by James Swedberg

the South Branch is a swirling, boiling, cascading, stampeding beast, something best left to river gods and insane kayakers. A relatively straight-forward section follows the second Route 12 bridge, until the river doubles under Route 12 again (in a left turn) and passes an island and a small roadside turnoff. In low to medium levels, these sections are class III; in high water they are class IV, again because of the current's continuity. Along the way the paddler should watch out for small islands supporting tree growth; if you're not careful, you'll be wearing a new laurel wreath, roots and all. It's difficult to explain brush burns on your face when you've just come off a river.

Near the end of the trip, the South Branch makes a right turn and passes under Route 12 once more. The next left turn starts a rock garden that lasts for several hundred yards. It is fairly technical and about as far away from the road as the river gets. In high water the difficulty is only class IV, because the gradient isn't so steep as it is upstream. One should not be lulled into a false sense of security, however, since there are plenty of exposed and unexposed rocks waiting to jolt you back to reality. As these rapids wind down, you approach an old bridge and, very shortly afterward, a small dam, which you can run or not depending on water level. The dam is broken in the middle, although you can't tell this at high water levels. The gauge is on the right bank here. This is also a convenient takeout spot, although boaters can easily continue down to and beyond the next left turn, which goes under Route 12 again. Beyond that bridge, the gradient gradually decreases and the river gets shallow; in low water, this section becomes a real drag. There is one spot downstream, however, where low-lying islands break the river into many narrow channels and the danger of tree hazards is high.

There is a USGS gauging station on the right bank, just upstream from the dam at the takeout. There used to be a convenient outside staff, but it is no longer there. This is unfortunate, because the river-level readings for this description were correlated to it. A hand-painted gauge is now on the left downstream side of the bridge just above the dam. In the past, if the gauge at Gilsum on the Ashuelot read 7.5, the South Branch was judged to be high. If the Gilsum gauge read 6.0, the South Branch was medium.

Ball Mountain Brook (Vt.)

Metcalf Road to Jamaica State Park

DISTANCE (MILES)	3.5		**TOO LOW**	
SHUTTLE (MILES)	3.5		**LOW**	6
AVG. DROP (FEET/MILE)	120		**MED.**	5
MAX. DROP (FEET/MILE)	130		**HIGH**	4
DIFFICULTY	III–IV		**TOO HIGH**	3
SCENERY	Good		**GAUGE LOCATION**	Route 30 Bridge
DATE LAST CHECKED	1997		**WATER LEVEL INFO.**	
RUNOFF PATTERN	n/f			

This small stream drains the south side of Stratton Mountain and feeds into the West River near the center of Jamaica, Vermont. In character and difficulty the rapids are similar to the Wardsboro and a little more difficult than the Winhall or the Rock. For those West release weekends when there's extra water around and you're in the mood for more challenge than the West provides, the Ball Mountain Brook is a good option.

Pikes Falls Road follows the river for its entire length, so you can choose your put-in. A convenient put-in is at or just above the bridge upstream of the center of Jamaica where Pikes Falls Road turns right to go over the bridge and a smaller dirt road continues straight ahead. You can also put in a quarter-mile farther up at Metcalf Road.

At medium water, the rapids are technical, with a few medium to large holes and numerous medium-sized boulders that form strong eddies. The water is very continuous with only a few class II and III sections interspersed among the steeper drops.

Before the second and third bridges that cross the river below Metcalf Road are larger, more constricted rapids that can pack a real punch at high water. After the bridge in the center of Jamaica the river turns right and enters Swimmers Hole—a large hydraulic in the center of the flow. The

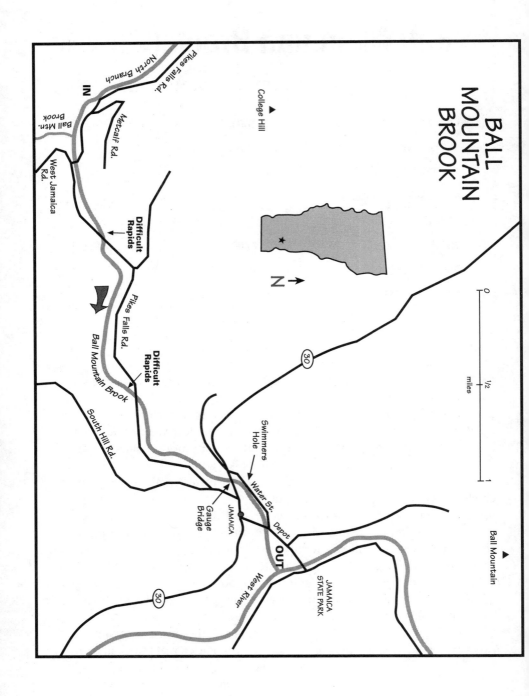

BALL MOUNTAIN BROOK

N →

College Hill ▶

Ball Mountain ▶

North Branch

Pikes Falls Rd.

IN

Ball Mtn. Brook

Metcalf Rd.

West Jamaica Rd.

Difficult Rapids

Pikes Falls Rd.

Ball Mountain Brook

South Hill Rd.

Difficult Rapids

Swimmers Hole

Water St.

Gauge Bridge

JAMAICA

Depot

OUT

West River

JAMAICA STATE PARK

30

30

0   ½   1
miles

strange thing about Swimmers is that the hole is out of proportion to the river. It is as if Swimmers were transported from the mighty Kennebec to the tiny little Ball Mountain Brook and dropped smack-dab in the middle of this otherwise innocuous rapid.

Following Swimmers, heavy (or technical, depending on the level) water continues until the Ball meets the West in another quarter-mile. Take out on the West at the entrance to Jamaica State Park. When flow conditions make the Ball runnable, the West is usually so flooded that it is a trivial matter simply to paddle upstream to the bridge at the entrance to the state park following the large eddy on river right.

There is no standard gauge for the Ball Mountain Brook, but local paddlers judge the level by the number of blocks showing on the downstream side of the center abutment of the Route 30 bridge in the middle of Jamaica. Since they count down from the top, the fewer blocks visible, the higher the water. Somewhere around six blocks is the lowest runnable level, while it has been run as high as three blocks (huge and very definitely class V).

Bearcamp River (N.H.)

Bennett Corner to Whittier

DISTANCE (MILES)	3.5		**TOO LOW**	0.5
SHUTTLE (MILES)	3.5		**LOW**	1
AVG. DROP (FEET/MILE)	32		**MED.**	
MAX. DROP (FEET/MILE)			**HIGH**	
DIFFICULTY	II–III (IV)		**TOO HIGH**	
SCENERY	Good		**GAUGE LOCATION**	Whittier
DATE LAST CHECKED	1997		**WATER LEVEL INFO.**	
RUNOFF PATTERN	n/l			

The Bearcamp is an interesting river located just south of the White Mountains. Depending on water level, it can be run by class II–III boaters, although they will have to exercise caution in several spots and will probably choose to walk or line the two most difficult rapids. The major rapids are well defined, each is less than 100 yards in length, and they are separated by stretches of flat or class I–II water. There is one dam that requires a portage, and two rapids may need scouting. Route 25 parallels the river, but is not obvious enough to detract greatly from the scenery.

Start the trip west of South Tamworth by turning off Route 25 onto Route 113, where a bridge crosses the river. There is also a Route 113 turnoff in Whittier. At the put-in the Bearcamp is about 60 feet wide with a class I current and a sandy bottom. Proceeding downstream, the riverbed meanders gently, with trees possibly blocking part of the passage; since the current is mild, they should present little hazard. After about fifteen minutes' paddle, the first rapid is seen; it is class II+ at low water, class III at higher levels. The total length is around 100 yards, and there is an abundance of small rocks to maneuver around. There are many routes through to the pool that sits at the bottom. A rock ledge across the river follows very shortly. The left side is easier; the right side has more drop.

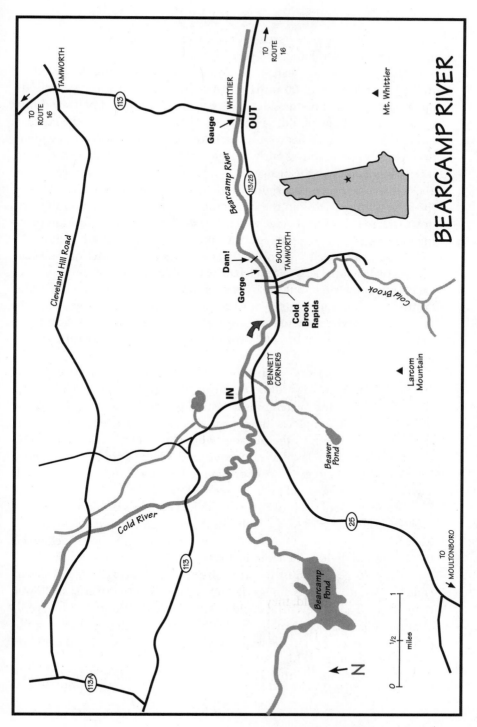

Bearcamp River   75

Class II rapids interspersed with flatwater follow. Soon, Route 25 approaches the right bank, and several houses come into view.

The quiet-flowing Bearcamp terminates in Cold Brook Rapids (class III–IV). Starting some 100 yards above an iron bridge, the current speeds up and large rocks line the sides. The water is choppy, and halfway down to the bridge a large boulder in center stream forces most of the current to the right, where the heaviest water is located. If you stay with the main flow, Cold Brook Rapids is fairly straightforward, although there are many little drops leading to the bridge and some nice haystacks underneath. Just above the bridge, on the right, Cold Brook picturesquely cuts its way through solid rock to join the Bearcamp. There is a big eddy on the left, downstream side of the bridge which you should pop into before attempting the final part. The rapids continue on past the bridge, and in about 30 yards there's a sudden drop over a ledge. A rock in the center of the ledge defines two channels, right and left. The left side drops a bit more sharply (3 feet) than the right, but the right channel has several small rocks at the bottom just waiting to push your bow into the cockpit. At a gauge reading of 1.0 this whole stretch is class III, harder at higher levels. Scout it if in doubt. The outflow travels down to and around the next turn, where the Bearcamp Gorge can be seen.

The Bearcamp Gorge is enshrouded by vertical rock walls rising 15 to 20 feet. It lasts 50 to 75 yards and is S-shaped. The entrance is via a sharp right turn where the current rushes hard against the outer rock wall. In the left turn that completes the S-turn, there's a 2- to 3-foot abrupt drop (low water), steepest on the outside right. This whole section is narrow, fast, and turbulent (class III+ at low water). A large pool below is handy for picking up the pieces. Scout the gorge before running, since its narrowness means you could be up a creek if a tree is down.

Below the pool is a broken dam with lots of debris blocking the channels. It should be portaged or run on the far right, where a 5-foot drop leads to a small channel that rejoins the main river. Immediately below the dam an island divides the river. Flatwater and class II rapids follow.

The next goodies, just upstream from a small bridge, are a series of small ledges. Route 25 is alongside on the right, and the river is shallower than above. The last eventful rapid is just before the Route 113 bridge in Whittier. It consists of a narrow S-shaped channel with large rocks on the sides and smaller ones in the water. It's class III in low water and could be exciting in medium or high water.

There is a hand-painted gauge on the left, upstream side of the Route 113 bridge in Whittier.

Big Branch (Vt.)

Big Branch Trail to Tabor Mountain Road Bridge

DISTANCE (MILES)	1.3		TOO LOW	
SHUTTLE (MILES)	1.7		LOW	
AVG. DROP (FEET/MILE)	400		MED.	
MAX. DROP (FEET/MILE)	n/a		HIGH	
DIFFICULTY	V+		TOO HIGH	
SCENERY	Excellent		GAUGE LOCATION	None
DATE LAST CHECKED	1997		WATER LEVEL INFO.	
RUNOFF PATTERN	n/f			

Big drops, big scenery, big danger, big hike out. For the seasoned class V creek-boater who's ready for a big challenge, here it is: nonstop rapids at a gradient of 400 feet per mile, with incredible scenery and no mandatory portages. Discovered by some paddlers at Middlebury College in 1997, the Big Branch has quickly become a test piece for New England creek-boaters.

What's most unusual about the run is that the gradient is absolutely unrelenting, there are no easy sections, and everything is runnable. From the put-in at the base of the Big Branch Trail to the takeout bridge one and a half miles downstream, the river demands complete concentration, absolute respect, careful judgment, and impeccable technique. Breaking a paddle, swimming, and pinning are all distinct possibilities, no matter how good you are.

From the Big Branch picnic area on Mount Tabor Road just east of Danby, follow the Big Branch Trail a quarter of a mile and about 500 feet downhill to the river. The rapids start immediately; the put-in rapids are fairly indicative of the rest of the run, although those downstream are, if anything, more difficult. Extremely narrow chutes, boulder sieves, constant blind 4- to 8-foot drops, and right-angle turn after right-angle turn

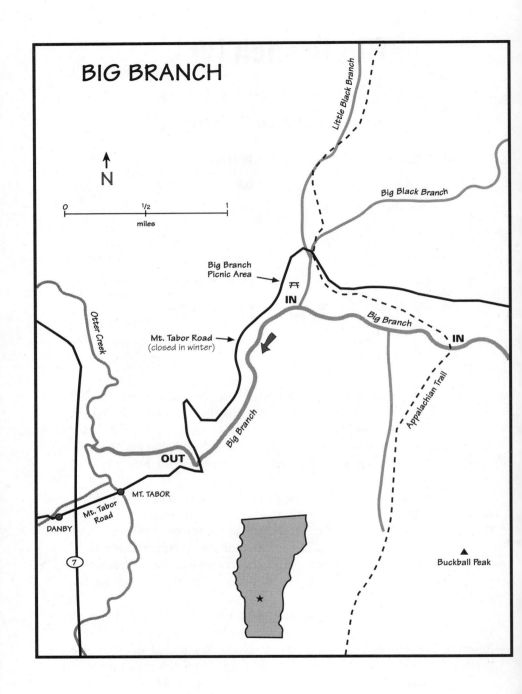

BIG BRANCH

N

0   1/2   1
      miles

Little Black Branch

Big Black Branch

Big Branch
Picnic Area

IN

Mt. Tabor Road
(closed in winter)

Big Branch

IN

Otter Creek

Big Branch

Appalachian Trail

OUT

MT. TABOR

Mt. Tabor
Road

DANBY

7

Buckball Peak

are par for the course. There are so many rapids it would be pointless to describe them all. Only three are described in detail here. If you need a guidebook to tell you how to run the rapids on this kind of river, you should be standing on the shore with a camera, not sitting in your boat.

About half a mile into the run the steepest drop yet appears after a left bend. Ahead, a 3-foot ledge leads to a much larger drop that is followed by a kind of minigorge. The lead-in ledge is straightforward, but don't let the angled hole mess you up, since the big drop downstream is about 6 to 8 feet high and has a piton rock at its base on river left and a cave in the wall on river right where the current pushes. Both right and center work when running the second ledge, but don't go too far right or you risk eddying out in the cave or getting splatted on the wall just downstream of it.

In another quarter-mile, a pair of bridge abutments appears and an island divides the river. The right channel is the route. Several large drops lead to a short section where the channels reconverge, then divide again as another island appears. Here the main channel is to the left of the island. Soon another blind rapid appears with a large flatiron toward the bottom that splits the channel abruptly, with most of the water going left and a messy boulder sieve just below the flatiron. The drops leading into this are not trivial, and getting left at the flatiron depends on running them precisely—a definite scout, and a possible portage.

More big drops lead, in about half a mile more, to the largest single plunge on the river. Here a 10-foot ledge extends from river left, becoming more broken and bouldery as you go right. Most of the water goes over the ledge through a very narrow crack in the rock with a nasty-looking rock rib on its right. The trick is to boof the small drop just above this rock, staying left so you don't get dragged through this crack but instead boof the large drop where the ledge is a clean apron on the left.

From this drop on down, more of the same leads to the takeout bridge. Difficult rapids extend downstream of the bridge for another hundred yards, where the first pool of the run signals the takeout. Climb the steep bank back up to the road and count your companions and equipment. If you have the same number you started with, consider yourself: a. lucky; b. good; c. both of the above.

There is no gauge for the Big Branch. If you are up to running it, you are able to judge its runnability by looking at the rapids upstream of the takeout. Needless to say, water level is critical on this one and runnable levels look almost too low. When it's low enough to run it appears very scratchy, but because it's so steep it's suicidal to run it with much water in it.

Black River (Vt.)

Whitesville to Perkinsville

DISTANCE (MILES)	5.5		TOO LOW	0.5
SHUTTLE (MILES)	5.5		LOW	1.5
AVG. DROP (FEET/MILE)	27		MED.	
MAX. DROP (FEET/MILE)	40		HIGH	
DIFFICULTY	II+		TOO HIGH	
SCENERY	Fair		GAUGE LOCATION	Covered Bridge
DATE LAST CHECKED	1997		WATER LEVEL INFO.	
RUNOFF PATTERN	n/d/l			

The Black is a medium-sized river in southeastern Vermont that offers a straightforward trip for advanced beginners. The usual run depends to a large extent on how much water is being released at the power station in Cavendish. A road parallels the river, so much of the trip can be viewed prior to launching. The river valley is not particularly attractive, and even less so during hunting season when abundant red-coated bipeds run through the woods. The riverbed is larger than most, so there's much room for what little maneuvering is needed. The rocks are mostly small, although several sections do have boulders that would be rather tough to displace with a moving canoe. In high water the current can be fast, although that would be the only danger. The most distinctive aspect of the Black, however, is the unrunnable Cavendish Gorge.

Blocked on its upstream end by a 30-foot dam, the Cavendish Gorge extends nearly a half-mile to the power station at its base. If this place is an example of how Mother Nature cuts through things, you definitely don't want to let her carve your Christmas turkey. Vertical rock walls spaced 20 to 30 feet apart and up to 50 feet high, abrupt 90° turns, under-cut passageways and ledges, and huge semispherical potholes gouged out

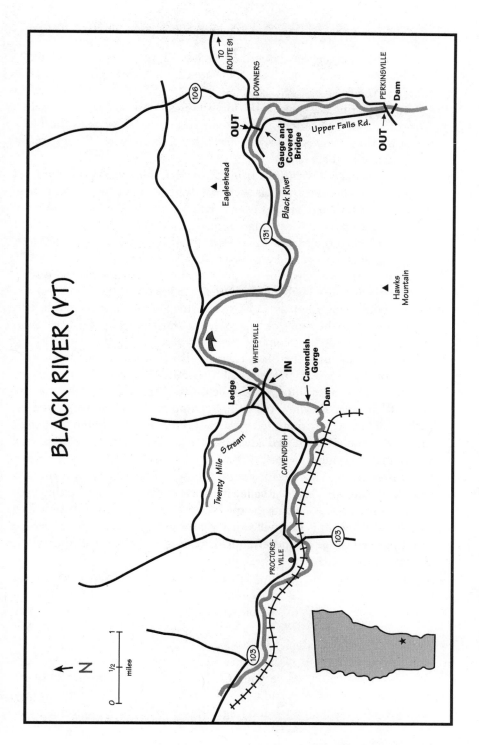

BLACK RIVER (VT)

TO ROUTE 91

DOWNERS

106

OUT

Gauge and Covered Bridge

PERKINSVILLE

Dam

Upper Falls Rd.

OUT

Black River

131

Eagleshead

Hawks Mountain

WHITESVILLE

Cavendish Gorge

IN

Ledge

Dam

Twenty Mile Stream

CAVENDISH

103

PROCTORS- VILLE

103

N

1

1/2

miles

0

of solid rock characterize this stretch of class VII water. You would have to be mad to attempt this in a boat; there are channels through which a boat couldn't even fit.

After visiting the Cavendish Gorge, launch your boats at Whitesville. Turn off Route 131 onto Carlton Road and drive 50 yards to the Black where a bridge crosses the river. The Black is fairly narrow here, and it flows with a good current.

Immediately downstream from the bridge is a ledge that extends all the way across the river. This is the most difficult single rapid on the trip. In normal water, there are passages at either extreme; the left channel is a less abrupt drop. From the bridge, approach the ledge in the right or right center, and when the current splits stay left. The total drop is about 2 feet. The left side is narrow and almost anything can block it, so look closely before you run. The drop in the right channel is abrupt and requires a sharp turn to enter. Higher points of the ledge block the middle of the river. A pool follows shortly and Twenty Mile Stream enters from the left. If you don't like the looks of this ledge for starters, put in farther downstream where Route 131 comes close to the river.

For the next mile the Black is class I–II in difficulty. You pass an old section of Route 131, then there's another mile of class II water.

About 3.5 miles into the trip, be on the lookout for rocks that are larger than normal. They mark the beginning of a section that is a bit more difficult. At one point in this section very large rocks line the banks, narrowing the riverbed and creating a fast, class III turbulent channel where maneuvering is necessary.

Approaching a covered bridge, small rocks force some easy turning in low water. After this bridge, the Black turns right and less-interesting paddling commences. A takeout by the covered bridge is probably best. Just below the bridge in Perkinsville, in a slight right turn, is a dam. There is a hand-painted gauge on the left, upstream side of the covered bridge near the takeout.

Blackwater River (N.H.)

Route 127 to Snyder's Mill

DISTANCE (MILES)	2.5		TOO LOW	
SHUTTLE (MILES)	2.5		LOW	3.8
AVG. DROP (FEET/MILE)	24		MED.	4.7
MAX. DROP (FEET/MILE)	50		HIGH	6
DIFFICULTY	I–IV		TOO HIGH	
SCENERY	Fair		GAUGE LOCATION	Webster
DATE LAST CHECKED	1997		WATER LEVEL INFO.	
RUNOFF PATTERN	d/r			

The Blackwater is a small, little-known stream that offers a short, racy run between slalom gates made of summer homes. The river is dam controlled, so it is possible to know exactly how much water to expect on any one weekend. Looking at the gradient figures, one would suspect the Blackwater cannot offer much whitewater, and in places it doesn't. There is the flatwater, and there are the rapids, and the two are quite distinct. In the upper half of the trip, the rapids are well defined and short. In the lower half, the rapids are narrow, technical, fast, and tend to blend together, forming several continuous thrillers. The Blackwater is not far from Concord, New Hampshire, and can serve as a follow-up run to the Contoocook.

Start a trip from a small side road that connects with Route 127 and approaches the river. At the start the river is relatively calm, and parts of it are pool-like in low water. If this spot proves difficult for a put-in because of posted land, an alternative start is on the right, downstream side of the Route 127 bridge. The bridge is just downstream from Blackwater Dam. The outflow from the dam is rather dramatic, and, below the bridge, the river forks around an island in class II–III fashion.

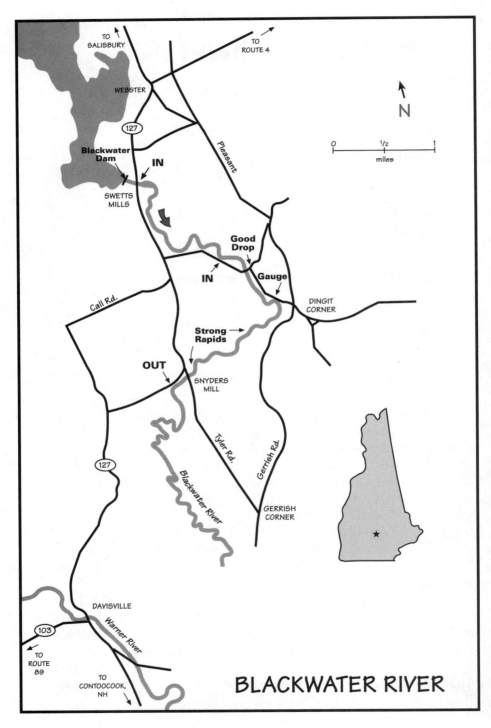

TO
SALISBURY

TO
ROUTE 4

WEBSTER

N

127

Blackwater
Dam

IN

Pleasant

SWETTS
MILLS

Good
Drop

IN

Gauge

Call Rd.

DINGIT
CORNER

Strong
Rapids

OUT

SNYDERS
MILL

Tyler Rd.

Gerrish Rd.

127

Blackwater River

GERRISH
CORNER

DAVISVILLE

103

Warner River

TO
ROUTE
89

TO
CONTOOCOOK,
NH

BLACKWATER RIVER

84 *New Hampshire, Vermont, and Maine*

When Clothespin Bridge (the name is bigger than the structure) is spotted, the boater should prepare for a real neck-jerker. Just before the bridge, the riverbed narrows and drops precipitously about 4 to 6 feet into an even narrower channel that can cause real problems if not run just right. This section often holds strainers. Scouting is a smart option. In the approach, the boater first paddles some calm water; then comes a short stretch of slightly S-shaped class II–III rapids that terminates in the big plunge. At the bottom, a series of boulders comes out from the left bank, forcing some furious last-second maneuvering in midair. It is very difficult to see the details of the drop from boat level, so your memory and instincts must be your guide. People have run this drop at various levels, but each boater should scout and judge for himself. The whole scene can be viewed from the bridge, but be aware that the surrounding area is heavily posted against swimmers, waders, parkers, loiterers, procrastinators, and urinators. The outflow from the drop down to the bridge is fast and tight. Below the bridge there's a little rocky rapid that splits around a tiny island. Calm water follows.

From Clothespin Bridge onward there are many summer homes, some with angry dogs in residence. In less than a half-mile of easy paddling, the gauge is visible on the left bank at Dingit Corner. The gauge has a dual purpose: it reads the river level, and it marks the beginning of the lower half of the run. From here on, there is either flatwater or good whitewater. Both are obvious when spotted. Almost directly below the gauge, the river turns right and falls over a short rock pile, which is very scratchy at a reading of 3.4. Beyond, the water turns flat.

The Eggbeater is the second set of long rapids in the lower part of the trip. The first set, called "A" Rapid, is about 100 yards long. If you think "A" is hard, wait until you encounter Eggbeater. There is some flatwater between them. Eggbeater is easily recognized because the whole river suddenly turns white, like a bowl of meringue beaten to a froth. It starts in a right turn and soon narrows into an extremely fast, tight, rocky chute that has the boater aiming first at one bank, then at the other. Turbulence, holes, and an extremely powerful current combine to make the Eggbeater a class IV, even in low water. On occasion, even good boaters manage to get turned around and are forced to run backwards. This is certainly not recommended, although it does have an advantage—you can't see what's coming next. Any swim you take here probably will be a long, brutal one. At the end of it you qualify for the Humpty Dumpty award. Eggbeater terminates rather dramatically in a right turn, just upstream from Snyder's Mill Bridge. A series of ledges cross the river in this turn. Depending on

Approaching Magic Falls on the Kennebec River. Photo by Shirley Griffin

where you cross their line, you'll have an easy or hard time of it. The steepest drops tend to be on the inside part of the curve. Avoid the right side if you can. The ledges continue beyond the bridge, with the rapids growing easier all the while.

Take out somewhat downstream of Snyder's Mill Bridge on the right bank. A small sandy road leads to Route 127, where there is a house (a cape with a bay window) and a small store.

The gauge is on the left bank, 0.2 mile west of Dingit Corner. It is hard to find it from the road. Make that impossible to find.

Blue Hill Falls (Maine)

Blue Hill Falls

DISTANCE (MILES)	100 yds.	**TOO LOW**	n/a
SHUTTLE (MILES)	None	**LOW**	n/a
AVG. DROP (FEET/MILE)	n/a	**MED.**	n/a
MAX. DROP (FEET/MILE)	n/a	**HIGH**	n/a
DIFFICULTY	II–III	**TOO HIGH**	n/a
SCENERY	Good	**GAUGE LOCATION**	None
DATE LAST CHECKED	1997	**WATER LEVEL INFO.**	tide tables
RUNOFF PATTERN	t		

Blue Hill Falls is a tidal rapid on the coast of Maine between Penobscot Bay and Mount Desert Island. Since it is not affected by runoff, Blue Hill Falls can be paddled any time of year when the tides are right. The setting is classic Down East coast, with fishing and lobster boats moored on the Blue Hill Bay side and upscale summer homes on the inland pond that is fed by the rip.

Blue Hill Falls is really two rapids in one: one on the incoming tide, and a different rapid on the outgoing tide. Things start to become interesting about two hours before high tide and again two hours before low tide. Tide tables are available in local newspapers. As with all tidal rapids, Blue Hill Falls changes throughout its run, challenging boaters constantly to deal with new conditions. Also typical of tidal rapids, the rocks are covered in barnacles and seaweed, making them either as abrasive as sharkskin or as slippery as an eel.

Access is easy: Park on Route 175 just south of Blue Hill, Maine, where a concrete arch bridge crosses the rapid. The roadway is narrow here, so watch for fast-moving vehicles barreling down the hill from the south side of the bridge. A set of steps on the inland, north side of the bridge leads to a convenient put-in on the outflowing tide. When the tide is coming in, the path on the bay side of the north end of the bridge is the easier put-in.

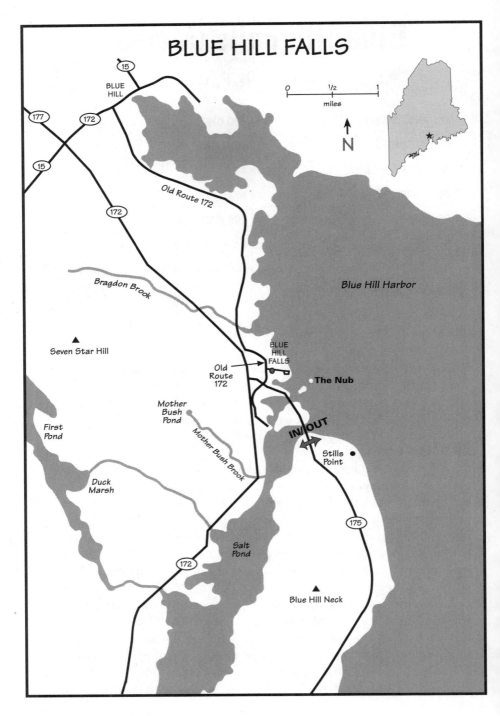

BLUE HILL FALLS

0   1/2   1
miles

N

BLUE HILL

BLUE HILL FALLS

The Nub

Blue Hill Harbor

Old Route 172

Bragdon Brook

Seven Star Hill

Old Route 172

Mother Bush Pond

Mother Bush Brook

First Pond

Duck Marsh

IN/OUT

Stills Point

Salt Pond

Blue Hill Neck

Racing in Twisted Sister on the Concord River in Lowell, MA. Photo by Bruce Lessels

On the outflow, the rapid is a 60-foot-wide tongue with compression waves formed where the outlet from Salt Pond narrows down at the Route 175 bridge. On river right (the south side of the rapid), a beefy hole forms and becomes steeper throughout the run, eventually turning into a pourover. There is a large eddy on river left below the bridge and a much smaller one on the right just above the hole. A train of diagonal waves develops at the bottom, with eddies extending into the bay below on both sides.

The incoming tide holds a smooth, regular surfing wave in the center of the channel, with a large eddy on either side that provides easy access to it. At higher tides (near the full moon) the wave gets big (5+ feet) and starts to curl, while at lower tides it is very regular and about 3 feet high. The river right (north) eddy line is a deep squirt line, and the upper part of it, where it comes off the bridge abutment, looks like mystery-move material.

Cold River (N.H.)
South Acworth to Vilas Pool
Trip A

DISTANCE (MILES)	5.5		TOO LOW	3.4
SHUTTLE (MILES)	5.5		LOW	
AVG. DROP (FEET/MILE)	43		MED.	5.2
MAX. DROP (FEET/MILE)	53		HIGH	8
DIFFICULTY	II		TOO HIGH	
SCENERY	Good		GAUGE LOCATION	Drewsville
DATE LAST CHECKED	1981		WATER LEVEL INFO.	
RUNOFF PATTERN	n			

The Cold is a small, snappy stream that offers nearly continuous current, pleasant scenery, fallen trees, and barbed wire. In low water the pace is relatively slow, while in medium to high levels the Cold offers a nonstop run. The Cold is an excellent place for advanced beginners to practice, because while none of the rapids is extremely difficult, they do require a certain finesse to negotiate gracefully. The valley is alternately attractive and civilized, and the water is polluted only by furry beasties and cows. When canoeable—generally only in the spring—the water temperature lives up to its name. A road passes alongside almost the entire route, so starts and stops are flexible.

Put in below the gorge, downstream from South Acworth where the road comes close to the river. This gorge has several sharp drops, the last being a 10-foot waterfall. At the put-in, the river is 20 to 25 feet wide, moving swiftly over small rocks with a scattering of larger boulders. A mile or so downstream, the river turns left against a 5-foot rock on the right, and a bit downstream a 6-inch rock dam should give no trouble. Farther down, the stream narrows and seems to double back on itself in several sharp turns where the risk of fallen trees is high. This section also

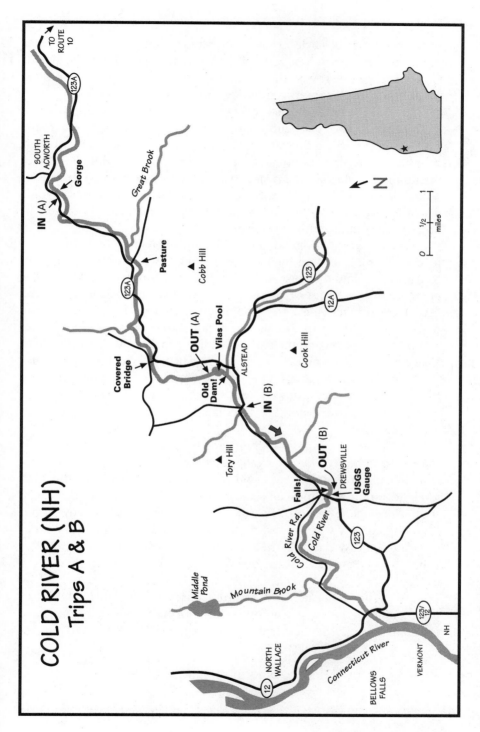

COLD RIVER (NH)
Trips A & B

TO ROUTE 10

123A

SOUTH ACWORTH

Gorge

IN (A)

Great Brook

123A

Pasture

Cobb Hill

Covered Bridge

OUT (A)

Vilas Pool

Old Dam!

ALSTEAD

Cook Hill

123

12A

IN (B)

Tory Hill

OUT (B)

DREWSVILLE

Falls!

USGS Gauge

Cold River Rd.

Cold River

123

Middle Pond

Mountain Brook

123/12

NORTH WALLACE

12

Connecticut River

BELLOWS FALLS

VERMONT

NH

N

1

1/2

0

miles

suffers from such obstacles as footbridges and makeshift dams. The boater should be particularly watchful for barbed wire, especially in the area of Great Brook, a side stream that enters from the left. A little bridge crosses Great Brook just before its confluence with the Cold.

Beyond the next bridge, the Cold flows through a pasture, where a curious cow or two (or twenty) may follow the funny-looking water animals. Passage to the following bridge has some crisp rapids and one left turn that is sharper than usual; otherwise there is nothing difficult. Under the Route 123A bridge, the river forks, with channels on the extremes of both sides. Continuing downstream, the Cold offers more brisk rapids where the narrow riverbed forces the canoeist to plan ahead carefully in order to zig and zag around rocks and fallen trees.

Near a covered bridge, be on the lookout again for more barbed-wire fences. You may not find them—consider that a good omen. About 0.25 to 0.5 mile below the covered bridge, the road leaves the river. At that point there is a series of particularly good class II–III rapids, spaced between swiftly moving water. The first one, in a left turn, is one of the best sections of the trip. The danger of fallen trees in every turn is great. The pace accelerates and the river twists like a snake until the entrance to Vilas Pool, about 1.5 miles from the covered bridge. When you enter Vilas Pool, take out immediately on the left side where the road is near, in order to avoid the dam on the downstream side of the pool. The outflow orifice of this dam is usually below the waterline, and it is just big enough to trap a body or a boat.

The Cold is runnable at almost any level, assuming, of course, that there is some water. Even at a gauge reading of 8.0, the Cold is manageable, but the current is strong and rescue will be difficult. At this high level, the rapids are almost all standing waves, with few or no rocks to be seen. The sideline trees are also in the water, which makes eddying out more difficult. At a gauge reading of 8.0 the Cold is rated a heavy-water class II or an easy class III. The route is usually straightforward, but class II boaters who are just starting out should exercise caution at these higher levels.

The gauge is located in Cheshire County on the left bank 50 feet upstream from the bridge on Route 123A, north of Drewsville. The gauge is just upstream from a short but impressive gorge where the Cold plunges down an almost vertical staircase.

Cold River (N.H.)

Alstead to Drewsville
Trip B

DISTANCE (MILES)	2	**TOO LOW**		3.4
SHUTTLE (MILES)	2	**LOW**		
AVG. DROP (FEET/MILE)	40	**MED.**		5.2
MAX. DROP (FEET/MILE)	40	**HIGH**		8
DIFFICULTY	II	**TOO HIGH**		
SCENERY	Good	**GAUGE LOCATION**		Drewsville
DATE LAST CHECKED	1981	**WATER LEVEL INFO.**		
RUNOFF PATTERN	n			

This trip may be made in conjunction with the previous one or as a separate trip. Just below the dam on Vilas Pool, immediately after a right turn, there is another dam. This dam is broken and may be runnable depending on the water level and your ability. Look it over and decide for yourself. Since you have to portage the dam at Vilas Pool, you might as well carry down to Alstead if you want to continue on from the upper part (trip A). Because trip B is only 2.0 miles long, it presents a good opportunity for new paddlers to practice without having to tackle the longer upper section of the river.

This section of the river is similar to the preceding section, and, although the rapids diminish somewhat, the swift current continues. The river is still narrow and fallen trees can aggravate the paddler and slow the trip drastically. Approach each blind curve cautiously, looking for obstacles. Beyond the trees there are no major difficulties—except for the take-out.

The trip ends as the river takes an awesome plunge down a vertical staircase filled with boulders and shrouded by vertical rock walls. These horrendous falls start immediately under the Route 123A bridge, which

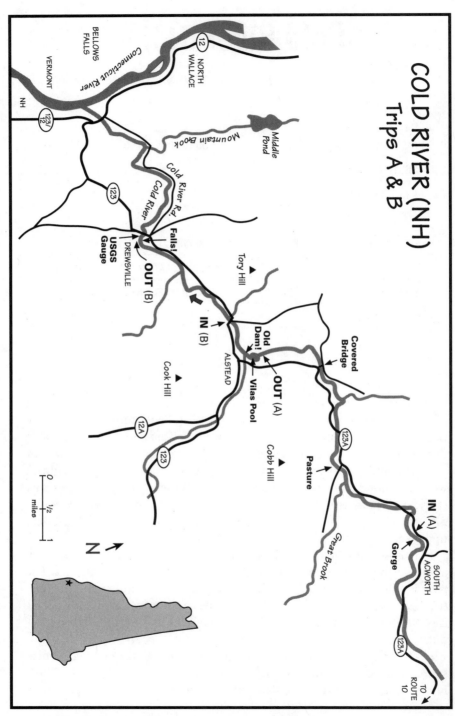

COLD RIVER (NH)
Trips A & B

crosses the river at the takeout. Paddlers would do well to familiarize themselves completely with a convenient takeout spot that is sufficiently far upstream from this drop to ensure a safe exit.

When the Cold is running high, it is certainly worth one's time to see water blasting through the Drewsville gorge; with large, stair-step drops concealed by abrupt rock walls, this gorge is as impressive as any in New England. Even thinking about boating it is a frightening prospect.

The gauge is on the left bank just upstream from the bridge and the entrance to the Drewsville gorge.

Another nearby river similar in difficulty to the Cold is the Black in Vermont.

Connecticut River–
Sumner Falls (Vt./N.H.)

Sumner Falls

DISTANCE (MILES)	0.25	TOO LOW	700 cfs
SHUTTLE (MILES)	none	LOW	
AVG. DROP (FEET/MILE)		MED.	5,000 cfs
MAX. DROP (FEET/MILE)		HIGH	10,000 cfs
DIFFICULTY	III	TOO HIGH	
SCENERY	Good	GAUGE LOCATION	Wilder Dam
DATE LAST CHECKED	1997	WATER LEVEL INFO.	888-356-3663
RUNOFF PATTERN	d/r/l		

Sumner Falls, or Hartland Rapid, as it's known in some boating circles, is runnable at almost any water level and interesting enough to occupy the better part of a day at most levels. Only a quarter-mile long, Sumner Falls is not a river run, but as reliable summer play spots go, it's tops.

Sumner Falls can accommodate a range of boating abilities, from beginners who may choose to stay in the eddy at the bottom and work their way across the current jets below the ledge, to intermediates who are challenged by catching a few eddies on their way down the rapid, to advanced boaters who spend the entire day blowing off enders and trying for the perfect pirouette.

The whitewater is formed by a slate outcrop that lies roughly parallel to the main flow of the river and creates an abrupt 3- to-8-foot drop. Below this drop the rapid quickly dies out in a deep, flat pool. There are three distinct areas where current flows over the ledge; the most upstream area is about 50 feet wide and is the most extreme, with a couple of large munchy holes waiting to chomp on boaters who miss their line. Be careful as you enter the rapid not to wander too far to the right unless you

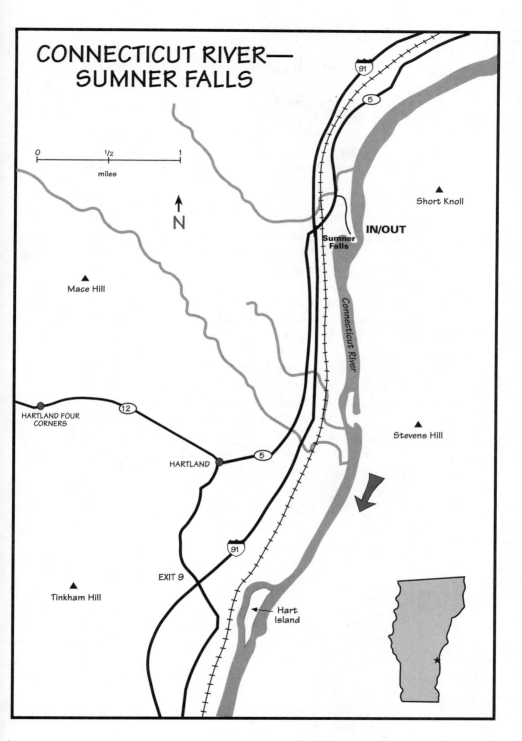

CONNECTICUT RIVER— SUMNER FALLS

0   1/2   1
miles

N

Short Knoll

IN/OUT

Sumner
Falls

Mace Hill

Connecticut River

HARTLAND FOUR
CORNERS

Stevens Hill

12

HARTLAND

5

91

EXIT 9

Tinkham Hill

Hart
Island

intend to run it, since the current splits subtly just above this drop and an unwary boater can easily end up running it without meaning to.

The next area where water runs over the ledge is much wider—about 100 yards or more—and consists of a steep hole in the center with clear lines on the left and right. The difficulty in running this drop is reading the sideways current above it, since to run it you have to turn at right angles to the main river. Following the main current to the bottom, the remainder of the river stays fairly straight and crosses the ledge in two smaller drops of 2 to 3 feet each.

Minimum flow at Sumner Falls is 700 cfs—a normal release level on the Deerfield. Since the Connecticut is somewhat channelized at Sumner Falls, even this water level provides reasonable playing opportunities. The flow is regulated at Wilder Dam, about 7.0 miles upstream of Sumner Falls, where, according to predicted power demand in New England for that day, water is released from either one or two turbines. Each turbine has a capacity of approximately 4,200 cfs, so the approximate level at Sumner Falls varies between 700 cfs and 9,000+ cfs. Of course, during high-water periods, the flows are much greater when they are spilling water at Wilder.

To get to Sumner Falls, take Interstate 91 to Exit 9 (Hartland). Go left at the end of the ramp onto Route 5 north. Stay on Route 5 through the center of Hartland. About 3.25 miles from the exit, you will cross the interstate and, immediately after it, the railroad that parallels the interstate. After crossing the railroad, take your second right onto a dirt road. There is a New England Power Company sign at the gate. Follow this road for about 0.25 mile to a parking area at the end. The rapid is right in front of you. Walk a hundred yards or so back up the dirt road to find a short put-in trail that leads to the top of the rapid.

Contoocook River (N.H.)

Hillsboro to Henniker

DISTANCE (MILES)	6.2		**TOO LOW**	5.6
SHUTTLE (MILES)	6		**LOW**	7.4
AVG. DROP (FEET/MILE)	23		**MED.**	9
MAX. DROP (FEET/MILE)	60		**HIGH**	10
DIFFICULTY	III–IV		**TOO HIGH**	
SCENERY	Good		**GAUGE LOCATION**	Henniker
DATE LAST CHECKED	1990		**WATER LEVEL INFO.**	
RUNOFF PATTERN	n/l		http://water.usgs.gov/public/realtime.html	

The Contoocook is one of New Hampshire's largest rivers and offers some of the best heavy-water paddling in all of New England. Because it holds water much better than smaller streams, the Contoocook can be run late in the season and even after heavy rains. In terms of personality, this section is definitely schizophrenic and manic-depressive; it is either disquietingly calm or ragingly mad, changing almost without warning. Rocks of all shapes and sizes populate this people-eating run, and the level of the water determines how they affect the boating. Low or medium water requires much maneuvering. At higher levels the rocks are responsible for the extreme turbulence. This trip is short; the first part can easily be eliminated and the rest can be repeated several times in a day. The lower half can be viewed from the road that follows the river except for two or three places, and, as things would have it, these places are class IV. The scenery is only OK, but you'll never notice.

One starting point is the old Route 202 bridge crossing about 3.0 miles below Hillsboro. You have to turn off Route 202 to reach old 202, now known as Western Road, and this bridge. After a half-mile of flat but flowing water below this bridge, the Contoocook turns quietly left, then shortly right. This right turn starts a long section (about 2.8 miles) of

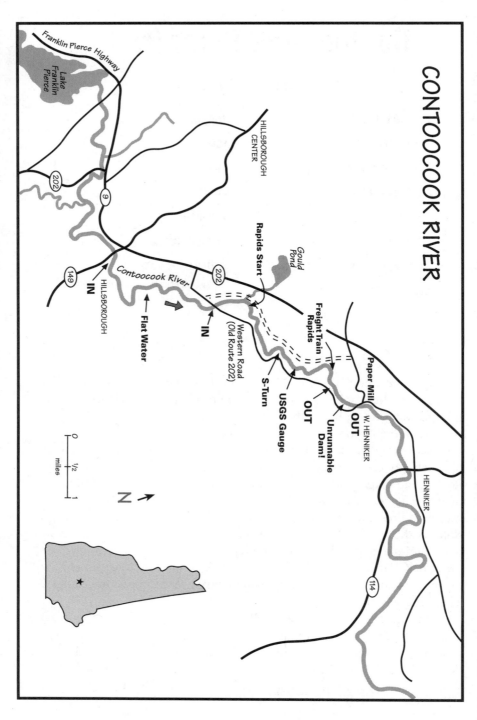

heavy, turbulent water. This is the more popular of the put-in spots. It is reached from a small dirt road off old Route 202.

In the first rapid, the water funnels to the center and creates haystacks measuring 3 to 4 feet at a gauge reading of 9.5. Far from regular, they clutch and slap at the boat, pushing, then pulling, always trying to disorient or overturn it. Looking at this spot in low water, one sees a relatively horizontal riverbed and then, suddenly, just a very slight downward tilt. Put 3 or 4 feet of water here and this tilt is amplified like music at a rock concert. Aggressive paddling is needed to stay in control among the cross-currents and turbulence. At a gauge reading of 8.2–8.5, these waves are merely class III. After a brief pause of quieter water, there follows another heavy rapid that it is best to run on the left; on the right if you want the heaviest water. The road comes back here, so if the previous rapids have proven too hard, you can use the road as a safe exit. Next up is another goodie, more extended than the previous one and best run in the center, since rocks complicate the sidelines.

As the Contoocook leaves the road and then prepares to turn right, get ready for the second-hardest rapid of the trip: S-Turn (class III–IV). Composed of irregular waves, holes, rocks, and several sudden drops, this rapid should be scouted if you haven't seen it previously. There are several methods of attack; which is the best depends on water level. In high water the left side is the most straightforward, but it is also the most violent and turbulent. There are also several large boulders at the start of S-Turn near the right bank that create some sharp drops. There are some smaller boulders on the left, upstream from the start, and many more everywhere downstream. At lower levels, you must pick and choose among many obstacles. The entire rapid is in the shape of an elongated S, which extends beyond the next right turn and through the next left turn. Overall difficulty decreases near the end. Leave your boat near the top of this rapid and you'll have a long, tough swim. Just ask people who have frequently boated the Contoocook; they probably have seen S-Turn from (in, not on) the water. The start of S-Turn is not easily visible from the road, although the easier lower portions are. After the final left turn of the S, the gauging station appears on the right bank and, following that, there's a schizophrenic turn. The river suddenly becomes calm as old Route 202 approaches very close. After several minutes' paddling, the Contoocook lazily turns left, away from the road, then right again.

Just as mythological sirens lured passing sailors with their songs only to leave them wrecked on the rocky approaches to their island, so this calm water may tempt the unwary to launch a boat for a pleasant downriver cruise. The river is ever so peaceful looking here, just like a sleeping vampire. Any who do launch at this point are in for the surprise of the day. Just beyond the right turn is the hardest section of the trip: Freight Train Rapid.

In high water this one is a mind-boggler. Large haystacks, souse holes, strong hydraulics, and tricky crosscurrents start quite suddenly and continue for about 300 to 400 yards downstream beyond the next right turn. The difficulty decreases somewhat after this turn. Large boulders line the sidelines all the way down, so don't try to sneak along there or you'll find real trouble with abrupt drops and strong eddies. The best run is in the center; although it has the least security and the most turbulence, it is the safest. This isn't really a contradiction. The run is most difficult at the start and again halfway down. You'll never have a chance to observe this when paddling Freight Train, but it does have a slight S-turn.

Freight Train cannot be seen from the road; it is about as far away from old Route 202 as the Contoocook gets. On the left bank are a small dirt road and an old railroad bed, but you won't see them from the river unless you are looking. At a gauge reading of 9.5 and higher, Freight Train is rated hard class IV or class V because of its length and turbulence. A swim through it could easily result in serious injury. At a gauge reading of 8.5, Freight Train is still class IV. This trip can end in the calm water just above a dam where old Route 202 is once again nearby, or downstream from the dam at two closely spaced bridges where parking facilities are better. The dam is unrunnable and must be portaged.

At a gauge reading of 8.2 to 8.5, the 'Took is a good river for an advanced intermediate paddler. At 9.5 it is powerful and continuous. At any runnable level the river's continuous current and width make rescue efforts very difficult for everyone.

The gauge is on the right bank, on old Route 202 about 2.5 miles southwest of Henniker. It is in the Telemark system. Readings are also available on the USGS web page at http://water.usgs.gov/public/real-time.html.

For another river roughly the same size as the Contoocook, try the lower Ashuelot (Ashuelot to Hinsdale). If you want another class IV run for the same weekend and you don't want to travel a lot, try the Blackwater, the upper Ashuelot, or the Otter Brook.

North Branch of the Contoocook River (N.H.)

Route 9 to Steele Pond

DISTANCE (MILES)	9.5	TOO LOW	
SHUTTLE (MILES)	6.5	LOW	
AVG. DROP (FEET/MILE)	42	MED.	
MAX. DROP (FEET/MILE)	250	HIGH	
DIFFICULTY	IV–V	TOO HIGH	
SCENERY	Good	GAUGE LOCATION	None
DATE LAST CHECKED	1997	WATER LEVEL INFO.	
RUNOFF PATTERN	n/l		

This is probably the toughest run in southern New Hampshire, with several class V drops at medium levels. At high water, the North Branch is a continuous class V–VI run with a couple of very serious rapids. The North Branch is a study in contrasts, as you pass from calm marsh to 20-foot drop. In the past the river powered mills, as evidenced by the many millworks and the intricate stone archways that occur at a couple of rapids.

Start a trip either at the intersection of Routes 9 and 123 near Stoddard, New Hampshire, where the river crosses the road downstream (north) of the intersection, or at the Loverens Mill Road bridge. The largest drops are where the river emerges from Bland Pond at the upper put-in and just upstream of where Loverens Mill Road crosses it. Both of these are class V at medium water.

There are several class-IV-and-higher rapids on this stretch, many of which drop very steeply in a short distance. Most rapids are formed from bedrock, so ledge holes are common. One of the more notable drops occurs where Route 9 crosses for the second time (counting downstream). This one is a steep, creek-like cascade that flows under a beautiful stone-

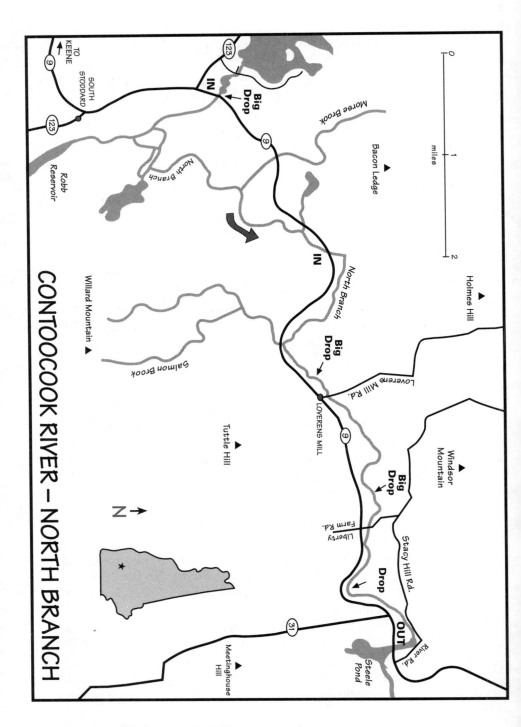

CONTOOCOOK RIVER – NORTH BRANCH

arch bridge and then under Route 9. Beware of metal in this rapid. Another drop, toward the end of the run, is seen easily from Route 9 and is an 8-foot falls with a class III lead-in. At high water, there is a huge rooster tail at the base of the falls where the water hits a flat rock. This one is fairly straightforward; paddle down the right at most levels.

Take out where the river enters Steele Pond and Route 9 crosses it. There is no gauge on the North Branch, but most of the run is seen easily from the road, and if you're good enough to consider running it, you should be able to judge the level for yourself.

Dead River (Maine)

Spencer Stream to the Forks

DISTANCE (MILES)	15		TOO LOW	
SHUTTLE (MILES)	20		LOW	800 cfs/3,000 cfs
AVG. DROP (FEET/MILE)	28		MED.	1,300 cfs/6,000 cfs
MAX. DROP (FEET/MILE)	50		HIGH	2,000 cfs/8,000 cfs
DIFFICULTY	II III/IV		TOO HIGH	3,000 cfs/10,000 cfs
SCENERY	Excellent		GAUGE LOCATION	Flagstaff Dam
DATE LAST CHECKED	1997		WATER LEVEL INFO.	800-557-3569
RUNOFF PATTERN	d/r/l			

The Dead River boasts one of the longest wilderness whitewater trips to be had in New England. By slightly altering the trip described here, a two-day expedition easily could be arranged for those who may prefer that. The Dead has two distinctly different personalities depending on the water level. At lower flows (800 to 2,400 cfs), the Dead is a fine open-boat or intermediate closed-boat run. At the higher flows (2,400 to 8,000 cfs) frequently released for whitewater rafters and advanced paddlers, the river becomes non-stop big whitewater. Waves reach heights of up to 8 feet and rapids continue without significant breaks for a mile or more.

Magnificent scenery, typical of the Maine backwoods, is a strong plus for this run. Once you start, however, you have little choice except to complete the trip in one way or another, since the river is isolated from any main roads, although a trail running alongside on the right does appear on topo maps. Because of the isolation and the possibility of quickly changing weather, inexperienced paddlers should carefully evaluate the consequences of an accident before deciding to run.

Since the trip is so long and the rapids are numerous, it is impractical to discuss them in detail, so only a general description of the trip follows. Also, since normal flows vary by as much as a factor of 10, the rapids

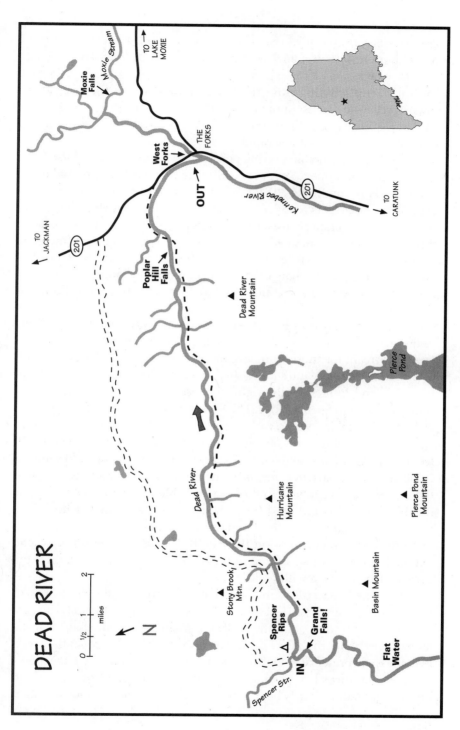

DEAD RIVER

are described primarily at the lower levels (800 to 2,400 cfs), with some notes about how they change with higher water. A paddler who is able to handle the class of rapids expected at the given level can easily complete the entire run scouting from the boat. Those running the river at the lower levels who are less sure of themselves may want to eyeball Spencer Rips and Poplar Hill Falls. At more than about 2,400 cfs, it becomes very difficult to stop to scout any rapids.

Arriving at a suitable starting point is as difficult as the run itself. For a put-in at the confluence of Spencer Stream and the Dead, proceed north from The Forks on Route 201 for 3.2 miles and take a dirt road that leads west to the river. This road has been improved in recent years, so it's not the old muffler-scraper it used to be. Directions on which turns to take on this road should be obtained from the local rafting companies (there are several outposts located along Route 201 south of and in the center of The Forks), since the road changes as the logging route changes. As an alternative to driving yourself, contact Webb's Campground in The Forks for a shuttle.

At its confluence with Spencer Stream, the Dead makes a big elbow to the right, and a fair-sized island sits in midstream, blocking the view of Spencer Stream for those who have just come down from Flagstaff Dam. The channel to the island's left is shallow. Just below the island, the Dead turns left and funnels to the right side, cascading over small rocks and standing waves in Spencer Rips. The Rips lasts for about 300 yards, the last 25 being the heaviest water, with waves reaching 2 feet at around 1,200 to 1,300 cfs. Toward the end of this rapid there is a rock wall extending 20 feet up the right bank, and a big eddy swirls on the left side at the end. At 7,000 cfs this constriction forms a smooth, 6-foot surfing wave, though there is no way to get back to it once you've blown off it. Spencer Rips is rated a straightforward class III at the lower levels. At higher flows it is class IV. It is a good place to play at any level and is probably the second or third most difficult spot on the trip. It can be run almost anywhere, although most canoeists take it on the right center at low flows, since the extreme left is loaded with rocks.

After the Spencer Rips introduction, the next several miles will seem tame, being mostly class II–II+ at low flows, III+ at higher levels. The current moves constantly, and the rocks are small. Notice all along that the larger rocks prefer the sidelines, and it isn't until high flows that they really make their presence felt. The Dead then drops into a very large, pool-like area that turns left, passing an old wooden logging drop ramp, high on the right bank. Shortly below are some class II rapids, a pool, and then some slightly harder rapids with larger rocks and a few 1- to 2-foot drops. At high water this section is rated class III. A very long stretch of easier water follows, where the paddler can relax and enjoy the luscious scenery. For those who like to drift along lazily sponging in nature (or sponging out their boats), this is truly heaven. The entire area is devoid of signs that encroaching bipeds have ever been here, except, of course, for an occasional broken boat or beer can. The conifers stand at strict attention, pointing skyward and contrasting with the gentle swaying of the white birches, while rocky faces protrude from the banks as if trying to break away from their earthly restraints.

The end of this section is marked by sharp rapids in a fairly straight 100-yard stretch where, at the bottom right, one large and one small rock point from shore toward a small but powerful hole at low levels. At high water the large rock, known as Elephant Rock, is mostly covered, forming a big nasty pourover. An eddy sits slightly downstream of the hole near the bank. These rapids are rated class II+ at low water, class IV at more than 2,400 cfs. They begin a section of drop/pool that becomes more continuous as the water rises. After this set of rapids there are some good class II and several II+s at low flows, followed by 0.75 mile of continuous rapids in the class III range. This last tickler has the heaviest water in the middle near the end and an abundance of rocks throughout. At higher levels, this section is class III–IV with a solid class IV section toward the end. Calm water again prevails for a long while, terminating in class II rapids and then class II–III rapids (low water) in a right turn.

Upper Poplar Hill Falls is located just after a right dogleg. It is a fairly wide rapid that can be run almost anywhere, although there are usually one or two groups of rocks that necessitate some deviation from a straight course at the lower levels. Upper Poplar Hill Falls is rated class III at about 1,200 cfs. Below, the Dead widens only to funnel left into Lower Poplar Hill Falls. The first 100 yards are the heaviest and hardest of the trip— tough class III at 1,200 cfs when they consist of turbulent, fast water rushing among a line of rocks. After this initial stretch, the difficulty gradually tapers off as the river approaches a bridge abutment in the next turn.

Poplar Hill Falls is a solid class IV at levels higher than 2,400 cfs. Large holes form at these levels, and the whole rapid requires good big-water-reading skills since the waves are over the heads of most boaters. From start to finish by the bridge abutment, Lower PHF measures 300 to 400 yards. From the abutment to the takeout at The Forks, the water is class I–II. It can be very scratchy if the discharge is less than 1,000 cfs. Along the way you pass a gauging station on the left bank, but there is no outside gauge.

The main discharge on the Dead is controlled by the dam on Flagstaff Lake. Because the Dead is dam controlled, scheduled water releases are possible during the summer months. In the mid-1980s the rafting companies located in The Forks negotiated with the dam owner for both more and higher releases on the Dead during the summer. There are now seven scheduled high-water (3,500 to 7,000 cfs) releases each summer and eleven scheduled low-water (1,500 cfs) releases. Information about release dates and levels can be obtained by calling CMP's river-information phone at 800-557-3569.

Flagstaff Dam can be reached by an 80-mile drive from The Forks. The reward for this extra trek is a view of the dam and Long Falls below it (class VI), plus a chance to canoe about 6.0 miles of flatwater and portage around Grand Falls. Grand Falls, which drops precipitously about 30 feet, is a quarter-mile above the confluence with Spencer Stream. It is well worth a visit upstream if you start at Spencer, since the view is spectacular.

Instead of starting at Spencer or Flagstaff, a trip also may be hauled into Fish Pond, which attaches to the northern waters of Spencer Lakes. After paddling eastward 6.0 or 7.0 miles on these lakes, you reach an outlet dam, and after a rough portage you can place the boats in Little Spencer Stream. Quite small and serene, this stream drowsily meanders about 4.0 miles before entering Spencer Stream proper. Two miles beyond, you join the Dead. The road to Fish Pond is class III and turns off Route 201 near Lake Parlin, 15.0 miles north of The Forks. If the dam at Spencer Lakes is delivering 200 cfs, the trip is fairly enjoyable; much more and the trees would have canoeists for company in the woods.

Fire and camping permits must be obtained through the forest ranger in Caratunk, Maine, for the whole Dead River area. There are several campsites near the confluence of the Dead and Spencer Stream. Local rangers have been known to get very upset if you go without a permit or "reinterpret" a permit that you have by camping at a site not specified on the permit.

Area Code 207 672 3761

Deerfield River–
East Branch (Vt.)
Somerset Reservoir to Searsburg Reservoir
Trip A

DISTANCE (MILES)	6	**TOO LOW**	150 cfs
SHUTTLE (MILES)	7	**LOW**	
AVG. DROP (FEET/MILE)	40	**MED.**	300 cfs
MAX. DROP (FEET/MILE)		**HIGH**	
DIFFICULTY	I-II	**TOO HIGH**	
SCENERY	Excellent	**GAUGE LOCATION**	Somerset Dam
DATE LAST CHECKED	1997	**WATER LEVEL INFO.**	888-356-3663
RUNOFF PATTERN	d/l		

Before the European settlers arrived, Vermont must have looked very much like the valley of the East Branch of the Deerfield. From this tight, winding creek, views of the Green Mountain National Forest are unspoiled by signs of man. For just a moment you can imagine you are alone in the world. The broad, marshy flood plain is covered with grasses and wildflowers—a perfect habitat for beaver, moose, and blue heron. The steeply forested Green Mountains rise serenely from the expansive valley as they have since their formation. Rapids are secondary to the appeal of this scenic 6.0-mile stretch, so levels as low as 150 cfs, while a bit scratchy, still offer a pleasant experience.

The East Branch begins as a spout of water shot from a tube out of Somerset Reservoir. The river channel here is a narrow, ledgy class III+ gorge that widens half a mile below the dam. The best put-in avoids this first half-mile via a trail on river left. If you feel up to a no-warm-up lead-in, however, a primitive path on river right emerges immediately below

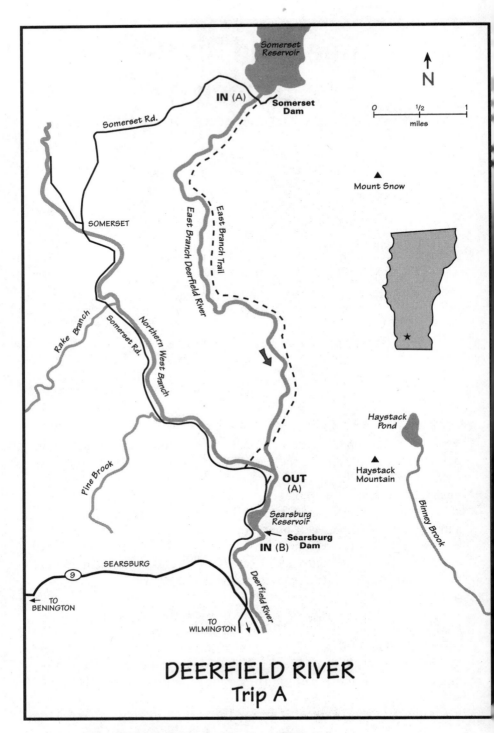

DEERFIELD RIVER
Trip A

the dam. Either way, the first 4-foot ledge is only marginally runnable because of nasty rocks at its base.

After this introduction, the river settles into narrow class I–II rapids interspersed with the slow-moving backwaters of beaver ponds. Downed trees can be especially hazardous in this constricted stream bed—even a small blowdown can easily block the entire passage. In most cases, the banks are not steep, however, so portaging around strainers is neither time-consuming nor difficult.

The other hazard that appears frequently on this stretch is beaver dams. While most can be run, the sticks forming them can act as spears. To avoid an impaling experience, canoeists should try to run the dams where smooth passage is evident.

About two-thirds of the way down, the river valley widens and the river slows, forming the largest of the beaver ponds on this section. Several side channels lead to interesting inlets where you can spot wildlife or eat a quiet picnic lunch. As it leaves this pond, the river again enters a small gorge. The first rapids below the pond can be somewhat technical and shallow at low water, so use caution here, since it is still a couple of miles to any roads. (If you have trouble, look for the trail on river left.)

Easier rapids continue to the confluence with the Northern West Branch of the Deerfield above Searsburg Reservoir. The takeout for this stretch is below the confluence where the river enters Searsburg Reservoir. The first sign that you are approaching the takeout is when you pass under a footbridge. About 0.35 mile downstream, a dirt road leads to the reservoir on river right where boats can be beached.

The runoff characteristics of the East Branch are somewhat complex, since the power company uses the East Branch principally to feed water from Somerset Reservoir into Harriman Reservoir during the summer months when natural flow diminishes. Hence, the East Branch runs when everything else is dry—usually in July, August, September, and October. For those who pray habitually for rain all summer long, this opportunity to paddle a beautiful stretch of river under the hot summer sun has a powerful appeal.

Water levels for this stretch can be obtained by calling the Deerfield flow phone at 888-356-3663. The water levels are reported as the Somerset discharge.

Deerfield River– Searsburg Section (Vt.)

Searsburg Dam to Harriman Reservoir
Trip B

DISTANCE (MILES)	4.5		TOO LOW	500 cfs
SHUTTLE (MILES)	4.5		LOW	700 cfs
AVG. DROP (FEET/MILE)	50		MED.	
MAX. DROP (FEET/MILE)			HIGH	1500 cfs
DIFFICULTY	III		TOO HIGH	2000 cfs
SCENERY	Good		GAUGE LOCATION	Searsburg Station
DATE LAST CHECKED	1997		WATER LEVEL INFO.	800/356-3663
RUNOFF PATTERN	d/f			

The Searsburg Dryway is about 4.5 miles long, with boulder gardens, ledges, and good-sized wave trains. The river's flow is normally diverted into a black wooden penstock that dries up the riverbed for the first 3.0 miles of this run. The penstock is visible as you follow Route 9 just west of Wilmington, Vermont, above the north end of Harriman Reservoir. The last half-mile of river is fed by the powerhouse and often runs at a scratchy, but runnable, 300–400 cfs.

The put-in is on the dirt road that leads to Somerset Reservoir. This road is the first right turn off Route 9, a half-mile after you cross the Deerfield going west out of Wilmington. The pavement stops in a short distance, and the road turns to dirt. Follow the dirt road for about 0.75 mile, until you see Searsburg Dam and Reservoir on the right. Park here and walk over the diversion tube on a little wooden bridge and through the woods a short distance to the river.

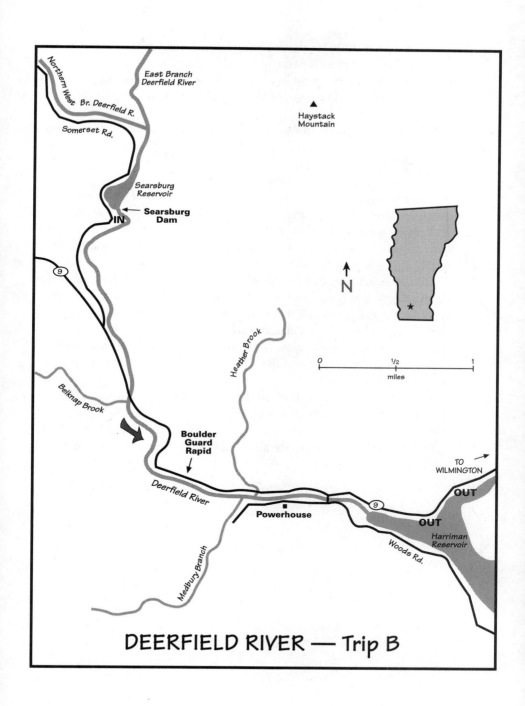

DEERFIELD RIVER — Trip B

The rapids build nicely from the dam downstream, starting off with about 2.0 miles of class II+ warm-up. As you approach the Route 9 bridge, the river turns sharply right in a rapid with a few small surfing waves and some crisp eddies. Be careful of the bridge abutment in the center of the river.

Below this bridge, things heat up. Around the next big left bend, a ledgy drop deposits you in a pool with swirly eddy lines—an excellent squirt spot and a handy place to gather your group and your wits before the next rapid, which is the heaviest of the trip.

In this one, named Boulder Guard Rapid, a large boulder guards the entry on river right, forcing you left and into the largest waves. Several eddies line both banks. The center is a relatively straight shot if you aren't worried about swamping. A short pool below provides a good spot for rescue and regrouping. This rapid is III+ at about 1,600 cfs.

Another half-mile of class II–III rapids brings you to the powerhouse on the river-right bank. The outflow from the powerhouse follows a narrow channel on the right side of an island just below the station. The rest of the river follows the left channel around the island. After the two channels join, another mile of class II paddling brings you to Harriman Reservoir, where the takeout is on the left, up a steep bank to a roadside pull-off on Route 9.

To catch this excellent class III run, watch the weather patterns in southern Vermont and call the Deerfield River-information phone 888-356-3663 if you suspect it's up. You won't be disappointed if the dam is spilling at least 700 cfs. Above about 1,400 cfs the more difficult middle section becomes class III+ to IV.

Deerfield River–
West Branch (Vt.)
Readsboro Falls to Readsboro
Trip C

DISTANCE (MILES)	3		**TOO LOW**	
SHUTTLE (MILES)	3		**LOW**	1
AVG. DROP (FEET/MILE)	190		**MED.**	3
MAX. DROP (FEET/MILE)	200		**HIGH**	5
DIFFICULTY	V		**TOO HIGH**	
SCENERY	Fair		**GAUGE LOCATION**	Chair Factory Bridge
DATE LAST CHECKED	1997		**WATER LEVEL INFO.**	
RUNOFF PATTERN	n/f			

In 1987 a sign on the dilapidated chair factory building in Readsboro, Vermont read: FOR SALE—100,000 SQUARE FOOT HUNTING CABIN—$7,000. The old chair factory and mill remained on the market despite the clever sales pitch. But more than one boater entertained thoughts of setting up a small industry just for the pleasure of working next to the tumbling West Branch as it negotiates some of its more intimidating and exciting rapids: High Chair and Low Chair. The chair factory is gone now—plowed into a hole when it became unsafe as a structure—and the green field in its place certainly makes a more appealing riverbank.

An old mill is also evident 3.0 miles upstream at the put-in, known as Readsboro Falls, where a water wheel and its works stand idle in a native chestnut barn that the river is slowly reclaiming through endless seasons of freeze, thaw, flood, and storm. To reach Readsboro Falls, drive 2.8 miles The falls cascades over two 4-foot drops and into a huge pothole that it only reluctantly abandons.

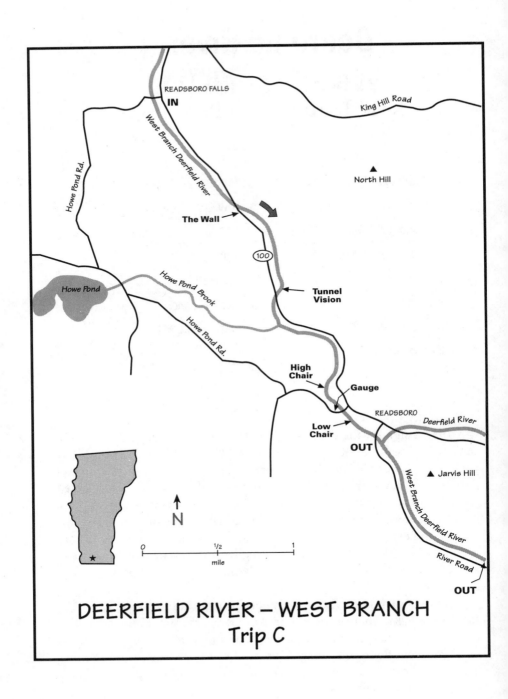

DEERFIELD RIVER – WEST BRANCH
Trip C

Putting in above the falls is like taking your first swimming lesson in the middle of the Atlantic Ocean. A few people have run Readsboro Falls, but most paddlers cross the footbridge over the falls and put in below the old mill. The recirculation at the base of the falls is deceptively powerful, and more than one boater has swum in it only to be rescued by a rope dangled from the bridge above.

There's another way to enter the West Branch that provides an adrenaline pump and makes exciting photos. Try an otter entry on river left just below the falls. You'll find a smooth spout eroded from the bedrock during high water. Just the width of a boat and blessed with a soft, easy landing about a boat's length below, what this slot lacks in machismo it easily makes up for in the assurance that you'll be around to run the second rapid. At either put-in, avoid parking on private property.

Water levels are crucial on this 300-foot-per-mile creek. The gauge is painted on a rock on river right just upstream of the bridge next to the former chair-factory site in Readsboro. At 1.0 on the gauge the river is barely runnable, and, although not as powerful as at higher water, the drops are more abrupt, causing more of a bow-pinning hazard. Three on the gauge is optimum for a first run—a medium level that makes all rapids fluid but relatively distinct. At 5.0 and over, which is about 700 cfs, things happen very quickly on this class V stream. While extra water provides welcome padding on certain rocks, it also greatly reduces reaction time and worsens the consequences of a mistake.

After the put-in, you immediately encounter Holey, Holey, Holey. Actually two distinct drops, HHH provides a good indication of what lies ahead in its power, gradient, and general chaos. Start by boofing right over the first hole, then drive hard as the river tries to slam you into the left wall. Punch the next hole wherever you end up in it, or surf it out to the eddy on river right. The next drop is a straightforward slide into another river-wide hole. While the hole is not bad, both ends are blocked by rocks, making your exit something of a trick.

Beware of trees in the slots of the next rapid, where the river disappears into a boulder sieve. All three options involve blind runs through extremely tight drops. Then settle into some leisurely paddling as a half-mile or so of class III–IV water follows before the river passes under a road bridge and turns right toward the Wall.

Somehow the river gods knew when they designed the Wall that every boater would be tempted by this fluvial siren. As you approach, something tells you things can't be as simple as they appear, and they aren't. There's a rock just below the surface in the eddy on the left below the drop that's just waiting to stop your bow dead and send your feet through your foot pedals. So have yourself lashed to the mast if you will, but beware the hidden rock in the eddy.

Immediately below the Wall, avoid bow pinning in the steep jumbled zone. After a short respite, the river turns left into the turbulent Cauldron. You can portage or scout from river left. Keep your bow up on Cauldron and recover quickly as you pass sculptured, water-worn boulders, because following this is Face Plant. The huge boulders, steep drops, and sharp turns in Face Plant demand quick reflexes. Face Plant begins with a jump over a 3-foot pourover, then a sharp turn to the right followed by an equally sharp turn left. After a short rest there follows a pillow move where 90 percent of the river slams into a boulder shaped like a UPS truck. You can make a super-high-speed turn into the river-left eddy with a hairball exit back across the pillow, or retreat to the left of the rock where the river becomes a shallow gravel bed.

Half a mile of easier water interspersed with a class IV drop or two leads into the Tunnel Trio as the river turns left and enters a partially man-made gorge. A cliff forms the river-left bank and the road is directly above on river right. Tunnel Trio includes Tunnel Falls, Breather, and Tunnel Vision, and is the crux of the West Branch.

The beginning of the Tunnel Trio is a good place to end a shorter run or to spot a car if a group is not sure of its abilities. It lies about halfway through the run. You can also portage down the road to rejoin the river below the tunnel. To consider running either of the first two drops, you must be absolutely sure of your roll. A swim after Breather could be terminal.

Tunnel Falls is a 12-foot drop with a clean but narrow line on the right where the water cresting the lip of the falls creates a slight saddle. Consider this one only if there is adequate flow, since even at high levels the line is shallow and the rocks are sharp. Breather is an otherwise harmless class IV slosh from one bank to the other, except that less than 25 feet from its end is the point of no return where Tunnel Vision takes off downhill.

Tunnel Vision, a genuine class VI rapid, has a total vertical drop of around 40 or 50 feet in less than 100 yards. Tunnel Vision drops more in this short distance than many whitewater rivers do in a mile. The river plunges first down a steep slide, then over several ledges that create steep, twisted drops and large holes. Much of the rock has been blasted by road builders and has sharp edges. Tunnel Vision ends as the entire river enters a huge concrete culvert under the highway. There are two car-sized flat boulders blocking the tunnel at its upper end, and they can come equipped with strainers. A class IV rapid continues through the tunnel, where you can come as close as anyone would ever want to running the River Styx.

Following the tunnel, the river returns to continuous big-boulder rapids that last about 0.75 mile until the next break. The most notable features in this section are the possibility of downed trees from the river's steep slopes and the bow-pinning rock in the second drop, just after a steep waterfall enters from the right bank. Take the far left channel in this drop to avoid the bow-pinning rock.

After a brief pause, the river narrows for a half-mile alongside the road and passes over several tricky ledges and grabby holes called Tumble. These tight drops have one sneaky suck hole and a couple of boulder walls toward the bottom. You can see this one from the road on the way up to the put-in.

A short shallow section leads under a small footbridge and into the final stretch of rapids. The footbridge marks another good takeout. In the coming drops—High Chair and Low Chair—man's impact is evident in the development on the riverbanks and in several important local graffiti sites.

As High Chair begins, just upstream and out of sight of the former factory, the river turns sharply right, then left over a ledge into a frothy hole. Recovery from this entry must be quick, since High Chair continues with a steep slide to the right. In the slide, the left wall is an undercut cliff, and all the current carries you in that direction.

Below High Chair the river runs past the gauge rock and under the small road bridge. Be careful to catch an eddy just after the road bridge, because Low Chair begins here and should be scouted even by those who have run it before; its rocks move frequently, causing the runnable lines to change. Road work on the left bank a few years ago significantly modified the drop, the most prominent feature of which is a pointed widow-maker rock in river center.

Decent takeout opportunities exist at the chair-factory bridge above Low Chair and at the next bridge downstream from Low Chair, or you can paddle down to the confluence with the main Deerfield and take out at a convenient spot on river right. Two more class IV drops can be paddled on the main stem, with a decent takeout just below the last drop where it meets Sherman Reservoir. Avoid parking at the American Legion.

The upper section of the West Branch offers a good class IV–V alternative when the section described here is too high (above about 5.0 on the Readsboro gauge), although the shuttle for the upper section is sketchy and the walk to the put-in is a bushwhack through the woods. To get to the upper section, follow Route 100 upstream from Readsboro Falls until Route 8 joins it from the right. In another quarter-mile take a right into a Green Mountain National Forest road. The pull-off just off Route 100/8 is the takeout. Continue up the dirt road a couple of miles until you reach a height of land and a small pond appears through the woods about 100 yards away on the right. Bushwhack to the pond and follow the very small, steep brook from the pond to the main river— about a quarter-mile of river so steep you'll feel like your ears will pop from the rapid descent and so narrow you can reach both shores with your paddle from the middle of it.

Ellis River (N.H.)

Route 16 to Harvard Cabin

DISTANCE (MILES)	3		**TOO LOW**	1.3
SHUTTLE (MILES)	3		**LOW**	2.1
AVG. DROP (FEET/MILE)	87		**MED.**	2.9
MAX. DROP (FEET/MILE)	100 +		**HIGH**	
DIFFICULTY	IV		**TOO HIGH**	
SCENERY	Good		**GAUGE LOCATION**	Route 16
DATE LAST CHECKED	1997		**WATER LEVEL INFO.**	
RUNOFF PATTERN	n/f			

The Ellis River typifies the White Mountains. Starting near the slopes of Mount Washington, it cascades down the very heart of Pinkham Notch, contorting among rock formations and rapids to drop finally into the Saco River near the junction of Routes 16 and 302. In its upper part the Ellis displays some of the most tempting class V and VI rapids in New England. It's intriguing to scout these sections, wondering how you would run the blind 90° turns or squeeze through the narrow slots when the water itself has trouble doing so. Lower down rapids become more manageable, with stretches of calm water and some variation in sophistication and difficulty. This is the section for sport, not stunt.

The Ellis is relatively small, with a watershed to match. It seldom has enough water for paddling, but when the snow melts and the whitewater eggs hatch, it does offer a fine adventure. It is interesting to note that the Ellis can be run with as little flow as 129 cfs (gauge of 2.1). A modest flow of 350 cfs means water a foot deeper (gauge of 3.0).

Since Route 16 parallels the river, you can start a trip from any number of places. The standard put-in is at a roadside picnic area approximately 1.0 mile north of the Route 16 bridge that crosses over the Ellis. This bridge is where the Ellis, descending from the mountains, crosses from the east to the west side of the road about 0.25 mile north of Dana Place Inn.

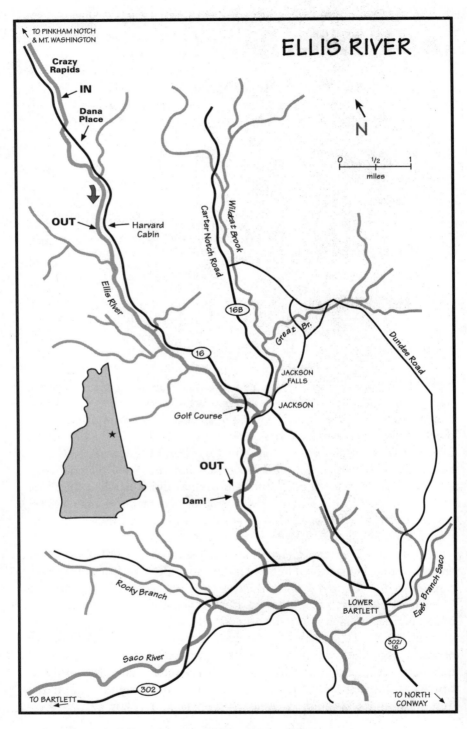

ELLIS RIVER

TO PINKHAM NOTCH
& MT. WASHINGTON

Crazy
Rapids

IN

Dana
Place

OUT

Harvard
Cabin

N

0   1/2   1
miles

Carter Notch Road

Wildcat Brook

Ellis River

16B

Great Br.

16

JACKSON
FALLS

Dundee Road

Golf Course

JACKSON

OUT

Dam!

Rocky Branch

LOWER
BARTLETT

East Branch Saco

Saco River

302

302/
16

TO BARTLETT

TO NORTH
CONWAY

124   New Hampshire, Vermont, and Maine

The very brave (or foolish) can put in a little upstream of the picnic area, allowing a class V run through Crazy Rapids. This put-in can be found by driving north on Route 16 approximately 0.25 mile past the picnic area. As the road goes uphill it gets very steep and curves to the left, with a guardrail on the right. The USGS gauge is located about 100 yards before the end of the guardrail, down a steep embankment. The gauge isn't visible from the road, so park past the guardrail and walk downhill along the road until you see the gauge house. From the gauge you're smack in the middle of Crazy Rapids and can, with a bit of effort, climb up- or downstream to get a close look at what you'd really like to watch someone else run. This section is a steep, narrow creek with many must-make moves, big rocks, and no room for error. Once in it, you're committed. If you must run it, scout the entire length first, checking for recent strainers and other surprises. Put in a few hundred yards upstream of the gauge, where the road levels off and is close to the river. If you reach a second picnic area, you've gone too far.

Below Crazy Rapids you'll reach the standard put-in and Commencement Rapids. This spot offers plenty of hiding areas for changing clothes and parking cars. Access to the river is via any number of paths leading down from the picnic area to the river. Directly adjacent to the picnic area the trek to the river is short and steep. To avoid climbing, follow other paths downstream a bit for easier river access that also avoids the bulk of the rapid.

Putting in on Commencement Rapids is not easy. The river here looks as if it has more rocks than water. Finding a calm spot to launch a boat and fasten a spray skirt is a challenge. Above, the channel bounces down a relatively narrow slot that seems nearly impassable (and isn't passable at low water). Below, the rapids are uninterrupted and technical, and usually there is only one practical route through the labyrinth. Water level is crucial for this stretch. At a gauge reading of 2.1, the going is a tight class III. Higher levels will most certainly be class IV or more. At any level, the boater must make one quick decision after another to negotiate the maze successfully; the correct path is not obvious, the current is pushy, and broaching opportunities abound. If this section appears too hard, skip it by putting in at any convenient spot off Route 16, or do it at the beginning of a second run.

An easy put-in below Commencement Rapids is at the Route 16 bridge 0.25 mile north of Dana Place. Here the river descends at a moderate class II–III pace, avoiding the upstream class IV and V rapids. First comes a relatively straightforward chute, near a contemporary house on the left bank. Rapids then alternate with calmer water for the remainder of the trip. The unbroken difficulty of Commencement Rapids is behind you. From now on, the Ellis's course is generally away from Route 16.

There is one drop through a narrow rock gorge that should be portaged. This cataract, about 25 yards in length, requires that you negotiate several stair-step drops and hydraulics while placing your boat in the middle of the only runnable channel. Each boater should judge for himself whether to attempt a run. The walk around is easiest to manage on the left. Preceding this drop is a left turn, a short stretch of calm water, and then a right turn into the falls. This one is class V, even in low water.

Another noteworthy rapid occurs where a rock ledge blocks the river. In low water, the channel funnels to the left into the only runnable path. At higher levels, the water will pass more directly over the ledge, opening up new routes and new problems, but that's the fun of it all.

One convenient takeout is near the Appalachian Mountain Club's Harvard Cabin. The cabin cannot be seen from the river; a large summer home near the river on the left bank is a landmark. The house is close to a 1- to 2-foot stair-step drop into a pool. Ask permission if you plan to cross the land. Harvard Cabin is 6.1 miles up Route 16 from the junction of Routes 16 and 302. A small dirt road off Route 16 leads to the cabin (about 100 yards).

From Harvard Cabin the Ellis continues for 5.0 miles more to the dam at Goodrich Falls. Parts of this section are flat and uninteresting, but there are rapids, some of which pack a wallop at high water. You'll find nothing on a par with Commencement Rapids, but there are some you should scout, particularly one set where the river seems to disappear over some rocks. Another obstacle to note in this lower section is a golf course just north of Jackson. Flying balls and golf carts are definitely extraordinary whitewater hazards, but you might have to deal with them here. Consider yourself "fore" warned. Take out at any one of the several public picnic areas along the road, which provide excellent river access. One can be found slightly upstream of Eagle Mountain Road. Continuing into the town of Jackson, another takeout is found at Greenhill Road where the river crosses under a bridge. The dam at Goodrich Falls is just after a Route 16 highway bridge; the actual drop looks as if it plunges straight into hell.

The gauge is in Carroll County on the right bank, 1.3 miles upstream from the bridge near the put-in. There is an additional, hand-painted gauge on the Route 302 bridge 2.0 miles south of Jackson near the intersection of Routes 16 and 302 where the Ellis flows into the Saco. It doesn't always correlate to the USGS gauge many miles north, since the river rises and falls rapidly during the day, and it takes many hours for the water to travel from the put-in down to the Saco. It does give you a general idea of the water level, however, and lets you avoid a thirty-minute drive just to check the official gauge.

Gale (N.H.)

Franconia to Ammonoosuc River

DISTANCE (MILES)	7.5		TOO LOW	
SHUTTLE (MILES)	5.5		LOW	0.5
AVG. DROP (FEET/MILE)	25		MED.	1
MAX. DROP (FEET/MILE)	80		HIGH	2
DIFFICULTY	I–IV		TOO HIGH	
SCENERY	Excellent		GAUGE LOCATION	Streeter Pond Bridge
DATE LAST CHECKED	1997		WATER LEVEL INFO.	
RUNOFF PATTERN	n			

The Gale River is one of New Hampshire's finest. It has everything that counts in a whitewater trip—in abundance. Isolation, natural beauty, distinctive rapids, and even a gorge all combine to make this an unforgettable voyage. The Gale even has a most picturesque spot for eating lunch or watching skinny-dippers. But the most remarkable thing about the Gale is that it is seldom boated. The parts that can be seen from the road are rather dull and uninteresting and would escape the attention of a casual observer. Like an iceberg, the important parts of the Gale are hidden: varied and nearly uninterrupted rapids. If that weren't enough, the Gale's rapids progress in sequence from class I to class II to class III and end with a very definite set of class IV. Except for the Gorge section, which can be portaged with difficulty, intermediates could handle all the rapids—and have a good time at it.

Draining parts of Mount Lafayette and Mount Garfield, the Gale flows quietly through Franconia, New Hampshire, displaying only class I–II difficulty. You can start from several different bridges depending on the amount of warm-up you desire. At a gauge reading of 1.0, the depth here is 3 to 12 inches, depending on where you stick your paddle. If you put in by Church Street, you get to pass an old iron kiln on the left bank that has been standing there since the nineteenth century. A road marker on Route 18 opposite discusses its history. After the kiln, Route 116 crosses the river. From Church Street to Streeter Pond Road Bridge (2.5 miles), the river is mostly class I and

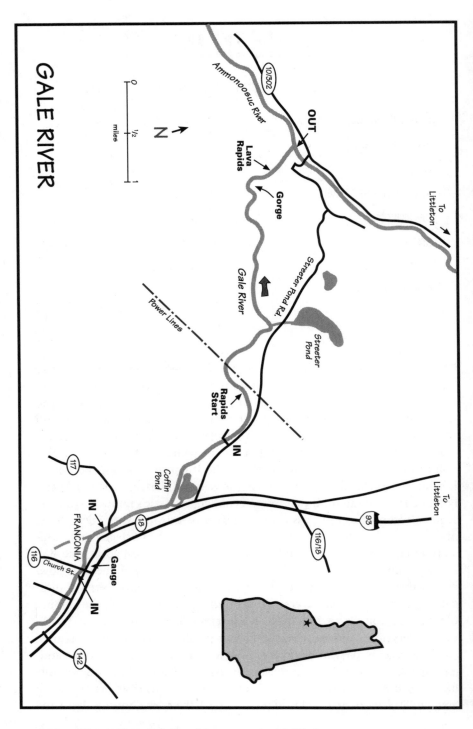

GALE RIVER

N

0   ½   1
miles

Armmonoosuc River

10/302

OUT

To Littleton

Lava Rapids

Gorge

Gale River

Power Lines

Streeter Pond Rd.

Streeter Pond

Rapids Start

IN

Coffin Pond

117

IN

FRANCONIA

18

116

Church St.

Gauge

IN

142

116/18

93

To Littleton

shallow, with fairly unattractive scenery, but this is the admission price you pay to the river gods for the good times ahead.

A second put-in appears where Route 117 crosses over the river, approximately 0.5 mile downstream from Church Street. Past the Route 117 bridge, the river is class I and continues another 2.0 miles to an old iron bridge where Crane Hill Road branches off from Streeter Pond Road. A hand-painted gauge is found on the river-left abutment. This section is also a handy put-in if you want to avoid most of the shallow and easy sections.

Within a half-mile of the Streeter Pond Road Bridge, the paddler turns left and enters a rather isolated valley surrounded by hills that come into view before the turn. After the next right turn, an overhead power line is the last sign of civilization you'll see until you approach the bridge at the Ammonoosuc at the trip's end. From here on, the river runs through woods; the current is uninterrupted and the rapids nearly so. At the beginning, rapids are class II, with distinct stretches of calmer water in between; then distinctions begin to vanish as the rapids pack closer and closer together. At a gauge of 1.0, most rapids toward the beginning of the trip are class II, but they are technical and require some maneuvering.

As the rapids increase in intensity and frequency, be especially careful of a particularly deceitful one. This little devil appears to be a straight chute in river center between two boulders in left and right center. It has an abrupt drop of about 2 feet and falls onto a flat rock directly downstream from the drop. The flat rock is difficult to see from upstream, and unwary paddlers will blast right into it. An angled run to either side avoids the problem. Stop and scout if you recognize this spot beforehand; otherwise, say hello to the rock.

The Gale continues its descent, and by now it should be obvious that the gradient is picking up, as are the waves. Continuous class II and III rapids (gauge of 1.0) are common. Rocks everywhere make maneuvering a must. For competent boaters, this section is a playground. You can dart in and out almost at will, catching eddies and hydraulics and skirting rocks in various ways. In this section the unskilled will find several opportunities to redesign the lines of their boats. The scenery, if nothing else, is worth the trip. The next thing to look out for is a huge rock outcropping on the left bank, followed by an S-turn (right turn, then left). This is the first warning of the upcoming gorge section, where the difficulty increases instantaneously.

As you complete the left turn of the S, look downstream for a large rock outcropping jutting out from the right bank at a point where the river continues to turn left underneath and then appears to double back on itself. The Gorge (class IV) is imminent, so pull over immediately to scout. The Gorge is narrow and rock lined, with nearly vertical sides. There are three major drops. Fortunately, there are well-located eddies where you can rest and reconsider your previous decisions to run.

The first drop is directly under the signal rock. It is a river-wide ledge, steepest on the right (3-foot drop at a gauge of 1.0) and with rocks in the middle. It becomes less steep as you move left, but the shallow water makes it hard to paddle, and you may get turned around by the many rocks. In addition, the fast current could mash you against the solid rock wall of the left bank as the river turns back on itself and bends sharply right. Several smaller drops upstream determine your approach. The hydraulic at the bottom of the ledge can be strong. Sneak through by hugging the left edge of the river and back-ferrying into the eddy around the turn to avoid slamming into the rock wall.

After the right turn, a series of rocks across the river creates the second drop. Water level will determine your route. At medium levels, a course on the extreme left opens up and a trickier path in the middle still remains.

The third drop closely follows the second drop. It is another river-wide ledge, most abrupt on the left but with a relatively smooth tongue in the right center. At medium levels, watch out for the vicious-looking hydraulic on the left side. Standing waves form the outrun. Several smaller drops downstream should cause no concern. The Gorge veers right into more-open surroundings—the steep walls fall back into the woods. There is no pool at the end of the Gorge, as you might expect or hope; instead, there is a short stretch of class I–II water. At a gauge reading of 1.0 the Gorge is for experts only, and then only after careful scouting.

The rapids that follow the Gorge are class II–III depending on the level. A small wooden aqueduct on the right bank signals the approach of Lava Dam Rapid (class IV). The last major rapid of the trip, Lava Dam drops between 5 and 6 feet through a break in an old lava flow. Rocks and hydraulics clutter the approach, but the drop itself is rather straightforward, or so it seems until you try to run it. An angled wave running diagonally down the drop masks some rocks below it; this wave also will threaten to flip any boat not set up properly. The outflow from the drop is fast, the swim is longer than you want to take, and there are several important rocks to avoid. After Lava Dam Rapid, it's a short distance to the confluence with the Ammonoosuc River, where, as at the start of the trip, the Gale wears a class I–II facade.

There is a hand-painted gauge on the Gale, on the river-left abutment of the Streeter Pond Road Bridge. Any prospective boater should realize that even though the Gale River valley holds excellent scenery, it is isolated. Help in an emergency will be difficult to find.

Kennebec River (Maine)

Harris Station Dam to The Forks (Route 201)

DISTANCE (MILES)	11		TOO LOW	
SHUTTLE (MILES)	11		LOW	1,500 cfs
AVG. DROP (FEET/MILE)	23		MED.	4,800 cfs
MAX. DROP (FEET/MILE)	53		HIGH	7,000 cfs
DIFFICULTY	IV		TOO HIGH	
SCENERY	Excellent		GAUGE LOCATION	Harris Station
DATE LAST CHECKED	1997		WATER LEVEL INFO.	800-557-3569
RUNOFF PATTERN	d/r/l			

The Kennebec is one of the few big-water runs in New England, and one of only two with reliable summer flows. Until the mid-'70s the Kennebec was a logging river, with annual log drives that littered the eddies with dangerous lumber and made it nearly impassable by whitewater boats. After the last drive in 1976, the river became boatable. Whitewater is now a major industry in this region, utilizing the Dead and the Penobscot Rivers as well as the Kennebec. While commercial rafters originally were responsible for persuading Central Maine Power (CMP) to release water on a regular basis for recreational use, private boaters have benefited as well from the utility's scheduled flows.

The Kennebec is released daily throughout the spring, summer, and fall at levels varying from 1,500 cfs to 8,000 and higher. While each level has its advantages and disadvantages, generally levels below about 3,600 cfs are considered low—Magic hole is grabby and powerful, and the waves in the rest of the gorge are on the small side. From about 3,600 to 5,600 cfs the river is big, continuous, and most features are pretty soft. At these medium flows Magic hole has two distinct foam piles and a soft spot in the middle. At 6,000 to 8,000 cfs and higher, the river is characterized by

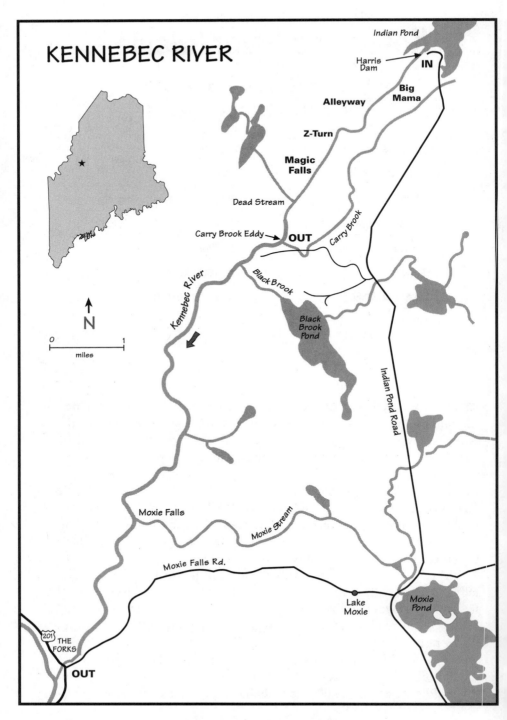

KENNEBEC RIVER

Indian Pond

Harris Dam

IN

Alleyway

Big Mama

Z-Turn

Magic Falls

Dead Stream

Carry Brook Eddy ➤ **OUT**

Carry Brook

Black Brook

Black Brook Pond

Kennebec River

Indian Pond Road

N

0   1
miles

Moxie Falls

Moxie Stream

Moxie Falls Rd.

Lake Moxie

Moxie Pond

201 THE FORKS

OUT

lateral breaking waves, and already scant opportunities for rescue are nonexistent. The first mile and a half are very continuous and the water is very turbulent.

The Kennebec runs through a slate gorge north of The Forks, Maine. It is released from Indian Pond at Harris Station Dam and fed at its source by Moosehead Lake.

Putting in on the gorge for the first time can be intimidating, since the Kennebec's reputation precedes it and you know that once you round the first bend there's virtually no other way out but down the river. To run the Kennebec, you must have a strong roll that's been proven in combat situations. A swim can be serious because of the size and continuous nature of the water. Walking out, while possible, is difficult.

Put in at the outflow of Harris Station and enjoy the first quarter-mile of warm-up as the river gathers speed and you have a brief opportunity to get used to the power of the water before the real fun begins. Soon the rapids start to build and waves of 4 to 5 feet become common. Eddies are fairly abundant on the shore at levels below 8,000 cfs, and there are brief fastwater sections between the first two or three rapids.

Soon an old log sluice appears on river right, signaling the start of the first really big rapid, which contains the largest single wave on the river: Big Mama. Big Mama used to be called the Three Sisters, but in the mid-'80s, when a rock moved during high water, the first of a three-wave train became much bigger than the other two and earned its new moniker. Whatever you call it, Big Mama starts off with a series of waves on the right and a jumble of waves and breaking curlers on the left. The water accelerates and is really zipping downstream in anticipation of the mother of all waves. There is a good eddy at river right just as the current accelerates. If you're quick enough to catch it, this is a handy stopping place to look over your shoulder and see what's coming up. Big Mama appears just below as a river-wide wave about 8 to 10 feet high depending on the volume. It usually curls somewhat on top, but not enough to hold a boater for more than a brief moment before releasing him into the turbulence below. There are strong, boily recovery eddies on either side of the river just below Big Mama, but the pool is very short between this and the next rapid, so get to shore quickly.

The next rapid is the Alleyway, a half-mile-long series of waves with a couple of holes thrown in for good measure. If you're comfortable playing in big class IV whitewater, this is a great place to surf, catch jet ferries, and perfect your big-water eddy-hopping.

At the beginning of the Alleyway on river right is the aptly named Goodbye Hole, which is famous for emptying rafts or other boats of their occupants, who then wind up swimming to the bottom of the rapid—a marathon swim if there ever was one. Past Goodbye Hole the river turns left and then right, with large, regular waves. On the outside of this right turn is the Whitewasher—a breaking wave that blinds you if you crash through it. This can be avoided easily by staying center or right.

The river then turns back to the left where a large midrapid recovery eddy appears on river left. This eddy also leads to a great jet ferry on the large wave at its top. Below here the rapid eases a bit, and several eddies on either side create excellent surfing, jet-ferrying, and ender opportunities.

Cathedral Eddy marks the end of the Alleyway and is a huge, turbulent vortex on river left at the bottom of the final wave train. Cathedral Eddy is a great place to stop and get your bearings if you're expecting it, but it is heavily guarded against entry by swimmers due to its wide and fluctuating eddy line. After the exhaustion of swimming the Alleyway, Cathedral is not a welcome sight. For this reason, it is better to swim to the right at the bottom of the Alleyway and use one of the more reasonable eddies on river right as a resting spot. Cathedral Eddy is where the raft companies keep a backboard for emergency use only. If your group has an emergency and uses this backboard or any other on the river, you must replace it immediately, since other river users count on it.

Below Cathedral Eddy the river is calm, with fast-moving flatwater for about a quarter-mile before Z-Turn Rapid. Z-Turn is an easy class III with an interesting surf/ender wave on river left and an escalator eddy on river right. Below these play spots the river turns sharply left and Z-Turn continues as a series of medium-size waves that lead to the fastwater above Magic Falls.

Magic Falls is the single most difficult rapid on the Kennebec (class IV+) and the only one that can be scouted easily from shore. Scouting is a good idea, especially on your first run. Take out on river left at any of several well-worn landing spots after the waves from Z-Turn have petered out. A trail leads you to Magic hole and a clear view of the top of the rapid where most of the difficult spots are located.

There are two major features in Magic—Magic hole and Maytag. Above 4,800 cfs, Magic hole is a large, but generally fairly harmless foam pile with a soft spot in the middle and a tongue against the shore. It extends about 25 feet from the left bank at the top of the rapid. Above 4,800 cfs, you can punch Magic on either the center or the left tongue, although an error of a couple of feet on either side could result in cart-wheels. Below 4,800 cfs, most boaters stay away, since Magic hole gets violent, the soft spot in the center disappears, and the rapid just below the hole is shallow.

Maytag is a large, flat hole midriver and somewhat below Magic hole. It makes sneaking Magic by running the rapid down the middle a bit more difficult than a walk in the park. Maytag is not a play hole at any level. Its size, violence, and strong recycle make it one to avoid. This is generally not difficult to do, although if you're inexperienced at reading big water, the lack of solid landmarks can make finding the line you saw from shore far from trivial. Below Magic hole and Maytag, the left and center of the river are dotted with smaller holes and pourovers, while the right side is a straight shot with medium-sized waves for another quarter-mile before the pool at the bottom.

The river becomes easy, with small waves and fastwater for another quarter-mile before Dead Stream enters on river right, signaling the final rapid of the gorge section. Dead Stream Rapid is a straightforward class IV with a jumble of 4- to 6-foot waves, a few mostly benign holes, and not a lot of stopping places. Toward the bottom some eddies appear on river left, but by this time most of the rapid is over. Dead Stream has some excellent on-the-fly surfing spots if you're alert enough to catch them as you float downstream, and the river-left eddies at the bottom give access to a couple of challenging surfs as well.

The final rapid before the takeout for the gorge section is a wide class III with one particularly insidious pourover in the middle. Difficult to see from above, this pourover is just right of center about halfway down the rapid and should be avoided unless you enjoy window-shading.

A bluff appears on the left shore at the base of this rapid, marking Carry Brook Eddy and the end of the upper section. Access here is not for the lazy, but it has been improved dramatically over what it was in the early 1980s when boaters crawled and clawed their way up the steep scree slope. The parking area is about 100 feet above the river, and you and your boat ascend that height along a steep wooden stairway. Parking is at an obvious pull-out a few hundred feet back from the river. Moose sightings in this area are common.

Putting in at Carry Brook Eddy, or continuing downstream from the gorge, the rapids are considerably easier, with the most difficult being Black Brook—a long class III 0.75 mile below Carry Brook. From Carry Brook to The Forks is about 8.0 miles and fast moving all the way. On a summer's day when your most pressing concern is where to set up your tent for the evening, this float can be a nice way to wind down from the gorge. Many boaters choose instead to take out at Carry Brook Eddy and run the gorge several times in a day. For intermediates who are not sure they are ready for the gorge, the lower section is a good test piece. If the hardest rapids on the lower section seem simple and your roll is solid, it may be time to challenge the gorge.

The takeout for the lower section is at a small riverside park with a picnic pavilion, on river left just above the bridge in The Forks. This bridge is the only one encountered on this section.

For information on when and how much water Harris Dam is releasing, call Central Maine Power's flow-information line at 800-557-3569. Once a year (usually around the 4th of July weekend) CMP schedules a "generator check" when, for a day, they flush as much water through their plant as possible to establish the maximum capacity of their generators. Due to the popularity of this day with boaters, the utility now schedules the generator check well in advance.

With the federal relicensing of Harris Station Dam, there is talk of establishing a higher minimum flow for fisheries, which will likely be boatable but very different from levels described above. At this low flow, the river is much more technical, with mid-river rocks and much smaller waves than at the higher levels.

To reach the put-in from Route 201 heading north into The Forks, go right just south of the only bridge across the Kennebec onto Moxie Falls Road. Follow this until it comes to a T intersection. Go left onto Indian Pond Road, where you will immediately pass Moxie Pond and cross a small metal bridge over Moxie Stream. From here the road is dirt for 7.5 miles until you reach the gate leading into Harris Station. You will be required to pay a parking fee at the gate and to sign a waiver absolving CMP of liability. To reach the Carry Brook Eddy takeout, follow the road back from the dam toward Moxie Pond and turn right in 3.4 miles. Follow this dirt road to its end.

For class III boaters who are not yet ready to challenge the gorge, a section just upstream of Harris Station known as the East Outlet offers a less intimidating alternative. The put-in is at the Route 6 bridge in Moosehead on Moosehead Lake. The 2.5-mile trip to Indian Pond is big and wide, but not nearly as difficult as its downstream cousin.

Lamoille River (Vt.)

Slide Falls to Jeffersonville

DISTANCE (MILES)	11.5	**TOO LOW**	
SHUTTLE (MILES)	11	**LOW**	
AVG. DROP (FEET/MILE)		**MED.**	
MAX. DROP (FEET/MILE)		**HIGH**	
DIFFICULTY	I–II	**TOO HIGH**	
SCENERY	Good	**GAUGE LOCATION**	
DATE LAST CHECKED	1997	**WATER LEVEL INFO.**	Umiak Outfitters
RUNOFF PATTERN	d/l		802-253-2317

The Lamoille River is a good way to see Vermont's Northeast Kingdom. With alternating rapid and flat stretches, the whitewater is not a draw in itself, but the varied scenery and late season make it worth the trip. The river got its name as a result of a map maker's laziness. Champlain discovered the river in his travels and named it La Moitte (the seagull), but when a cartographer failed to cross his Ts, Champlain's name for the river was forever lost to history.

The Lamoille traverses terrain similar to the Winooski. The put-in is just upstream of Johnson, Vermont, on Patch Road. There are two class IV–V rapids in a row here—Dog's Head and Slide Falls. Enter the river just below Slide Falls. The run is mostly fast moving, with some riffles here and there. The town of Johnson is not the scenic high point of the run, with a talc factory on the river-left bank, but once past Johnson the view improves.

A mile and a half after the factory the river passes under the Route 15 bridge. About half a mile past this is the first of two class II drops—Ithiel Falls. These drops can be scouted from river left and are straightforward. The banks of the river are steep and rocky, and this minigorge is one of the more interesting features on the trip.

From here to Jeffersonville the river is fast moving with alternating rapid and flat stretches, but no significant difficulties. You'll know you're approaching town when you pass under a railroad trestle. Take out at the

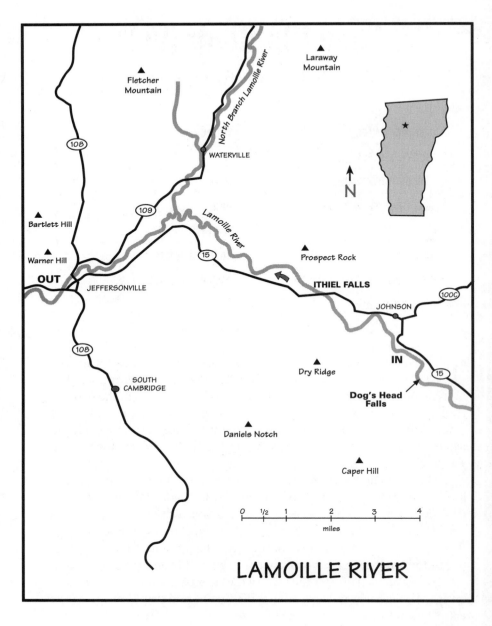

Fletcher
Mountain

Laraway
Mountain

North Branch Lamoille River

108

109

WATERVILLE

Lamoille River

Bartlett Hill

Warner Hill

15

Prospect Rock

OUT

JEFFERSONVILLE

ITHIEL FALLS

JOHNSON

100C

108

IN

SOUTH
CAMBRIDGE

Dry Ridge

15

Dog's Head
Falls

Daniels Notch

Caper Hill

N

0   ½   1   2   3   4
miles

LAMOILLE RIVER

second road bridge in Jeffersonville (Route 15) on the upstream left side
of the bridge.

The entire run is 11.5 miles long and is runnable well into the summer most years. Call Umiak Outfitters (802-253-2317) in Stowe, Vermont,
for water-level information.

Mad River (N.H.)

Waterville Valley to Goose Hollow

DISTANCE (MILES)	6.3		**TOO LOW**	
SHUTTLE (MILES)	6.3		**LOW**	1.5
AVG. DROP (FEET/MILE)	85		**MED.**	2.5
MAX. DROP (FEET/MILE)	100+		**HIGH**	
DIFFICULTY	III–IV		**TOO HIGH**	
SCENERY	Excellent		**GAUGE LOCATION**	Upper Mad River Rd.
DATE LAST CHECKED	1997		**WATER LEVEL INFO.**	
RUNOFF PATTERN	n/f			

The Mad is well worth the wait. Beautiful scenery, challenging rapids, and clear water all characterize this fine whitewater stream, even though there is hardly enough watershed to keep the river filled for more than a few short weeks in midspring. But, oh, those weeks! Then the Mad presents one of the nicest, most continuous sets of frothing water in the entire state. Once the water is down, however, boaters just have to wait it out through a long summer, fall, and winter to get another shot at the Mad.

Start your trip on the Mad in Waterville Valley where the road crosses the river. To get there, turn left off Route 49 at Tripoli Road. There is also a gas station near this turn. The turnoff is almost 10.0 miles from Campton Pond Dam. At the start, the river is rather small and relatively straightforward. The current, however, is moving at a very healthy pace, since the average gradient is 85 feet per mile. First-time Mad paddlers will find the current decidedly pushy.

Shortly after the start comes a big boulder on the left with a hole right beside it; then farther downstream the river turns right and moves away from the road. There are plenty of rocks, hydraulics, and drops to keep you busy in this loop, but nothing really spectacular. The Mad, then

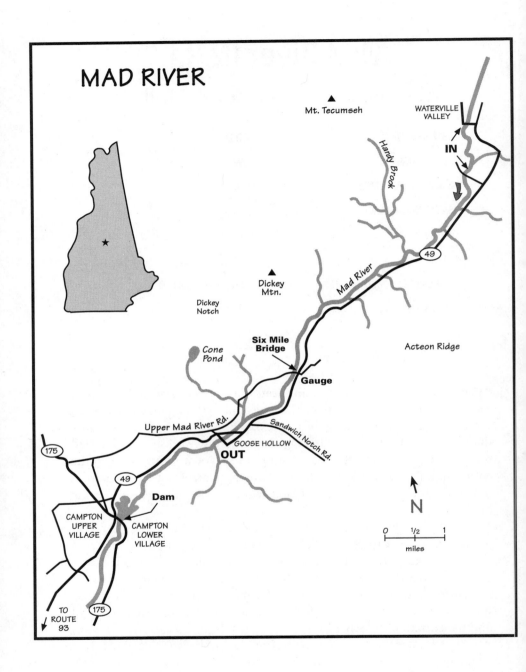

MAD RIVER

Mt. Tecumseh ▲

WATERVILLE VALLEY

Hardy Brook

IN

49

Dickey Mtn. ▲

Dickey Notch

Mad River

Acteon Ridge

Cone Pond

Six Mile Bridge

Gauge

Upper Mad River Rd.

Sandwich Notch Rd.

GOOSE HOLLOW

OUT

175

49

Dam

CAMPTON UPPER VILLAGE

CAMPTON LOWER VILLAGE

N

0   1/2   1
miles

TO ROUTE 93

175

returning to the road, bends sharply right and drops over Ho Hum Rapid. Short and intense, Ho Hum forces the paddler to make quick maneuvers in a tight channel and a fast current while pounding down a stair-step descent. Ho Hum is class IV in medium levels, and still tough in low water. It is the most difficult rapid encountered so far on the trip, and it is indicative of what follows. A roadside turnoff shortly downstream from Ho Hum makes scouting by car easy. Route 49 is on the left.

What follows Ho Hum Rapid is more of the same. If each subsequent set of rapids had a name, this description would resemble a dictionary, so no detailed description is given here. Suffice it to say that there are lengths of calmer water, but they are the exception. If the water is at a decent level, boaters will be very busy reading what lies ahead, then trying to act upon that knowledge. Several spots of continuously difficult rapid must be taken as they come; they're mostly away from the road, so you can't scout by car. Abrupt stair-step drops, large rocks, and a serpentine course make it necessary to run several rapids without really knowing where the best route lies. Planning ahead is a real asset here. If in doubt, get out and walk a bit. The run's continuity and fast pace are exhilarating if all is going well, dismaying if someone needs to be rescued—especially if that someone is you. At medium levels, this trip is rated a strong class IV—difficult without being overwhelming. It is sport, not survival. It is fun. It is intoxicating. It is beautiful.

The approach to Goose Hollow is easy canoeing. The river still has a steep gradient, but the channel is wide and the rocks are relatively small. You can take out at any of the bridges.

If you would like a longer journey, Campton Pond Dam is another 2.5 miles downriver. The river slows as it approaches the pond, though. Below the dam is a steep-sided, gorgelike stretch that is quite playful if you want to carry down the slopes. This stretch has been the scene of slalom races. It frequently has water when the upper section does not.

There is a hand-painted gauge on a rock on the left bank just upstream from Upper Mad River Road bridge. You can't see the gauge from the bridge; you must walk upstream on the river-left bank and look back downstream at the rock to read it. If you can't see the top of the gauge (3 feet), you should think twice about running the river. There is also a gauge measuring the water level at Campton Pond. This gauge is in the Telemark system, so the Corps of Engineers can get remote readings. The gauge is not well correlated with the hand-painted gauge, although it is estimated that a reading over 11.0 is needed for a good run.

Magalloway River (Maine)

Aziscohos Hydro to Wilsons Mills

DISTANCE (MILES)	1.75	**TOO LOW**	
SHUTTLE (MILES)	1.75	**LOW**	640
AVG. DROP (FEET/MILE)	91	**MED.**	
MAX. DROP (FEET/MILE)		**HIGH**	
DIFFICULTY	III	**TOO HIGH**	
SCENERY	Good	**GAUGE LOCATION**	Aziscohos Hydro
DATE LAST CHECKED	1997	**WATER LEVEL INFO.**	800-557-3569
RUNOFF PATTERN	d/r/l		

The Magalloway is a close cousin to the Rapid. A little easier and not nearly as long or continuous, the Magalloway is, however, much more accessible. The put-in on Route 16 below Lake Aziscohos is a mere hop, skip, and a jump off the main road, and the takeout is right on the highway. The run is very short at just over 1.5 miles. The scenery is not quite as panoramic as that on the Rapid, since the Magalloway is a bit smaller and surrounded by more dense, low-lying forests, but the area around the Magalloway is mostly unspoiled, so the surroundings are pleasant.

The two rivers have complementary release patterns, since they are the two main sources of water for Lake Umbagog. In order to maintain the level in the lake and provide water for the Androscoggin downstream of the lake, the Magalloway and/or the Rapid runs much of the summer. There is also an annual fall drawdown, when the Magalloway often runs for months at a time.

Upstream of the put-in for the normal run is a series of class V and VI cascades just below the dam at Lake Aziscohos. This spectacular set of rapids (falls?) has been run (by a drunk in an inner-tube, according to local rumor), but the presence of such logging artifacts as steel spikes in

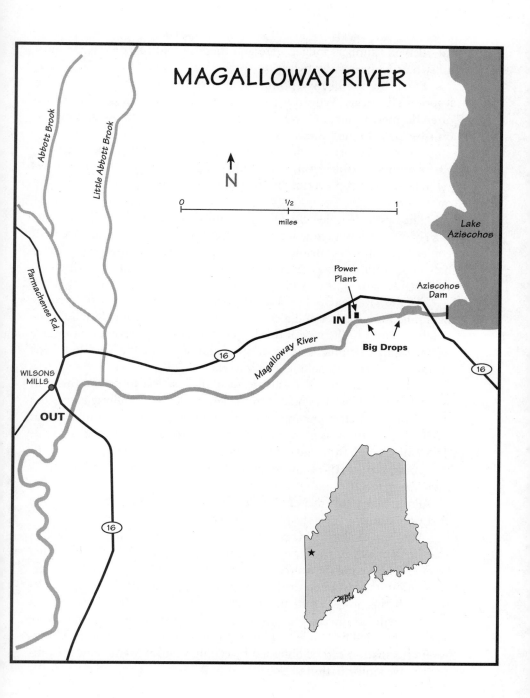

MAGALLOWAY RIVER

N

0   1/2   1
       miles

Abbott Brook

Little Abbott Brook

Lake
Aziscohos

Parmachenee Rd.

Power
Plant

Aziscohos
Dam

IN

Big Drops

16

Magalloway River

WILSONS
MILLS

OUT

16

16

the rock and timbers lodged here and there should make even the most gutsy hair-boaters think twice.

Enter the river below a power station that bypasses these cascades. An 8-foot vertical class V drop is immediately below the tailrace, but this is often deemed an inappropriate warm-up. A narrow path leads around it on river right to the easier water below.

The rapids start off with characteristic tight, technical rock gardens, where a missed stroke easily can result in a pin. The water at normal levels (640 cfs) is not powerful, but it packs enough of a punch to keep you on your toes.

The first half-mile below the put-in is continuous class III that ends at a river-wide (not saying much on a river this narrow) surfing wave with eddies on both sides. Below this wave, class II water follows for another half-mile, until the river turns sharply left and a house appears high on the outside bank of the turn.

As the river turns left it drops over a 2-foot ledge with a sticky hydraulic in the center and a clean chute on the left. Just below, a diagonal hole stands in the way of this left channel, forcing the boater to move left or right. This hole is an interesting and fairly mellow surf and feeds strongly to river left, making it easy to exit.

Below, 50 feet of easier water leads to the heaviest stretch on this run, where a 3-foot ledge extends from the left bank about halfway across the river. There is a clear channel with medium-sized waves (up to 3 feet at 640 cfs) just right of center, and a couple of strong holes on the far right. This entire rapid, from the left turn with the house on the outside of it to this point, is class III- at low levels, and can become a difficult class III at higher water as the holes get punchier.

From here to the takeout is half a mile of class I–II water. Take out the first time Route 16 crosses the river downstream of the dam.

Water levels for the Magalloway tend to be constant due to the hydroelectric dam, which runs most of the time at 630 to 640 cfs. In the spring or after a heavy rain, however, the overflow channel can run, adding various amounts of water to the run. At press time, negotiations were underway with the power company, which could result in 900+ cfs releases being scheduled during the summer. It is estimated that at levels above 1,000 cfs the first half-mile is class IV, due to its continuous nature. Water-level information can be obtained by calling Central Maine Power Company's river-information phone at 800-557-3569.

Mascoma River (N.H.)

Mascoma Lake to Lebanon

DISTANCE (MILES)	4		**TOO LOW**	
SHUTTLE (MILES)	3.5		**LOW**	340 cfs/2.3
AVG. DROP (FEET/MILE)	38		**MED.**	1,000 cfs/3.5
MAX. DROP (FEET/MILE)	80		**HIGH**	
DIFFICULTY	II–III (IV)		**TOO HIGH**	2,600 cfs/8
SCENERY	Fair		**GAUGE LOCATION**	Rte. 4A/Mascoma
DATE LAST CHECKED	1997		**WATER LEVEL INFO.**	
RUNOFF PATTERN	d/l		http://water.usgs.gov/public/realtime.html	

The Mascoma River is formed at the outflow of Mascoma Lake, near the junction of Routes 4 and 4A. The lake acts not only as a water source, but also as a flow regulator for the Mascoma, keeping it flowing in relatively dry weather and checking the effect of heavy rains. The river is medium sized, with numerous fallen trees that narrow the channels. The scenery is only fair—there are many signs of civilization. Except for Excelsior Rapids, the difficulty is rated class II–III. Excelsior, which ends the trip, is class III or IV depending on water level. Excelsior is just upstream from a 4-foot dam. This height may not be impressive, but the hydraulic at the bottom is. Avoid it. A slalom race used to be held at Excelsior, but due to access problems it is now held on a rapid upstream.

To start, put in at the Mascoma Lake outlet where there is a little roadside pull-off, reached after driving a short distance on a side road off Route 4A. The river starts out rather wide, but quickly narrows. Just below the remains of an old railroad bridge there is a gauge on the left. Between the start and the Route 4 bridge are a few standing-wave rapids. From the Route 4 bridge to the Route 89 bridge, rapids are short class II–III (at medium levels) with spaces of calmer water. There is really nothing here that merits scouting, except perhaps for fallen trees. A poorly maintained

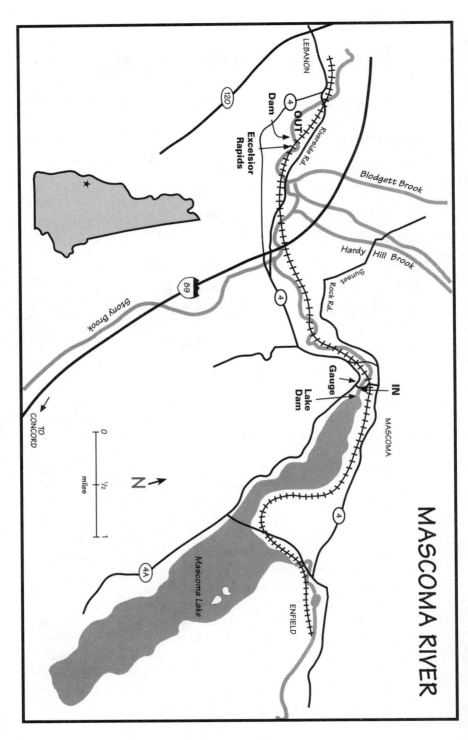

MASCOMA RIVER

Surfing the wave at Blue Hill Falls on the incoming tide. The tide is low in this photo. Photo by Bruce Lessels.

dirt road follows on river left in this section. It is blocked at the upstream end but can be reached just upstream of the Route 89 bridge. After the Route 89 bridge, the Mascoma follows the interstate (class I–II).

The Mascoma bears left, away from Route 89, then eventually right again to begin a more interesting section of river (less than a mile long). After the right turn comes a standing-wave rapid under a small stone bridge. There are eddies on either side, and the route is easy to discern. This is where members of the 1972 Olympic team trained. In the right turn below, the river starts a short, tight S-turn with a good hydraulic on the left in the right-turn part, and a few rocks and some good standing waves in the left-turn part. What follows then is 100 to 200 hundred yards of class III water taking you up to a railroad bridge in a right turn. This bridge marks the beginning of Excelsior Rapids.

Excelsior is harder than anything met on the trip so far, rated class IV at medium water levels and class III at low levels. It is about 100 yards long and runs reasonably straight through most of its course, ending in a left turn. The right bank is steep, but there is a footpath on the left bank. Excelsior has everything—rocks, holes, and standing waves that punch back. The usual run starts in a slot on the right or right center, traverses to the left halfway down, and finishes on the left. Several mean hydraulics halfway down on the right are good cause for a traverse. When you sight another railroad bridge after the final left turn, exit from the river; the next right turn immediately below holds the 4-foot dam with the powerful hydraulic. Cocky boaters whose rolls have failed them have been known to watch their boats being sacrificed to the river gods here.

The usual takeout is on the left just before the dam. A short walk across the railroad bridge brings you to a moving-and-storage company's parking lot, and from there it's a short walk to the main road. It's also possible to carry your boat upstream along the railroad tracks for 100 yards and run Excelsior again. Park next to the road rather than in the moving company's lot. Access has been an issue here in the past and respecting the landowners will help to ensure future access. Another takeout can be reached farther downstream where a side road (Bank Street) off Route 4 crosses over the river. Portage around the dam and continue downriver to reach this spot. The river is swift, but there are no rapids or obstructions once you are past the dam.

From here down, the Mascoma meanders lazily toward Lebanon, New Hampshire, where there is at least one dam. This stretch is not particularly recommended. There is a steep, jumbled class V rapid in the middle of town known as "Downtown Hair," a favorite of local hair-boaters.

The dam at Mascoma Lake is controlled by the New Hampshire Water Resources Board (603-271-3406). Call them for a release schedule. The USGS gauge is on the left bank, 250 feet downstream from a railroad bridge and 1,000 feet downstream from the Mascoma Lake outlet. Levels for the Mascoma are reported on the USGS web page at http://water.usgs.gov/public/realtime.html.

Mattawamkeag River (Maine)

Mattawamkeag Wilderness Park to Lower Gordon Falls

DISTANCE (MILES)	3.5		TOO LOW	
SHUTTLE (MILES)	3.5		LOW	2,000 cfs
AVG. DROP (FEET/MILE)			MED.	6,000 cfs
MAX. DROP (FEET/MILE)			HIGH	
DIFFICULTY	III–IV		TOO HIGH	12,000 cfs
SCENERY	Excellent		GAUGE LOCATION	Mattawamkeag
DATE LAST CHECKED	1997		WATER LEVEL INFO.	
RUNOFF PATTERN	n/l		http://water.usgs.gov/public/realtime.html	

The Mattawamkeag is Maine's longest undammed river, but it usually runs throughout the summer on natural flow due to its very marshy watershed. It flows through a wilderness park that is classic backwoods Maine, and its rapids are interesting, though not as plentiful or as difficult as such better-known Maine classics as the Kennebec, Penobscot, and Dead.

Like the Penobscot, the Mattawamkeag is pool-drop, with several long stretches of flatwater in the 3.5-mile run. Each rapid is no more than a quarter-mile long, and all but one is a straightforward wave train at low to medium levels.

Put in at the Mattawamkeag Wilderness Park 7.5 miles east of the town of Mattawamkeag. The single-track dirt road that leads to the park follows the river unobtrusively all the way, so it is easy to bail out, but the feeling of wilderness on the river is undisturbed by the presence of the road. By walking upriver a quarter-mile from the beach area at the park, you can add a class III rapid with an interesting surfing wave called Rams Head to the trip, or you can put in just below this rapid at a large pool. In early spring when the road to the park is closed (generally until the mid-

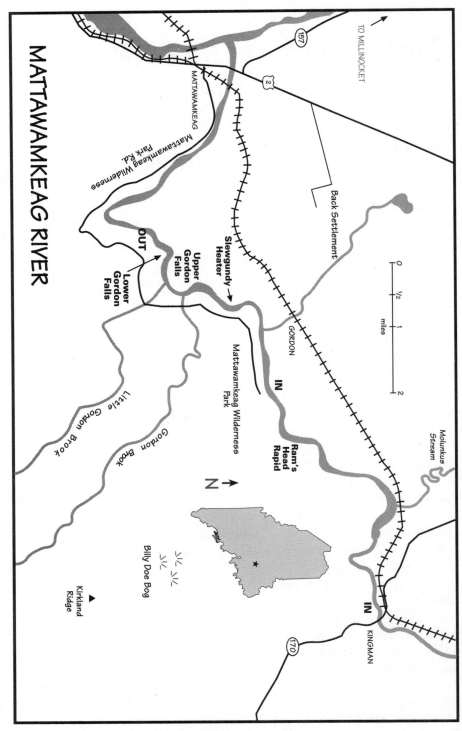

MATTAWAMKEAG RIVER

TO MILLINOCKET

157

US 2

MATTAWAMKEAG

Mattawamkeag Wilderness Park Rd.

Back Settlement

Slewgundy Heater

OUT

Upper Gordon Falls

Lower Gordon Falls

Mattawamkeag Wilderness Park

GORDON

IN

Little Gordon Brook

Gordon Brook

Ram's Head Rapid

Molunkus Stream

0

½

1

miles

2

N →

Billy Doe Bog

Kirkland Ridge

IN

170

KINGMAN

dle of May), it is usually necessary to enter the river upstream in Kingman. This adds 4.0 miles to the run, but at this time of year the river typically carries 6,000 to 12,000 cfs, so the fastwater goes by quickly.

The first mile below the park is flat, with an occasional riffle and slow-moving current. As you round a wide right bend, the water picks up speed, and soon the river narrows as it enters a small slate gorge called Slewgundy Heater. The biggest waves are down the right on this one, and there are plentiful shoreline eddies at medium water. After about 300 yards the river again slows, although gorge walls still contain it. As it bends to the right, the second half of this rapid appears with a 4-foot ledge that is steepest on the left and more gradual as you move right. The center holds a steep pourover, so the best lines are on either side of center. These first two rapids are rated class III at medium levels. At high water Slewgundy Heater develops large diagonal waves, and the lower ledge forms big holes that can gobble a boat and paddler.

Another mile of flatwater follows with fast current and beautiful scenery, until the river again bends to the right and begins to pick up speed. Downstream on the outside of the bend, a rock promontory signals that you have reached Upper Gordon Falls. This rapid is the biggest on the run and a solid IV at medium water. At high flows, the holes become monsters and the turbulence is awesome. Scout from either shore, and run any one of several lines starting generally left and moving right above the biggest drop (8 feet), then plunging over it almost anywhere (it's big no matter where you run it). An easy outflow with a steep play wave leads to the pool at the bottom. Both Upper and Lower Gordon Falls can be seen from the road on the way up to the put-in.

After a left bend, Lower Gordon Falls soon appears. This is considerably easier (class III- at medium levels) than Upper Gordon Falls and consists of a wave train that moves from river left to river right in a small, short gorge. A few interesting surfing waves can be found here. Take out a quarter-mile below Lower Gordon Falls where a cable for a gauging station crosses the river. There is a small roadside pull-off here.

Water levels for the Mattawamkeag are reported on the USGS web site at http://water.usgs.gov/public/realtime.html.

Other runs of similar difficulty in the area are the lower West Branch of the Penobscot (below the Cribworks) and the Roll Dams section of the West Branch of the Penobscot.

North River–Halifax Gorge (Vt.)

Route 112 to Route 112
Trip A

DISTANCE (MILES)	3		TOO LOW	
SHUTTLE (MILES)	3		LOW	3.4
AVG. DROP (FEET/MILE)	100		MED.	3.8
MAX. DROP (FEET/MILE)	125		HIGH	
DIFFICULTY	IV (V)		TOO HIGH	
SCENERY	Excellent		GAUGE LOCATION	Shattuckville
DATE LAST CHECKED	1997		WATER LEVEL INFO.	
RUNOFF PATTERN	n/f		http://water.usgs.gov/public/realtime.html	

This upper section of the North is better known for the nude sun-bathers who used to hang out on the rocks before the town closed the area than for its boating potential, but the 3.0-mile run holds some very interesting drops for advanced creek-boaters and the scenery is beautiful, varying from Vermont farm country to a vertical-sided slate gorge. There are three really big drops in the run; all are 10 feet or more, and all require scouting and class V boating skills. The rest of the difficult drops are class IV. There is a mile of easier water (class I–II) above the first gorge, and a mile and a half of class II between the two gorges. Despite these easy sections, however, this run is only for class IV–V paddlers, since the big drops are very serious and the approaches to them are not suitable for intermediate paddlers.

There are two distinct gorges that make up this run. Both lie along Route 112 in Halifax, Vermont. The downstream gorge is just a couple of miles north of the Massachusetts line, while the upper one is about a mile and a half north of that. The first big drop is visible from Route 112 at the top of the first gorge, although the land next to it is posted, so don't go traipsing across the lawn to view this one. You can walk down to it from

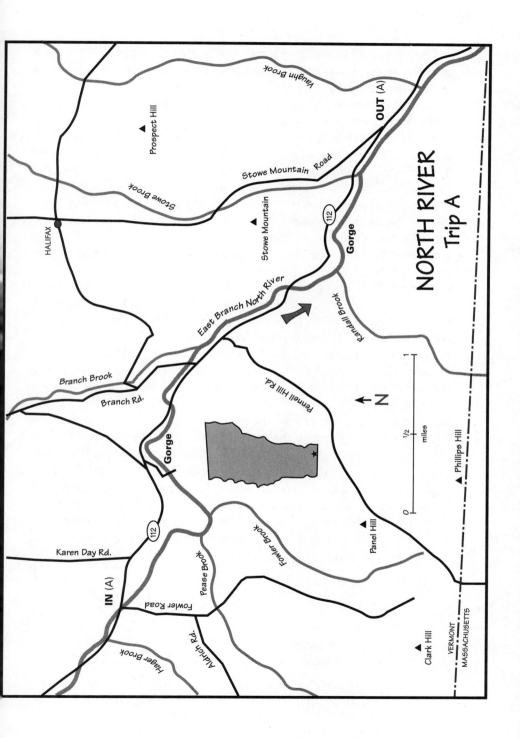

an eddy above once you're on the river. The two big drops in the second gorge are accessible via a trail leading from a small roadside pull-off about halfway up the gorge.

Put in where Route 112 crosses the North about a mile above the upstream gorge at Fowler Road. The first mile is an easy, scenic warm-up with lots of strainers but no rapids of any consequence. When you pass under a small private road bridge, the river turns left shortly, and the top of the first gorge is imminent. Eddy out river left to scout the first biggy— The Shallow End. After a winding approach, a 10-foot drop lands in a very short, shallow pool. Boof with lots of left angle to avoid pitoning at the base of the drop. The runout leads to a rocky class IV chute that's best started left and finished right after crossing the eddy in the middle. Two more class IVs complete the upper gorge, and a mile and a half of easy water follows.

The downstream gorge begins as the river narrows and ledgy rapids lead to a sharp left turn. Just below this turn, the rapids come to the brink of the next big drop—No Diving Allowed. Scout this one from left and/or right, but beware the tree jammed in the right slot. It's not clear whether it has branches underwater, but some mysteries are better left unsolved. Handle NDA by driving off the 12-foot falls left of center and angling somewhat left. The hole at the base of the parallel ledge below is easily surfed downstream into the recovery eddy on river left.

Just across this short pool the final falls, the Deep End, is best scouted from the left. This one is the highest (14 feet) and most powerful of the three big ones. Start right and drive hard left, landing where the strong current from the right merges with the main flow. Beware the decapitation rock at the base on river left where the current is forced against the left wall of the gorge. A few more class III and IV drops lead to an easier section as the river rejoins the road. Take out anywhere on river left.

Water level is critical on this run, as on most class V creeks. This description is based on a run at 3.6 on the Shattuckville gauge.

Otter Brook (N.H.)

East Sullivan to Otter Brook Park

DISTANCE (MILES)	3.3		**TOO LOW**	
SHUTTLE (MILES)	3.3		**LOW**	1.5
AVG. DROP (FEET/MILE)	80		**MED.**	350 cfs
MAX. DROP (FEET/MILE)	100		**HIGH**	3
DIFFICULTY	III–IV		**TOO HIGH**	
SCENERY	Fair		**GAUGE LOCATION**	East Sullivan/Otter Brook Dam
DATE LAST CHECKED	1997		**WATER LEVEL INFO.**	
RUNOFF PATTERN	d/f		http://water.usgs.gov/public/realtime.html	

If the water is up, this trip on Otter Brook presents one of the most delightful small creek runs in all of New England. The rapids are uninterrupted, with no pools or flatwater. There are plenty of rocks, and yet no rapids are extremely complex, though the difficulty can reach class IV. The water is not usually overpowering or scary, but it is fast and turbulent in a very narrow riverbed—maneuvering is a challenge, and you need to do quite a bit of it. Eddies are plentiful; the competent boater can zip in and out playfully like an otter. Route 9 follows the Otter Brook closely for the entire trip. The rapids are continuous, so only the highlights are presented here.

Put in where Otter Brook crosses Route 9 near East Sullivan, New Hampshire. The river is 40 to 60 feet wide here, with gentle rapids (in low or medium water) among a scattering of small rocks. A little way downstream come the first rapids, a 100-yard collection of class III haystacks, souse holes, and turbulence. These rapids are typical and put you in the mood for the rest of the run. After a short stretch of calmer water, the Otter Brook turns a right corner into a long section of continuous rapids, class III–IV depending on water level. Waves are up to 3 feet at medium

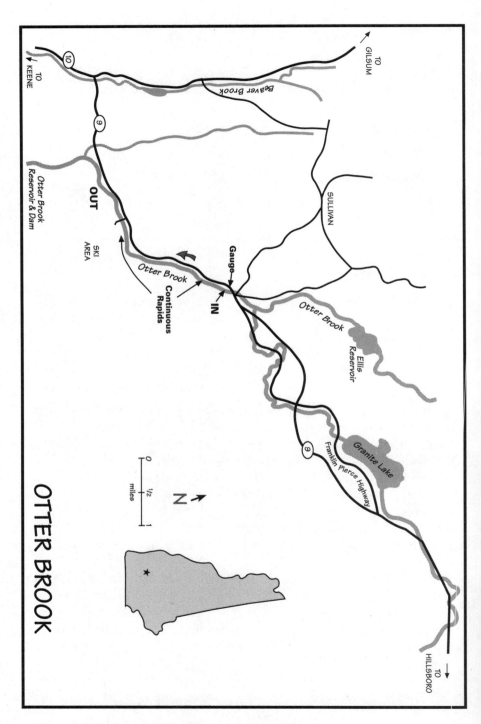

OTTER BROOK

TO KEENE
TO GILSUM

Beaver Brook

10

9

Otter Brook Reservoir & Dam

OUT

SKI AREA

Otter Brook

Continuous Rapids

Gauge

IN

SULLIVAN

Otter Brook

Ellis Reservoir

9

Franklin Pierce Highway

Granite Lake

N

0

miles

1/2

1

TO HILLSBORO

levels, and large rocks introduce themselves at the very beginning. The road is close to the right bank.

Very shortly after the river leaves the immediate vicinity of the road, there is a right turn and then a sloping drop of 3 to 4 feet into standing waves and holes (class IV in medium water), followed closely by another right turn and another similar drop. The road reappears and the rapids continue.

Slightly past a brown house on the right bank, there is a 2- to 3-foot drop over a ledge in a right turn. Following this are several tight S-curves and some easier drops. This type of rapid continues past an old iron bridge.

By the time you reach the site of a former ski area where a small bridge crosses the river, the tough rapids seem to have exhausted themselves, and the river becomes a little shallower. From this spot to the take-out, about 0.8 mile, the rapids are less intense (class II–III), but the current is still strong and there are plenty of small rocks, though the curves are not so sharp. Take out by the bridge in Otter Brook Park. If the main gate is locked, walk your boat several hundred yards to reach Route 9. If the water is low, you may want to take out at the ski area.

Special mention should be made of the 3.0-foot gauge reading. At this level, the upper part of the run is nearly unbroken class IV rapids. Several drops (see the third paragraph of this description, above) feel as if the bottom has fallen out, and the elevator is falling free toward an unseen depth. A swimmer will take a pounding and may even resurface occasionally. However, if you are well beyond the learning stage—i.e., you no longer lean upstream in a hole—you should find the Otter Brook a truly delightful challenge.

There is a hand-painted gauge on the right, upstream side of the center support of the Route 9 bridge in East Sullivan. There is also a Corps of Engineers dam just downstream from the takeout. Levels are posted daily on the USGS Water Level Information page on the web (http://water.usgs.gov/public/realtime.html). Information is provided both in cfs and feet on the gauge. It is estimated that 350 cfs will create a medium level for closed boats.

If you would like another nearby trip of similar difficulty, try the Ashuelot or the South Branch of the Ashuelot.

Pemigewasset River– East Branch (N.H.)

Kancamagus Highway to Loon Mountain
Trip A

DISTANCE (MILES)	2.5		**TOO LOW**	0.2
SHUTTLE (MILES)	2.5		**LOW**	1
AVG. DROP (FEET/MILE)	72		**MED.**	1.5
MAX. DROP (FEET/MILE)	80		**HIGH**	2
DIFFICULTY	IV		**TOO HIGH**	
SCENERY	Good		**GAUGE LOCATION**	Kancamagus Bridge
DATE LAST CHECKED	1997		**WATER LEVEL INFO.**	
RUNOFF PATTERN	n/l/f			

The East Branch of the Pemi lies on the western edge of the White Mountains, and its valley offers good boating and good hiking. Two characteristics predominate in the Pemi's personality. First, it is a big river—big for the area and big for New England. Second, it has a relatively steep gradient. These two traits combined make a rugged trip for anyone who dares venture forth when there is a respectable amount of water running. Because the Pemi has a large riverbed to fill, it takes a heavy runoff or a recent rain to satisfy its voracious appetite. The Pemi has plenty of rocks, although most are rounded and friendly, or at least as friendly as a rock can get. Due to the nature of the riverbed—gravel bars with a few large boulders scattered liberally about—the rapids on the Pemi change frequently as high water reshuffles the bottom, opens new channels, and rolls boulders bigger than a Mack truck downstream. For this reason, you should take the following description as a general guide, but rely on your own judgment when it comes to assessing each individual

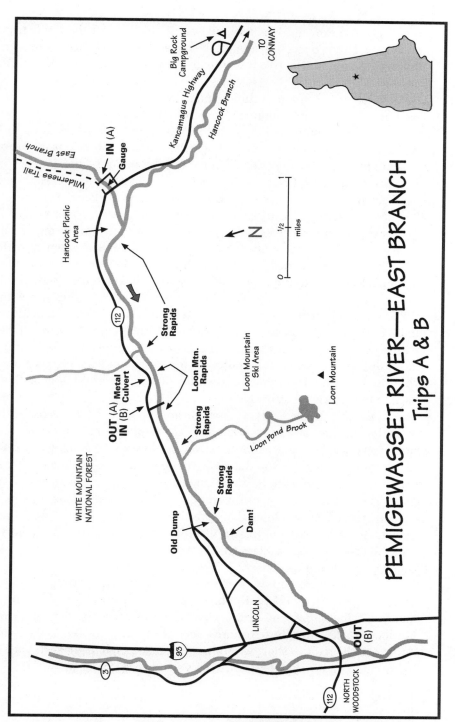

PEMIGEWASSET RIVER—EAST BRANCH
Trips A & B

TO CONWAY

Big Rock Campground

Kancamagus Highway

Hancock Branch

East Branch

IN (A)

Gauge

Wilderness Trail

Hancock Picnic Area

N

0   1/2   1
miles

112

Strong Rapids

Loon Mtn. Rapids

Loon Mountain Ski Area

OUT (A)
IN (B)
Metal Culvert

Strong Rapids

Loon Mountain

Loon Pond Brook

WHITE MOUNTAIN NATIONAL FOREST

Strong Rapids

Old Dump

Dam!

93

LINCOLN

3

OUT (B)

112

NORTH WOODSTOCK

rapid. The Kancamagus Highway follows the riverside for the whole trip, but it can't always be seen. Trip A can be repeated several times in one day; however, if you include trip B with trip A, you can have a full day's outing.

The rapids combine technical maneuvers and turbulent waves. In medium or high water the turbulence is overpowering and it cannot be appreciated merely by looking at the rapids from the road. Because the rapids are uninterrupted, only highlights will be described here, so keep in mind that water not specifically mentioned is still difficult.

Traveling west from the Swift River basin, the Kancamagus Highway parallels the Hancock Branch as it descends to meet the Pemi. This tributary of the East Branch can be an interesting steep creek run, but you have to time it just right, since its runoff pattern is very flashy. At the put-in on the Pemi, there is a convenient parking lot, a small visitor center with facilities, and a suspended footbridge. This is also the start of several hiking trails leading into the Pemi Wilderness, one of which travels along an old logging railroad that parallels the upper Pemi to its confluence with the Franconia Branch (3.0 miles). This section is seldom canoed because there is no access road for boat-carrying vehicles—and a 3.0-mile hike with a boat in your knapsack isn't much fun. This upper section is similar in difficulty to trip A. The railroad crosses the Franconia Branch and continues up the East Branch in the direction of Crawford Notch. Now back to the Kancamagus bridge.

At the put-in, the Pemi is some 35 yards wide, and it is loaded with many breadbasket-sized rocks. Larger rocks populate the sides. The section of river near the put-in almost always looks scratchy and low, regardless of the water level. If you don't have to do some rock-picking here, the rest of the trip is going to be a real challenge. Looking downstream from the start, the Pemi is straight for some 400 to 500 yards, finally turning right in the distance. Other than possibly being fast and choppy, this straight section holds no great difficulties. The right turn has a short, tricky stair-step descent (class III–IV at a gauge of 1.3) as the Hancock Branch enters from the left.

After Hancock Rapids, you'll be heading toward the 2,680-foot, dome-shaped peak of Potash Knob. Just when it seems to be on the immediate right, the Pemi swings left. The channel is turbulent on the right, and hordes of rocks cover the left shore. More of the same follows as the road returns to the river. A short way downstream is a slight right turn with a heavy chute. In lower water this chute is somewhat technical.

Below an old gauging station on the right bank, a gravel island divides the river; the main flow is on the right, swinging left and then sharply right at the island's downstream end. There is a rather powerful rapid at this spot. In low water several routes are possible among the large rocks found there. In high or medium water, the rocks are mostly covered, but they are replaced by turbulence. You may want to scout this one if you are unfamiliar with the river. The approach around the island is relatively straightforward if the holes and violent water don't upset you.

Shortly thereafter comes another gravel island with trees. The right side around the island is narrow and fast with the trickiest rapids on the trip. One-third of the way down are two hydraulics that extend across the width of the channel. Near the end, a collection of three huge boulders blocks the center route. The largest is dead center, and the two smaller ones are slightly upstream to the right and left. The right boulder is underwater at medium levels, so when the paddler comes blasting down this narrow chute he must suddenly make several quick maneuvers through a short, tight slalom course where last-minute decisions can be followed by a swim. The road is very close, so you can easily look the whole thing over beforehand. Upstream and downstream from the three boulders you may come upon scattered remains of an old metal culvert, which, although sometimes submerged, are a menace at any level. Don't take this right-side channel without scouting it. A trapped tree or other debris in such narrow confines easily could lead to an ugly situation. The left side of the island is another typical Pemi staircase descent. It offers a class IV sneak route that avoids the class IV route on the right side.

Below, Loon Mountain Rapid starts. This rapid does not look particularly difficult, but it requires a great deal of maneuvering around an abundance of rocks, and the paddling is always heavier than it would appear from the road. The takeout is in the middle of Loon Mountain Rapid at the bridge—you can choose left or right for your exit. Loon Mountain Rapid continues beyond the bridge, becoming more malicious along the way, so plan your departure carefully (and in advance). The drop under the bridge itself is steeper than it appears until you get very close to the lip. The rocks are also jagged, since they appear to have been moved during reconstruction of the bridge. The left side is the clearest line here.

At a gauge reading of 2.0 (maybe even 1.5) and higher the Pemi deserves special attention: most boaters should exercise discretion, not valor. At these levels the current is savage. The rapids are like barbarians trying to ram the door of a castle, and if you make a mistake you'll find the swim just a bit more death defying than that in a moat. At lower levels, Loon Mountain Rapid is merely challenging; at these higher levels, it's a malicious labyrinth where the wrong choice of path leads not just to a dead end, but to a high-speed collision with a boulder as well. The run is continuous class IV, and the whole trip varies between borderline class V and solid class V. The paddler must maneuver around numerous rocks and gaping holes in heavy water, while trying to stay out of hydraulics that can easily drown a boat. Rescues are nearly impossible. Although eddies exist, they are few and hard to capture. Competent people boat this section at these levels, but it requires the utmost in skill and performance, and one should be prepared to challenge an angry giant.

There is a hand-painted gauge on the right, downstream side of the middle bridge support of the Kancamagus bridge at the put-in. Since the Pemi is a wide river and the gauge is in a particularly wide spot, any change in height means more than it would on a lesser river. Be attentive to small changes in gauge readings here, especially if the river is rising. There is also a gauge on the Pemi at Woodstock that is listed on the U.S. Army Corps of Engineers Water Level Information page on the World Wide Web at http://water.usgs.gov/public/realtime.html under the New Hampshire page. A rough correlation between the gauge at Woodstock and the one on the Kancamagus bridge is given in the following graph.

If you would like a run of similar difficulty to the Pemi (class IV) try the Swift.

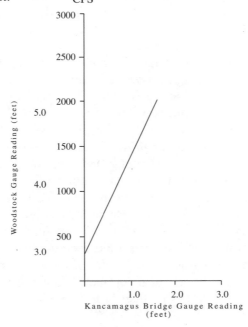

Pemigewasset River– East Branch (N.H.)

Loon Mountain to Route 93
Trip B

DISTANCE (MILES)	3.4		**TOO LOW**	
SHUTTLE (MILES)	3.4		**LOW**	1
AVG. DROP (FEET/MILE)	65		**MED.**	1.5
MAX. DROP (FEET/MILE)	100		**HIGH**	2
DIFFICULTY	IV		**TOO HIGH**	
SCENERY	Fair		**GAUGE LOCATION**	Kancamagus Bridge
DATE LAST CHECKED	1997		**WATER LEVEL INFO.**	
RUNOFF PATTERN	n/l/f			

The Lower Pemi, as this run is known, is similar in all respects to the previous trip. The rapids are just as interesting, maybe even more so: there's a dam either to run or to portage, and when the water is high this section will offer a ride you will not soon forget. This trip is paralleled by the Kancamagus Highway, though it is seldom in view. You do get a view of the Lincoln town dump, several new condo projects, and the backside of the new mall. So much for progress. The lower Pemi can be run as a continuation of the upper Pemi or as a separate trip. In either case, it is usually the better of the two runs if the water is low.

Starting at Loon Mountain bridge, the paddler is immediately faced with difficulty, namely the continuation of Loon Mountain Rapid. The area below the bridge was once the site of a dam, but what a recent flood didn't destroy, the bulldozers did. Now the river is relatively wide, housing an immense boulder field. There are two main channels here, and they run close to either bank. The middle tends to be dry except in high water. Both

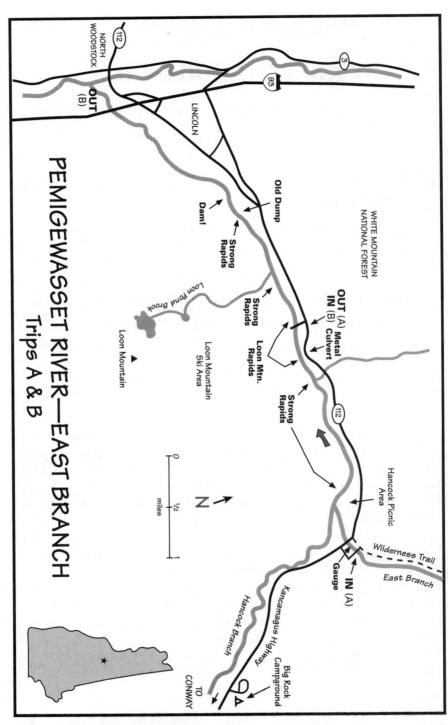

PEMIGEWASSET RIVER—EAST BRANCH

Trips A & B

channels are difficult, filled with holes, sharp drops, and lots of rocks. In low water the left side is a bit easier, but it is also longer. The right side is shorter, but it has more difficult drops and sharper rocks. In high water, trying to decide which side is harder is about as difficult as telling which of two maddened attack dogs has the more unpleasant breath. The rapids are prone to change, so give this whole section a good look. Loon Mountain Rapid usually paddles harder than it looks.

Shortly downstream from Loon Mountain, the whole river condenses to pass through a narrow slot. In low water, this spot is a class III–IV rapid where exposed rocks force the boater to maneuver in a heavy current. A small change in the gauge reading will mean a big difference in the character of this drop.

Next comes Decision Rapid. A gravel island in the middle of the river has been broken by the current in at least four places, and you have to choose which route is best, a harder decision in low water than in high. The river generally moves from left to right, and each route has its own set of peculiarities. The whole area is unstable and changeable, so pay your money and take your chances. Scout before running.

The Pemi is relatively calm for a while, then a left turn starts some more action in an extended drop. There are lots of rocks in low water and standing waves in high. After a pool come more good rapids—relatively long and definitely exciting. Again, much maneuvering is required, so boaters should count on being really busy to avoid trouble spots. At a gauge reading of 0.8, these rapids are rated a good class III or class IV. In high water consider this stretch a real bruiser.

A condominium complex near the site of the old Lincoln town dump is located on the right bank at the base of these rapids. Just after this, a steep, ledgy drop leads immediately to a dam. The current is continuous to the lip of the dam, so when you see the condos, start moving left. The dam has a rock ledge extending out from the left bank. The total drop is about 4 to 5 feet, with a steep, powerful hydraulic at the top formed by the remains of the timber crib. It has been run on the extreme left over the rock ledge, but look it over for yourself. At the base of the dam are a couple of powerful play holes that are a challenge to get out of in your boat.

From this spot to Route 93, you will come upon several islands and more rapids similar to what has already been met. The river will narrow and widen several times because of islands; when it constricts, be ready for a roller-coaster ride. After the Route 93 bridge and the railroad track below, it is a short distance to the takeout on the right bank near a small grocery store that is out of business (and cannot be seen from the river)

A typical drop on the lower West Branch of the Penobscot. Photo by Shirley Giffin

on the outskirts of Lincoln. To find the takeout from the road, proceed on the Kancamagus Highway past Route 93 until you see the store on the left. There is a small dirt road to the left of the store that leads to the river.

The Lower Pemi becomes a real bear in high water and should be given infinite respect. The difficulties are continuous and the entire run approaches, or jumps into, the class V range. Rescues are very difficult. The trip should be attempted only by strong groups.

There is a hand-painted gauge on the middle of the downstream bridge support of the Kancamagus bridge at the start of trip A, or you can consult the USGS gauge referred to in the trip A description.

Pemigewasset River–
Bristol Gorge (N.H.)

Ayers Island Dam to Coolidge Woods Road
Trip C

DISTANCE (MILES)	1		TOO LOW	
SHUTTLE (MILES)	1		LOW	500 cfs
AVG. DROP (FEET/MILE)	25		MED.	1,500 cfs
MAX. DROP (FEET/MILE)			HIGH	
DIFFICULTY	II–III		TOO HIGH	
SCENERY	Good		GAUGE LOCATION	Ayers Island Dam
DATE LAST CHECKED	1997		WATER LEVEL INFO.	603-634-FLOW
RUNOFF PATTERN	d/r/l			

Having gathered all the water flowing from the western White Mountains, the Pemigewasset is a very different river in Bristol from the technical boulder garden of the East Branch a mere 20 miles upstream. Bristol Gorge, in fact, drains such a large area that it runs throughout the summer and is an excellent site for beginning boaters to learn the tricks of the trade and for advanced boaters to keep their blades wet while waiting for the summer spate that will open up smaller runs to their explorations.

The run is located below the Ayers Island Dam just east of Bristol. From the dam to the takeout is just a mile, but the river has some interesting play spots that make the run worthwhile, especially for a desperate summer paddler.

To reach the put-in, take Ayers Island Road just east of a lumberyard in Bristol off Route 104. Bear right after the ball field on the right, then go past the dump and turn left at the bottom of a hill just after passing a gravel pit on the right. Follow this road past another dump down a steep dirt road to the river.

The outflow from the dam holds a surfing wave or two, with a large eddy in the center and the main flow on river right. Below this the river is

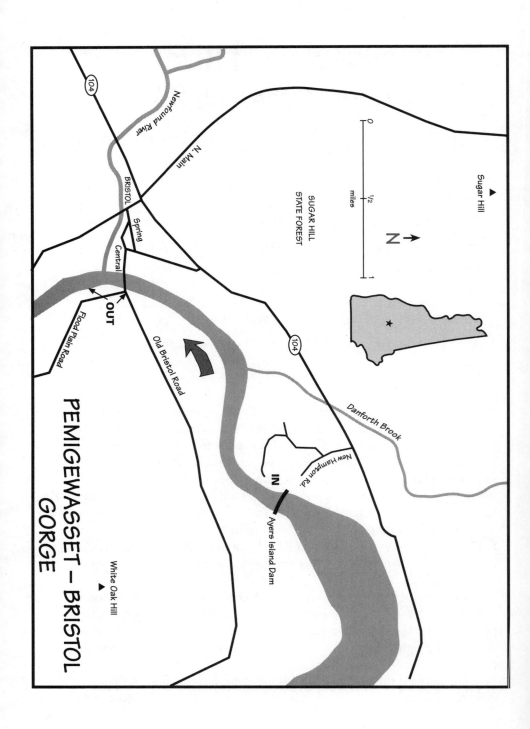

flat but fast moving for a couple of hundred yards as it approaches a right bend with a large eddy on the outside. Just after this bend, several ledges extend from river left, creating large waves and holes depending on the level. Downstream of this a large rock divides the river, with the main current on the left. This sluice has large eddies on both sides and interesting playing/surfing/endering possibilities at most levels. The outrun from this rapid is fairly clean, so this is also a good place to work on perfecting a whitewater roll.

Continuing downstream, the takeout soon becomes visible as a wide, featureless class II rapid with a few small surfing waves leads under the bridge. You can take out on river left just after the bridge or continue one rapid farther downstream. After the Newfound enters rather spectacularly on river right, another class II with some small ledges on the left runs out into fastwater. Take out at the beach on river left at the base of this rapid and walk through the woods to Coolidge Woods Road, which leads upstream to the bridge in a few hundred yards.

Water-level information for this section can be obtained by calling Public Service of New Hampshire's River Flow Information Line at 603-634-3569.

West Branch of the Penobscot River–Roll Dams (Maine)

Seboomook Dam to Roll Dam Campgrounds

Trip A

DISTANCE (MILES)	2.5		**TOO LOW**	
SHUTTLE (MILES)	2.5		**LOW**	400 cfs
AVG. DROP (FEET/MILE)	15		**MED.**	1,000 cfs
MAX. DROP (FEET/MILE)	70		**HIGH**	1,500 cfs
DIFFICULTY	III		**TOO HIGH**	
SCENERY	Excellent		**GAUGE LOCATION**	Seboomook Dam
DATE LAST CHECKED	1997		**WATER LEVEL INFO.**	207-723-2328
RUNOFF PATTERN	d/r/l			

The Roll Dams section of the Penobscot is considerably easier than its downstream cousin, Ripogenus Gorge, but it still provides interesting whitewater and a beautiful setting for intermediate paddlers in search of a challenge. The run is short—only 2.5 miles—so it can be repeated several times in a day. The ledgy character of the Roll Dams is unusual for a New England river, and creates mazes of channels where the river runs through various breaks in the ledges. This section also has more holes per square foot than any other run in New England, and some of them have strong recirculations formed by the regular nature of the ledges.

Put in below Seboomook Dam on Poulin Road about 35.0 miles west of Ripogenus Dam. There is a small parking area on the river-right side of the dam, and a short fisherman's path leads to the river. After the fastwater below the dam, a half-mile of flat paddling brings you to a small, rocky island that divides the river with most of the flow going left. A right turn

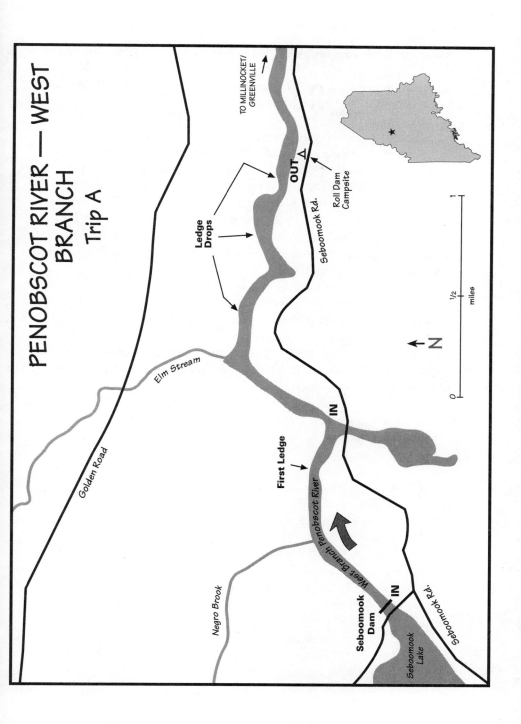

PENOBSCOT RIVER — WEST BRANCH

Trip A

TO MILLINOCKET/ GREENVILLE

OUT

Roll Dam Campsite

Seboomook Rd.

Ledge Drops

Elm Stream

N

miles

1   ½   0

IN

First Ledge

Golden Road

Penobscot River

West Branch

Negro Brook

IN

Seboomook Dam

Seboomook Rd.

Seboomook Lake

Penobscot River, West Branch   171

follows immediately, and then the first rapid is upon you. This one is a double ledge drop with a beefy hydraulic in the center. At the first ledge, there is a small tongue on the right and a larger one left. The second ledge follows about 20 feet after the first and is best run on the right. This drop is fairly typical of the rest of the run, though the holes are some of the more grabby ones to be encountered.

Another half-mile of flatwater leads to the next rapid, which begins a mile of continuous ledge drops. There are far too many to describe in detail, and the joy of running a river like this is in discovering different lines down the rapids with each run, so suffice it to say that the individual drops vary between 2 and 4 feet, and the holes vary from benign to keeper. Most of it can be boat-scouted by a competent intermediate, although a few of the steeper drops are blind unless you're willing to eddy out just above them, so scouting from shore may be prudent.

Seboomook can be run as low as 400 cfs (scratchy) and gets pushy at around 1,500. A medium level is 1,000 cfs. Information on levels can be obtained by calling Great Northern Paper's recorded message at 207-723-2328.

Take out at a small camping area called, appropriately, Roll Dams, on the right after the last ledge. This is also a good place to stage a weekend of West Branch exploration.

West Branch of the Penobscot–Ripogenus Gorge and Lower West Branch (Maine)

McKay Station to Pockwockamus Falls
Trip B

DISTANCE (MILES)	11		TOO LOW	
SHUTTLE (MILES)	11		LOW	1,800 cfs
AVG. DROP (FEET/MILE)	22		MED.	2,400 cfs
MAX. DROP (FEET/MILE)	80		HIGH	3,000 cfs
DIFFICULTY	IV–V		TOO HIGH	
SCENERY	Excellent		GAUGE LOCATION	McKay Station
DATE LAST CHECKED	1997		WATER LEVEL INFO.	207-723-2328
RUNOFF PATTERN	d/r/l			

The Penobscot is the most difficult of the trio of summertime big-water rivers in Maine, which also includes the Kennebec and Dead. Located about 40.0 miles from Greenville and 30.0 miles from Millinocket, the Penobscot is not near anything. Moose are plentiful in this area, as are hawks, salmon, and mosquitoes, which sometimes seem like the area's largest (and certainly most effective) predators. Views downriver often encompass the jagged profile of Mount Katahdin, and the rugged wilderness feel of the area attracts fishermen and hikers as well as boaters.

There are two sections to the lower West Branch. The Ripogenus Gorge stretch ends at the Cribworks and contains the hardest drops and

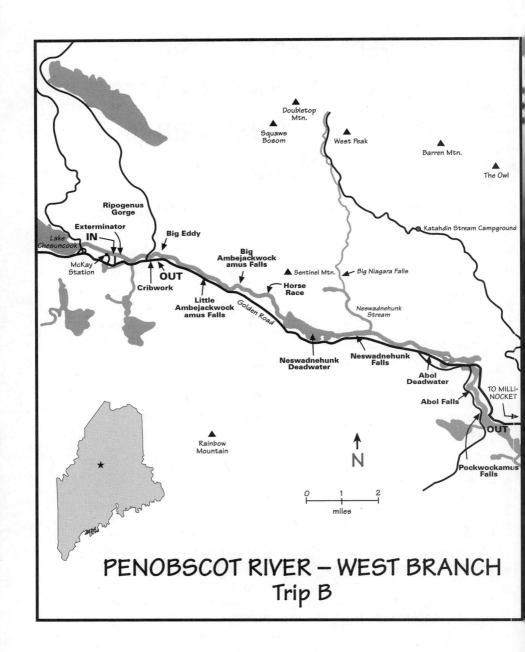

PENOBSCOT RIVER – WEST BRANCH
Trip B

the most continuous whitewater, with only a brief bit of flatwater. Below this the river is alternately frenzied and calm, with long pools interspersed among class IV and V rapids. Paddling both sections involves a long day with lots of pond crossings, so many boaters choose to run Ripogenus Gorge and then drive down to one or two rapids below as a finale. The gorge is the most difficult section, with at least three bona fide class V rapids, one of which, the Cribworks, is among the more difficult drops in New England.

Start a run of the gorge at McKay Station below Ripogenus Dam off the Golden Road, owned and maintained by Bowater/International Paper, which charges a fee for out-of-state cars ($4 per carload for a one-day permit at this writing) for use of the road. From the boaters' parking area you can easily walk to a vantage point that allows you to scout most of the gorge. Step gingerly, and note the features below, especially the abundant holes and diagonal waves. The most upstream hole is the Exterminator—now nearly river-wide since some rocks moved in the early 1990s. This one, while not a keeper, is large enough to cartwheel a closed boat, thrash an open boat, and flip a raft as if it were a pancake on a griddle. Swimming from here is not recommended, since very little separates the Exterminator from Staircase, where several pourovers lead to a turbulent runout, and the only eddy you'd have a hope of swimming into is the one at the bottom of the rapid. Both the Exterminator and Staircase, if you consider them to be separate rapids, are class V.

A short distance below Staircase, the river splits around a large rock island. Most of the water goes left, but the most interesting drop is in the right channel. Called the Heater, this drop is not long, but consists of a double ledge where the move is left, then right to follow the main flow.

Following a quarter-mile of easy water, the river, now much wider (200–300 feet on average), becomes ledgy with frequent holes and waves, many of which are excellent for surfing. At the beginning of this section on river right, a large hole with a somewhat flat recycle, known as Troublemaker, provides a challenge for adept surfers but can trash those not comfortable in powerful holes. This ledgy section (class III–IV) continues for the better part of a mile until a sharp right turn appears and the river narrows and goes under a small bridge. This marks the entrance to the Cribworks—time to get out and scout!

The Cribworks is long, big, and technical—everything a class V rapid should be. If you're not sure of yourself in difficult water, this is not the rapid for you, but if you want to challenge one of the most difficult rapids in the area, check out the Cribworks.

As its name implies, this rapid was the site of a timber-crib dam that washed out in the late 1970s. Little remains of the timbers in the main rapid, but the rings in the rocks and the unnatural-looking boulder piles tell the story to the observant boater. The rapid consists of three sections: the entrance, which is big, wide, and holds a couple of surprise holes for the unsuspecting; the Turkey Chute, where most of the flow funnels into a narrow passage and drops about 6 feet, with turbulent eddies on both sides at the bottom; and the bottom section, with two flat holes leading to the Final Chute on river right, the Boulder Pile in the middle, and a sneak chute on river left. All this happens in a little under a quarter-mile.

The usual line is down the center in the entrance rapid, avoiding Telos Hole to the left, then through the Turkey Chute (catch the river-left eddy if you dare) and right toward the island. Avoid the hole at the top of the island to the left (or surf till they turn the river off), avoid the next hole to the right, and drop into the Final Chute. All this takes anywhere from thirty seconds to a minute if it works as planned—much longer if you hang out in any holes along the way.

From the Cribworks to Big Ambejackwockamus (Big A) is just over a mile of flatwater. Many boaters take out at Pray's Big Eddy Campground just below the Cribworks. Either way, be respectful of fishermen who come to the Penobscot for some of the best landlocked-salmon fishing around.

You first pass Little A, an easy class II–III with a few play spots. Half a mile farther is Big A (class IV)—a long rapid (1.0 mile plus) with lots of standing waves, holes, and ledges scattered throughout and plentiful eddies at normal flows. The whole rapid does a big S-turn as the river bends first left, then right. Just below Big A, a mile of class I–II water known as the Horserace leads to Neswadnehunk Deadwater.

After a little more than a mile of flatwater Neswadnehunk Falls appears, a one-shot 10-foot drop with multiple lines and great playing opportunities. Neswadnehunk is formed by a river-wide ledge that dams up the river and lets most of the water through a deep channel on river left. Here the river falls steeply off the ledge and into a raft-flipping, cartwheeling hole with an easy outflow. You also can run several more shallow lines to the right of the main tongue wherever the pool below the ledge is deep enough and the hole is not too munchy (this varies considerably with water level). That's the beauty of this rapid—on a hot summer day, you can drive or paddle here and run it again and again, each time trying a different line or going for a different number of enders in the hole.

A couple more miles of flatwater lead to Abol Falls. Not a real waterfall, this rapid is a challenging class IV with a few large pourovers, ample eddies for boat-scouting or playing, and a few interesting surf spots. A couple of hundred yards from top to bottom, Abol is followed shortly by Pockwockamus, a fitting finale to a classic river.

Take out about 100 yards below Pockwockamus on river left where a sand beach appears on the shore. To access this takeout from the Golden Road, backtrack toward Millinocket from either the Cribworks or the put-in. The first bridge you cross will be just above Abol. Take your next right onto a gravel road and continue down it for about 100 yards until you see the trail to the river on the right.

The Penobscot is released daily to provide power to the paper mills in Millinocket. Normal levels vary from 1,800 cfs to 3,600 cfs. Above about 3,000 cfs the river gets very powerful. At levels over 3,600 (which generally occur when water is being spilled from the floodgates at the dam) every rapid is class V with several large, violent holes and few, if any, rest spots in the upper section. Paddlers should seriously consider staying out of the gorge and the Cribworks at these levels. You can obtain expected release levels by calling Great Northern Paper Company at 207-723-2328.

Pond Brook (N.H.)
Baker Pond to Wentworth

DISTANCE (MILES)	3		TOO LOW	
SHUTTLE (MILES)	3		LOW	
AVG. DROP (FEET/MILE)	117		MED.	
MAX. DROP (FEET/MILE)	200		HIGH	
DIFFICULTY	IV–V		TOO HIGH	
SCENERY	Good		GAUGE LOCATION	None
DATE LAST CHECKED	1997		WATER LEVEL INFO.	207-723-2328
RUNOFF PATTERN	n/f			

Pond Brook is a small but very steep creek that is born in the Baker Ponds just west of Wentworth, New Hampshire. Narrow, fast flowing, and ledgy, Pond Brook holds creek-boating of a nature rarely found in New England. In the short 3.0-mile run are several slides, many rapids that drop 15 feet or more in a span of a couple of hundred feet, and a clean 8-foot plunge. Combined with beautiful scenery and relatively predictable water levels during the spring runoff, the Pond is a great choice for advanced creek-boaters looking for a challenge.

Strainers are frequent throughout the run, and the narrowness makes it easy for even a small tree to block the entire channel. Old millworks and such other signs of early hydropower facilities as stone retaining walls and millraces follow the river where it becomes steepest and leaves the road.

Put in on Route 25A where Pond Brook leaves Lower Baker Pond just downstream of a summer camp. Here it is just slightly larger than a drainage ditch.

The rapids start immediately with a couple of steep class III drops over 1- to 2-foot ledges. These last for a quarter-mile until the river becomes fast moving as it winds through a wide, marshy area. As it enters

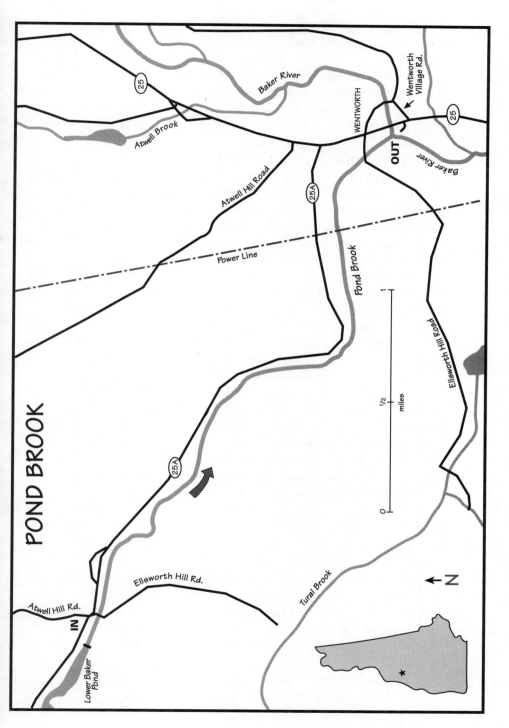

POND BROOK

this section, a very low footbridge blocks the channel, creating a mandatory portage.

After this swampy area, the river leaves the road again and begins dropping more steeply, with class III and IV drops that become larger, more frequent, and more technical. When the road again approaches, the rapids temporarily ease for a short distance until the river bends away from the road once more and starts dropping in earnest.

The fun starts as you leave the road for the last time. For the next mile and a half the rapids are continuous, difficult, and unremittingly steep. From here on the run is class V—a swim or pin could be very serious, since at times the distance between drops is less than a boat length. As the rapids increase in difficulty, you approach a drop with a channel on river left blocked by a flatiron standing on end a few feet below the entrance to the chute. The water hits this rock and splits abruptly, creating tempting channels on each side. At this writing the left channel was blocked with a tree, and the right channel appeared very difficult to make, with the consequence of missing it being a broach on the flatiron rock and almost certainly a very dangerous pin. Boofing the ledge to the right of the drop provides a reasonable way out, and the rest of the rapid goes easily down the right.

Immediately downstream of this doozy is the biggest drop on the river—a serious class V slide that drops a total of about 30 feet in 100 feet. The first two bumps are no problem, but the third bump is a 20-foot slide into a rocky point on river left that creates a large hole/pillow. The chance of the point being undercut makes this rapid a very serious class V at even low water levels. Continuing below this, more difficult rapids lead to a power-line cut where a two-stage slide with a tricky move at the bottom is followed by a narrow section where the river is confined between two ancient stone walls—probably an old millrace. As if to end with a grand finale, the next three drops are some of the best on the run, and the final drop is probably the most satisfying. First, a steep slide leads to a pinball-like ride as the river sloshes from side to side; then, as the river turns sharply right, a narrow chute followed by a 6-foot slide deposits you in the pool before the grand finale. In this last rapid, 3- to 4-foot drops lead to the brink of an 8-plus-foot plunge into a short eddy that flows over a 3-foot drop into the final pool. Boofing the 8-foot drop, your boat smacks into the eddy below before a quick couple of strokes set you safely at the bottom.

Since the land around the bridge at the bottom of the run all appears to be privately owned, the best takeout is to continue a quarter-mile downstream to the Baker River and take out on the far shore of the Baker just downstream from a small baseball diamond off Route 25 east of the center of Wentworth. Pond Brook meets the Baker about 100 yards downstream of the public access, but it's a simple matter to either walk up along the far bank or paddle and pole the short distance upstream.

Pond Brook does not have a gauge, but any party running it should scout it extensively before putting in. Boaters with the skill and experience to paddle this kind of water should be able to judge whether a given water level is appropriate for their group on a given day.

Rapid River (Maine)

Middle Dam to Cedar Stump

DISTANCE (MILES)	4.5		TOO LOW	
SHUTTLE (MILES)	4.5		LOW	
AVG. DROP (FEET/MILE)	40		MED.	1,400 cfs
MAX. DROP (FEET/MILE)	80		HIGH	
DIFFICULTY	IV		TOO HIGH	
SCENERY	Excellent		GAUGE LOCATION	Middle Dam
DATE LAST CHECKED	1997		WATER LEVEL INFO.	800-557-3569
RUNOFF PATTERN	d/r/l			

It certainly can be—rapid, that is. Heavy turbulent water, huge holes, and a scattering of rocks for good measure characterize this fine whitewater river. The Rapid really is special. It starts out from Lake Richardson, drops quickly to Pond in the River, and then plunges again to Lake Umbagog. It is this last section that holds most of the heavy water. For advanced boaters this is truly one of the best playgrounds in the Northeast. Normally you wouldn't expect a river that starts and finishes in a lake and passes another on the way to have such fine whitewater, but there it is. The blue sky, the green vegetation, and the whitewater make this one of the most aesthetically pleasing trips anywhere.

Because of its isolation in the Maine woods, the Rapid is moderately difficult to paddle. Paddlers used to arrive via a one-hour motorboat ride across Lake Umbagog or fly in on a floatplane, but since no one in the area offers these services anymore, most now opt for a class IV drive in from the south on unmarked logging roads. If you choose to drive in, bring a detailed Maine atlas and a vehicle with four-wheel drive. Check in with Northern Waters in Errol for any changes in logging road locations and leave plenty of extra time for flat tires.

RAPID RIVER

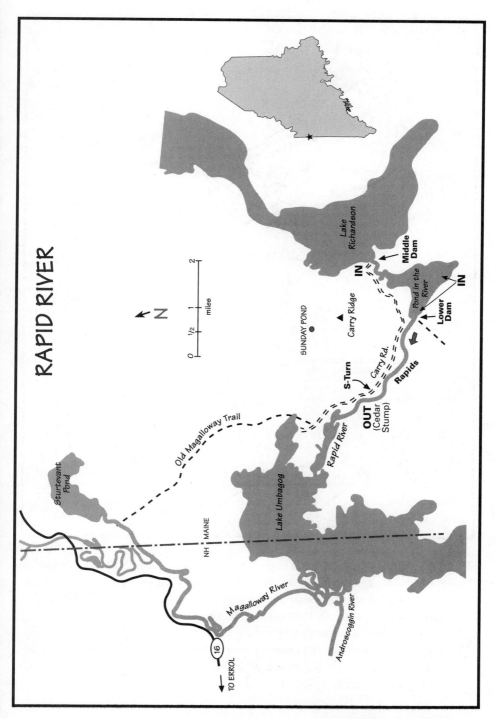

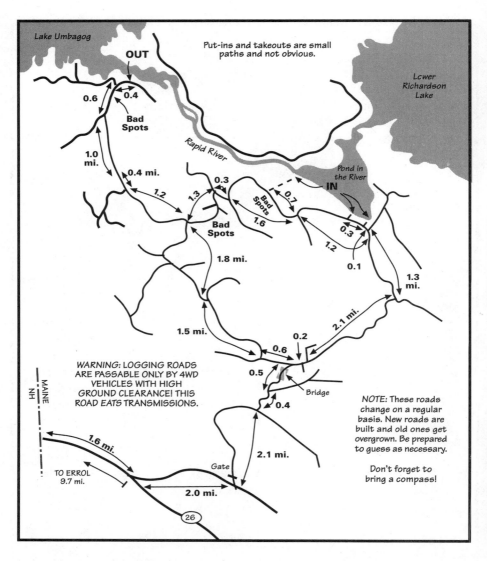

Map labels:

Lake Umbagog

OUT

0.6 0.4

Bad Spots

1.0 mi.

0.4 mi.

Rapid River

Put-ins and takeouts are small paths and not obvious.

Lower Richardson Lake

Pond in the River

IN

1.2 1.3 0.3 0.7 0.3

Bad Spots

1.6

1.2

Bad Spots

1.8 mi.

0.1

1.3 mi.

2.1 mi.

1.5 mi.

0.6 0.2

0.5

Bridge

0.4

WARNING: LOGGING ROADS ARE PASSABLE ONLY BY 4WD VEHICLES WITH HIGH GROUND CLEARANCE! THIS ROAD EATS TRANSMISSIONS.

MAINE
NH

1.6 mi.

TO ERROL 9.7 mi.

Gate

2.1 mi.

2.0 mi.

26

NOTE: These roads change on a regular basis. New roads are built and old ones get overgrown. Be prepared to guess as necessary.

Don't forget to bring a compass!

Middle Dam is owned and operated by the Union Water Power Company. Water release levels for the next twenty-four hours can be obtained from Central Maine Power's river-information line at 800-557-3569. The river runs periodically throughout the season most summers.

The dam is a wooden structure in various states of repair, just waiting for Hans Brinker. The water immediately below is very turbulent, and the eddy near shore is almost a whirlpool. The easiest put-in is below the dam on the right side, just around a slight right turn in the river. Anyone who attempts to run the dam, even as a stunt, has rocks in their head, or soon will have.

At 1,000 cfs, the drop to Pond in the River is mostly heavy water—class III—over a distance of about half a mile. The water is a series of moderately turbulent standing waves with a few rocks and a sweeping left turn. At Pond in the River the current stops, and a 1.5-mile paddle across flatwater ensues.

If you drive in from the south, the put-in is at the far end of Pond in the River. After dragging boats down a long path in the woods, a similar 1.5-mile paddle from a different corner of the pond is required.

The outlet to this lake used to be Lower Dam, but now it is just a hulking skeleton of old memories that can be run just about anywhere (although the passage can be shallow, even at 1,000 cfs). The middle channel has the largest drop, about 1.5 feet. On the right below, there's a nice small notch for resting and swimming. A turnoff from Carry Road on the north leads to Lower Dam, where trips may also be started if you don't want to paddle the lake.

The outflow from Lower Dam is smooth and shallow, leading shortly to easy class II rapids. For the next mile, till the first of the big drops, the paddler passes several islands and a few summer homes on the right shore. Rapids are mostly class II–III, and some can be shallow with a few interesting play spots. Even though the water is relatively easy, a detailed inspection of the water's motions will forewarn the boater of what lies ahead. Enshrouding all creatures within, the Maine woods march right up to the river's edge in one of the few really isolated whitewater spots in New England.

The first big drop (class IV), First Pitch, takes place where the river curves right at the end of this fairly straight section and it is easy to recognize. Slanting in a slight angle to the right, this rapid is about 100 yards long and made up of large, irregular standing waves and holes. Rocks are scattered about but generally remain invisible until the last second. The safest run is dead center, where the turbulence is greatest. As with the other rapids here, there are more rocks on the sides, creating abrupt drops, so a boater looking for an easy route will find trouble instead. At the end is a left turn and, in several hundred yards, the next big one.

The heaviest rapid on the trip, the second drop, Second Pitch, starts out with standing waves measuring 4 to 6 feet at 1,000 cfs. Again, they are in the middle but can be safely avoided by paddling in the left center, around them. Run 'em head on and they'll drive you vertical—both ways. The rest of the drop is quite similar to the first: mean. After 100 to 200 yards of quieter water, the next goody, Third Pitch, appears. Assuming your eyes have been open so far, this one doesn't display anything different from those above: turbulence, engulfing souse holes, and several lines of rocks crawling out from the right bank halfway down. Negotiating these three rapids is the acrobatic equivalent of a drunk running a bobsled track on roller skates.

Shortly below the third drop is Smooth Ledge. Whether you're swimming or paddling, it is a great timeout place for lunch, sun worshipping, or playing a hydraulic. Smooth Ledge is a large, flat rock advancing from the right ahead of the woods. It extends underwater to midstream, creating a nice hole-curler combination for the more energetic to play in, so bring along your sand pail and shovel. It is usually not big enough for enders in long boats, but shorter play boats may be able to do retentive moves. Dropping on a slant of about 2 feet with a 2-foot wave following, it can be avoided on the left side.

Immediately below Smooth Ledge, one sees more white stuff, with the waves flickering upward, licking an ethereal face. This is the beginning of the famous S-turn, which is the most difficult of the course. Slanting downward, the paddler first sees a several-hundred-yard section that's class III–IV, but a blind right turn hides all hell breaking loose. For approximately a quarter-mile, this whole rapid is as deceptive as a grand-motherly con artist. Previously, most standing waves were just that—standing waves. Here, there's a good possibility that they're pillows hiding rocks, and when you charge through… ##$*!! The water is very fast, with few eddies and much turbulence. It is somewhat shallower than previous rapids, mainly because the riverbed is wider. Near the end, before the final flick of the S, the river turns right. Stay in the center or to the right here and then left again, falling into a blaze of standing waves, foam, and spray at the end. There is a nice play wave at the bottom in the center.

Following is more smooth fastwater forming a large, flowing, pool-like expanse that empties to the right into an easy class IV rapid. Go down through the center, avoiding the large hole hidden around the right cor-ner. This is the first of perhaps six sets of rapids spaced between short stretches of calmer water. This series extends about three-quarters of a mile, and the rapids are rated class III–IV at 1,000 cfs, probably a little lower with less water. Although not so turbulent as the first three drops, the ever-present, boat-devouring rocks and pushy crosscurrents still make them difficult. The rapids end rather abruptly, and Cedar Stump campsite is then but a few minutes' paddle away.

There is no gauge on the Rapid. The flow is regulated entirely by Middle Dam.

Roaring Branch–Arlington (Vt.)

Kelly Stand Road to East Kansas

DISTANCE (MILES)	3.5		**TOO LOW**	n/a
SHUTTLE (MILES)	3.5		**LOW**	n/a
AVG. DROP (FEET/MILE)	230		**MED.**	n/a
MAX. DROP (FEET/MILE)			**HIGH**	n/a
DIFFICULTY	V		**TOO HIGH**	n/a
SCENERY	Good		**GAUGE LOCATION**	None
DATE LAST CHECKED	1995		**WATER LEVEL INFO.**	n/a
RUNOFF PATTERN	n/f			

Tucked away in a crease of the Green Mountains, this class V creek holds one of the most continuous runs in the region. The Roaring Branch is born in the Stratton Pond area in the Green Mountain National Forest. It is followed by a dirt road for its entire length, so access is easy—except when the dirt road is 3 feet deep with mud, which is most any time there's enough water to run the river.

The Roaring Branch is an experts-only run that averages about one eddy every half-mile—and most of those are big enough only for one boat. Pinning is a major hazard, and swimming in this 230-foot-per-mile run could be terminal.

On the bright side, if you're into class V creek runs that don't stop for miles and challenge your ability to dodge rocks, scout from the boat, and catch true microeddies, wait until the weatherman predicts several inches of rain in central Vermont and check it out. You can put in anywhere along Kelly Stand Road. Depending on the level, the upper stretches can be too scratchy to run or can extend the run by a mile or two.

Water level is critical here. The steep, boulder-strewn rapids can easily run so fast that there isn't an eddy to be found and rescue is out of the question. There is no gauge on the run, so you'll have to use your own judgment on level. Suffice it to say that if you're up to running this kind of river, your judgment is good enough to decide on the runnability of a given level.

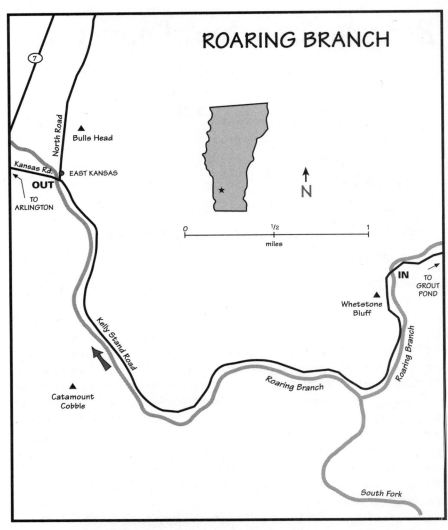

ROARING BRANCH

Because of the continuity of the rapids, it's difficult to distinguish one from another. It is impractical to scout the whole run from shore, so boat-scout carefully. There are two or three rapids that end with plunges onto rocks—likely portages. Also be on the lookout for strainers and rocks that have moved from season to season. The last rapid is probably the most interesting—a double slide that drops about 20 feet in all and ends with a meaty hole in the middle of the river. This one is definitely worth a look. A hundred yards or so below this last drop the river passes under a small bridge; this is the takeout. In all, the run is about 3.5 miles if you put in just after the point where Kelly Stand Road crosses the river for the first time.

Rock River (Vt.)

Williamsville to Route 30

DISTANCE (MILES)	3.5	TOO LOW	
SHUTTLE (MILES)	3.5	LOW	
AVG. DROP (FEET/MILE)	66	MED.	
MAX. DROP (FEET/MILE)		HIGH	
DIFFICULTY	III–IV	TOO HIGH	
SCENERY	Good	GAUGE LOCATION	None
DATE LAST CHECKED	1997	WATER LEVEL INFO.	
RUNOFF PATTERN	n		

The Rock enters the West River just upstream of Brattleboro, Vermont. Its scenery, rapids, and accessibility make it one of the more interesting of the many runnable West River tributaries (five at last count), and its runoff pattern causes it to run frequently during the spring snowmelt or after a summer freshet. While the rapids on the Wardsboro and Ball Mountain Brook are bouldery in character, the Rock is unusually ledgy. The three major rapids on this section all have significant ledge holes, and in two cases they are river-wide. The setting is classic Vermont: a covered bridge; a quaint town center; and a narrow, high stone arch bridge on the upper section give way to a steep wooded valley with few man-made intrusions on the lower half.

Start the run 1.2 miles past the center of Williamsville on Williamsville Road where the river is right next to the road and the shoulder is wide enough to pull off. The first mile is a fast-moving class II–III warm-up, as the river runs under a covered bridge and approaches the center of Williamsville. About a quarter-mile past the covered bridge, an island appears on river left. The left channel is dry in all but high water, but the island indicates you are nearing the first difficult rapid—a broken dam (class IV). To scout or portage this, you must stop on river left when you first see the island, since the only eddy past the island is the one on river right at the top of the rapid, and access from this eddy is very difficult at best.

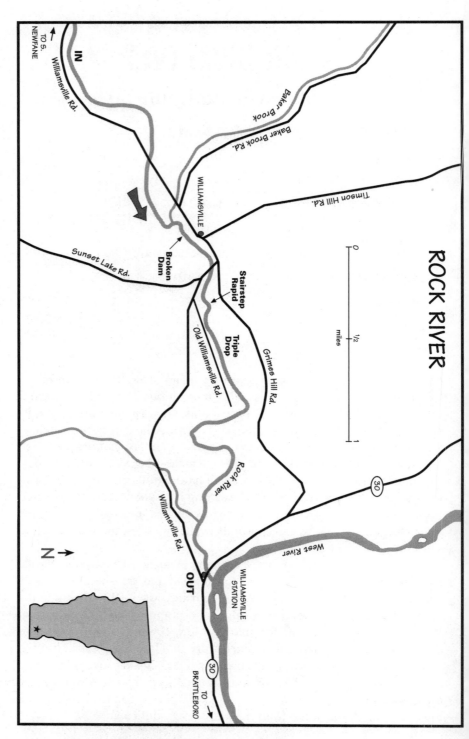

ROCK RIVER

IN

TO S.
NEWFANE

Williamsville Rd.

Baker Brook

Baker Brook Rd.

WILLIAMSVILLE

Timson Hill Rd.

Sunset Lake Rd.

Broken Dam

Stairstep Rapid

Triple Drop

Old Williamsville Rd.

Grimes Hill Rd.

Rock River

0   ½   1
miles

30

Williamsville Rd.

N →

OUT

West River

WILLIAMSVILLE STATION

30

TO BRATTLEBORO

★

190 New Hampshire, Vermont, and Maine

Little debris remains at this former dam site, but the debris still in the riverbed is hidden, making it more dangerous than if it were obvious. The approach to this rapid is a sharp left turn with a landslide on the outside bank. The eddy at the base of the landslide is useful for boat-scouting. The rapid is short, with a couple of grabby ledge holes where the river drops over 3- to 4-foot ledges. The cleanest line threads the needle to the left of the first obvious hole, then runs the next ledge in the center. The second ledge is the one with the most remaining timbers, making a swim here more dangerous than the whitewater would otherwise indicate.

A few playful ledges follow in the lull before the next rapid, then a class III–IV boulder drop leads to a miniature gorge under the stone bridge in town. Below here a few vacation homes appear on river right, and half a mile below the dam Stairstep Rapid begins.

This one is a double ledge drop, with about 50 feet of quick, turbulent water separating the two ledges. There are several places to run the first ledge, but the left has the most defined tongue. The hole is grabbier than it looks and could hold a boat and a person for a time before spitting them out to be worked by the second drop. The second hole takes up most of the center, leaving narrow tongues left and right.

Another quarter-mile of class III rapids follows, then Triple Drop, the most difficult of the run. This one is class IV at pretty much any level. The whole river makes an S-turn where the current moves first right, then left. At the outside of the first curve there is a small slot that appears runnable at certain levels, but at this writing it contained a large tree that could prove fatal, so making the turn is not optional. The second ledge is river-wide and a straightforward boof on the left, where it is lowest. The hole is grabby, so those choosing to run it elsewhere should be ready for a wild surf if all does not go as planned. Following this ledge, a large hole with a strong recirculation dominates the center right, while a smooth surfing wave/hole lies just below it. This is a great intermediate to advanced play spot, since both the wave and the hole are accessible from a large eddy on river right.

Triple Drop marks the end of the difficult rapids. The last mile and a half to the West is mostly class II and III, but the scenery is pretty, with steep wooded slopes ending abruptly at the water and an occasional side creek cascading into the main flow. Take out just after the Route 30 bridge on river right. The short walk to the parking area is fraught with poison ivy, so don't touch that shiny leaf.

There is no gauge on the Rock, but the level is easy to read from the Route 30 bridge. If it appears runnable there, it probably is runnable farther upriver as well.

Saco River (N.H.)

Crawford Notch to Bartlett

DISTANCE (MILES)	6.5		TOO LOW	0.5
SHUTTLE (MILES)	6.5		LOW	1
AVG. DROP (FEET/MILE)	40		MED.	
MAX. DROP (FEET/MILE)	60		HIGH	4
DIFFICULTY	III–IV		TOO HIGH	
SCENERY	Excellent		GAUGE LOCATION	Bartlett
DATE LAST CHECKED	1997		WATER LEVEL INFO.	
RUNOFF PATTERN	n			

The watershed valley of the upper Saco is one of the most impressive in all New England. Driving west on Route 302 near the river, the traveler is ringed on all sides by tall peaks, as if some mythological giant rested his crown on the earth, encircling the entire valley. Giants in their own right, these peaks possess such non-mythological names as Hancock, Jackson, Clay, Jefferson, and that titan from Massachusetts, Webster. On a clear spring or summer day, the majesty of this view is breathtaking, which accounts for visits by many landscape artists.

The Saco River itself is born out of Saco Lake, in the middle of Crawford Notch. It flows generally southeast to Conway, then on to the Atlantic. Paddlers, however, have scant opportunity to enjoy the scenery, because the rapids offer such good whitewater sport. For advanced boaters the Saco is at its best when the water is roaring, which usually happens when the other White Mountain rivers are too high for safe boating. At these levels, the run is unremittingly fast and rescues can be really tough. The rapids hold choppy standing waves and countless souse holes. These conditions prevail when the gauge approaches 3.0 and beyond. At lower levels rocks show themselves, and the run becomes more technical and more interesting to open-boaters. At a gauge reading of 1.0 the run is rated class II–III and offers numerous opportunities to pin your boat. Regardless of level, be aware that spring thaws can raise the river level dramatically within hours.

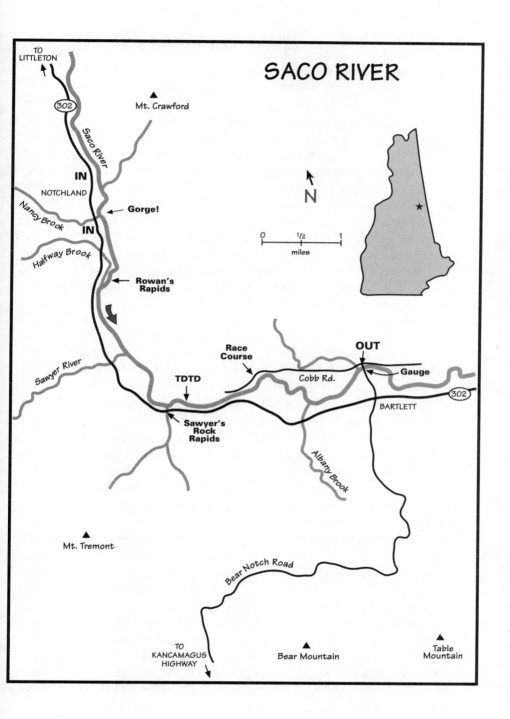

An enjoyable class II–III trip can change into a class IV challenge if you don't stay alert to what's happening.

To start a trip on the upper Saco, put in south of Notchland, just downriver of the Saco gorge where a small stream (Nancy Brook) passes under Route 302. You can see the last portion of the gorge by looking down this stream. The gorge itself is class IV at low to medium levels. It is very narrow, presenting the unappetizing possibility of broaching end to end between the walls. As the water level rises, so do your chances of getting hurt. Most of the passage is narrower than a boat's length, the walls are solid rock, and there are several sharp 2- to 3-foot drops scattered around. It is well worth a visit—on foot or in the boat, depending on conditions and your skill level.

To start above the gorge, put in at a roadside pull-off 0.25 mile upstream of Nancy Brook. At the put-in below the gorge, the "trail" from the highway to the river is down a steep bank to a railroad track and then down an even steeper bank to the river—a solid class IV put-in at any water level. At this point the Saco is about 75 feet wide and flowing fast from the drop through the gorge. The first rapid, which commences immediately, is a very long run through haystacks in a fairly straight section of river. In high water these waves are quite pushy and turbulent. This section terminates in a sharp right turn where the current tries to force the paddler over a small drop on the outside. Eddies rest upstream on the left and on either side downstream from the drop.

Directly below this turn is a brief, smooth-flowing area followed by another drop, heaviest in the middle and easiest on the left. Arriving shortly is another long rapid broken by a calmer spot squeezed in the middle. These two sections comprise Rowan's Rapids. The first stage is easier; it consists of haystacks and rock. The second stage is heavier but similar. You should scout it in high water if you are uncertain or have a weak group. A cluster of rocks in the middle, halfway down, causes sudden drops into holes and tricky crosscurrents. In high water these rocks are partially covered and deceptive. At the bottom is a left turn. You can see Route 302 here, high on the right shore. Lower down the hill there is an older, unused road. The entire section just described is continuous, rated class IV in high water. At a gauge of 1.0, it is class III with lots of rock—some people would even go so far as to call it annoying at this lower level.

From here to the trip's end, the Saco displays more difficult sections, but they are generally spaced with calmer stretches. The run will be rocky and technical if the level is low, full of standing waves if the water is high.

Below, in a slight left turn, there is a 50-yard chute with shifty haystacks and, farther on, two more sets of similar rapids. As the Saco approaches a high dirt bank on the left and turns right underneath, there is yet another chute. Depending on water level, this is class II-IV, and the most obstacle-free path is in the center. A railroad bridge is next as the river turns left. On the right, the Saco drops about 3 feet (at high water only) over a rock into a very ugly looking hole that can devour anyone who might pop in for dinner.

Following this is Sawyer's Rock Rapid. In a left turn, a large rock ledge extends from the right bank, creating an abrupt drop that tapers down gradually as it moves out to the center of the riverbed. This is Sawyer's Rock (named after Benjamin Sawyer, who in 1771, after pushing a horse through Crawford Notch for the first time, performed the ecological equivalent of throwing a beer bottle against the rock). It is run most easily on the left. Hydraulics and haystacks await below. One hydraulic in particular is rather tricky—in high water it can stop a boat or even pull it back in if you're not careful. A big eddy sits just below Sawyer's Rock. Sawyer's Rock Rapid is easy to see from Route 302, and this area is often full of curious onlookers.

Several hundred yards downstream from Sawyer's Rock is Tweedle Dum–Tweedle Dee. Named for two large boulders 30 to 40 yards apart in the left and left center, this rapid comes on the outside of a right turn with an island on the inside. The right side of the island is a trivial route. On the left the main channel speeds up and forms a series of powerful haystacks (up to 3 feet in high water) and holes. Tweedle Dee is upstream and not much of an obstacle, while Tweedle Dum is downstream and closer to the center, with its upstream pillow pouring into a boat-eating hole. Ten yards below Tweedle Dum is another sizable standing-wave-plus-hole combination to catch those who have relaxed a bit. Run TD–TD in the right center. It is rated class III when the gauge reads 1.0.

Just in front of the next railroad bridge is another drop, creating some huge—up to 4 feet in high water—waves in the right center and some interesting play holes. To avoid them, stay on the left. Below, the river takes a sharp right, where the last heavy water awaits—standing waves, class III or III+. This is sometimes the site for a slalom. From here to the takeout, the Saco meanders 1.5 miles or so, mostly class II, between low-lying gravel banks. Tucked into this class II stretch is a little class III surprise ledge drop with some long, gradual surfing holes and one with lots of rocks that requires some maneuvering. The channel on this last one is S-shaped. Take out near the Bartlett Bridge by a dirt parking lot on the left side.

The gauge is a hand-painted one, on the right downstream support of the Bartlett Bridge. It is difficult to read, since it is covered by riprap.

If you are looking for other nearby rivers with class IV difficulty, try the Ellis, Swift, or Pemi. If you want class II–III, try the Ammonoosuc.

Smith River (N.H.)

Route 104 to Old Route 104

DISTANCE (MILES)	2		TOO LOW	- 0.5
SHUTTLE (MILES)	2		LOW	0.5
AVG. DROP (FEET/MILE)	90		MED.	
MAX. DROP (FEET/MILE)	100		HIGH	1.5
DIFFICULTY	IV		TOO HIGH	
SCENERY	Good		GAUGE LOCATION	Cass Mill Bridge
DATE LAST CHECKED	1997		WATER LEVEL INFO.	
RUNOFF PATTERN	n/l			

From its origin on Mount Cardigan, the Smith flows primarily eastward and empties into the Pemigewasset. It is a short, tricky run that can be repeated easily several times in a day. In character, it is typically New England—small and rocky. The section that is usually run is continuous whitewater for the most part. It is class III–IV depending on the level. Because of this, rescues can be difficult. The majority of the rapids offer many paths, although several have just one or two practical routes. Turns and maneuvers must be done with authority, lest the rocks gobble up your boat. Eddies are not uncommon, but you must work to get in and stay there, usually crunching over several rocks in the process. A road parallels the river and, although it is no longer a major public thoroughfare, it can still be used for access. It is not plowed in the winter. Five miles downstream from this section, the Smith drops through scenic Profile Gorge, which ends in a picturesque waterfall. This portion is unrunnable, but you can see it by taking Route 3A out of Bristol, New Hampshire.

There are several spots from which a trip may be started. Route 104 parallels the river, but a new addition removes it from direct sight. To reach the river, proceed west from Bristol on Route 104 to Cass Mill Road,

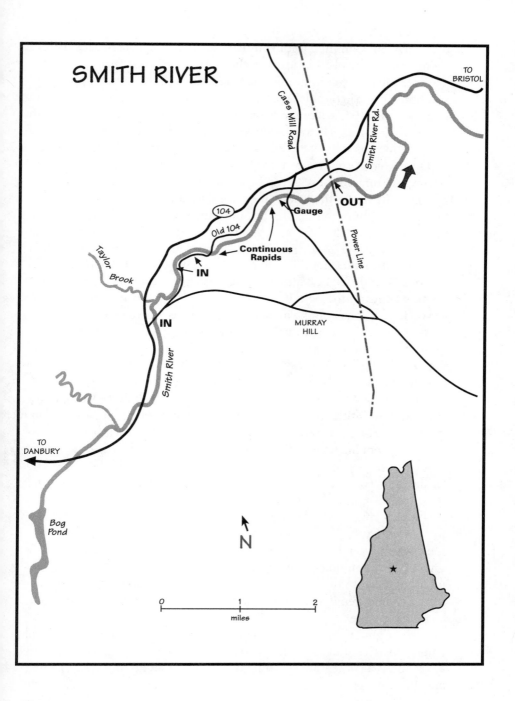

SMITH RIVER

TO BRISTOL

Cass Mill Road

Smith River Rd.

104

Old 104

Gauge

OUT

Power Line

Continuous Rapids

Taylor Brook

IN

IN

MURRAY HILL

Smith River

TO DANBURY

Bog Pond

N

0   1   2
miles

then turn left. Continue until you see the river. At the crossroads there, a right turn on the old 104 leads to the start, while a left turn goes to the takeout. You may put in near a bridge crossing the river or continue until you find a more agreeable location. Old Route 104 parallels the river and intersects new 104, where a trip may also begin. Above this spot, the Smith is mostly class I–II. The rapids directly upstream from the old 104 bridge are quite like the rest—a fast current that's pushier than it looks and many rocks to avoid. A small pool at the head of the rapids permits a convenient start where unused muscles can be warmed up in safety.

Directly under the bridge the pace slackens slightly. Below, there's a big rock in right center before the Smith turns hard left. The approach to this turn is filled with haystacks and hydraulics; a heavier rapid follows in the turn, with a 2-foot drop into a hole on the right and a smoother tongue in the left center. After 30 feet of straight, fast water, a line of rocks juts out from the right bank, pointing to a chute on the left. Then there's another chute on the right if you miss a rock in the center; it won't move, so you have to. Next on the menu is a fast staircase rapid where steps measure 1 to 1.5 feet and are carpeted with turbulence. The Smith continues in this manner, making it necessary for boaters to stay on their toes, thinking and acting fast. A detailed list of difficulties would be too much to remember.

In one right turn just above Cass Mill Road, you'll find a short, tricky spot. As the Smith rounds the corner, the riverbed narrows and gains momentum to pour over a rock blocking the center; then it falls into a menacing-looking hole. In the approach, upstream in left center, is another drop over a small rock. Enter this short class IV rapid in the center and let the pillow on the rock throw you left or right, usually left. Immediately below, an island divides the Smith into a larger right channel and a smaller left channel. If you don't look closely, the island is easy to mistake for the left bank. The left way around this island is definitely easier than the right, although three-quarters of the way to the left there is a rock directly in the middle. Going right of this rock is easier, but the current forces the boat to the outside and into another rock downstream, requiring a Z-maneuver. In medium or high water, this latter rock will not cause so much trouble.

The right channel around the island can be the toughest of the trip. Approach it cautiously. It has three abrupt drops several boat lengths apart and is a comparatively straight shot if you set up properly. The first and third drops are 2.5 to 3 feet; the second is somewhat smaller. The whole thing is 20 or so yards long. At low levels, it is a plastic-boats-only rapid. At the downstream side of the island is Cass Mill Road Bridge, which is now closed but scheduled to be rebuilt soon. It offers a nice view of the whole mess upstream.

Below the bridge the Smith turns left, and in a bit there's a friendly/unfriendly double hydraulic in the left center. A snaggletooth at dead center complicates an otherwise straight approach. At low water the first drop-hole combination is 2 to 3 feet and the second is 2 feet. If you choose left, paddle hard so the not-so-friendly aspects don't pull you back in for a friendly hug and kiss. The rest of the trip is typical class III. Take out under a set of overhead power cables.

A hand-painted gauge is located on the left upstream wing of Cass Mill Road Bridge. There is a USGS gauge in Merrimack County on the right bank in Hill, 1.5 miles upstream from the mouth and 1.8 miles southwest of Bristol. This gauge is very difficult to find, but it is reported on the USGS web site at http://water.usgs.gov/public/realtime.html. The web site also converts gauge readings to cfs. It is estimated that 4.0 on the USGS gauge is low, while 6.0 is high.

For another nearby river similar to the Smith, try the Mad.

Souhegan River (N.H.)

Greenville to Wilton

DISTANCE (MILES)	3.5		TOO LOW	0.5
SHUTTLE (MILES)	4		LOW	1
AVG. DROP (FEET/MILE)	50		MED.	2.5
MAX. DROP (FEET/MILE)	65		HIGH	
DIFFICULTY	II–III		TOO HIGH	
SCENERY	Good		GAUGE LOCATION	Old Powerhouse
DATE LAST CHECKED	1981		WATER LEVEL INFO.	
RUNOFF PATTERN	n			

The Souhegan River meanders in southern New Hampshire, moving north by east. There are two distinct parts to the section described here: the upper is a harder class III and the lower stretch is an easier class II. Your main difficulties are over once you've paddled 1.0 mile down from the put-in. Enough rocks sprinkle rapids to make things interesting but not especially technical, with two or three exceptions. Most rocks are small, and they are covered in medium or high water. At these levels, difficulty rarely exceeds tough class III. Because of its southern location, the Souhegan is usually one of the first New Hampshire rivers canoed in the spring. Early in the year, ice shelves on the banks frequently extend into the river, creating dangerous situations. Route 31 follows the river, although the lower part is more isolated and prettier than the upper.

Start your trip on the Souhegan at the sparse remains of an old powerhouse that can't be seen from the road about 1.0 mile north of Greenville on Route 31. The road moves diagonally toward the river. Looking upstream from the old powerhouse, you'll see a narrow riverbed with more rocks than below. At the put-in the Souhegan is 40 to 50 feet wide, with a steep-faced left bank. A fairly straight section occurs directly

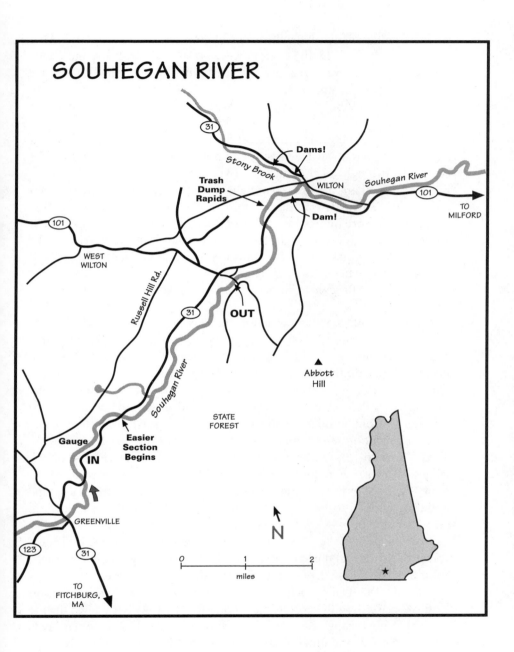

SOUHEGAN RIVER

31

Dams!

Stony Brook

Trash
Dump
Rapids

WILTON

Souhegan River

101

TO
MILFORD

101

Dam!

WEST
WILTON

Russell Hill Rd.

31

OUT

Abbott
Hill

Souhegan River

STATE
FOREST

Gauge

Easier
Section
Begins

IN

N

GREENVILLE

0   1   2
        miles

123

31

TO
FITCHBURG,
MA

below the old powerhouse, with a rock outcropping on the left bank. Difficulty here depends on the level; however, it should hardly ever go above class III. At lower levels, rock patterns are visible; at higher levels there are standing waves. The rapids are generally straightforward, with large rocks on the sidelines. About 300 yards below the put-in, the rocks thin out a bit.

In another 100 yards you'll meet the next set of rapids, followed by a shallow section in low water. At the end notice a large boulder in the right center. To the right of this rock the river is about as wide as a boat; the main channel here, naturally enough, is on the left or left center. Then move center, since there are several more rocks on the left side below. This is one of the more interesting rapids of the trip. The outrun is easy. You'll see Route 31 high on the right bank downstream. After more easy rock-picking and haystacks, you pass into a left turn amid larger rocks. A small island appears where the main channel on the right side is narrow and fast. It may be difficult to notice the island as you go whipping downstream.

Shortly comes a narrow left turn. Stay on the inside; this is the entrance to the most difficult rapids (class III+ in high water). After this turn, the current is on the left. It races madly 50 to 75 yards toward a group of rocks on the left, through which there is a twisting, boat-length-wide channel. At higher water levels, the right side also becomes feasible. Quickly after this group of rocks come two ledges spaced about 10 to 20 feet apart. A big boulder sits in the middle at the start of the first ledge. After a fast runout and then a pool, the Souhegan turns right in the distance. Turn to turn measures 200 to 300 yards. In the vicinity of the ledges, the current follows an S-curve. The ledges can be paddled on either the right or the left side, depending on water level. Both ledges slope and drop about 1 to 1.5 feet, with hydraulics and other nasties following.

From the pool below to the Route 31 bridge crossing, typical Souhegan rapids are in order. A sharp right turn leads to the bridge itself. Just under the bridge on the left upstream side is a playful hydraulic you might want to try to surf. There's another on the downstream side.

Below the bridge calmer water prevails and the easier section begins—class II, with more difficult rapids occasionally to spice up the afternoon. At a gauge reading of 1.0, this section is low for open boats paddled tandem and dull for hard-nosed closed-boaters. At this level, typical haystacks measure up to 1 foot.

Just before a left turn, and 5 feet upstream from a large boulder in left center, is a 6-inch drop over a rock wall spanning the river—class II. After the left turn there is a nice pool, and shortly thereafter another left turn with a trick ending. A rock at dead center and a rock ledge extending from the right narrow the path. The turn is sharp and fast.

After the Souhegan passes a large gravel pit set back on the left, the river accelerates, turning left very sharply. There are large rocks on the right bank and more below where the current pushes hard against the rocks. This is a tricky rapid if you are inexperienced. In a right turn a half-mile or so downstream, there's a chute that ends with a touch of turbulence. Farther down there's a large boulder on the left, then an island divides the river into narrow channels. This part of the river is away from the road—as deep a wilderness as you'll see on this trip. There are beaver dams, and canoeists should look out for dams that might block the river—this is reported to have happened on several occasions. To the right of one of the islands is a 1- to 2-foot drop at the start of the channel. Take out by a small bridge that crosses the river.

This trip can continue to the town of Wilton itself. If you decide to travel onward, you get to run Trash Dump Rapids, which are next to...guess what! You may also portage a dam just on the outskirts of Wilton. There is a hand-painted gauge on the concrete wall next to the old powerhouse at the put-in. For a similar trip on a nearby river, try the Sugar in N.H.

Sugar River (N.H.)

Newport to Route 103

DISTANCE (MILES)	2.5		TOO LOW	1.8
SHUTTLE (MILES)			LOW	2
AVG. DROP (FEET/MILE)	34		MED.	4
MAX. DROP (FEET/MILE)	40		HIGH	4.5
DIFFICULTY	II–III		TOO HIGH	5
SCENERY	Good		GAUGE LOCATION	West Claremont
DATE LAST CHECKED	1997		WATER LEVEL INFO.	
RUNOFF PATTERN	n		http://water.usgs.gov/public/realtime.html	

The Sugar River flows in southwestern New Hampshire, emptying into the Connecticut River at Claremont. The section reported here is class II–III, with continuous rapids for much of its length; it is generally removed from heavy civilization. Lots of rocks make an easy technical run, and there's one short stretch of tricky rapids. It is an excellent trip for advanced beginners without fear of overpowering rapids, holes, etc. It is also short and easy to repeat in one day. Fairly close are the Black (Vermont) and the Cold (New Hampshire), which are of similar difficulty.

After consulting several road maps and some local natives for directions, put in by a new covered bridge where the North Branch of the Sugar flows into the Sugar. From Newport, drive about 1.5 miles north of the town on Route 10 and turn left on Corbin Road by a small airfield. The put-in, at Corbin Bridge, is about two-thirds of a mile down. The river here for the first half-mile ranges from quickwater to easy class II. It's an excellent spot to warm up before you reach an alternate put-in and more-challenging water.

The second put-in is where Oak Street crosses over the Sugar in North Newport. Be aware that there have been problems with landowners here in

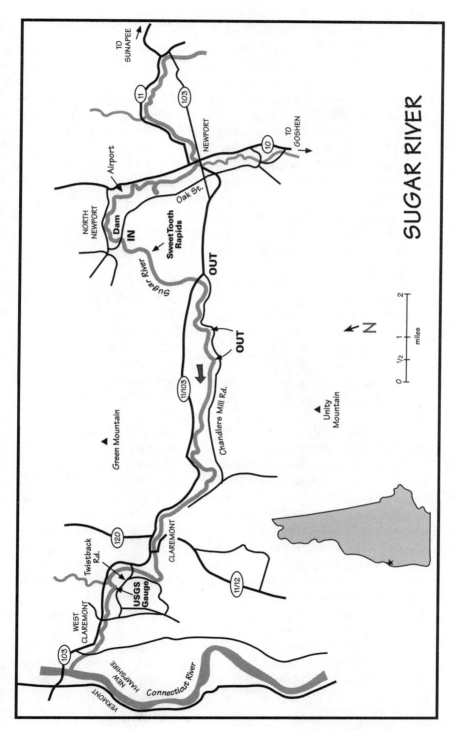

SUGAR RIVER

the past, so be sure to treat the area with courtesy and park only in public areas. The river here contains the remains of an old railroad bridge and an old dam. The railroad bed is now used as a mountain-bike path and follows the river for almost the entire run. If you look closely, you'll see that the middle section of the dam is missing; it is found about 1.0 mile downstream. A flood years ago apparently placed it in its present position.

At the start, the Sugar is 75 feet wide, going right past an old brick building that used to tap part of the river for its power. The river here is class I–II, with the small rocks covered in medium water. A railroad bridge is next. Below is an easy class II rapid, then a slightly more difficult one that lasts for some time and passes the middle part of the dam. Again a railroad bridge crosses the river, and a right turn follows; soon there's a pool and a short class III rapid. Railroad tracks now on the right bank continue to Route 103.

The Sugar widens and grows shallower. A right turn follows opposite a high left bank of dirt, which is badly eroded. Sweet Tooth Rapid, the toughest (class III) on this trip, occurs just before and during this turn. The river is congested with unpassable boulders on the left three-quarters of the river, forcing the bulk of the water down a narrow channel on the right. Pull out on river right slightly upstream to scout. Be aware that the drop comes up quickly, so you want to pull out around the corner before you see it. Look for the sharp turn in the river with the eroded high bank on the left.

The course, which runs 20 to 25 yards, is a complicated array of large and small rocks. Two large ones sit in the left center of the channel, with lots of smaller ones scattered around. Follow the main channel down past the first set of boulders, then cut either right or left around a set of submerged rocks at the bottom of the drop. Low levels (2.0 feet on the gauge) demand some fast maneuvering to avoid the rocks. At medium levels (3.0 feet on the gauge), expect the drop to be fast and pushy. The combination of pushy water with lots of rocks makes this a prime spot for an inexperienced party to wrap rocks with plastic. At high levels (4.0 feet plus) it's more of a straight shot with turbulence; the submerged rocks just form a hole at the bottom of the chute. At any level there is a short section of quickwater immediately below where rescue boats and throw ropes can wait. This also makes a great lunch spot from which to view the action.

In the next left turn there is a sporty class II–III rapid as the Sugar turns sharply against the right bank, which is cluttered with sharp stones that were used to build the railroad. Calmer water follows, then there's a long class II section past a set of old bridge supports on either shore. The last significant rapid follows shortly. It is a long class II–III rapid that gets harder as it progresses. Near the end the rocks get larger and more numerous, necessitating some maneuvering. This is probably the second most difficult section. An island then divides the river; both channels are OK but can be shallow. This marks the end of the interesting water. It's only a short paddle to the first takeout by the Route 103 bridge in Kelleyville. There's room for a large number of cars under and at the base of the bridge on river right.

From this point the trip can be extended for another 5.0 miles. Sugar River Drive follows the river on the left bank for almost the entire way. There are a number of takeout opportunities in the first few miles. You'll also pass two covered railroad bridges now used as part of the bike path. The river's pace slackens here. The rocks are smaller, and at lower levels the course mainly involves picking your way between them. At higher levels this section washes out into straightforward fastwater.

The takeout for the lower section is found at a fire-department training site located approximately 5.0 miles from the Route 103 bridge. Look for an area where the road has wandered away from the river and then comes close to it again. The countryside opens up and flattens out, farms appear, and the road becomes paved again. The most convenient spot for pulling out is a farmers' boat launch that appears shortly after the road rejoins the river. Boaters are allowed access, but do not park here or otherwise block the path. Park instead a hundred yards downstream at the fire-department training building.

The most difficult part of the Sugar is finding the gauge. The concrete house is in Sullivan County on the right bank, 0.2 mile downstream from Redwater Brook in West Claremont and 2.4 miles upstream from the mouth. It is in a section of the river that loops away from the road. The most useful outside calibrated staff is on the left bank, directly across the river on a rock ledge. To get there, cross the Sugar on a small bridge near a blinking yellow light about 3.0 miles from the mouth. Drive straight until you hit Twistback Road, then turn right. Proceed until the river comes very close by a red house (0.25 to 0.5 mile from the bridge). The gauge can be found by tramping through the woods for 25 yards down to the rock ledge. When last seen, the staff had no numbers indicating foot markings, although it did have staples. Take the top foot marking as 4 feet and count downward for readings. Higher levels are measured on a staff attached directly to the gauge house itself. For those who are inclined to skip the search for the gauge, levels are reported on the USGS Water Level Information page on the web at http://water.usgs.gov/public/realtime.html. Oh, the wonders of technology!

SWIFT RIVER (N.H.)

General

If veteran boaters were to pick five of the best whitewater rivers in New England, the Swift would surely be on everybody's list, so when the Swift is up, most good boaters somehow turn up here. Arising in the White Mountains and flowing eastward along the Kancamagus Highway, it offers one of the most challenging runs in the Northeast. Although only a medium-sized riverbed, even by New England standards, it boasts unusually big hydraulics and a pushy current. Its real specialty, however, is rocks and ledges. There are more abrupt drops on the Swift than on any other commonly paddled river in the area—two of them are waterfalls. If the water level is medium or higher, the pace is very fast, with little or no interruption between rapids. The pauses between major rapids on the lower two sections are generally good class III, while most drops are solid IV. In high water, two sets of rapids on the lower Swift are rated class V. At low or medium levels, the Swift is a long, hard day's paddle, requiring exact boat placement and careful planning. In high water the entire run becomes very difficult, physically demanding, and dangerous. If you scout, you'll spend your day walking instead of canoeing—every other drop appears to need eyeballing. Since most of the water comes from snow runoff, the Swift is cold as well as mean.

Swift River (N.H.)

Bear Notch Road to Rocky Gorge
Trip A

DISTANCE (MILES)	4		**TOO LOW**	2.4
SHUTTLE (MILES)	4		**LOW**	
AVG. DROP (FEET/MILE)	22		**MED.**	3.1
MAX. DROP (FEET/MILE)			**HIGH**	
DIFFICULTY	I–III		**TOO HIGH**	
SCENERY	Excellent		**GAUGE LOCATION**	Bear Notch Road
DATE LAST CHECKED	1997		**WATER LEVEL INFO.**	
RUNOFF PATTERN	n			

Known as the Upper Upper Swift, this run offers a pleasant trip for those who want stunning scenery and an easy warm-up period before the real excitement begins. The first half of this trip is principally class I, with many downed trees and meanders: The current here is continuous and the bottom is sandy. Halfway into the trip the rapids start, and they too become continuous, reaching class III difficulty in places at a gauge of 3.1 and above. The trip ends at Rocky Gorge Scenic Area, where the Swift plunges over an abrupt 10-foot falls. Obviously you should scout the take-out in detail to eliminate any possibility of tangling with this drop unexpectedly.

Start your trip where Bear Notch Road crosses the river. If you turn off the Kancamagus Highway, you should reach the river with no trouble. If you are trying to come over from Bartlett, however, Bear Notch Road may be blocked by snow early in the season. At the put-in, the river is 60 feet wide and flowing gently. There are several summer houses. The gauge is on the downstream side of the right bridge support. In the distance, the Swift executes an **S**-turn, and shortly you'll see another summer house high on the left bank. The water is class I and will remain so for quite some

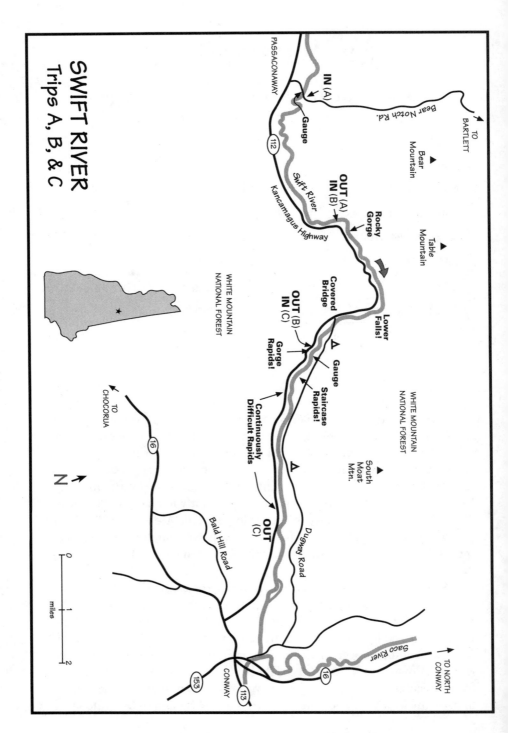

SWIFT RIVER
Trips A, B, & C

PASSACONAWAY

TO BARTLETT

Bear Notch Rd.

IN (A)

Gauge

112

Bear Mountain ▲

Swift River

Kancamagus Highway

OUT (A)
IN (B)

Rocky Gorge

Table Mountain ▲

Lower Falls!

Covered Bridge

OUT (B)
IN (C)

Gorge Rapids!

Gauge

Staircase Rapids!

Continuously Difficult Rapids

WHITE MOUNTAIN NATIONAL FOREST

WHITE MOUNTAIN NATIONAL FOREST

South Moat Mtn. ▲

OUT (C)

Dugway Road

TO CHOCORUA

16

Bald Hill Road

N →

0   1   2
miles

153

CONWAY

113

16

Saco River

TO NORTH CONWAY

210 *New Hampshire, Vermont, and Maine*

time. Be particularly watchful for downed trees, especially in the turns; there are always plenty of trees just waiting to drop in for a bath. The number of angled trees in this section bears silent witness to the power of previous high water.

Although by now it might seem that the whole trip won't get beyond class I, rapids do start after a right turn; first just standing waves and a noticeably faster current, then one little rocky rapid in a left turn, and another set farther below. The maneuvering is not difficult, and the rapids are spaced out at first. However, these spaces shrink progressively as you move downstream. Rapids up to this point have no outstanding difficulties, so they are not described in detail.

There is one rapid that does deserve special notice. It is a double river-wide ledge, with the two drops separated by 10 to 15 yards. These ledges are the hardest rapids you'll encounter on the trip, and you may want to stop and scout the best route. Several courses are possible, and water level plays an important role. The approach to these ledges is continuous class II at a gauge reading of 3.1. You can sight this spot from the Kancamagus Highway if you are looking carefully for it. Below Double Ledge Rapids, the water is uninterrupted class II–III, with the going generally rougher than it is above. The rapids continue right down to Upper Falls (Rocky Gorge), so it is important that you recognize the correct takeout spot. The bridge across the Swift at Rocky Gorge Scenic Area is below the falls.

The gauge for this section of the Swift is located on the right downstream side of the Bear Notch Road bridge.

Swift River (N.H.)

Rocky Gorge to Gorge
Trip B

DISTANCE (MILES)	3.5		TOO LOW	0.5
SHUTTLE (MILES)	3.5		LOW	1.3
AVG. DROP (FEET/MILE)	40		MED.	2
MAX. DROP (FEET/MILE)			HIGH	3
DIFFICULTY	III–IV		TOO HIGH	
SCENERY	Good		GAUGE LOCATION	Gorge
DATE LAST CHECKED	1997		WATER LEVEL INFO.	
RUNOFF PATTERN	n			

The Upper Swift is definitely easier than its downstream brother, but it too becomes difficult in high water. When the gorge gauge reads 1.5 to 2.0, most rapids are class III or III+, and several pass into the class IV column. This trip begins in one parklike area and ends in another, so you can be sure of a sizable audience if the weather is good and Dad wants to bring the family out for a trip. The Kancamagus Highway follows the whole run and is almost always visible, so an impromptu exit can be executed without much bushwhacking.

To start, put in below the Rocky Gorge Scenic Area just off the Kancamagus Highway. This spot is also called Upper Falls because the Swift plunges 10 feet in vertical falls into a narrow, box canyon–like area that lasts for 100 to 200 yards. This area has been "civilized" by the Forest Service and it swarms with tourists in the summer. The banks are steep, almost vertical, and carrying your boat down to the river can be quite eventful. If there's snow or ice, the banks make a fantastic sliding board with a big surprise at the end. The rapids start immediately below the put-in, but they are not difficult—in the class III range.

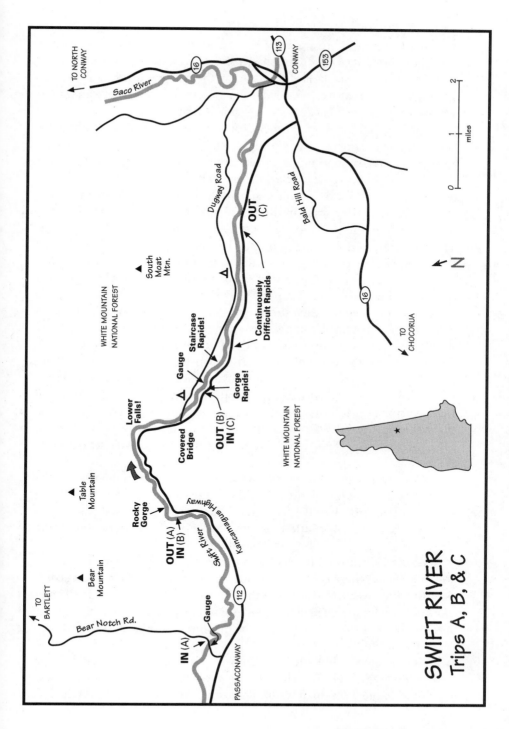

SWIFT RIVER
Trips A, B, & C

In a left turn, there are some good standing waves, then some large rocks in the middle as the road takes a short break from the river. Another left turn has haystacks and a hydraulic; the next right meander houses a 1-foot drop over a river-wide ledge where several large rocks wait on the left bank for the next ice age. The left side is best here.

The next left turn has another drop between rocks on the right bank and in the left center—take it straight on. Then more rapids just below, and another really good one between large boulders (class IV). The river then turns right into a heavy class IV rapids that has two parts, the second being a 2- to 3-foot drop into a gaping hole with a large stopper punctuating the end. A large rock on the right bank constricts the channel here. A center run is the worst, or the best, depending on how you look at it. The road then comes into view on the right bank. Next, some islands split the channel. They can be run on either side among rocks and whitecaps.

Several turns down, in a dogleg to the right, large rocks appear to choke the flow, a landmark for the start of the final set of major rapids. There are three ledges; each drops 1 to 3 feet. The suggested route is to start in the center for the first ledge and move left for the remaining two. Alternative routes are possible, but don't get overzealous, because Lower Falls is waiting for you only 50 yards downstream. Each drop in these rapids is followed by its fair share of hydraulics and haystacks. Without proceeding too far downstream, take out on the right side, where you'll find a picnic area full of spectators rubbernecking at the crazy people in the water, just waiting to see someone bounce down the falls. This last rapid may be inspected from the roadside turnoff when you set the shuttle.

To start a trip at Lower Falls is one hell of an introduction to the Swift. At this point it is about 1.75 miles to the Gorge, and most rapids are class II–III according to the water level. Along the way, you'll pass a covered bridge and have a little more time to enjoy the scenery. Rapids are mostly discrete, relieved by pools or calmer water.

Lower Falls drops about 10 feet in stages. It is quite wide compared to Upper Falls. There is a runnable line down the far left that is best scouted from the river-left shore; another, more-technical one in the center runs the first ledge where it is highest, then threads the needle through the intricate maze of holes and ledges below. Either run is class V and very level dependent.

Immediately below the falls, the water is fast from the outflow, and soon a long rapid appears. This rapid is a rowdy class III+ at medium levels and a vicious IV in high water. There are several large rocks on the left, halfway down, where you'll find the toughest water. The real problems, however, are the smaller rocks and turbulence they create. The current is fast and the waves are choppy, so you must maneuver frequently to avoid being pushed into a broaching situation. This rapid extends around the first right turn, tapering off a bit as it goes. You can scout most of this stretch from the road.

Most people will choose to take out before the Gorge, which is a mile below the covered bridge. The Gorge starts just after a rather sharp right turn, although you should not use this turn as a marker, because once you are past it you are into the middle of the Gorge, and you may not want to be. Upstream from the Gorge, the road is very close to the river.

The gauge appropriate for this section is painted on a rock, on the right bank at the bottom of the Gorge. A newer one is painted on the rock wall opposite it on river left at the bottom of the Gorge. The newer gauge is easily visible from the road and is easier to read, since the water fluctuates on it less than on the old gauge. It reads about half a foot lower than the old one. If the river right gauge rock is unreadable because water is flowing over it, the level is above 3.5 feet and you may want to consider doing another river.

Swift River (N.H.)

Gorge to Kancamagus Highway
Trip C

DISTANCE (MILES)	3	**TOO LOW**	0.5
SHUTTLE (MILES)	3	**LOW**	1.3
AVG. DROP (FEET/MILE)	80	**MED.**	2
MAX. DROP (FEET/MILE)	100	**HIGH**	3
DIFFICULTY	IV	**TOO HIGH**	
SCENERY	Good	**GAUGE LOCATION**	Gorge
DATE LAST CHECKED	1997	**WATER LEVEL INFO.**	
RUNOFF PATTERN	n		

If the upper section of the Swift doesn't get you, the lower one will. Considered one of the classic runs in New England, this part of the Swift offers challenge almost without pause. After two class IV–V sets of rapids for openers, the Swift then drops 200 feet or so in the next 2.5 miles, for the most part in discrete jumps. The Kancamagus Highway is close all along the run, so you may terminate the trip anywhere. This lower section is runnable even when the upper section isn't, although under such conditions there will be much boat scraping. A guardrail on the river side of the road occasionally makes parking difficult, but there aren't any parking meters yet.

The start of this trip is most impressive: the Gorge. This is not strictly a gorge, but rather a particularly difficult rapid that has been given this ominous name. The Gorge is about 100 yards long, and the total drop is 10 to 15 feet. Paddlers must move around large rocks in a fast, tricky current. The swiftness of the descent and some car-sized boulders obstruct the view ahead. In addition the Gorge also harbors some rather mean holes, as well placed as mischievous sand traps around a green. The approach to the Gorge is a sharp right turn that is narrow and fast. Many

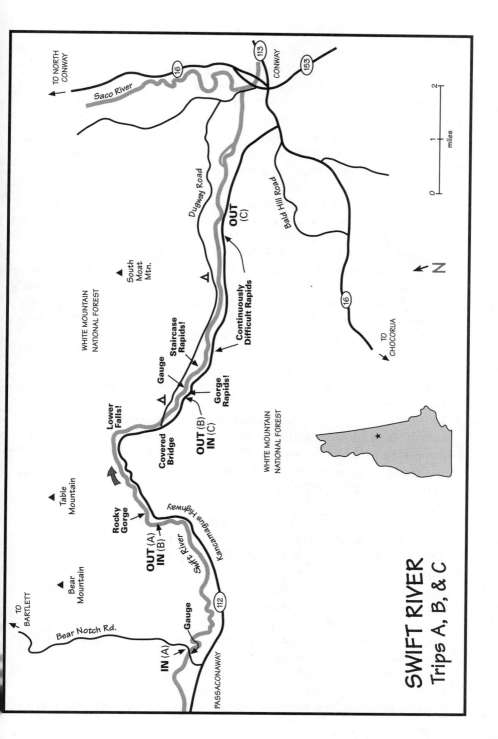

SWIFT RIVER
Trips A, B, & C

TO NORTH CONWAY

Saco River

16

113

CONWAY

153

Dugway Road

OUT (C)

Bald Hill Road

South Moat Mtn.

WHITE MOUNTAIN NATIONAL FOREST

Continuously Difficult Rapids!

Staircase Rapids!

Gauge

Gorge Rapids!

Lower Falls!

Covered Bridge

OUT (B)
IN (C)

N

16

TO CHOCORUA

WHITE MOUNTAIN NATIONAL FOREST

Table Mountain

Rocky Gorge

OUT (A)
IN (B)

Swift River

Kancamagus Highway

Bear Mountain

112

TO BARTLETT

Bear Notch Rd.

Gauge

IN (A)

PASSACONAWAY

0   1   2
miles

people underestimate this turn, and they end up swimming the whole Gorge before they've even seen it from their boats. Access to this right turn is via a left turn that runs away from the road. Water level means a lot when running the Gorge—different passages become more attractive at different levels. In low or medium levels, try a zigzag course on the left side, making good use of the eddies there for the first three-quarters of the way down, then moving to the right side to complete the very last drop. Just upstream from this turning point is a rock with potholes in its downstream side (Turnstile Rock), directly in the middle of the river. Turnstile also deflects the current to either side, creating an ugly upstream hole as it does so. Just upstream from Turnstile Rock, one of the many abrupt drops in the Gorge complicates the whole situation even more—definitely a place to avoid flipping over. Below Turnstile Rock at the end of the Gorge, a hole extends from the left and tapers into a smooth tongue on the extreme right side, where the only easy passage lies. At its deepest, this hole is about 3 feet lower than the water immediately about it, and it can be strong enough to hold a boat or a boater. Below the Gorge, the banks are almost vertical and the water is quick but smooth, handy for the recovery work that is sometimes needed. This area is known as the Shirley Siegel Pool. At low or medium water levels, the Gorge is rated a technical class IV; at high levels, it is a class V. Even those who are familiar with it should scout the Gorge every time.

Paddlers who wish to avoid this down payment to the river gods can start in the calmer water below the Gorge. The put-in here is tough because the banks are very steep. The subsequent third of a mile is class III–IV depending on water level. There is one sharp drop of 2 to 3 feet in this section, and the current is speedy and pushy. And then comes Staircase.

Lying in wait in a slight left turn, Staircase is short but very intense—the meanest and most sinister rapid on the trip, as well as an absolute stern-smasher. Staircase is basically three abrupt drops, about a boat length apart from one another, and it is 15 to 20 yards of concentrated fury. You can run it on the left or right. There are numerous holes in Staircase. One in particular will make a milkshake out of you if you do not run it correctly. If the best route isn't patently clear, stop and scout before running. In high water, Staircase is a clear-cut class V, and a class IV even in low; make your own decision on this one.

A shallow rock island just before and alongside of Staircase separates a narrow, rocky channel from the main stream. To avoid Staircase entirely, take a route to the extreme left of this island. Be alert for a very sharp right turn on the downstream side of the island. If you don't make the turn, you smash directly into a large boulder and end up dropping 2 to 3 feet into a hungry hole. Other than that, the going should be easy.

Below Staircase, the Swift goes into its drop, turn, and twist act. It contorts like a bucking bronco for the next couple of miles over one ledge after another. It is impractical to describe all the difficulties in detail—they would be impossible to remember. Rocks are numerous and passages intricate; the pace is nonstop and, although there are plenty of them, eddies are hard to capture. There are many abrupt drops of 2 to 3 feet in heavy chutes, and tight curves with powerful water pushing to the outside, where there is always a rock. The water is extremely turbulent. In medium or high levels, many hydraulics have the power to hold a boat. At high levels, class III rapids can be considered a rest stop. Among the rapids you will run along the way are Screaming Left Turn, Race Course, and Big Rock.

There are two takeouts on the lower Swift. The uppermost is right after Big Rock, by a flat rock ledge that juts out from the right bank to create an abrupt drop. The second is after shallow rapids near a billboard-like sign on the right bank (which most recently advertised Darby Field Restaurant). In both cases, the road is only a short walk away. The first takeout is a good place for lunch—the hole created by the rock is fun to play in unless the water is too big, in which case the hole plays you.

The Swift is not for everybody. It is an advanced run suitable for paddlers with sharp skills and blunt boats. It takes great familiarity with the river and precise boat control, not to mention some luck. It is best for inexperienced boaters to stay off the Swift.

There are two hand-painted gauges on the Swift. The old gauge is on a rock on river right at the bottom of the Gorge. It is on the upstream face of the rock and only reads as high as 4. The new gauge is on the river-left wall at the gorge across from the old one. This one is easier to read, fluctuates less, and is calibrated for higher levels. It reads about half a foot lower than the old one; that is, 2.0 on the old gauge is 1.5 on the new gauge. Levels given in this description are based on the old gauge. If the old gauge rock is underwater, go home, go to lunch, go to another river— but don't run the lower Swift unless you are prepared for a class V trip.

Waits River (Vt.)

Waits River to Route 25B

DISTANCE (MILES)	10	TOO LOW	0.4
SHUTTLE (MILES)	10	LOW	
AVG. DROP (FEET/MILE)	38	MED.	2
MAX. DROP (FEET/MILE)	50	HIGH	
DIFFICULTY	II–III	TOO HIGH	
SCENERY	Good	GAUGE LOCATION	Route 25B Bridge
DATE LAST CHECKED	1997	WATER LEVEL INFO.	
RUNOFF PATTERN	n		

The Waits is about two-thirds of the way up Vermont and is a tributary of the Connecticut. It is a good advanced-beginner run. Possessing a steady current, it has several large, sloping ledges; many sharp turns; an abundance of haystacks; and the smell of cow dung in the air. For most of its course, the Waits can be run straightforwardly, and it is a good place for boaters to learn their craft. In three separate places the upper river is punctuated by ledges that generally require skill to negotiate. The part directly below Waits River, Vermont, is decidedly unattractive, although the left bank of the lower part is as scenic as any. For intermediate boaters, the water must be high to generate excitement.

In Waits River, near a white church, turn left off Route 25 and proceed 100 to 200 yards to a small bridge crossing the river. The Waits is about 30 feet wide here, flowing smoothly with very few rocks and looking very much like the countryside stream it is. Moving downstream there are many sharp curves, which become trickier as the water level rises. Houses and farms populate the left bank, as does a collection of old junk cars. Waves and small rocks continue for about 1.5 miles to the first Route 25 bridge crossing, where the approach has a nice chute. Below, the pace increases to form continuous class II–III rapids—fast current, rocks, crosscurrents, and sharp turns. Next, look out for a large, dug-out gravel pit set back behind some trees on the right bank (and visible only when

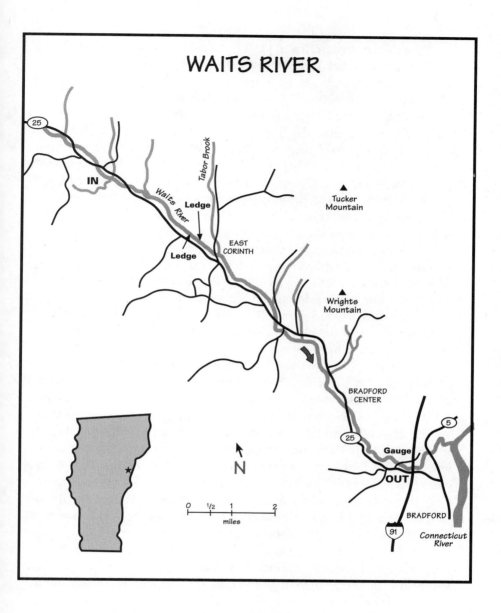

WAITS RIVER

the leaves are off the trees): the next left turn has a small ledge extending from the right. A surfing wave follows. The extreme left side avoids the 6- to 12-inch drop.

A short distance downstream, in another left turn, is a more extensive ledge. Extending across the entire channel, it can be run in the center. There is a rock directly in the center at the bottom of this drop, but it is usually water covered, so it will push boats aside. The total drop is 2 to 3 feet over a distance of 10 to 15 feet. Eddies await downstream on either side, and flatwater precedes the actual drop. The Waits then broadens out, and you'll see a gas station high on the right bank.

A series of small ledges follows—a 6-inch ledge that extends the width of the river, then the first of two large ledge systems. In a fairly straight section of river, the first system is river-wide and lasts for about 50 yards. It has a short, flat spot midway down. The whole thing resembles a large washboard. One-quarter of the way down this ledge, a small stream enters from the right side. Different water levels will make different routes more attractive, so look this one over before running. A suggested route starts on the left, angles right to just above where the small stream enters, and then goes down from there. After traversing the brief plateau, the last part drops more abruptly, 1 to 2 feet. A rooster tail sticks up in the right center, so pass to either side (the right side being better in low water). The whole ledge angles slightly left to right.

In the distance, the river drops from sight again over another large ledge. Smaller than the previous one but similar in character, this one is also river-wide and has been run on both the left and right side depending on water level. Look it over. Lower down are some smaller, easy ledges and the remains of an old bridge. The road reappears, and then comes the concrete bridge at East Corinth. This is the end of the most difficult section.

From East Corinth to the takeout at Route 25B, 6.0 miles or so, the Waits is class I–II. Directly below the bridge at East Corinth, several small streams add their water, deepening the river. If the upper section is too low, then this lower section is usually just low. Past the first bridge, the passage is quite easy. The valley is attractive, the left side particularly so. The steep-sided left bank occasionally pulls back its rouged mantle of conifers and broadleafs to expose a more picturesque rocky face that extends sometimes to the depth below.

In the approach to a small, dark-colored bridge there is a 1- to 2-foot drop over a rock ledge in the middle, with easier channels to the right and left. Below the bridge there is a long class II rapid with the road close to the left side. After this, the rapids become fewer and consist mainly of haystacks. Below a brown bridge are some islands that divide the river into many channels, all of which are passable except for tree hazards. The difficulty here is mainly class I. Take out by the Route 25B bridge, just upstream from Interstate 91. A hand-painted gauge is located on the right downstream side of the Route 25B bridge.

For a trip of similar difficulty that is close by, try the Winooski.

Wardsboro Brook (Vt.)

Wardsboro to West River

DISTANCE (MILES)	4.5		TOO LOW	
SHUTTLE (MILES)	4.5		LOW	
AVG. DROP (FEET/MILE)	90		MED.	
MAX. DROP (FEET/MILE)	160		HIGH	
DIFFICULTY	III–IV		TOO HIGH	
SCENERY	Good		GAUGE LOCATION	Route 100 Bridge
DATE LAST CHECKED	1997		WATER LEVEL INFO.	
RUNOFF PATTERN	n/f			

The Wardsboro is a small tributary of the West River. Its season is limited to only a couple of weeks, unless there are heavy rains. But when the water is up, the Wardsboro presents a demanding run. The current is continuous for the entire run, as are the rapids. It is definitely harder than its nearby cousin, the Winhall—the rocks are larger, the gradient steeper, and the rapids generally more complex. As with the Winhall, a road parallels the entire trip, so impromptu exits and entrances are possible.

The basic character of this stream changed dramatically after the flood of 1975 and again after the floods of the mid-'80s. Huge volumes of water passed down all the rivers in the area, altering not only their courses but their complexions as well. In the clean-up period that followed, bulldozers reportedly manhandled the riverbed, so that many parts now look like an uneventful sluiceway. The Wardsboro is far from dead, however, and it still holds a surprise or two. Since there are so many rapids on the Wardsboro, only the highlights are discussed in detail here.

Several starting points are possible. You can put in as high up as the West Wardsboro bridge, where Route 100 first crosses. This upper section holds interesting class III drops and a few IVs, although it takes high water

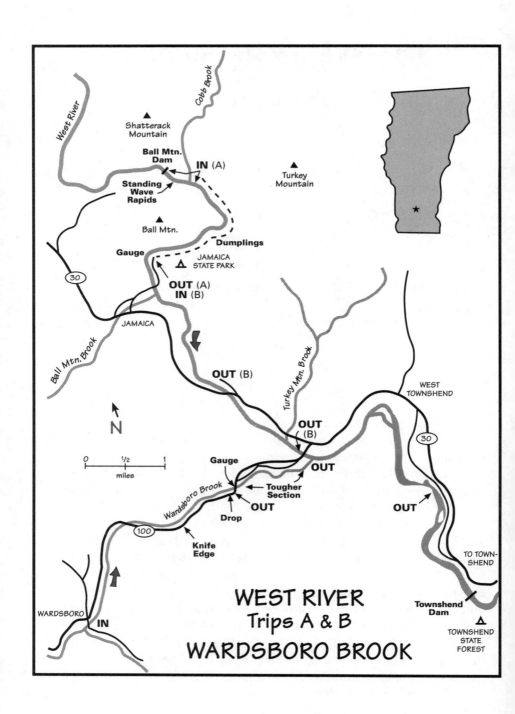

WEST RIVER
Trips A & B
WARDSBORO BROOK

to make it runnable. A more popular put-in is in the town of Wardsboro, where Route 100 turns sharply and meets a small side road with a bridge over the river. The drop just upstream of the bridge is a steep, ledgy stair step that falls about 5 feet in less than 30 feet. For more of a warm-up, put in just below the bridge. There is also a lower put-in by a bridge 1.2 miles downstream from Wardsboro Center. From the town to this bridge, the river is an uninteresting class II–III, although this section would be useful for a warm-up.

Shortly below the bridge, the river turns right and the difficulty begins. Stay on the inside of this turn at first, then move quickly to the center to align yourself for a series of drops among some boulders. Paddle hard, since the water is turbulent throughout. A section of numerous rocks follows, where maneuvering through tight channels is necessary. One narrow channel should be scouted; it holds a number of nasty rocks and holes that may be unavoidable depending on water level. This particular stretch occurs when the channel pinches as it bears left around what was once an island. This rapid also tends to change from year to year.

Knife Edge Rapid is about 200 yards long and consists of two parts. It is narrow, fast, and requires good boat control. The approach begins in a right turn, and the rapid then continues through the next left turn. The first part is a boulder patch with a landslide on the left bank. Depending on the level, there are runnable courses both on the extreme right and left. The right channel is probably better in lower water levels. Shift left as the river turns left and approaches the road. The lower part of Knife Edge is a sloping 3-foot drop, straightforward except for two rocks that run longitudinally with the current and stick up like knife edges in the right center. Pass between them or to their left. Between the upper and lower parts, the current is fast and the eddies are tricky because of complex crosscurrents. Knife Edge can be seen and scouted from the road.

Just upstream of the Route 100 bridge, near the end of the trip, is a long and possibly heavy rapid. This one lasts for several hundred yards, with an S-shaped course and numerous rocks and hydraulics. The fast runout leads into another 100-yard-long rapid directly below the Route 100 bridge. The run to the bridge goes around an island, which you probably won't recognize as such, especially in low water. In high water you won't care. This rapid is a strong IV in high water, less at lower levels. It probably should be scouted if the water is high. A big eddy forms on the left upstream side of the bridge. Since this rapid looks like a Japanese rock garden in low water, one questions whether it could generate any excitement. The drops seem like mouse steps. Put 3 feet of water over them, however, and the mouse roars.

A trip could end here at the Route 100 bridge, although a mile remains until the confluence with the West. However, that mile is a little harder than what has been paddled so far. Route 100 vanishes from view at this point, and a smaller dirt road, the access to a number of houses, roughly parallels the river. Banks are sometimes extremely steep and scouting may be difficult. Myriad riverbed rocks and several islands complicate things. The pace is fast, the maneuvering is demanding, and downed trees can cause real problems. If the water is up, this section should be reserved for the experienced. You can also run this section when the upper section is too low.

The river in this lower part is very broad in places. There will be a great deal of turbulence if the water is high. However, at medium levels the difficulty is a technical class III.

There is one spot, though, where everyone should exercise caution: where the Wardsboro flows around an island with the main channel on the left side. This channel is very narrow, and there are a series of ledges, drops, and rocks that must be dealt with for a successful passage. A large boulder sits on the left bank near the end, and it takes some effort to miss it. Following this boulder, the boater must immediately paddle around a tight S-turn, trying to avoid the right bank at the end. Even at low water, this rapid is rated class IV. At higher levels the right side of the island will open up as a possible route, but you should judge this for yourself. You can spot an overhead power line below—but only if you are looking at the sky. This rapid cannot be seen from the road.

The rest of the way to the West is relatively easy, but still fast and sassy. At the confluence, two bridges make a convenient takeout.

There is no gauge as of this writing. There was one on the river-right abutment of the lower of the two bridges at the confluence with the West; when a new bridge was built, however, the gauge was wiped out. The AMC Gauge Restoration program plans to put a new gauge at the Route 100 bridge just upstream from the confluence with the West.

Warner River (N.H.)

Melvin Mills to Warner

DISTANCE (MILES)	2.5		TOO LOW	
SHUTTLE (MILES)	2.5		LOW	
AVG. DROP (FEET/MILE)			MED.	
MAX. DROP (FEET/MILE)			HIGH	
DIFFICULTY	IV		TOO HIGH	
SCENERY	Fair		GAUGE LOCATION	Laing Bridge Lane '
DATE LAST CHECKED	1997		WATER LEVEL INFO.	
RUNOFF PATTERN	n			

The Warner is a small technical stream in the Sunapee region that runs in the spring during periods of snowmelt and occasionally during the fall after a heavy rain. It is a short but exciting run, beginning with easier sections and terminating in a series of pushy, technical class IV drops.

Put in on Melvin Mills Road by a small bridge that crosses the river about a quarter-mile south from where the north end of Melvin Mills Road intersects Route 103. The first part ranges from flatwater to easy class III, providing the paddler a good warm-up. The river curves away from the road here. After this section, the first interesting rapid begins slightly downstream from where old Route 103 intersects Route 103. Look for the river curving back to the left and approaching Route 103. This is a short and pushy class III rapid that ends as it comes up against the road. It is easily visible from Route 103, and onlookers frequently stop to watch boaters strut their stuff. The best path follows the right side of a narrow channel filled with rocks. Once through here, the river curves away from and then back to Route 103, where the first class IV section appears.

This section can be found slightly upstream of the intersection of Route 103 and Laing Bridge Lane. The drop is formed by a small dam with

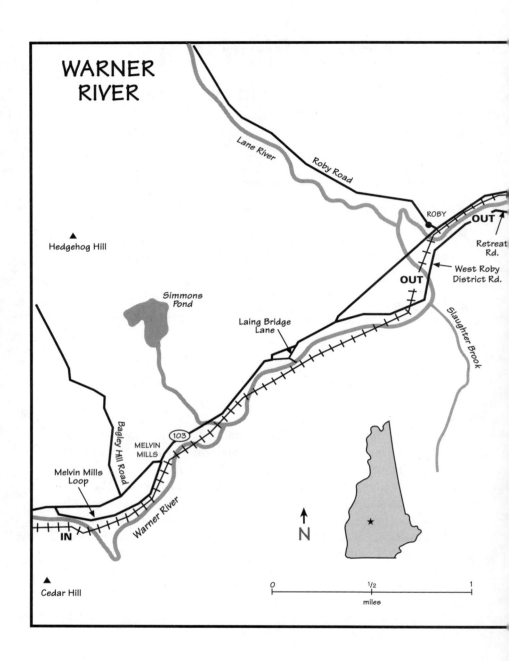

WARNER RIVER

Lane River

Roby Road

ROBY

OUT

Retreat Rd.

West Roby District Rd.

OUT

▲ Hedgehog Hill

Simmons Pond

Laing Bridge Lane

Slaughter Brook

Bagley Hill Road

103

MELVIN MILLS

Melvin Mills Loop

Warner River

IN

N

1/2

miles

0   1

▲ Cedar Hill

a runnable slot in it. At the base of the slot are the remains of old railroad-bridge abutments. It can be scouted easily as you drive to the put-in or by pulling off the river when you reach the pool formed by the dam. If you pull off on river left, be careful to avoid the diversion channel that leads to a small, nonfunctioning powerhouse.

After this, the river follows Route 103 and the old railroad bed for a short distance. Be on the lookout for a section where the riverbanks are built up with stone-and-rock walls from the remains of several old mills. This is the beginning of the most difficult section, with a series of three class IV drops. Pull out on river left, then climb up and walk along the old railroad bed to view the entire section. The drops are short and steep. The first one is a center run through a slot that forms a hole and curler on the bottom that tends to flip boats. Start slightly left and paddle to the right as you go over the drop. A small pool immediately below provides a good opportunity to rescue boaters who get flipped by the curler. Below here, the second and third drops appear in quick succession, with only a few microeddies between them. At the very bottom there is a large pool on river left close to where West Roby District Road intersects Route 103. This section easily can be scouted ahead of time by pulling off at this point and walking up along the old railroad bridge.

A takeout is found several hundred yards below here on West Roby District Road, where the river flattens out and provides excellent access only a few feet from the road.

Past this point, the river continues with more class III sections separated by small areas of flatwater. Another takeout is located downstream on river right where Retreat Road follows the river. From the intersection of Route 103 and East Roby District Road, drive down East Roby District Road about 0.5 mile and take out where the road branches up and away from the river.

A hand-painted gauge is located on the right bridge abutment slightly downstream of the small hydro dam at Laing Bridge Lane. At press time, this new gauge had not yet been calibrated for runnability.

West River (Vt.)

Ball Mountain Dam to Jamaica State Park
Trip A

DISTANCE (MILES)	2.5	**TOO LOW**	
SHUTTLE (MILES)	3.8	**LOW**	6.3/1,000 cfs
AVG. DROP (FEET/MILE)	40	**MED.**	7.0/1,600 cfs
MAX. DROP (FEET/MILE)	50	**HIGH**	7.7/2,500 cfs
DIFFICULTY	III	**TOO HIGH**	
SCENERY	Excellent	**GAUGE LOCATION**	Jamaica State Park
DATE LAST CHECKED	1997	**WATER LEVEL INFO.**	
RUNOFF PATTERN	d/r/l		

One of the principal waterways of southern Vermont, the West has been the site for important national slalom championships. Although it is blocked by two large flood-control dams, there are still several parts of the West that can present some sport. In its watershed are several smaller but exciting streams—the Winhall, the Wardsboro, the Rock, and the Ball Mountain Brook. Since the West is dam controlled, scheduled water releases on the last weekends of April and September permit boating when nearby rivers are often dry. The rapids on the West are mostly straightforward, although one stretch may require scouting if you haven't seen it before. Competent boaters will find several good spots to play, and intermediates will still find a challenge.

Starting a trip from Ball Mountain Dam is not the easiest thing to do. There is an old railroad bed that has been converted into a one-lane class III road, which runs from the parking lot of Jamaica State Park up the left side of the river. The state park usually runs an inexpensive shuttle service up this road on release weekends. This shuttle leaves you a half-mile below the dam, where the biggest rapid of the trip is located. If missing this rapid is not in your game plan, you can walk the last half-mile to the dam. The

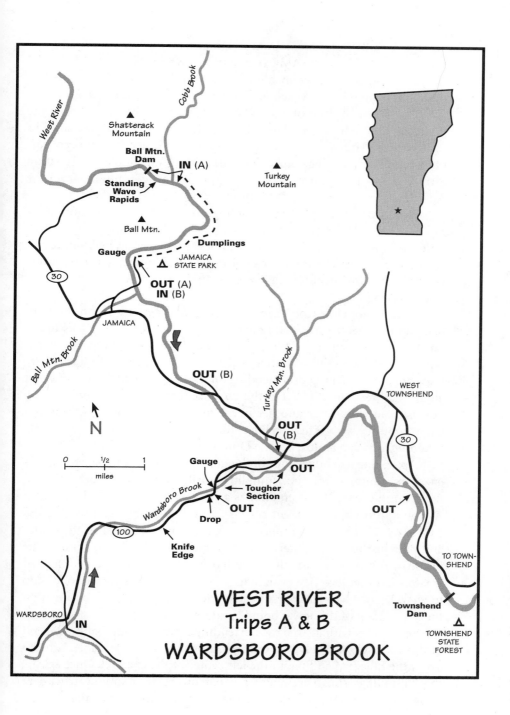

WEST RIVER
Trips A & B
WARDSBORO BROOK

portage over Ball Mountain Dam is somewhat easier than it used to be since volunteers from the AMC built a trail down the face of the dam. The Corps of Engineers generally allows access to the parking lot just below the spillway on release weekends, facilitating this access option as well.

The first half-mile of the West was dramatically altered after the floods of 1987, when water crested the spillway for the first time since its construction. The initial rapid on the trip is now bigger and more continuous than it used to be, and a dynamic surfing wave-hole combination formed below the spillway. This first rapid is now continuous from the dam down to the put-in at Cobb Brook.

From Cobb Brook to the Dumplings, the West is mostly continuous rapids of class III difficulty at a level of 1,500 cfs (6.9 on the gauge), and a little less at lower levels. There are countless rocks, waves, hydraulics, and 1- to 2-foot drops. This section can be run by intermediates; it is not overwhelmingly difficult, although a rescue could be hard because of the continuous current.

Somewhat below Cobb Brook, where a rock face forms on the right bank and the river turns gently left, the frequency of rocks picks up, as does the excitement, at least for a short stretch. Below, the water is flatter, but it still moves as the West then makes a wide, looping right turn where there are class II–III rapids depending on the level. A rock line extends out almost halfway from the left in the turn itself, creating a nice hole on the downstream side. After another left turn, the river drops gently into a large pool-like area where a huge rock face decorates the right bank. Straining, one can almost see the Dumplings farther downstream.

Appearing like huge blobs of dough left by some giant baker to harden in the summer sun, the Dumplings easily present the most technical rapid on the river. However, there is a clear passage through their midst. As you approach, the current speeds up and larger rocks appear on the banks. As you see the Dumplings, look for a huge boulder in the center and pass just to its left, then turn diagonally right and stay close to the inside of this turn as a smaller rock blocks the lower left-center channel (mainly in lower levels). As you make this right turn, the passage opens up to view. Pass between this first large boulder and another lower down on the left. Once past this lower boulder, turn sharply left to enter a fast chute that terminates with a large rock extending from the right bank. The end of this rock supports a hefty pourover known as the Ender Hole. You can avoid the hole by paddling in the left center of the channel. Once set up, the Dumplings run is a regular but narrow S-curve among truck-size boulders and turbulent water. For the more adventuresome, the slots on

Open boats on Split Hair Rapid on the Dryway section of the Deerfield River.
Photo by Zoar Outdoor

the right at the top have all been run and provide interesting alternative routes as well as excellent advanced ender holes.

The Dumplings is a tough class III or an easy IV at 1,500 cfs. It looks more fearsome than it actually is. The outrun is fast, with standing waves and large rocks scattered throughout for a good length. There are even some strong eddies that nimble boaters may want to pop into. Once past the outrun from the Dumplings, you won't meet anything difficult before the takeout at the Salmon Hole in Jamaica State Park. The most difficult thing here is waiting in line for the restroom so you can change your clothes in relative comfort.

With the cooperation of the Army Corps of Engineers, there are two yearly water releases on the West that are planned in advance. These usually fall on the last weekends of April and September. Because of the popularity of these releases, expect large crowds and make your camping reservations six months or more in advance. The West also runs frequently in the spring and after heavy rains any time of year. In contrast to the usual crowded release weekends, running the river at one of these "off-peak" times is like walking down a sidewalk in New York City at 5:00 on a Sunday morning.

The gauge on the West is located in Jamaica State Park on the left shore near the Salmon Hole. However, the external staff read by boaters is directly across on the right side of the river, attached to a rock ledge. So, get into your boat, paddle across the pool there, and read the gauge to determine if you should paddle back. The gauge is underwater at levels of 10.5 and over. It is also sometimes hard to spot because of debris. This gauge is not listed on the USGS water-level information site on the Internet, but the gauge downstream in Townshend is. The site lists both gauge readings and cfs.

There is an upper section of the West known as the Londonderry Ledges located about 6.0 miles upstream of Ball Mountain Dam along Route 100. This section is free flowing and provides an excellent class III run when there is sufficient water. The rapids are chock-full of hydraulics formed by the frequent low-angle ledges. The hydraulics get very big and grabby at higher flows.

West River (Vt.)

Jamaica State Park to Townshend Reservoir
Trip B

DISTANCE (MILES)	5.5	TOO LOW	
SHUTTLE (MILES)	6	LOW	6.3/1,000 cfs
AVG. DROP (FEET/MILE)	30	MED.	
MAX. DROP (FEET/MILE)	40	HIGH	
DIFFICULTY	II–II +	TOO HIGH	1,600 cfs/7.0
SCENERY	Fair	GAUGE LOCATION	Jamaica State Park
DATE LAST CHECKED	1997	WATER LEVEL INFO.	
RUNOFF PATTERN	d/r/l		

This lower portion of the West is easier than the upper stretch; it is a pleasant paddle at almost any water level. With a larger cross section, the lower part is shallow in places and in low water it is a bottom-scraper. This broadness also allows enjoyable paddling for beginners even when the upper section is too high. Although there are well-defined rapids, none is difficult or requires scouting, and a straightforward approach and run will suffice. Also, it is possible to avoid all the heavy water by paddling the sidelines. The road is fairly close to the river almost all the way and there are many signs of civilization, yet the valley is not totally unattractive.

Begin the trip just inside Jamaica State Park at the Salmon Hole, which is a pool that's flanked on its left side by a sandy beach. There are also a paved parking lot, many drive-in campsites, and an outhouse complete with flush toilets. (Ah, for the real wilderness.) Rock-lined on the right side with the main current nearby, the Salmon Hole reportedly was the scene of an early Indian battle; nowadays the only battles are for parking spaces. At its downstream end, on the left, is a low island and below that a class I–II rapid that leads to an iron bridge. Under the bridge is an easy class II rapid, rocky in low water and stuffed with waves in high water. After a pause there is a short, intense rapid with heavier waves (2 feet at a gauge of 7.4) where the Ball Mountain Brook comes in from the right.

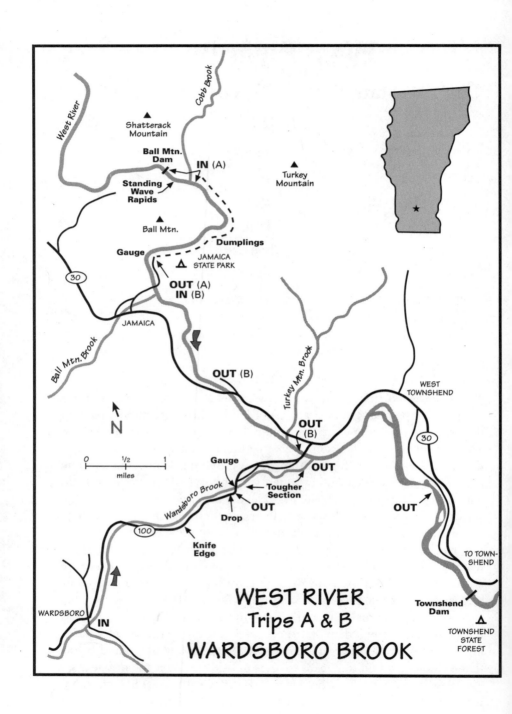

West River

Cobb Brook

Shatterack
Mountain

Ball Mtn.
Dam

IN (A)

Turkey
Mountain

Standing
Wave
Rapids

Ball Mtn.

Dumplings

Gauge

JAMAICA
STATE PARK

30

OUT (A)
IN (B)

JAMAICA

Ball Mtn. Brook

OUT (B)

Turkey Mtn. Brook

WEST
TOWNSHEND

N

30

0   ½   1
miles

Gauge

OUT
(B)

OUT

Tougher
Section

Wardsboro Brook

OUT

OUT

Drop

100

Knife
Edge

TO TOWN-
SHEND

WARDSBORO

IN

WEST RIVER
Trips A & B
WARDSBORO BROOK

Townshend
Dam

TOWNSHEND
STATE
FOREST

Shortly below this the river splits, with the larger flow going left of a large island and a smaller portion going right.

On the left channel, shortly after the split, there's a short, tricky stretch where the water is forced away from the left bank into a center channel by a rock ledge. In high water this tickler becomes rather angry. The far right is calmer, and an eddy lurks below on the left. Next, a sweeping right turn houses an extended series of small haystacks and rocks. After a period of quieter water, there is another long, easy rapid terminating in a left curve, where the two channels rejoin and a heavy but short rapid appears with a boily eddy on the right center halfway down.

The right channel around the large island is narrow, fast, and winding, with the potential for multiple strainers. A paddler was killed in a strainer here in 1989, so be cautious. Also, about three-quarters of the way down this channel a very low covered bridge of recent vintage could present problems at very high water.

The beginning of a trailer camp on the right bank marks the last rapid before the Route 30 bridge. This one is 50 to 75 yards long and consists of a few small midriver eddies at the top and a series of standing waves spread across the river. It can be run almost anywhere. Since most of the sporty rapids are exhausted, the boater may decide to take out just upstream of the bridge on river left and run again or, alternatively, continue down about 3.5 miles to the Townshend Reservoir. In this lower stretch, there is an interesting ledge rapid with several surfing holes and waves above the Route 100 bridge and a maze called the Corkscrews below the bridge, where the river is divided into several channels by islands and the sharp turns in between are good exercises in class II boat handling. Take out at the old Route 30 just downstream of West Townshend Center (don't blink!). The road is sometimes flooded in the spring, making it necessary to paddle across some flatwater to reach it. An alternate takeout is the Route 100 bridge a couple of miles upstream.

Jamaica State Park offers camping, for a fee (more for out-of-staters). There is also the Winhall Brook Camping Area near the Winhall River and an area near the Townshend Dam.

The gauge on the West is located in Jamaica State Park on the left shore near the Salmon Hole. However, the external staff read by boaters is directly across on the right side of the river, attached to a rock ledge. So, get into your boat, paddle across the pool there, and read the gauge to determine if you should paddle back. The gauge is underwater at levels of 10.5 and over. It is also sometimes hard to spot because of debris. This gauge is not listed on the USGS water-level information site on the Internet, but the gauge downstream in Townshend is. The site lists both gauge readings and cfs.

West River   237

White River (Vt.)

North Royalton to South Royalton

DISTANCE (MILES)	7.5		**TOO LOW**	
SHUTTLE (MILES)	7.5		**LOW**	
AVG. DROP (FEET/MILE)			**MED.**	
MAX. DROP (FEET/MILE)			**HIGH**	6
DIFFICULTY	I–II		**TOO HIGH**	
SCENERY	Excellent		**GAUGE LOCATION**	West Hartford
DATE LAST CHECKED	1997		**WATER LEVEL INFO.**	
RUNOFF PATTERN	n		http://water.usgs.gov/public/realtime.html	

Draining central Vermont, the White River offers many miles of pleasant canoeing through some of the most beautiful countryside New England has to offer. Like the Green, the White is known more for its attractive watershed than for its rapids. Whereas the Green typifies the backwoods, the White characterizes the farmlands of Vermont. Nestled between high, tree-shrouded hills, these tiny farms are tucked among the giant folds of the Green Mountains. Typically a house attached directly to the barn and other buildings for protection against fierce winters, these fertile farms provide the backdrop for the White. The rapids (what rapids there are) consist of class I and II water; they need a very heavy spring runoff to make them more difficult. The water itself is as clear as distilled, allowing the lazy paddler to observe fish 10 feet below the surface. If it weren't for the cows, of which there are many, the White could provide a natural source of water for a town. This section of the White tends to hold its water better than other sections, often remaining runnable throughout the summer.

Put in at the Fox Stand fishing access off Route 14 just behind the Fox Stand Inn in North Royalton. From North Royalton to Royalton is all moving water with a few riffles, except for one class II drop just above South Royalton. There is a good spot to stop for lunch just downstream of this rapid on river right at Lions Club Park.

Just below the green bridge in South Royalton is another class II rapid. Take out at a fishing access past the South Royalton–Sharon line

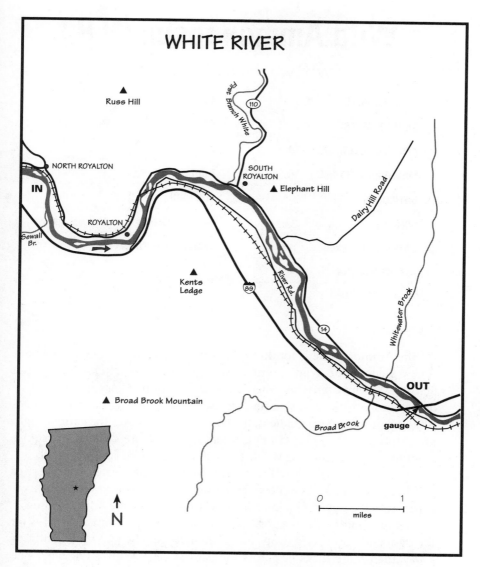

WHITE RIVER

Russ Hill

First Branch White

110

NORTH ROYALTON

IN

ROYALTON

Sewall Br.

SOUTH ROYALTON

▲ Elephant Hill

Dairy Hill Road

Kents Ledge

89

River Rd.

14

Whitewater Brook

▲ Broad Brook Mountain

OUT

Broad Brook

gauge

0   1
miles

N

where a large gravel pit is close on river left. Just downstream of this is the Route 89 bridge. There is a hand-painted gauge on the bridge abutment for Route 89. When the slab at the bottom is wet (0 feet), this run is low. Up to 3.0 feet the run is mostly class I and II, above and 3.0 feet the rapids at South Royalton become class III. This section is good for teaching beginners, because the rapids are far enough apart that it is not intimidating but there are enough of them to keep things interesting.

Wild Ammonoosuc (N.H.)
Swiftwater to Route 302

DISTANCE (MILES)	2		TOO LOW	1
SHUTTLE (MILES)	2		LOW	
AVG. DROP (FEET/MILE)	90		MED.	
MAX. DROP (FEET/MILE)	100		HIGH	
DIFFICULTY	II–III		TOO HIGH	
SCENERY	Good		GAUGE LOCATION	Covered Bridge
DATE LAST CHECKED	1997		WATER LEVEL INFO.	
RUNOFF PATTERN	n/f			

If the Ammonoosuc is too high for comfortable boating, or if you want new scenery, the Wild Ammonoosuc presents a short class II–III run. Starting at Swiftwater, where there's a waterfall, the paddler can ease his way down among rocks and standing waves, never venturing far from a road. Although it has a steep gradient, the drop is averaged over the entire length, presenting a continuous, fast run where no rapids are difficult or require scouting. In high water the whole trip will turn into one long waterfall.

Put in below the covered bridge and waterfall in Swiftwater. Here the river is 50 to 75 feet wide and fast flowing over small rocks. It continues in this manner most of the way until it joins with its larger brother, the Ammonoosuc.

At one point, notice a gorge-like area; above, the main channel is on the right and the current drops over a small ledge. The water is smooth for a way, then more rocks lie across the path. A center run is OK here. The next couple of hundred yards are cluttered with larger rocks, and 0.2 mile farther, after a right turn with large rocks on the right bank, there's a good chute with rocks. Again, a center run is fine.

The trip may be ended where the Route 302 bridge crosses the river or, alternatively, continued down to the Ammonoosuc.

There is a hand-painted gauge on the center abutment of the covered bridge at the put-in. This gauge was new as of this writing, and it is not known how it correlates to runnability, although 1.0 is thought to be too low.

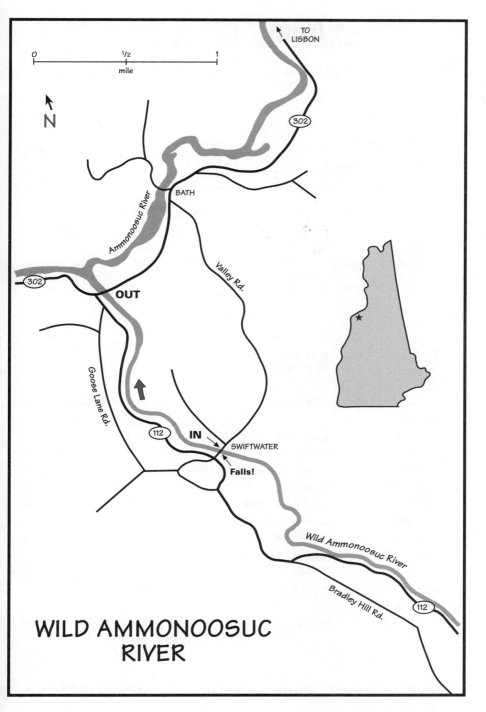

WILD AMMONOOSUC
RIVER

Winhall River (Vt.)

Grahamville School to Londonderry Road

DISTANCE (MILES)	4.5		**TOO LOW**	
SHUTTLE (MILES)	4.5		**LOW**	
AVG. DROP (FEET/MILE)	62		**MED.**	
MAX. DROP (FEET/MILE)	100		**HIGH**	
DIFFICULTY	III–III +		**TOO HIGH**	
SCENERY	Fair		**GAUGE LOCATION**	Route 30 Bridge
DATE LAST CHECKED	1997		**WATER LEVEL INFO.**	
RUNOFF PATTERN	n/f			

The Winhall is a rather small stream that can offer an exciting ride in high water and a challenging class II–III run in medium or low water. Because it has a small watershed, the Winhall has a relatively short season—normally it's up for only a few weeks in early April. The current is continuous and the rapids nearly so. There is a healthy assortment of rocks, but in medium or high water the turbulence is most noticeable and maneuvering is done to avoid hydraulics and haystacks. In low water the rocks necessitate a moderate amount of maneuvering. There is only one set of rapids that should be scouted, and it is easy to avoid. A road passes alongside almost all the way, so most of the river can be seen before running. The Winhall enters the West River above the Ball Mountain Dam. It is not practical to list all the rapids, since there are so many and they are so similar.

A suggested starting spot is near a small bridge behind the Winhall Memorial Library, just off Route 30 about 1.0 mile upstream of the Stratton Mountain Access Road in Bondville. Here the Winhall is about 30 feet wide with a scattering of small rocks. Just below, the river has gentle curves and easy standing waves as the paddler looks directly into a morn-

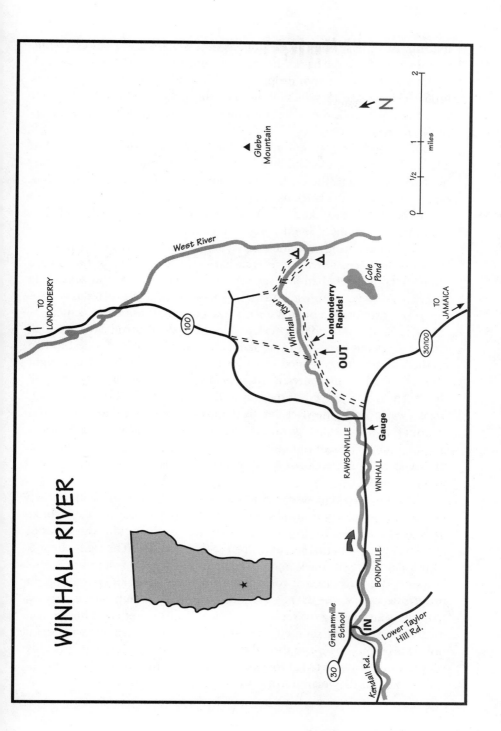

WINHALL RIVER

ing sun. In early spring this section, as others, has ice shelves extending into the river from the banks. In the beginning of a left turn, there's a rock in the middle and a 1-foot drop. Go to either side, although the right is a little trickier. Standing waves follow, then shortly another rock in the right center and a 1- to 2-foot drop into more turbulence. Typical class II–III rapids follow.

By a wooden restaurant up on the left bank, the Winhall turns left in a fast, narrow chute blocked by a large rock in the middle. The left channel is S-shaped and the outflow is turbulent for 100 yards downstream, where under a small bridge there are several good hydraulics. This section is hard class II or easy class III at low water. The rapids taper down below the bridge, and houses line the river for a while.

To the next bridge and the one beyond, the rapids are quite similar to those already seen. There are several sharp curves, and one section after a left turn has heavier-than-average haystacks (1 to 2 feet at a gauge reading of 1.0). Just as you glimpse houses in Rawsonville, a left turn has a sloping 3-foot drop with a big haystack at the bottom. Run it dead center.

The Route 100 bridge is next, and in the first left turn below it, a rock ledge pushes out from the right bank, creating a drop. It is easiest to run on the left or center (inclined 1 to 2 feet) and hardest on the extreme right (abrupt 2 feet). A small stream enters below from the left, and the Winhall then turns right. The rest of the way to the takeout is class II–III, depending on water level. The river here is shallower and wider than above. The takeout is at the next bridge on the Londonderry Road (dirt). Care should be taken not to proceed too far downstream, since the next left turn has the most difficult section—Londonderry Rapids (class IV even at low water).

The left turn that starts Londonderry Rapids is sharp, with a steep right bank and a beginning almost completely blocked by a huge, slablike rock in the middle. To drop directly over this rock would mean a 4-foot fall. The approach must be made from either extreme. The right channel angles sharply right to left, then straightens out for 100 feet in some easier water. After this distance rocks again choke the river, and a right or left route is necessary. The left is more technical while the right side is narrow, with the water falling over a sloping ledge. If this channel is chosen, you must keep your bow pointed downstream and blast through a powerful hole. This rapid obviously should be scouted before running. It probably should not be attempted at low water. Most intermediate boaters should walk around if they plan to continue the trip down to the West.

Decision making on the Winooski River's Junk Yard Rapid. Photo by Bruce Lessels

There is a hand-painted gauge on the downstream side of the river-left abutment of the third bridge on Route 30, going toward the put-in from the intersection of Routes 100 and 30. This gauge is new and it is not known how the markings correspond to runnability. If, during the spring runoff, the Ball Mountain Dam is discharging 2,500 cfs or more, it is probably a good bet that the Winhall is runnable. This is certainly not always true, but it may prevent a long trip for nothing.

The Wardsboro, Ball Mountain Brook, and Rock are nearby cousins of the Winhall and are of similar character, but they are more difficult at comparable water levels.

Winooski River (Vt.)

Dam to Waterbury

DISTANCE (MILES)	5.5	TOO LOW	
SHUTTLE (MILES)	6	LOW	
AVG. DROP (FEET/MILE)		MED.	
MAX. DROP (FEET/MILE)		HIGH	
DIFFICULTY	I–II	TOO HIGH	
SCENERY	Good	GAUGE LOCATION	None
DATE LAST CHECKED	1997	WATER LEVEL INFO.	
RUNOFF PATTERN	n/l		

The Winooski is a narrow, scenic run in northern Vermont that holds its water well into the summer most years. The rapids are mostly easy and there are significant stretches of flatwater, but the run is worthwhile for the scenery, which is mostly classic Vermont. There are a few blemishes on the scenery, such as a highway that follows closely for a stretch and a few town centers, but the marshes and small stone gorges make the run interesting nevertheless.

Put in just below a hydroelectric dam near Exit 9 on I-89 off Route 100B about 6.0 miles east of Waterbury. The river is contained within a small gorge here, but soon widens as it drops over a small class I drop. Fastwater takes you through a marshy area for half a mile or so, and shallow riffles are frequent until the Mad River joins from the left. A short distance up the Mad is a shale gorge worth exploring.

Below the confluence with the Mad, the Winooski passes under Route 2 and turns left. Shortly after this, Junk Yard Rapid (class II) appears just after a car junkyard on the left shore. At this drop the water pushes up against the left bank—a low-angled rock ledge. After moving right, it piles up on a rocky island midstream and splits, with about 60 percent of the flow filling the left channel while 40 percent goes right. Run left, or right if necessary, but no matter what, lean into the rock if you broach on it. Scout from the left bank.

After Junk Yard the river winds through several rocky gorges with a

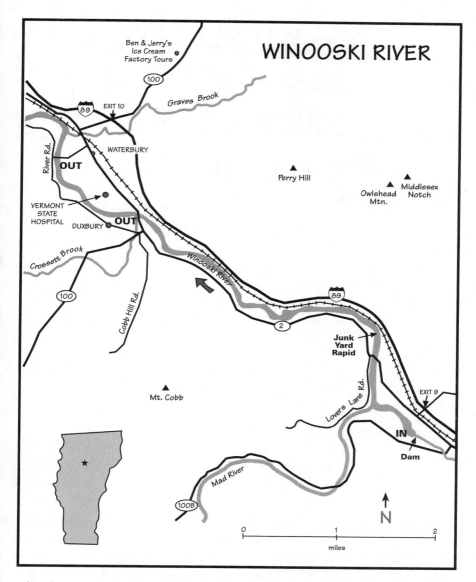

WINOOSKI RIVER

Ben & Jerry's
Ice Cream
Factory Tours

100

89 EXIT 10

Graves Brook

River Rd.

WATERBURY

OUT

Perry Hill

Middlesex
Notch

Owlshead
Mtn.

VERMONT
STATE
HOSPITAL DUXBURY OUT

Crossett Brook

Winooski River

100

Cobb Hill Rd.

89

2

Junk
Yard
Rapid

Mt. Cobb

Lovers Lane Rd.

EXIT 9

IN

Dam

Mad River

100B

N

0   1   2
miles

few fast-moving riffles. Birds of all types sing from both banks and from
the islands that often appear midstream. Take out the next time Route 2
crosses the river just east of Waterbury or a mile farther downstream at the
Winooski Street bridge in Waterbury.

There is no gauge on the Winooski. Call Umiak Outfitters in Stowe
(802-253-2317) for water-level information.

MASSACHUSETTS, CONNECTICUT, and RHODE ISLAND
Bantam River (Conn.)
Stoddard Road to Shepaug River

DISTANCE (MILES)	5.4	**TOO LOW**	
SHUTTLE (MILES)	5	**LOW**	0.5
AVG. DROP (FEET/MILE)	25	**MED.**	
MAX. DROP (FEET/MILE)	32	**HIGH**	
DIFFICULTY	I–II	**TOO HIGH**	
SCENERY	Good	**GAUGE LOCATION**	Route 47 Bridge
DATE LAST CHECKED	1997	**WATER LEVEL INFO.**	
RUNOFF PATTERN	n/f		

The Bantam is traditionally one of the early trips. Along with the Shepaug, it nestles in the western Connecticut hills. Several groups usually run both rivers on the same weekend. The Bantam provides an easy introduction to the bigger and far more exciting Shepaug, since it is class I–II depending on the water level. To a hardy closed-boater, the Bantam is as exciting as riding the crest when someone pulls the plug of your bathtub. All foolishness aside, however, the water should be respected, because in March it is very cold and a swim then could dampen your enthusiasm for later trips.

To start a trip on the Bantam, proceed west on Route 202 from its junction with Route 209 for about 0.4 mile and turn left on West Morris

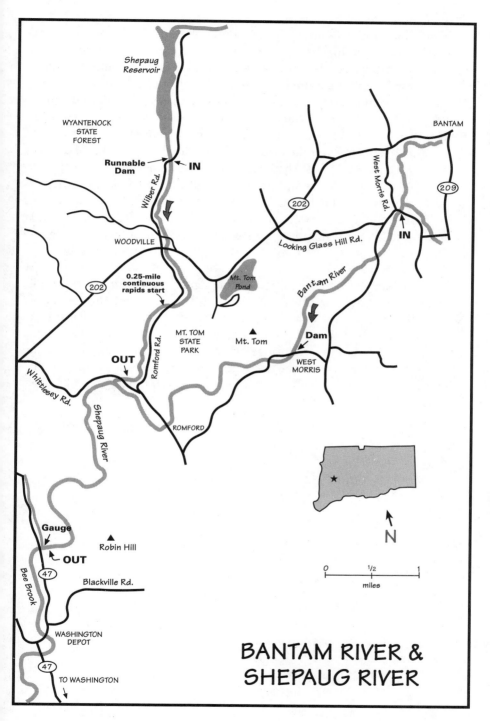

Shepaug Reservoir

WYANTENOCK
STATE
FOREST

BANTAM

Runnable
Dam → IN

Wilber Rd.

West Morris Rd.

209

202

WOODVILLE

Looking Glass Hill Rd.

IN

0.25-mile
continuous
rapids start

202

Mt. Tom
Pond

Bantam River

Romford Rd.

MT. TOM
STATE
PARK

Mt. Tom

Dam

OUT

WEST
MORRIS

Whittlesey Rd.

Shepaug River

ROMFORD

Gauge

Robin Hill

OUT

47

Bee Brook

Blackville Rd.

N

0   1/2   1
miles

WASHINGTON
DEPOT

47

TO WASHINGTON

BANTAM RIVER &
SHEPAUG RIVER

Road. Continue for a little less than a mile and take a left onto Stoddard Road, which leads to a bridge crossing the river. Here the Bantam is 2 to 3 boat lengths wide, with rapids above the bridge and smooth water flowing below. The river continues flowing smoothly most of its length, and it takes very high water to make it anything but an easy class II. In 0.8 mile, after a bridge, the river widens a bit but becomes no harder. The main danger in this stretch is downed trees, of which there can be many.

Just upstream from the bridge in West Morris, is a broken dam that drops a total of 3 to 4 feet. There are many rocks at the bottom, which may be covered at high levels and present a challenge at low levels. Scout or portage on river right. The dam is breached on the right and can be run at most levels. The river on the downstream side is slightly faster than above, and in high water there are even little ripples. Another set of standing-wave rapids sits just in front of the next bridge, and there's also one after the bridge.

The Bantam then stays smooth. One right turn has some little rapids and below, in a left turn, there's a six-inch ledge. Downstream a short distance is a right turn with a large rock in the left center. Below that there's another drop over a small ledge. These ledges are gone in high water. The next landmark is the steel bridge at Romford, which is about 1.0 mile from the confluence with the Shepaug. Once the Shepaug is entered, the tempo picks up. For details, see the Shepaug description.

Blackledge River (Conn.)

Route 66 to Salmon River

DISTANCE (MILES)	5.9	**TOO LOW**	1.4
SHUTTLE (MILES)	5	**LOW**	3
AVG. DROP (FEET/MILE)	20	**MED.**	
MAX. DROP (FEET/MILE)	30	**HIGH**	
DIFFICULTY	II	**TOO HIGH**	
SCENERY	Good	**GAUGE LOCATION**	Comstock Bridge
DATE LAST CHECKED	1981	**WATER LEVEL INFO.**	
RUNOFF PATTERN	n/f		

The Blackledge is a narrow, winding stream that is sometimes used for entering the Salmon. Since it has a very small watershed, it is up only during heavy spring runoffs. When it's up, standing waves are the order of the day; when it's low, rocks appear, making a nuisance of themselves. At this lower level the Blackledge is not worth the effort.

From the junction of old Route 2 and Route 66 in Marlborough, Connecticut, proceed about 1.5 miles east on Route 66 to a spot where a small bridge crosses the river. Here the river is about two boat lengths wide, and the current's speed depends on the water level. Put in on the upstream side of the bridge, as the lower part has been posted against trespassers. An alternative starting point is along old Route 2 where the river approaches the road. Here, there is a small dam crossing the stream and several closely spaced meanders. The entire river is narrow, with no special difficulties other than tree hazards and the narrowness, which restricts maneuvering. Approach curves with caution, because a tree could be down almost anywhere. From Route 66, the Blackledge runs for about 3.3 miles through the Salmon River State Forest, away from roads,

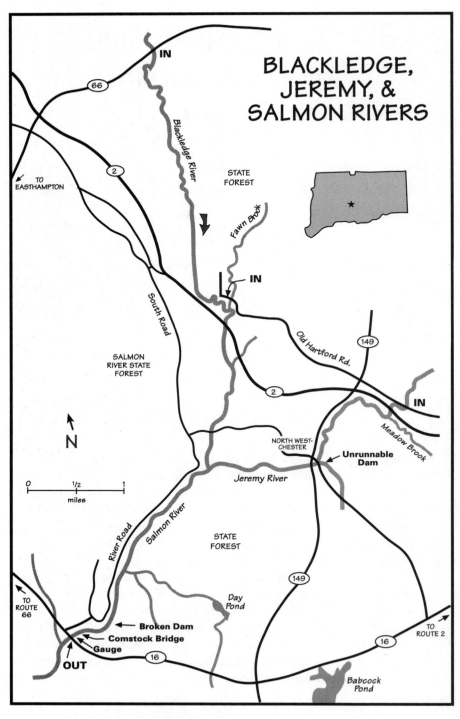

BLACKLEDGE, JEREMY, & SALMON RIVERS

IN

66

2

TO EASTHAMPTON

STATE FOREST

Blackledge River

Fawn Brook

IN

SALMON RIVER STATE FOREST

South Road

Old Hartford Rd.

149

2

IN

Meadow Brook

N

0   1/2   1
miles

NORTH WEST-CHESTER

Unrunnable Dam

Jeremy River

River Road

Salmon River

STATE FOREST

TO ROUTE 66

Day Pond

149

Broken Dam

Comstock Bridge

Gauge

16

OUT

TO ROUTE 2

16

Babcock Pond

Tandem paddling in the Hudson River Gorge. Photo by James Swedberg

before it approaches both old and new Route 2. After it finally leaves Route 2, it runs away from roads again for 1.5 miles, where it joins with the Jeremy to form the Salmon.

The gauge for this trip is on the Salmon at Old Comstock Bridge. For further details, see the Salmon description.

Chickley River (Mass.)

Route 8A to Deerfield River

DISTANCE (MILES)	4.4	TOO LOW	
SHUTTLE (MILES)	4	LOW	
AVG. DROP (FEET/MILE)	77	MED.	
MAX. DROP (FEET/MILE)	100	HIGH	
DIFFICULTY	II–III	TOO HIGH	
SCENERY	Good	GAUGE LOCATION	None
DATE LAST CHECKED	1997	WATER LEVEL INFO.	
RUNOFF PATTERN	n/f		

The Chickley runs through the rural landscape of Hawley, Massachusetts. Cow pastures, sugarbushes, and old mill sites are common along the river that takes its name from the Reverend John Checkley, an early landowner in the region. This pleasant class II–III creek becomes boatable after heavy rains or during spring snowmelt. The river is paralleled for its entire length by Route 8A and begins in Dubuque (formerly Hawley) State Forest.

You can put in almost anywhere below where the two branches of the Chickley join in the small village of West Hawley, and take out at its confluence with the Deerfield River in Charlemont. To avoid the most difficult (class III) drop, take out where you first cross the river on Route 8A going south from Charlemont.

The whitewater on the Chickley is as continuous as class II gets, but the narrowness of the river and the moderate gradient keep things manageable for competent class II–III boaters at low to medium water. The primary hazards on this run are downed trees that can block the entire channel, and wire fences strung by local farmers to keep their cows from wandering across the normally ankle-deep current. You can scout much

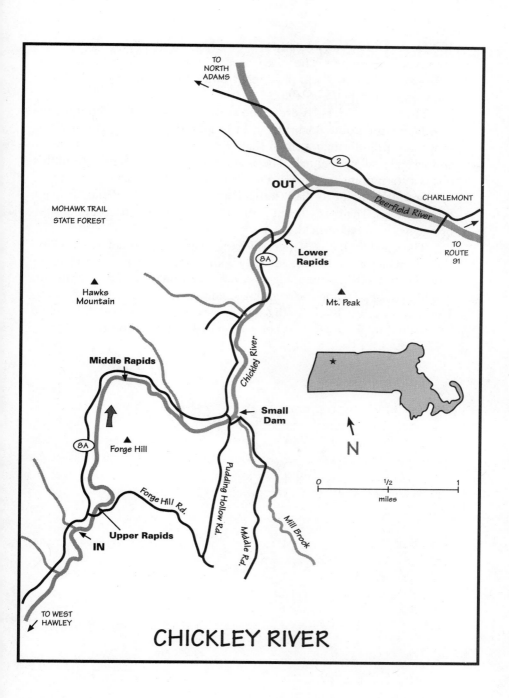

TO
NORTH
ADAMS

2

OUT

MOHAWK TRAIL
STATE FOREST

CHARLEMONT

Deerfield River

TO
ROUTE
91

8A

Lower
Rapids

Hawks
Mountain

Mt. Peak

Chickley River

Middle Rapids

Small
Dam

8A

Forge Hill

Pudding Hollow Rd.

Middle Rd.

Mill Brook

N

Forge Hill Rd.

Upper Rapids

IN

0   1/2   1
miles

TO WEST
HAWLEY

CHICKLEY RIVER

of it from the car, but any time you run the Chickley, be on the alert for both types of strainers. The wire fences are very difficult to see. Be especially careful just after you pass under Route 8A about a mile above the confluence with the Deerfield.

The toughest class III drop, known as Lower Rapid, is about a half-mile below the Route 8A bridge next to an old mill site. Here the river drops abruptly through a small shale gorge, forming a few meaty holes and several shallow channels. The easiest run is down the left side, but this one is a stern muncher wherever you run it unless the water is very high.

From this point to the Deerfield, another half-mile of class II ledge drops follows. The best takeout is on river left just as you pass under the bridge before the Deerfield.

The Chickley has no gauge. It is very flashy with a small, steep watershed, so its level can change abruptly with rain or snowmelt. At medium levels it is class II–III, but at higher levels it becomes much more difficult, as eddies disappear and the medium-sized rocks become holes and waves. Use caution at any level, and be sure to monitor the river carefully while you're on it to be sure it does not get too high for your group.

Clear-Branch Rivers (R.I.)

Harrisville to Glendale

DISTANCE (MILES)	4.8	TOO LOW	2.9
SHUTTLE (MILES)	3.5	LOW	
AVG. DROP (FEET/MILE)	8	MED.	
MAX. DROP (FEET/MILE)	90	HIGH	
DIFFICULTY	I–II	TOO HIGH	
SCENERY		GAUGE LOCATION	Forestdale
DATE LAST CHECKED	1997	WATER LEVEL INFO.	
RUNOFF PATTERN	n/a		

Although Rhode Island is not known as a whitewater haven, it would be erroneous to assume that there is no river running to be had in this state. What the Clear-Branch Rivers lack in whitewater thrills, they make up in idyllic beauty and serenity. Flowing along low banks and thickly settled with trees, these small rivers meander endlessly, as if they were trying to tie themselves into knots. The current is usually present, though it is weak in spots. Rapids are easy riffles and several abrupt drops over small, debris-laden dams. There is also one section of several hundred yards in Glendale where the pace increases and the boater faces some rocky class II rapids. Since the rivers are so narrow, trees can completely block the path, a hazard throughout the trip. These rivers are definitely for beginners or for those seeking an amiable commune with nature.

Start the trip on the Clear River, just downstream from the dam in Harrisville. Immediately upstream from the Route 107 bridge is a collection of rocks and stones that can be negotiated or not depending upon the water level. If the gauge is 2.9 or lower, carry your boat under the bridge and put in there. After passing a factory on the right bank, the water sets the pace—slow and even. After several turns, there is a 6- to 12-inch drop

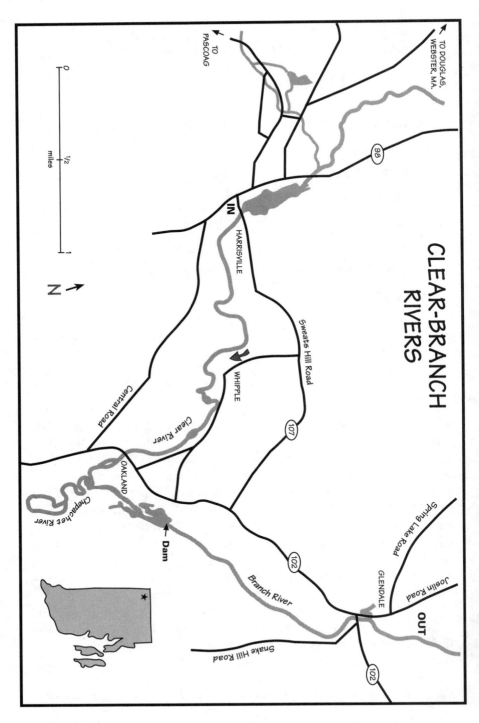

CLEAR-BRANCH RIVERS

TO PASCOAG

TO DOUGLAS, WEBSTER, MA.

98

IN

HARRISVILLE

Sweats Hill Road

WHIPPLE

Central Road

107

Clear River

OAKLAND

Chepachet River

Dam

Branch River

102

Spring Lake Road

Joslin Road

GLENDALE

OUT

Snake Hill Road

102

0   ½   1
miles

N →

258   Massachusetts, Connecticut, and Rhode Island

over a small dam that could easily change complexion every year. There are now woods on the right bank and houses on the left. After you pass the remains of an old bridge, woods populate both banks.

Following a right turn, there waits an old dam with a two-stage descent. In low water it is scratchy to get over; in medium water the drops should be easier. Look it over if you are unsure about where to go. There are some big boulders below, but they are easy to miss.

The Clear continues on in its typical sinuous manner, under two bridges and past the remains of several more. When the river turns sharply left and passes some old railroad-bridge supports, the paddler enters a marshy area where the channel is deeper and wider than normal. This is where the actual Branch River is formed by the confluence of the Clear and Chepachet Rivers. Also, this is the beginning of some backwater behind a dam. This dam is near a factory on the left bank; the portage should be made on the right bank. Below the dam the current is quicker than normal, but after the first turn the river reverts back to its characteristic temperament.

As you approach Glendale, a row of old bridge supports spans the river. You'll have to pick and choose your way through the debris piled up on them. Next are two closely spaced bridges, then the boat enters a section of continuous fast current that is peppered with rocks. This portion of the river starts by dropping over a small broken dam, passes to the left of an island, then continues down past more rocks and waves. This is probably the most continuously difficult part of the trip; at a gauge reading of 2.9, it is a very scratchy and annoying class II in difficulty. This stronger current lasts for several hundred yards.

Several takeouts are possible. The first is in Glendale, just at the end of the set of rapids there. A factory (Bruin Plastics) and also the Glendale fire and rescue station are in view on the left bank near this spot. An alternative is to continue to the junction of Routes 7 and 102 and take out there. If you do this, be careful of the dam just upstream from the Route 102 bridge.

The gauge is in Forestdale, about 400 feet downstream from a mill-dam. The gauge is at the bottom of a steep hill behind the former H&H Machine Tool Company, now Galaxy Computers, which is itself down and across the street from the Forestdale post office. The 2.9 gauge reading is rated too low for the section of rapids in Glendale. At this level, passage is possible, but it will lacerate the bottom of your boat.

Cohasset (Mass.)

Border Street

DISTANCE (MILES)	100 yds.	**TOO LOW**	n/a
SHUTTLE (MILES)	None	**LOW**	n/a
AVG. DROP (FEET/MILE)		**MED.**	n/a
MAX. DROP (FEET/MILE)		**HIGH**	n/a
DIFFICULTY	II	**TOO HIGH**	n/a
SCENERY	Fair	**GAUGE LOCATION**	None
DATE LAST CHECKED	1997	**WATER LEVEL INFO.**	tide table
RUNOFF PATTERN	t		

About half an hour south of Boston is an interesting tidal rip known to boaters in the area simply as "Cohasset." This short class II drop has amused summertime whitewater paddlers in and around Boston since at least the late 1960s, when dam releases for recreational boating were virtually nonexistent. It remains an interesting play spot with features that change constantly during the two- to three-hour window as the ocean rushes inland through a narrow gap.

The setting is unusual: a picturesque seaside town with yachts and fishing boats moored in the harbor and a marina jutting out over the water just above the tidal rip. Parking is not plentiful, and the narrow road leading to the rip is posted against parking for most of its length. Legal parking can be reached by taking a left just after the bridge at the tidal rip when coming from the center of town. On warm summer days this lot is often full, so you may have to park farther away and carry boats to the water.

The rip tends to get crowded as well during the summer—and not just with boaters. Despite a town ordinance forbidding it, local kids still jump from the bridge into the swift current at the base of the rapid.

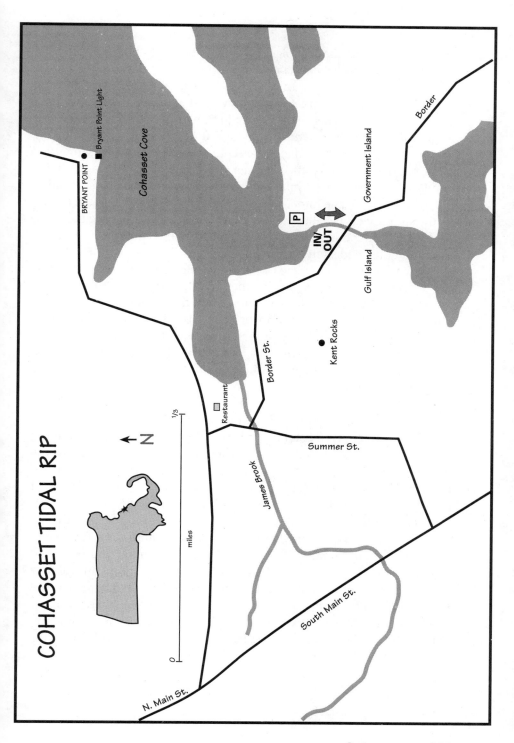

COHASSET TIDAL RIP

N

miles

1/3

0

Bryant Point Light

BRYANT POINT

Cohasset Cove

Border

Government Island

P

IN/OUT

Gulf Island

Kent Rocks

Border St.

Restaurant

Summer St.

James Brook

South Main St.

N. Main St.

Cohasset   261

Cohasset is one of the few places where you have to read not only the whitewater, but also when the next kid will jump.

The rapid is simply a 3-foot ledge that causes ocean water pouring into a tidal stream to form standing waves, an occasional hole, and some very swirly eddies. There is a large eddy on river right just below this ledge, a much smaller intermittent eddy left of center, and a pocket eddy against the river-left cliff. The entire rapid is less than 100 yards long.

Cohasset is ideal for the beginner, because the rapid ends in a huge pond, so recovery is easy. Intermediates find surfing the waves, catching the microeddies in the middle and on river left, and rolling in the turbulent water provide a challenge. And experts may enjoy attaining the drop, squirting in the boils and whirlpools, splatting the barnacle-covered far wall, and doing enders in the wave.

You must time your visit to Cohasset to coincide with the rising tide. You can obtain tide tables on the Internet at http://www.ceob.nos.noaa.gov/tides/nyneBOST.html, or look them up each day in the *Boston Globe* or other area papers. Many bookstores also carry tide tables for the entire year. Plan to arrive about three hours before high tide. By the time you're dressed and in the water (two and a half hours before high tide), the rip is beginning to get interesting and you have some time to warm up before it gets big. From about two hours to just under an hour before the peak, the rip is at its best.

The height of the tide is also an important consideration at Cohasset—higher tides (10 feet and greater) tend to create a larger and more powerful wave and, at times, a hole. The other factor that plays into the mix is the accumulation of barnacles on the ledge. Frequent Cohasset paddlers will tell you that the more barnacles there are, the steeper and larger the wave, and the more it tends to turn into a hole.

To reach the rip from Boston, take I-93 south to Route 3 south. Get off at Exit 14 (Cohasset, Hingham, Rockland, and Nantucket). Turn left at the bottom of the ramp onto 228 north. After 7.0 miles you will cross Route 3A. At 0.12 mile farther, Route 228 will bear left, but you will bear right (Cohasset) onto Main Street. Follow Main Street for 3.0 miles; at the second flashing light, turn left onto Summer Street. At the end of Summer turn right onto Border Street. Follow this for about 0.25 mile until you cross over a narrow stone bridge. Go left just after the bridge into the parking lot. The rip is upstream of the bridge.

Cold River (Mass.)

Dead Man's Curve to Deerfield River

DISTANCE (MILES)	4.25		TOO LOW	
SHUTTLE (MILES)	4.25		LOW	1
AVG. DROP (FEET/MILE)	125		MED.	3
MAX. DROP (FEET/MILE)	135		HIGH	6
DIFFICULTY	IV		TOO HIGH	8
SCENERY	Excellent		GAUGE LOCATION	Mohawk S.F. Bridge
DATE LAST CHECKED	1997		WATER LEVEL INFO.	
RUNOFF PATTERN	n/f			

You're lucky to run the Cold when it's completely free of ice, since most of its season is in the late winter or early spring just as the snow begins melting. It's not unusual for it to run briefly just after a summer rain, but the window of opportunity is very narrow, with the river sometimes staying at a runnable level only for four to six hours. The level is critical any time you run it, since above about 7.0 on the gauge the Cold becomes an awesome class V flush with perhaps one eddy every mile or two, powerful holes, and nonstop whitewater.

The put-in for the Cold is at the auspiciously named Dead Man's Curve on Route 2 about 7.5 miles west of the center of Charlemont. This sharp bend in the road after a steep downhill section is a regular site of truck accidents as panicked drivers lose their brakes, causing their entire rigs to jump the hefty guardrail and tumble down the steep slope below. At one point a few years ago, there were pallets of denim strewn on the slope—a grim reminder of the last cargo that truck carried.

The pull-off is three-quarters of a mile upstream of the only bridge that crosses the Cold on Route 2, where a small, extremely steep creek (Black Brook) enters from the side. For a slightly shorter run and to avoid

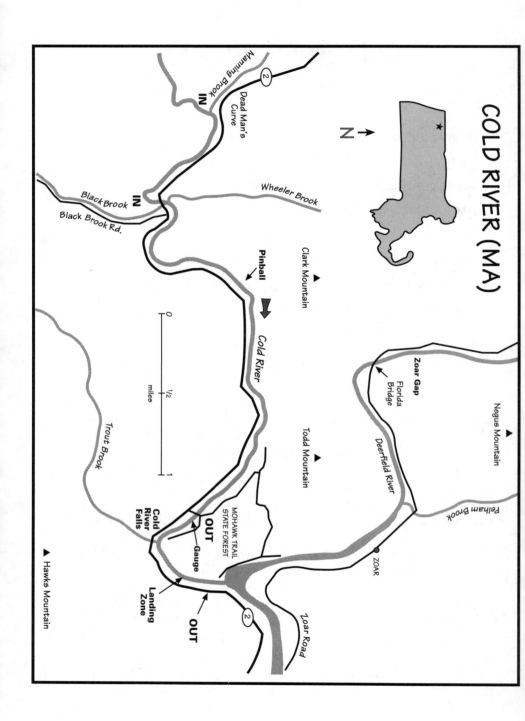

COLD RIVER (MA)

N→

IN

Manning Brook

Dead Man's Curve

Black Brook

Black Brook Rd.

IN

Wheeler Brook

Clark Mountain ▶

Pinball

Cold River

Zoar Gap

Florida Bridge

Negus Mountain ▶

Deerfield River

Pelham Brook

Trout Brook

0

½

miles

1

Todd Mountain ▶

MOHAWK TRAIL STATE FOREST

Cold River Falls

OUT

Gauge

Landing Zone

OUT

ZOAR

Zoar Road

2

▶ Hawks Mountain

the difficult carry to the upper put-in, many parties put in at the bridge itself. From the pull-off at Dead Man's Curve, walk over the guardrail and down a ridge to Manning Brook, which leads to the Cold.

At the start the river is narrow, steep, and very technical, with frequent eddies at medium flows. About a quarter of a mile past the put-in, a steeper drop with a few ledges and a pyramid-shaped rock appears. This one has a large hole at the bottom that can be a keeper. Below here, more of the same continues until Black Brook enters from the right and you approach the Route 2 bridge. Just below the confluence with Black Brook, a very short pool leads to Savoy Shuffle, a hole-ridden drop that slows shortly before passing under the highway.

Below the bridge, the next section contains more technical rapids with large rocks, interesting eddies, and an occasional ledge hole. Soon the river enters a calmer section, and a beach appears on river left at the same time as the rapid ahead appears to be a jumble of boulders and the river drops off steeply. This is Pinball. The left chute here is the most challenging, and a potential bow-pinning hazard exists at the base of this run. Running right at the beginning is more technical (scratchy at medium and low levels) but gets easier toward the end and avoids the pinning spot.

The classic run is to eddy-hop down the left chute until the river below falls over a 3-foot drop and turns sharply right where it rejoins the right channel. Be sure to make the sharp right turn and keep your bow up as you run this one, since pinning here can be serious. It's not a bad idea to station someone on the rock at the base of the chute for safety.

Below Pinball the rapids ease as you approach Mohawk Trail State Forest. Soon you approach a left turn with a large boulder on the inside and a big eddy on river right at the bottom. This is the Ender Hole. It provides good playing at any level, but as the water rises, the enders improve. From the Ender Hole to the state forest bridge is about three-quarters of a mile, with more class III–IV rapids and signs of the now-defunct footbridge and dams that used to span the river before being wiped out by floods.

The state forest bridge is a good takeout spot for paddlers who feel they've had enough. The rapids below the bridge are significantly more difficult than those above, and the whole section below the bridge becomes very continuous above 5.0 on the gauge.

In about a quarter-mile the river turns left and Cold River Falls appears abruptly. Scout and/or portage on river right. This one is runnable down a sluice in the middle or by boofing right in high water. At levels above 5.0 a large hole forms in the center of the river, complicating this drop considerably. Also at these levels, it is very difficult to stop before the falls.

Immediately below the falls, Joe's Rock threatens to pin paddlers who relax before they're in the eddy. For the next 100 feet, very technical water leads to a confluence with a small brook on river right. Below here a short pool lets you collect yourself before Stairway to Heaven.

Stairway is composed of several 3- to 4-foot drops in a short, turbulent 50 yards. These holes get very big above 5.0 on the gauge.

The final drop is Landing Zone, a Z-turn rapid with a fast, technical lead-in on river left that feeds a boulder sieve below. Make the sharp turn to the right, then immediately head back left before you hit the retaining wall. This one's quickly over, one way or the other.

Take out on the right about a quarter-mile before the Cold enters the Deerfield. Beware the poison ivy on the bank. The gauge is on the downstream side of the river-left bridge pillar at the Mohawk Trail State Forest bridge. The shifting riverbed here makes readings somewhat inconsistent: a reading of 3.0 one day does not always correspond to a reading of 3.0 another day after the bottom has shifted in high water. Use this gauge only as a general indicator. Use common sense to evaluate any reading you may have reason to question. There is also a gauge on the far side, but this gauge starts to get wet only at very high water.

In 1995, two paddlers put in on the Cold at somewhere around 9.0 to 11.0 on the gauge. They both swam within the first quarter-mile. One got out; the other drowned by flushing downstream in the turbulent water. His body was recovered 6 miles downstream on the Deerfield. This one gets very serious in high water: Don't underestimate it.

Concord River (Mass.)

Bradford Industries to Merrimack River

DISTANCE (MILES)	1.5		TOO LOW	400 cfs
SHUTTLE (MILES)	1.5		LOW	600 cfs
AVG. DROP (FEET/MILE)	35		MED.	1,000 cfs
MAX. DROP (FEET/MILE)	44		HIGH	1,400 cfs
DIFFICULTY	III–IV		TOO HIGH	2,000 cfs
SCENERY	Poor		GAUGE LOCATION	Olsen Electric
DATE LAST CHECKED	1997		WATER LEVEL INFO.	508-975-0400
RUNOFF PATTERN	n/d/r/l			

This run epitomizes urban paddling and is the closest class III–IV whitewater to Boston. Known as "Thoreau's Portage," history says that Henry David walked around these rapids on his journey to the Merrimack, which is chronicled in his classic *A Week on the Concord and the Merrimack*. But in actual fact, Thoreau bypassed the rapids by paddling the canal that paralleled the river even in his day. Moreover, if, as the city fathers claim, Lowell was the first city to employ hydropower (mechanical at the time), then the Concord may have been the first river dammed to create bypass canals. At any rate, thanks to a cooperative hydropower developer and large marshes upstream, the Concord tends to be runnable throughout the spring and into May. In a wet spring it can stay runnable well into June.

The river is ledgy, with lots of man-made debris and a nasty breached dam at the end. There are three distinct rapids in the mile-and-a-half-long section. The scenery is nothing to write home about, although there are some interesting industrial artifacts along the route, including household appliances, shopping carts, and the occasional discarded tire. There have been a few reported incidents with the locals, including an encounter with

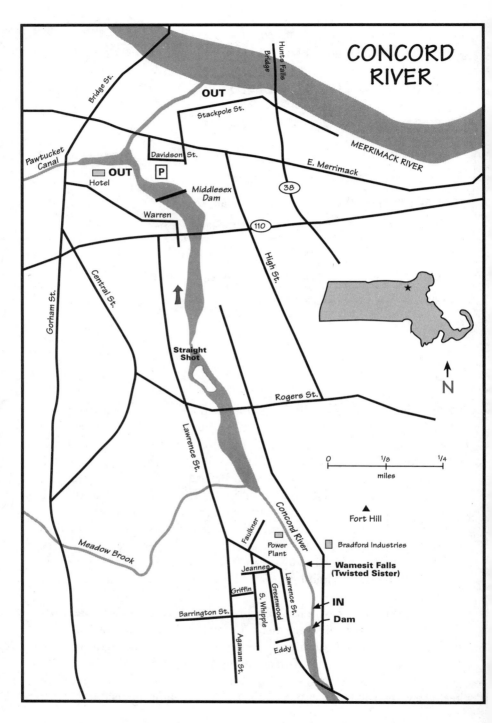

CONCORD RIVER

Bridge

Hunt's Falls

MERRIMACK RIVER

OUT

Stackpole St.

Bridge St.

Davidson St.

P

E. Merrimack

Pawtucket Canal

OUT
Hotel

Middlesex Dam

38

Warren

110

High St.

Central St.

Gorham St.

Straight Shot

Rogers St.

N

0   1/8   1/4
miles

Lawrence St.

Fort Hill

Meadow Brook

Faulkner

Power Plant

Concord River

Bradford Industries

Jeannes

Wamesit Falls
(Twisted Sister)

Griffin

S. Whipple

Greenwood

Lawrence St.

IN

Barrington St.

Dam

Agawam St.

Eddy

268   Massachusetts, Connecticut, and Rhode Island

a gang of rock-throwing teenagers who were repelled by brandishing a paddle, and a near miss from a juice bottle thrown casually off a bridge as boaters were passing beneath. Aside from incidents like these, however, the natives appear to be friendly.

With the rising popularity of whitewater boating in the late 1980s, the Concord was discovered by slalom racers as an interesting urban race site, and by suburban Bostonian paddlers for the opportunity it provides them to get out on weekday nights. Since the run is short and the setting somewhat blighted, it's not likely you'd choose the Concord as a weekend paddling destination, but if you find yourself passing through with a boat, or live around Boston and are sick of the tidal rip at Cohasset, check out the Concord for a little variety.

The rapids generally have well-defined features. A couple of interesting surfing holes and waves form at higher water levels. The run starts just below a low-head dam that is usually littered with various river debris. To get to the put-in, park in the Bradford Industries lot and walk upriver about a quarter-mile to where an access has been cleared by rafters and racers.

Below the put-in eddy, rapids begin immediately as the river is constricted by stone retaining walls on both sides that form a broad sluice with irregular waves and a couple of shoreline eddies on river right. In about a hundred yards the river-right wall disappears and the river broadens into a shallow pool before heading into the heart of Twisted Sister (class III–IV, more classically known as Wamesit Falls).

Below the pool, a cliff on river right causes the river to neck down again and a double ledge forms three holes—one in the center of the rapid and one each on the right and left just below it. There is a clean line on the right, or you can punch the holes with sufficient speed at medium levels. The river-right hole formed by the lower ledge is a fun surf and is easily accessible by a minor attainment from a shoreline eddy just below it.

A short pool leads to a 3-foot ledge jutting out from the left bank that forces the main flow to twist around to river right and then powerfully back left. At the far end of the ledge on river right a large, powerful hole guards the route against attempts to cut across the inside of the bend. This hole has been known to recirculate boaters for minutes, since both the eddy below it and the bend itself feed back into it.

Continuing past the hole, the river is again narrowed by another 3-foot ledge that extends out from the right shore. At the left end of this second ledge, where 99 percent of the water flows at normal levels, a channel-wide hole guards the way. Punch this with speed and you'll sail right through. Boof it from left to right and you'll be in the eddy in a flash. But float unsuspectingly into it, and you'll feel like you've just been to an all-night heavy-metal concert and stood in front of the speaker bank.

Twisted Sister continues with class II water for a couple of hundred yards below this second hole before petering out in a large pool above the Rogers Street bridge.

Just after the bridge, the river splits around an island. This rapid is known as "Straight Shot." The river-left channel is longer and has a small ledge across it about halfway down with an easy play hole. River right is steeper but lacks features. Just as the channels reconverge, the river steepens significantly and drops about 8 feet in a short 30 feet into another large pool. The water falling over this drop makes an excellent ender site even at medium and low levels.

Following this pool, the river passes under the Church Street bridge and turns left before negotiating the final rapid—Middlesex Falls. This is the site of an old timber-crib and stone dam that was breached by high water in the mid-1980s. The dam is runnable (class IV) but should definitely be scouted first, and is dangerous due to the timbers, spikes, and other debris left by the breach and still lodged at the base of it.

In another quarter-mile the Concord enters the Merrimack. There are numerous possible take outs, none of them ideal. On river left just below the Middlesex Dam a steep bank leads to the back of a parking garage at the Sheraton Hotel. To take out above Middlesex Dam, get out at the field on river right just below the Church Street bridge and walk to the municipal parking lot at Davidson Street (less than 100 yards). If you want to continue on to the Merrimack, paddle just downstream of the confluence and take out behind Archie Kenefick Manor at 50 Stackpole Street. Park on Fayette or Brown Street, and don't forget to feed the meter. Information about water levels can be obtained by calling Olsen Electric Monday through Friday 9:00–5:00 at 508-975-0400.

Deerfield River–Monroe Bridge Dryway (Mass.)

Monroe Bridge to Dunbar Brook Picnic Area
Trip D

DISTANCE (MILES)	3	**TOO LOW**	
SHUTTLE (MILES)	3	**LOW**	600 cfs
AVG. DROP (FEET/MILE)	60	**MED.**	1,000 cfs
MAX. DROP (FEET/MILE)	80	**HIGH**	2,000 cfs
DIFFICULTY	III–IV	**TOO HIGH**	5,000 cfs
SCENERY	Good	**GAUGE LOCATION**	#5 Dam
DATE LAST CHECKED	1997	**WATER LEVEL INFO.**	888-356-3663
RUNOFF PATTERN	d/r/l		

The Monroe Bridge Dryway is one of the great relicensing success stories of New England. Dewatered except for occasional spillage until 1991, the Dryway now has a schedule of 32 days each season when it's open for boating. Thanks to an agreement reached between the power company and several environmental and recreational groups, intermediate and advanced boaters in the Northeast no longer have to travel long distances or wait until spring to get a whitewater fix.

The Monroe Bridge Dryway is one of numerous dewatered sections on rivers throughout the country. To produce hydropower where no single large drop exists in a riverbed, a dam is built to divert water away from the natural riverbed into a canal that descends very gradually to a powerhouse some distance downstream (usually at the base of the whitewater section). Moving downstream from the dam, the canal rises higher and higher above the riverbed until it reaches the powerhouse, where the water now has significantly more "head" than it had at the dam. Under normal

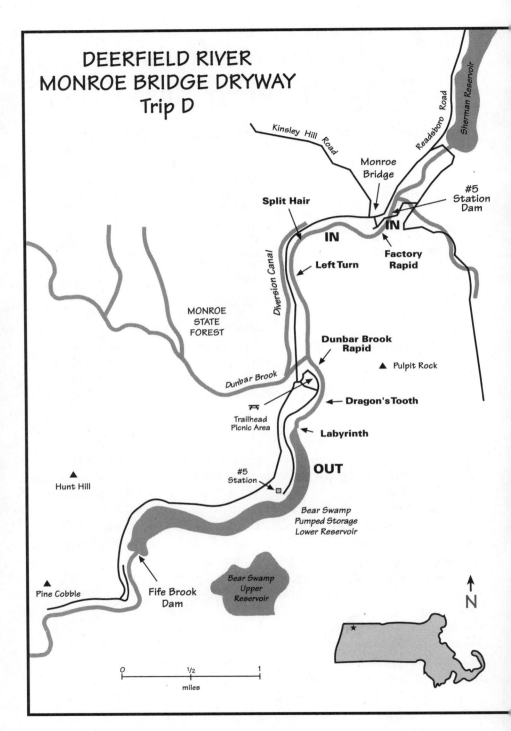

DEERFIELD RIVER
MONROE BRIDGE DRYWAY
Trip D

Kinsley Hill Road

Readsboro Road

Sherman Reservoir

Monroe Bridge

#5 Station Dam

Split Hair

IN

IN

Diversion Canal

Factory Rapid

Left Turn

MONROE STATE FOREST

Dunbar Brook Rapid

▲ Pulpit Rock

Dunbar Brook

Dragon's Tooth

Trailhead Picnic Area

Labyrinth

▲ Hunt Hill

#5 Station

OUT

Bear Swamp Pumped Storage Lower Reservoir

▲ Pine Cobble

Fife Brook Dam

Bear Swamp Upper Reservoir

N

0   1/2   1
miles

operations, every drop of water is run through the canal and into the powerhouse, emerging in the pond at the bottom after having spent its energy turning the turbines to generate electricity. When the water is diverted from the dam back into the riverbed, the hydropower operator loses money, but boaters gain valuable recreation.

Put in for the Dryway at the #5 Station dam in Monroe Bridge or just downstream of the town center, where a rough path leads to a lower access. The scenery at the dam is nothing to write home about, with a large, decaying factory littering the right bank and the dam just under the bridge. Access is down a steep, loose bank. This access is scheduled to be improved soon by the power company and can only become safer and more convenient.

Directly below the small pool is Factory Rapid, a sharp, debris-laden class III+ that runs out into a fast wave train at the bottom. Beware the debris on river right, especially where spikes and sharp metal edges are visible at low water. A quarter-mile of class II follows until the river turns left and a longer class III begins, with a popular surfing wave two-thirds of the way down. Another short pool leads to Split Hair, the first of the more difficult drops. Also known as Governor's Rapid, this one is class IV at most levels and holds several excellent eddies, inspiring surfing waves, and a somewhat nasty pourover on river left at the bottom. The Split Hair rock is the large one in the center halfway down—go left or right, but decide before you hit the rock.

Below the pool after Split Hair is Judy's Hole, an easier rapid with a bouncy play hole on the left halfway down. Judy's leads directly to the next rocky class III which leads into Left Turn, one of the longer, more complex class IVs on the run. The easiest line at Left Turn is on the left where the water is biggest, but there are several possible variations and numerous play waves along the way.

Where the valley widens below Left Turn, a popular lunch spot on a large rock on river right provides a good viewing spot for the bottom half of the rapid. Below this, easy water leads to another interesting class III drop. Soon after, Dunbar Brook enters from the right. The gravel bar here is a popular rest spot. From here down, the rapids generally become tougher and increase in difficulty until Labyrinth.

Dunbar Brook Rapid is narrow and powerful, with a very grabby hole at the top in the center. Play waves and eddies abound, but the length of the rapid makes rolling at the top critical. Shortly below Dunbar, Pine Tree, also known as False Tooth, entertains with several more surfing waves, a few steep holes halfway down, and a challenging slot move on the right. Class II water follows for another hundred yards to the top of Dragon's Tooth, which is intimidating because the water is powerful and a large hole blocks most of the river partway down the rapid. The basic run is from right to left to avoid the hole, then back right again below it. Sounds simple, but the water is zipping along, so you have to make the move with authority and stay upright in the big water. Scout or walk on the left.

There are several excellent play spots below Dragon's Tooth and a short pool before Labyrinth. Labyrinth sometimes is flooded from below by the Bear Swamp reservoir, but when it's all there, it's the longest, most complex, and most interesting rapid on the river.

After a long, fast tongue that pushes onto a submerged snaggletooth, a few small ledge drops lead to the Terminator hole, where the entire river drops into a large, powerful hydraulic over a 4-foot ledge with a nasty boulder sieve below on the left. The right is fairly clear down to the large eddy at the bottom.

At low reservoir levels another rapid appears below Labyrinth. This one has a large boulder in the center and lines on either side of it. Don't paddle below this rapid. The power company is required by their federal license to limit access to the reservoir, since it fluctuates up to 40 feet in a day and has an intake that draws 5,000 cubic feet per second of water up the mountain at a moment's notice.

Access to the takeout is via the Dunbar Brook Picnic Area access road. This road also leads to the power plant, so be careful to observe posted *No Parking* areas to keep the power company's access open. The residents of Monroe have complained of boaters speeding through town, so keep it down. The Dryway is too great a run to lose because of inconsiderate boater behavior.

Water-level information for the Dryway is available through the Deerfield River information phone (888-356-3663). Listen for the spill at the #5 Station dam. There is a hand-painted gauge on the factory abutment just opposite the put-in. While it is not calibrated to release levels, it is thought that 1.7 on the gauge represents roughly 900 cfs. Readings of 2.0 occur at levels around 1,100 cfs, and at 3.0 and higher the river is really ripping! A schedule of the release dates for the coming year can be obtained from a local outfitter.

Deerfield River–Fife Brook Section (Mass.)

Fife Brook Dam to Zoar Gap
Trip E

DISTANCE (MILES)	5		TOO LOW	
SHUTTLE (MILES)	5		LOW	600 cfs
AVG. DROP (FEET/MILE)	25		MED.	1,000 cfs
MAX. DROP (FEET/MILE)			HIGH	1,500 cfs
DIFFICULTY	II–III		TOO HIGH	5,000 cfs
SCENERY	Excellent		GAUGE LOCATION	Fife Brook Dam
DATE LAST CHECKED	1997		WATER LEVEL INFO.	888-356-3663
RUNOFF PATTERN	d/r/l			

From Fife Brook Dam in Florida, Massachusetts, to the Number 4 dam in Buckland, the Deerfield River flows unimpeded for 17.0 miles. The longest stretch without a dam on the main river, this run is also among the most heavily used by whitewater paddlers.

From a boating perspective, the most prominent feature here is Zoar Gap, a class III rapid 5.0 miles downstream from the dam. But there is much more of interest than whitewater alone. The history of this stretch is closely linked to the development of the railroad and hydropower. Environmentally, this section is important for the variety of bird species present, including red-tailed hawks, ospreys, bald eagles, and blue herons; its active beavers; and its potential as a trout fishery.

Put in down a steep embankment at a dead end where Old River Road runs into the river below the Fife Brook Dam 1.0 mile upstream of the Hoosac Tunnel. Finding the turnoff for the put-in can be tricky if you're not watching: After crossing the railroad tracks at the east entrance to the Hoosac Tunnel, pass through a small village with a couple of houses on each

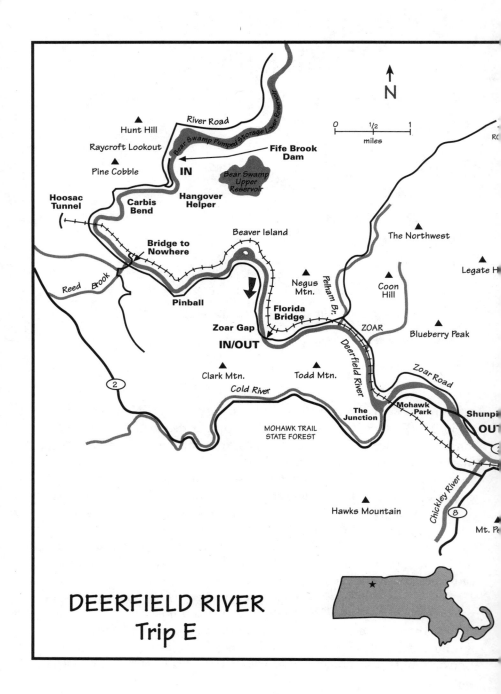

DEERFIELD RIVER
Trip E

side of the road. The road then turns sharply left, with a view of the river on the right. A more gradual right turn is then followed by a long, straight section with a farmhouse on the left. At the end of this straightaway, as the road begins curving left, the Old River Road leads off to the right.

The river begins with some fastwater followed in a couple of hundred yards by the first class II rapid, Hangover Helper. The lead-in contains a few moderate-sized surfing waves. On river left and right, large eddies offer good places to stop and paddle back up into the rapid to surf the waves. This first drop is an excellent teaching site, because the pool below it makes rescue a breeze and eddy lines and waves are well defined.

A mile or so downstream of the put-in, after a sharp left turn, a decaying dam abutment is visible deep in the woods on the left bank. Look carefully at the right bank and you'll notice that what appears to be a natural escarpment is in fact a man-made cut through bedrock, forming a canal that once carried water half a mile downstream to a stone mill building for mechanical hydropower. This power was used to ventilate the Hoosac Tunnel during its construction.

A couple of class II rapids follow the abutment. The second, Freight Train, following the channel left of the island, holds some interesting surfing waves and a swirly eddy-line for squirting at levels around 1,000 cfs. Looking to the right at the base of this rapid, the remains of the mill building are still visible as stone walls, columns, and lintels that have withstood the weather.

Just downstream of the mill building a railroad bridge leads to the eastern entrance of the Hoosac Tunnel. Originally conceived as an aqueduct connecting a nationwide system of canals, the tunnel took so long to plan and gain legislative approval that, by the time it was built, the trend favored railroads over canals. Engineers working on the tunnel pioneered the use of nitroglycerin in such construction applications, and showed their surveying skills by coming within one and a half inches of meeting dead-on as they dug from both ends toward the middle. In twenty years of tunnel construction, 195 men were killed.

At the time of its completion in the 1870s, the Hoosac ranked as the nation's longest tunnel, at more than 25,000 feet in length, and was hailed as an engineering marvel. While it is still in use, rail traffic on it has slowed to a crawl, making it more of a historic landmark than the crucial transportation link it once was from North Adams to Boston. There is talk in the Massachusetts State House of revitalizing the line to give Boston a competitive advantage as an international shipping center.

After the railroad bridge comes a section of shoals as the river widens and flattens out. Choose the deepest channels here, since there are several sections where a boat will easily run aground. As you float through these shoals, you pass under the Bridge to Nowhere, so named because it crosses from Florida into Rowe on what used to be a town road leading northeastward into the center of Rowe. The road is now maintained only as far as the two remaining homes on the Rowe side of the river, but its former path can be traced by walking up and over the mountain as it passes a few abandoned farms.

About a mile past the Bridge to Nowhere, the river turns sharply left and enters a mile-and-a-half-long class II section called Pinball, one of the more interesting rapids on this stretch. With numerous large boulders forming excellent eddies and a few tight slots, several small surfing waves, and plenty of places to rest or recover, this rapid is a great play spot for beginning to intermediate boaters, and it makes a perfect instructional area.

The final rapid in this section ends in a large, deep pool across from a rock outcropping. The small patch of sand on river left is known as Miami Beach because of its proximity to Florida, Massachusetts (which happens to be one of the coldest towns in the state). This is a nice place to stop for lunch or a breather. A few surfing waves appear in the rapid above the beach at most levels.

Continuing past Miami Beach, stay left of the large island, since at most levels the right side is too shallow to get down without scraping. Another class II rapid follows the island around, then back right, and ends in a pool with panoramic views straight ahead of Negus Mountain, named after a colonial British colonel.

Past the pool, the river becomes shoaly again as it prepares for the largest rapid on this section, Zoar Gap. A saddle in the ridge line on river right provides a geologic clue to the origin of the Gap. Downhill from the saddle, a hummock sits just above the river. Formed by an ancient landslide, the hummock is slowly calving off into the river, clogging the Gap with rocks of all sizes and creating the turbulent whitewater that makes it so popular with boaters.

The well-landscaped eastern face of the hummock is a sign of the highway department's frustration with nature. After losing sections of River Road into the Gap nearly every year, the state finally decided to hasten erosion a bit. Cutting the slope back to a lower angle of repose also caused a few more rocks to drop into the river, narrowing it in sections and forming more good eddies on river right.

You can easily be drawn into the Gap unprepared, so stay close to either shore as you run the shallows above it. There is a medium-sized eddy on river left above the Gap and a few small ones on river right. There is also a crude landing area well above the Gap on river right that is the easiest and

Kayaker rolling in the Funnel on the Lower Millers.
Photo By Zoar Outdoor.

safest point to scout from. Many parties scout or portage the Gap, not because of its difficulty per se, but because it is at least a grade harder than anything else on this section. Boaters capable of paddling class II should think twice before attempting the Gap. Zoar Gap can be scouted from either side of the river, but if you choose river left, be aware that the railroad tracks are in use and that you may be trespassing on railroad property.

There are three options for running the main drop. A ledge on river left and a large boulder on river right, both slightly submerged at levels around 1,000 cfs, form the central tongue, which is the main route through the Gap. After entering the tongue, the straightest route is slightly to river right to avoid two wave holes left of center. The sneak route hugs the right shore all the way down but is actually more technical than the main channel (although it is generally drier), making it attractive to open boats. The third option starts in the center of the main tongue and cuts left into the tail of the big left eddy. This leaves you heading straight for O.S. Rock, which you can then quickly sidestep to the right, following the current. This route is tricky because of the eddy currents you must cross, but it is probably the most fluid of the three runs, avoiding the stern-crunching drops of the other two lines. To get a sense of the power of Zoar Gap, catch the eddy on river left just above the three slots and ferry over to the eddy on river right, a class IV move in a class III rapid.

As the river forms a pool at the base of the main rapid, a surfing wave, accessible from eddies on both sides, spans the river. The river-right eddy also provides a good rescue spot or a resting place just below the drop. Following this eddy the river drops again through a maze of boulders where several U.S. team slalom racers have trained in the past and where the 1993 National Slalom Championships were held.

There are many good takeouts below the Gap. A trail leads up the slope on river left about 100 feet upstream of the bridge. Around the bend below the bridge, a trail leads up to the power company picnic area.

You can continue a run below the Gap for as much as 12.0 more miles. Several more class II rapids and some swimming holes are found in this section. There are many takeouts along the way, but be careful to respect private property: below Zoar Gap, river frontage belongs mostly to individuals who appreciate being asked before boaters begin tramping across their fields.

Water-level information for this section can be obtained on the Deerfield River information phone (888-356-3663). Select Fife Brook Dam from the menu options. The next day's release level is available after 5:00 P.M. each day. It takes the water about two hours to reach Zoar Gap from the dam. A schedule of release dates for each season can be obtained by calling Zoar Outdoor (413-339-4010) or Crab Apple Whitewater (413-625-2288).

Paddlers looking for a milder whitewater run can enter the river in Charlemont at the Shunpike rest area just east of the Indian Bridge on Route 2 for several miles of class I–II water. A couple of class I–II rapids follow before you pass under the Route 8A bridge in the center of Charlemont. Stay clear of the bridge abutments. The best route is right down the middle of the river. Two more class I–II rapids are found between this bridge and the takeout, about 6.0 miles downstream, but for the most part, the river is fast flowing and unobstructed.

A good takeout is a small boat launch next to Route 2 on river left as the river enters the dead water above the Number 4 dam. The section ends at the Number 4 dam, next to a bridge on Route 2 just upstream of Shelburne Falls.

Deerfield River– #2 Section (Mass.)

Wilcox Hollow to Stillwater Bridge
Trip F

DISTANCE (MILES)	7		**TOO LOW**	
SHUTTLE (MILES)			**LOW**	400 cfs
AVG. DROP (FEET/MILE)	17		**MED.**	1,000 cfs
MAX. DROP (FEET/MILE)	n/a		**HIGH**	2,500 cfs
DIFFICULTY	I–II		**TOO HIGH**	
SCENERY	Excellent		**GAUGE LOCATION**	#2 Dam
DATE LAST CHECKED	1997		**WATER LEVEL INFO.**	888-356-3663
RUNOFF PATTERN	d/l			

Number 2 is the first dam on the Deerfield counting up from the Connecticut River. Number 1 was planned but never built, and it is highly unlikely it ever will be. The river below Number 2 dam is remote. It runs 6.0 miles through a steep, wooded gorge before opening out into the rich, scenic farmland of Deerfield and joining the Connecticut River a few miles later.

The most inaccessible portion of the trip is from the highest put-in at Gardner Falls Dam to the Bardwell Ferry bridge. The most difficult part involves portaging the Number 2 dam itself. Bardwell Ferry is a popular put-in spot for canoeists and tubers. The bridge itself is something of a historic landmark—one of only a few lenticular spans in the country—and has even appeared in a daytime soap opera. If you put in at the bridge in the summer, you likely will find hundreds of other people with the same idea competing for the few parking spaces. Don't park on the bridge. It can't take the weight, and you wouldn't want to fish your car out of the Deerfield.

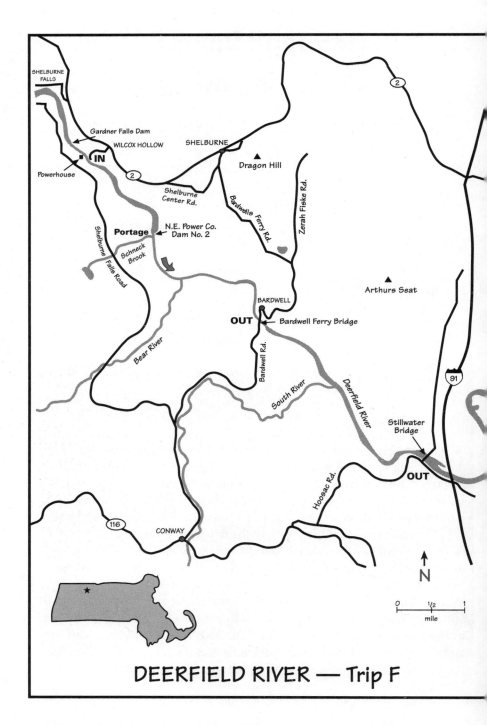

DEERFIELD RIVER — Trip F

If you put in at Gardner Falls, be prepared for the difficult and dangerous portage around the Number 2 dam. Cross the 2.0-mile-long impoundment. Just before you get to the dam, a cascade on the left bank is a nice place to stop for a picnic. Portage from the right bank well above the dam. At high water, when the river is spilling over the dam, getting too close could be fatal. A paved road, accessible only by power company personnel, leads to the power station and the fence around the station. Walk to the right of the fence, and traverse the loose side hill very carefully. Ropes are useful to lower your boats to the river, since the hill is unstable and a fall could lead to serious injury. (At press time, the power company was planning to improve this portage route in the near future.)

Put in again just below the power station. When water is not spilling over the dam, a large eddy on the opposite side of the river can be used to get a group together or to check outfitting.

The first rapid comes at you right away. An interesting class II, it has a few big waves and several microeddies on either side. Several more class II

Endering below the Dumplings on the West River. Photo by Bruce Lessels

rapids keep you occupied for the next 3.0 miles to Bardwell Ferry bridge. You know you're approaching the bridge when you see a stone railroad trestle.

You can take out at Bardwell Ferry or continue downstream to one of several other takeouts. To take out at Bardwell Ferry, find one of the trails on river right just above or below the bridge. Both trails are overgrown with poison ivy, so don't touch the shiny green stuff.

If you choose to continue below Bardwell Ferry, a few more class I–II rapids in the next 3.0 miles and an old abutment from a trolley bridge a short distance below Bardwell Ferry punctuate your trip to Stillwater Bridge. At Stillwater, the river pools up for about a half-mile. This is a popular summer spot for swimmers, sunbathers, and cliff divers.

Stillwater is the end of the whitewater on this section, although you can continue another 5.0 miles or so to the confluence with the Connecticut River. The lower run is primarily quietwater that snakes around the fields surrounding the historic town of Old Deerfield. On a good water release, it makes a beautiful excursion.

Trips below Number 2 dam are dependent on water releases from the dam. The power company releases pretty regularly here, although summer releases are often short. To calculate put-in times, add an hour and a half to the release time if your departure point is Bardwell Ferry bridge. You can, of course, put in at Number 2 station a few minutes after the release starts, although you should go slowly enough to avoid outrunning the bubble.

Water releases that last less than three hours are difficult to ride below Stillwater, since the widening river and the many pools on this section dissipate the release. To paddle below Stillwater, it's best to have a release of four or more hours, and to put in with several hours of water ahead of you so you don't outrun it.

Release information for Number 2 dam is available on the power company's river—information phone 888-356-3663.

Dunbar Brook (Mass.)

South Road to Dunbar Brook Trailhead

DISTANCE (MILES)	3	**TOO LOW**	
SHUTTLE (MILES)	5	**LOW**	
AVG. DROP (FEET/MILE)	223	**MED.**	
MAX. DROP (FEET/MILE)	354	**HIGH**	
DIFFICULTY	IV–V	**TOO HIGH**	
SCENERY	Excellent	**GAUGE LOCATION**	None
DATE LAST CHECKED	1997	**WATER LEVEL INFO.**	
RUNOFF PATTERN	n/f		

Dunbar Brook is one of the narrowest, steepest, most extreme creeks in the Deerfield River's watershed. For it to be runnable, you need lots of rain or snowmelt over a short period of time, and a small, very experienced group of paddlers.

The first descent was done by a party of four, and it took more than four hours to run 3.0 river miles with no major incidents. The river runs through Monroe State Forest and meets roads only at the put-in and take-out, so be prepared for a hike out if you have problems. A trail follows the river through the forest. It is on river left upstream of the footbridge and on river right downstream of the footbridge.

Put in where the river leaves the road between Monroe and Florida, just downstream of the old prison camp. A bridge on a dirt road spans the river here, and a major cascade located just downstream of the bridge gives you a taste of what lies below. The cascade was not run on the first descent. The river below the put-in is class IV–V, with virtually no pools longer than a couple of boat lengths. One-boat eddies are large for this river, and multiboat eddies are a rare treat. About 1.0 mile into the run, a 10-foot slide with several nasty rocks at its base should at least be scouted,

Dunbar Brook 285

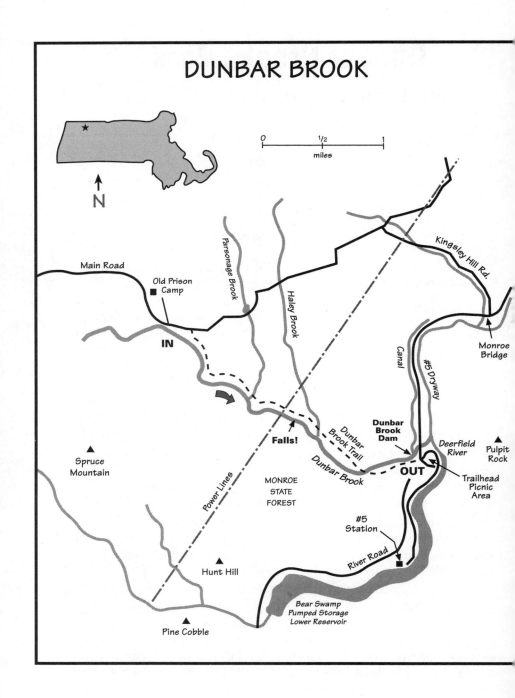

DUNBAR BROOK

O   1/2   1
miles

N

Main Road

Old Prison Camp

Parsonage Brook

Haley Brook

Kingsley Hill Rd.

IN

Canal

#5 Dryway

Monroe Bridge

Dunbar Brook Dam

Falls!

Spruce Mountain

Dunbar Brook Trail

Deerfield River

Pulpit Rock

Dunbar Brook

OUT

Trailhead Picnic Area

Power Lines

MONROE STATE FOREST

#5 Station

Hunt Hill

River Road

Bear Swamp Pumped Storage Lower Reservoir

Pine Cobble

if not carried. Below this drop, a half-mile class III–IV section provides a breather. Beware of downed trees here and on the entire run.

After a side stream adds its volume, things start to get very interesting as the size of the drops increases as well. A power line crosses the river just below here, signaling the approach of the largest drop on the river, which as of this writing has not been run. Getting out before this drop is not trivial, so take the power line as a serious warning. Scouting and portaging this series of falls is difficult from either side, but the left bank is a bit less steep. The lead-in to the drop is an angled slide where the current pushes from right to left over a 6-foot ledge. A tiny recovery eddy is all that separates this from the meat of the drop, where the river channelizes into a class V jumble before falling over a 15-foot ledge onto a rock. The outflow from this is another 6-foot drop with a nasty undercut rock on river right and severe pinning problems on river left. This is class VI boating, which means your paddling career could last longer if you avoid it.

Return to the river in the large pool below the falls and wind your way down among several serious strainers through the next series of drops, which lead to an interesting 4-foot plunge into a clean pool. In a short distance the river passes under a footbridge built by the inmates of the former Monroe Prison Camp. Class IV rapids continue below the bridge until you arrive at the last big drop.

This one features a 30-foot-long lead-in, where the river is only as wide as your boat, followed by an abrupt 5-foot drop that is mostly blocked by a boulder at the bottom. The lead-in is not a problem, but that last step....This one has yet to be run as well.

A few more rapids like those above empty into a small reservoir just above a dam that allows the water from Dunbar Brook to be swallowed up by the #5 diversion canal. Be careful not to get splatted against the trash racks on the dam. On the first descent the reservoir had been drained, and the current continued with few good stopping places right up to and through the trash racks. After taking out on river right, walk a short distance up and over the canal to the parking area at the Dunbar Brook trailhead on River Road. There is no gauge for Dunbar Brook.

Farmington River (Mass.)

Otis Bridge to Route 8
Trip A

DISTANCE (MILES)	2.4		TOO LOW	
SHUTTLE (MILES)	2.4		LOW	4
AVG. DROP (FEET/MILE)	27		MED.	5
MAX. DROP (FEET/MILE)	50		HIGH	
DIFFICULTY	II		TOO HIGH	
SCENERY	Good		GAUGE LOCATION	New Boston
DATE LAST CHECKED	1997		WATER LEVEL INFO.	
RUNOFF PATTERN	d/r/f			

Compared to portions farther downstream, this section of the Farmington is small and fairly slow moving at low levels, with few rocks and often a couple of strainers. Run either as a separate trip or as a warm-up for the more exciting section below, it offers only a minimal challenge to the competent boater, but it is good water for the novice. Route 8 passes alongside the entire length, so an exit anywhere is relatively easy, although most groups take out just before the iron bridge that is the put-in for trip B.

Put in at a bridge that leads to Otis Reservoir from Route 8, or farther upriver toward Otis for a longer trip. At the bridge, the Farmington is 50 to 75 feet wide and smooth flowing. After a couple of left turns, a few rocks appear, with some good-sized ones in the next turn. A nice pool follows. Then come some rocky class II rapids, a brief pause, then more rapids, then calmer water. The river next loops to the right around a picnic area and a camp on the right bank. Water here is class I–II. Downstream, after the river approaches Route 8 and turns left, lie more rapids. The rocks start sparsely but multiply; several large ones are located at the bottom on either side. There's a small drop and a hydraulic in the center.

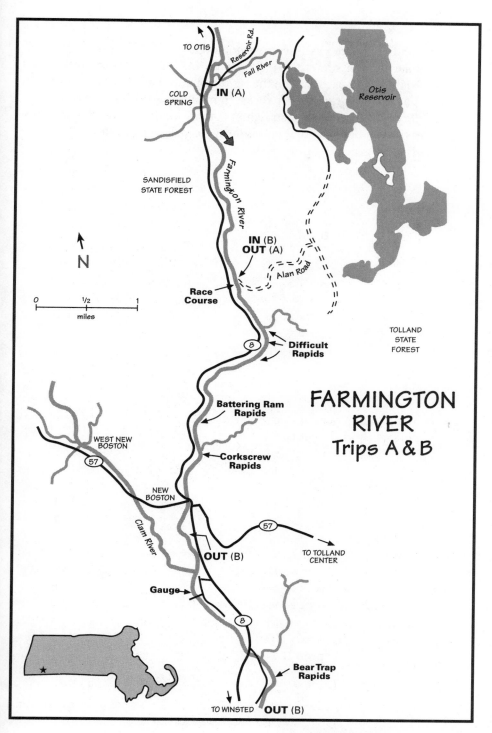

TO OTIS

Reservoir Rd.

Fall River

COLD SPRING

IN (A)

Otis Reservoir

N

SANDISFIELD STATE FOREST

Farmington River

0   1/2   1
miles

IN (B)
OUT (A)

Alan Road

Race Course

8

Difficult Rapids

TOLLAND STATE FOREST

Battering Ram Rapids

FARMINGTON RIVER
Trips A & B

Corkscrew Rapids

WEST NEW BOSTON

57

NEW BOSTON

Clam River

OUT (B)

57

TO TOLLAND CENTER

Gauge

8

Bear Trap Rapids

TO WINSTED   OUT (B)

The gradient is steep but the run is not too difficult. After a short breather, a similar though somewhat more strung-out rapid appears. At the end some large rocks extend from the right bank, so stay left where there is an avenue through several more rocks. In medium water all of these will be mostly covered, allowing a straighter course. Along the way the left bank is heavily wooded, and the right is fairly steep, leading to Route 8.

For the gauge location, see the next trip.

Farmington River (Mass.)

Route 8 to New Boston
Trip B

DISTANCE (MILES)	3		**TOO LOW**	3.6
SHUTTLE (MILES)	3		**LOW**	4
AVG. DROP (FEET/MILE)	75		**MED.**	4.5
MAX. DROP (FEET/MILE)	100		**HIGH**	
DIFFICULTY	III–IV		**TOO HIGH**	
SCENERY	Fair		**GAUGE LOCATION**	New Boston
DATE LAST CHECKED	1997		**WATER LEVEL INFO.**	
RUNOFF PATTERN	d/r/f			

The Farmington River above New Boston is a fine class III–IV run, provided there is enough water. The minimum level is critical. Three hundred cfs is adequate for a relatively fluid run, although the river is still passable at 250 cfs (with much bottom scraping and cursing). In general, lower levels require more maneuvering, and certain passages even become dry or unrunnable. Except for the spring runoff, the river is usually too low for canoeing, although the fall (October, most of the time) water releases from Otis Reservoir via Fall River raise the level sufficiently for a trip. The river is very fast flowing, with essentially no flatwater and many rocks of all shapes and sizes. Due to the narrowness of the riverbed, strainers are a common hazard. In several locations there is only one canoeable channel, so the party should stay well spaced to avoid a chain-reaction pileup in case of trouble. Route 8 follows the river, and most of the rapids can be scouted from the road.

A good meeting spot for this trip is near an iron bridge just off Route 8, 5.2 miles south of Otis. After putting in on the upstream side of this bridge, the paddler passes immediately into the area where an annual slalom race takes place. The river then bears right, passes a picnic area

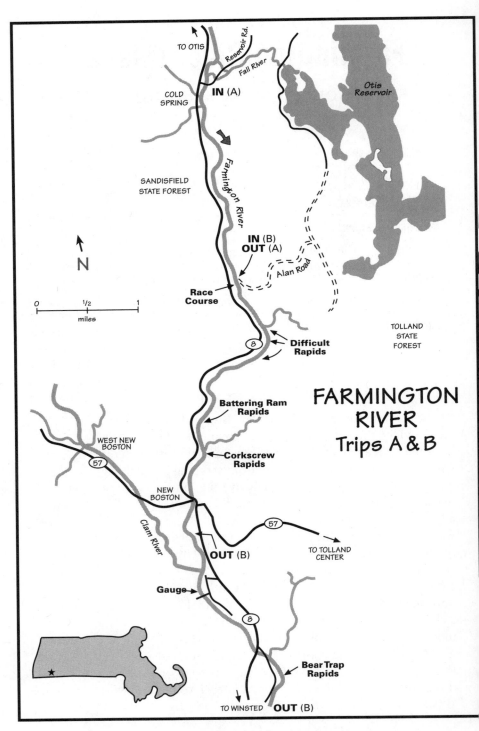

FARMINGTON RIVER
Trips A & B

TO OTIS

Reservoir Rd.

Fall River

Otis Reservoir

COLD SPRING

IN (A)

Farmington River

SANDISFIELD STATE FOREST

N

0   ½   1
miles

IN (B)
OUT (A)

Alan Road

Race Course

TOLLAND STATE FOREST

8

Difficult Rapids

Battering Ram Rapids

Corkscrew Rapids

WEST NEW BOSTON

57

NEW BOSTON

57

TO TOLLAND CENTER

Clam River

OUT (B)

Gauge

8

Bear Trap Rapids

TO WINSTED   OUT (B)

on the right shore, and then turns left again. A hundred yards or so downstream is an abrupt drop of 2 feet, best run on the right or left, with the center reserved for high water only.

The outflow is straight and the eddies are plentiful. This is the first in a series of closely spaced rapids in the upper section of this run. The Farmington continues to flow swiftly among rocks that clutch and grab at the canoe. Just before and on into the next right turn are some rapids best run on the extreme right, especially in low water. More adventurous boaters could start out on the extreme left and pass diagonally to the right halfway down, in front of several large rocks.

The next rapid appears after a downstream passage of several hundred yards, amid partly covered rocks and back-curlers. A center cluster of large rocks guards a drop over a ledge that is best run on the right. There are eddies below this rapid, then the river races toward the next drop—Decoration Rock Rapid—100 yards downstream.

Decoration Rock Rapid is very intricate in low water, requiring you to execute several sharp turns in quick succession. Look this one over briefly beforehand if it isn't familiar. The extreme right is the best passage at most levels, since there is less chance of pinning there than in the center or left. At a gauge reading of 4.5, Decoration Rock supports a large upstream pillow and either left or right is fairly straightforward.

The next right turn holds another drop over a ledge, best run to the extreme left of center. Several hundred yards below, where a group of rocks stands on the left side, is one of the best playing holes on the trip. A slanting 2- to 3-foot drop into a hydraulic is easy to punch through, but try coming back and sitting in it sideways. From this spot onward, the river's rapid flow over and around rocks creates standing waves and hydraulics. The general pace will be class III or a little harder. The gradient is not so steep as that of the first half-mile, but the afternoon sun will shine directly into your eyes.

Downstream, the river turns right, runs past a road turnoff on the right shore, approaches Route 8, and then turns left again. Shortly after this left turn, the channel narrows and there is an abrupt drop over a 2- to-3-foot ledge. The current runs diagonally, right to left. This is Battering Ram Rapid; your best approach is right center. This rapid got its name from an old tree trunk that formerly protruded into the paddlers' path. Several people tried to move the tree while running the drop. One might say that they "got out on a limb."

After Battering Ram Rapid, the river angles away from the road, turns right again, sweeps through another rock garden, then divides around a small island. Past the island on the left are the remains of an old concrete bridge and a stone wall. Below these landmarks of times past, the river turns right and drops over two sharp ledges. After another left turn, the approach to the last big rapid—Corkscrew—begins.

If the water conditions allow it, a center approach to Corkscrew is best because it provides the option of moving either left or right at the end. The serpentine route ends in a 2- to 3-foot drop, angling right to left, with an outrun that is a bit more complicated than it first appears: several angled hydraulics can catch an unwary paddler who thinks the worst is over. At a gauge of 4.5, Corkscrew becomes harder than at lower levels. The left side opens up as a viable route, but there are some gaping holes just waiting to swallow nice, shiny new boats. Look it over first to decide if you want to run it. The center route at 4.5 is considered the toughest path. If you botch the job and flip, there is usually a full complement of people sitting on the bank to applaud your lack of finesse. At a gauge reading of 4.5, Corkscrew is a short but intense class IV. You can scout both this drop and Battering Ram Rapid from the road. For paddlers who have survived this far, the last half-mile to New Boston should cause no great concern, although there are still plenty of rocks.

The takeout at the bridge in New Boston has become something of a problem, due to local residents and traffic congestion, especially during October when annual water releases bring hordes of boaters out for a good time. A better takeout is at the American Legion field several hundred yards downstream of the bridge on river left. In either case, show consideration to the locals and respect their wishes and their property. Arguments ultimately end in a no-win situation.

Even though this trip supposedly finishes in the town called New Boston, a post office at the takeout displays a sign that reads Sandisfield, Massachusetts. The local hostelry, on the other hand, is called the New Boston Inn. If you can figure this one out, let us know.

At 300 cfs, this trip is somewhat scratchy and annoying. Channels are narrow, and many rocks acquire new color as boats bounce over them. At 600 cfs (gauge of 4.5), the whole run is considerably more fluid, though many rocks still show and are therefore the targets of abuse. Should you make a mistake, remember that the Farmington is somewhat unforgiving: a paddlerless boat probably will broach on one of the many rocks. Consider yourself warned.

The gauge is in Berkshire County, on the river-left abutment of a bridge, 0.3 mile downstream from Clam River and 1.0 mile south of New Boston. To reach this spot, go south on Route 8 and turn right onto an old paved road. A half-mile ride takes you to the bridge. This gauge is part of the Telemark system, so the Corps of Engineers can phone to determine the water level.

There is also an interesting class II–III section below the takeout, known as the Bear's Den. It is often run as part of trip A, with a shuttle around the class III–IV section. There is one class III rapid at the takeout; the rest is class II paddling.

For another river of similar difficulty in the same general vicinity, try the Sandy in Connecticut.

Farmington River–
Tariffville Gorge (Conn.)

Route 189 to Route 187
Trip C

DISTANCE (MILES)	1.5	TOO LOW	n/a
SHUTTLE (MILES)	2	LOW	1.9
AVG. DROP (FEET/MILE)	15	MED.	3.2
MAX. DROP (FEET/MILE)	40	HIGH	n/a
DIFFICULTY	II–III	TOO HIGH	n/a
SCENERY	Fair	GAUGE LOCATION	Tariffville
DATE LAST CHECKED	1997	WATER LEVEL INFO.	http://www.nws. -
RUNOFF PATTERN	d/l		noaa.gov/er/nerfc/products/BOSWRKF1A.txt

Every club runs a section of river ominously known as "the gorge," and the Tariffville Gorge is probably the best known in the western Massachusetts–Connecticut area. This section of 1.5 miles is easy to do several times in one day, and it presents several opportunities for playing in the rapids. In low water it is a good place to train beginners. A slalom has been held here in the spring. Low water levels show the most rocks, whereas medium levels generally have haystacks and a fast current.

A put-in is possible near the Route 189 bridge. For another put-in, follow the main road through Tariffville to a Dead End sign, bear left, and continue onto a dirt road that eventually leads to a small park with tennis courts and a picnic area, and then to the river itself. At either spot, the river is very quiet and slow flowing. Slightly downstream from the upper starting point are the remaining pillars of an old railroad bridge, and beyond, as the river turns left, is a 6-inch drop that extends across the river at low water. The Route 189 bridge then crosses the river. About 0.25 mile

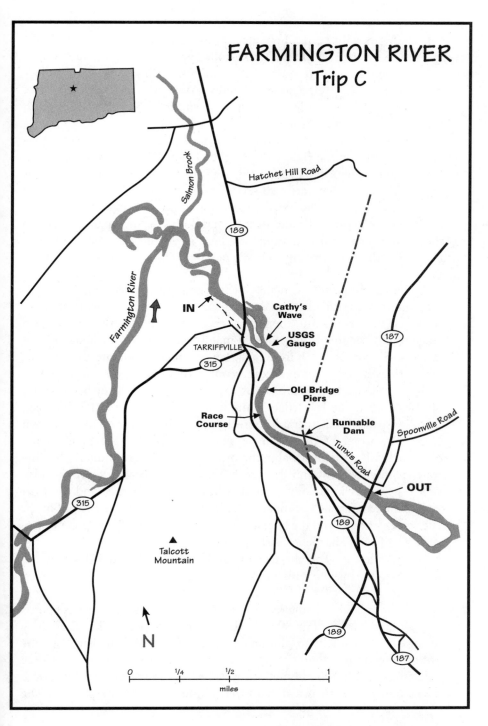

FARMINGTON RIVER
Trip C

Salmon Brook

Hatchet Hill Road

189

Farmington River

IN

Cathy's Wave

USGS Gauge

TARRIFFVILLE

315

187

Old Bridge Piers

Race Course

Runnable Dam

Spoonville Road

Turxis Road

OUT

315

189

Talcott Mountain

N

189

187

| 0 | 1/4 | 1/2 | 1 |

miles

below, after a right turn, the boater can see a concrete wall on the right and the nearly vertical walls of the so-called gorge forming in the distance. Next to the wall in high water, a silky-smooth surfing wave forms at levels over about 4.5 feet. Known as Cathy's Wave, this is one of the most consistent, yet challenging surfing spots in southern New England at high water.

Just inside the entrance to this canyon section, you can read a government gauge on the right bank. Slightly below the gauge is a right turn with a small ledge. Shortly after this right turn, the first extended rapids appear, in which there are two sets of four concrete blocks each, in the right center and left. The blocks are the remains of a bridge that connected Tunxis Road on both sides of the river. Both sets line up at an angle to the current. The most exciting ride here is on the extreme right side, although other passages are certainly possible. There is a small pool below on the right.

The Farmington next makes a left turn as the current quickens. The area surrounding this turn is the scene of the slalom. Immediately after the river straightens out, there is a rapid consisting of two sets of two ledges each. The first ledges, located mainly on the right, are about 15 feet apart and drop about 1 foot each. Several rocks populate the middle. When they are covered, in medium water, they can create wicked holes. Ledges in the next series are about 15 to 20 feet apart. They begin about 20 yards below the last ledge in the first set. Each drop is 1.5 to 2 feet. Standing waves and hydraulics greet the paddler before and after each ledge. The worst of these can be avoided by pursuing a path on the extreme left. In medium water, the drops are not so pronounced, but the water is more violent and the current is fast. This is a very popular play spot. The upper hole, known as the Clingon, is the biggest and can provide a challenging surf at most levels. The lower holes, the Pencil Sharpener on river right and the hole just next to it on river left, are polar opposites. The Pencil Sharpener is steep and nasty at most any level, while the hole on its left is generally friendly and washes out into a pool. As the water level increases, the hydraulics in this entire section can become very large and sticky.

A few seconds' paddle reaches the next rapid. The entrance is guarded right and left by a line of rocks that extend centerward, but they show up only in low water, so plot an initial center route. You then have the option of running center or right or cutting left. Rocks in the middle force a decision, and he who hesitates is wet. The left course is probably a little easier but has an S-turn outrun that requires several sharp turns. The right-side or center path ends in an abrupt drop over a ledge. In medium water, these rapids are replaced by a series of small ledges and standing waves, with the main current angling to the right. The only exposed rocks are a group in the left center at the end. These rapids are worth scouting.

Below looms a broken dam and the decision of whether to run or not to run. The dam is concrete and extends from the right bank. There is a 25-foot gap on the left side through which the entire river pours. It is easy to run in low water, if you don't mind banging your stern. Submerged obstacles of an unknown variety have been found at the bottom of the drop. Below the dam, the outflow pours into an undercut car-sized rock that supports a large pillow when the water is high.

At medium levels, the turbulence below the dam flows up and over the undercut car-rock, and an ugly hydraulic extends diagonally downstream from the right side of the break in the dam. Also, the drop itself is less abrupt at higher water levels. A large pool sits below the dam, and there is an outlet on the left side where there is a fast current and a sharp right into a narrow channel. This channel is a way around two islands, and the current can be strong, as can the eddies and crosscurrents. Once past this section, you will see the Route 187 bridge.

You can reach Tunxis Road by turning off Route 187 onto Spoonville Road, which is just north of the Route 187 bridge crossing. Tunxis Road runs alongside the river on its left side, but only from the racecourse down. It is not visible from the river.

If you want the gauge reading before put-in, the gauge is on the right bank 0.3 mile downstream from Route 189, behind a house at Tunxis Road (west side of the river). It is best reached by driving into the parking lot for Cathy's Needlepoint factory.

Green River (Vt.–Mass.)

Green River to West Leyden
Trip A

DISTANCE (MILES)	6.5		TOO LOW	
SHUTTLE (MILES)	6.2		LOW	
AVG. DROP (FEET/MILE)	30		MED.	
MAX. DROP (FEET/MILE)	50		HIGH	
DIFFICULTY	II–III		TOO HIGH	
SCENERY	Excellent		GAUGE LOCATION	None
DATE LAST CHECKED	1997		WATER LEVEL INFO.	
RUNOFF PATTERN	n/f			

The Green River is known more for its rustic scenery than for its challenging rapids. Snaking its way through the Vermont woodlands, the Green River valley typifies the New England outback. It's a wintry fairyland after a freshly fallen snow, with the white-covered limbs bending down to touch the water as it dances between snowcapped rocks. Springtime radiates all the wonder of rebirth in this narrow valley. If the weather is clear, an unchallenged serenity prevails and you see, smell, and hear the woods reviving after a long sleep. The rapids themselves are a mixture of standing waves with an occasional rock garden. They are pleasant but not difficult.

At Green River, Vermont, the river is barely 25 feet wide; a trip may be launched just below the dam and covered bridge there. A trip also may be started several miles upstream where the river is still narrower, with a great deal of fallen trees and brush. Although it is broken in at least one spot, a 4-foot dam about 0.5 mile north of the covered bridge must be carried. A dirt road (class II+ if it's wet) runs alongside the river for its entire length, crossing at Green River, Vermont, via a covered bridge. (There is a fine of $2 if you drive across the bridge at more than a hiker's pace.) The

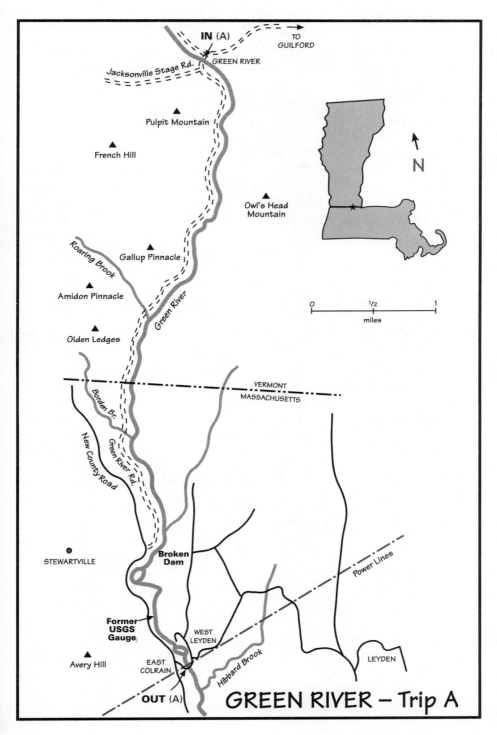

IN (A)

TO GUILFORD

GREEN RIVER

Jacksonville Stage Rd.

Pulpit Mountain

French Hill

Owl's Head Mountain

Roaring Brook

Gallup Pinnacle

Green River

Amidon Pinnacle

Olden Ledges

N

0   ½   1
miles

VERMONT
MASSACHUSETTS

Borden Br.

Green River Rd.

New County Road

STEWARTVILLE

Power Lines

Broken Dam

Former USGS Gauge

WEST LEYDEN

LEYDEN

Avery Hill

EAST COLRAIN

Hibbard Brook

OUT (A)

GREEN RIVER – Trip A

scattering of rocks and steady current at the put-in are typical of this small stream. The rapids should not challenge a competent canoeist. Water level is critical, and it is usually too low for an enjoyable trip. Only the spring runoff and very heavy rains raise the level sufficiently to offer good sport.

A third of a mile below the covered bridge, just prior to a right turn, is a small island dividing the river; then the river bends left. A hundred yards below, some snappy rapids appear; they should be easy to run. The river then loops away from the road. When it comes back, the Green narrows to between 5 and 10 feet, so a tree could easily block the passage. Downstream near a footbridge the riverbed deepens and widens a bit. This entire section is dangerous because of fallen trees. One hundred to 200 yards below the footbridge come some rapids in a slight left turn. Most turns here do have rapids. Roaring Brook enters from the right. Downstream there is a short drop over a rock dam that is easy to run. Another small stream enters from the right; the river then turns left with a chute. The best route is on the right or in the center; an eddy awaits on the right below.

To this point rocks have been mostly breadbasket sized. You should soon spot a slightly larger rock in midstream. Past this rock and the next left turn, a wall of small rocks seems to block the river's passage. This wall is the first of three sets of rapids in close succession. In low or medium water, the best path for the first is on the extreme left, moving diagonally right, down a 1- to 2-foot drop (some 2.5 miles from the covered bridge). This drop may be complicated by more rocks in the path, depending on water level. In medium or high water, other passages will open on the right. Five yards below is another 1- to 2-foot drop over a ledge, best taken either in the right center or on the extreme left if you spot this route quickly enough. Rocks in the center divide these channels. Immediately below, the river narrows and turns right and then quickly left, with standing waves in each turn. This three-rapid stretch is the most technically difficult one of the run. Whether to scout depends on the group's strength. These rapids are no more than class III, class II in low water.

The dam at Stewartville is broken and now forms a class III rapid with some debris from the former timber-crib structure still in the river. You will know you are approaching it when you see a sharp left turn with a ledge and a steep bank on the outside of it. The rapid is just downstream, so pull out river left or right above the turn to scout. From the road, the Stewartville dam is at a fork where Green River Road follows the river and becomes dirt again after being paved for a couple of miles. The paved road continues up a hill to the northwest. Below the dam, a long rapid flows (class II in low water, III in high) by a lumber mill on the right bank. From here to West Leyden, the Green shows mostly class II water and the river leaves the road for approximately 1.0 mile. Just before the takeout at the bridge in West Leyden, there's a small rock dam you'll pass over easily.

Green River, Vermont, may be reached by following Route 5 to Guilford. Turn west at the center of town and follow the main road until it forks. Take the right road (now dirt) and continue to the covered bridge at Green River. Just before it enters the noise and bustle of this large cosmopolitan town, the road forks again. The right fork leads upriver.

A USGS gauge is located in Colrain, Massachusetts, 0.5 mile upstream of the West Leyden bridge on the right bank. It is unreadable from the river since the staff has rotted away, and readings are not available on the USGS web page. On the hope that it will be resurrected in the near future, its location is described here. Look for the gauging-station hut beside the road (about 10 feet tall and 4 feet square). Then go downhill on foot to the river. The staff gauge used to be about 20 yards upstream.

Green River (Mass.)

West Leyden to Eunice Williams Road
Trip B

DISTANCE (MILES)	5	TOO LOW	
SHUTTLE (MILES)	5	LOW	
AVG. DROP (FEET/MILE)	31	MED.	
MAX. DROP (FEET/MILE)	40	HIGH	
DIFFICULTY	II	TOO HIGH	
SCENERY	Good	GAUGE LOCATION	None
DATE LAST CHECKED	1997	WATER LEVEL INFO.	
RUNOFF PATTERN	n/f		

The trip from West Leyden to the covered bridge by the Greenfield water-control dam is similar to the trip on the upper Green; however, the lower section is neither so difficult nor so pretty. There are no special difficulties, and no rapids need to be scouted. If the water is up, the run is continuous in that there's little slack water. In low water, the canoeing will be boring to those looking for challenging sport. In all, this is a good trip for open boats. The water-control dam is just upstream from the covered bridge on Eunice Williams Road off Leyden Road north of Greenfield, and can be recognized by the pool above it. The dam is about 9 feet high and runnable at certain water levels, although most boaters will choose to take out above it.

The gauge for this section and for the upper section of the Green is no longer readable.

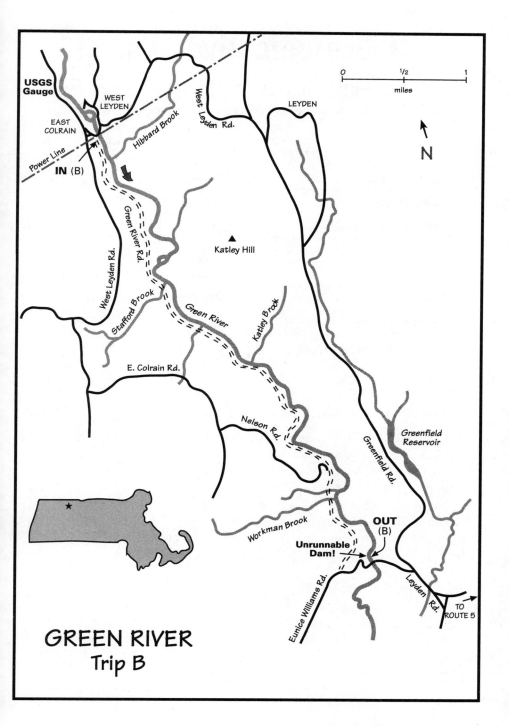

USGS
Gauge

WEST
LEYDEN

EAST
COLRAIN

Power Line

IN (B)

West Leyden Rd.

Hibbard Brook

LEYDEN

West Leyden Rd.

Green River Rd.

Katley Hill

Stafford Brook

Green River

Katley Brook

E. Colrain Rd.

Nelson Rd.

Greenfield
Reservoir

Greenfield Rd.

Workman Brook

OUT
(B)

Unrunnable
Dam!

Eunice Williams Rd.

Leyden Rd.

TO
ROUTE 5

0   1/2   1
miles

N

GREEN RIVER
Trip B

Housatonic River (Conn.)

Falls Village to Housatonic Meadows State Forest

Trip A

DISTANCE (MILES)	11	TOO LOW	n/a
SHUTTLE (MILES)	13	LOW	500 cfs
AVG. DROP (FEET/MILE)	12	MED.	1,500 cfs
MAX. DROP (FEET/MILE)	n/a	HIGH	2,000 cfs
DIFFICULTY	I–II	TOO HIGH	3,500 cfs
SCENERY	Good	GAUGE LOCATION	Falls Village Hydro
DATE LAST CHECKED	1997	WATER LEVEL INFO.	860-824-7861
RUNOFF PATTERN	n/d/l		

Tucked away in the northwest corner of Connecticut, the Housatonic is set in the quaint hill towns that are built on the eastern slopes of the Taconics. The Appalachian Trail crosses the river at the put-in to this upper section, and two outfitters rent canoes for this run. The river comes out of Massachusetts, where its source is in the central Berkshires around Great Barrington. Its watershed is fairly large. Two hydroelectric dams store a small amount of water that is released when the demand for power is greatest (usually midday), making the Housatonic runnable most of the year.

The river below Falls Village is mostly flat, with a few rapids, interesting scenery, a genuine New England covered bridge, and convenient put-ins and takeouts. In all it is about 11.0 miles from the Falls Village hydro station to Housatonic Meadows State Park. The river is paralleled by Route 7 for most of the run, so it is possible to shorten the trip by taking out at one of several intermediate areas.

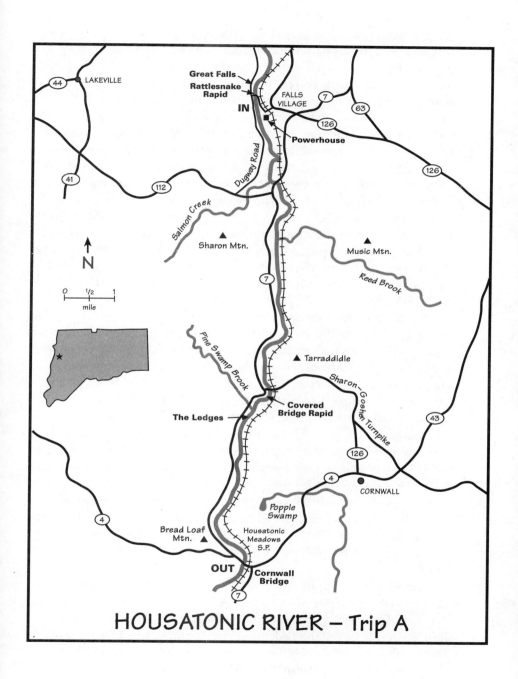

HOUSATONIC RIVER – Trip A

Launch at the small park across from the Falls Village hydro station. Just upstream of this park is Rattlesnake Rapid, a quarter-mile, challenging class IV run with an 8-foot drop at the bottom and lots of beefy holes and interesting surfing waves. The Snake, as it is known by locals, runs only when there is too much water for the hydro station to put through the generators and it spills over the dam above.

At the put-in the river is swift and shallow. Immediately downstream of the dam is a sweeping left turn with an easy class II rapid where slalom racers often train. There are usually practice gates suspended from wires above this rapid. Start in the center of the river and move gradually left as the river approaches the road. The cleanest line from here down is to stay on the unobstructed left half of the river, avoiding the large rocks directly in midstream and the smaller but more insidious ones on the right side.

A large recovery pool follows this rapid, which lasts a total of about 200 yards. Below, the river is swift but unobstructed as it meanders through fields and forests for about 4.5 miles until a few easy class II drops in the next mile lead to the covered bridge in West Cornwall.

Covered Bridge Rapid is a solid class II+ and fairly long. There is an access point about 150 yards upstream of the bridge for those who are unsure whether to walk or paddle and for canoeists who choose to tour downtown West Cornwall—a low-key New England tourist town with a couple of excellent lunch options and a few art and knickknack shops.

Covered Bridge Rapid starts with a shallow riffle as the riverbed steepens and picks up speed. The line here is just right of center as you pass under the bridge, where a couple of eddies on river left offer convenient stopping points. After the bridge the right side holds a few rocks and small holes, as well as several small but catchable eddies. The clearest path follows the middle of the river to the bottom of the rapid, where a large recovery pool awaits. In all, Covered Bridge is about 0.25 mile long.

The portage trail emerges on river left in the recovery pool. Don't try getting out on river right at the bottom of Covered Bridge—the landowner is understandably unhappy when uninvited boaters traipse across his property.

About half a mile after Covered Bridge are the Ledges—a short, easy class II—where the river drops a few feet over a couple of smooth ledges. Left and right are both clear; center holds some shallow surprises. A few hundred yards below the Ledges on river right, Clarke Outdoors maintains a takeout. Check with them before using this access.

Continuing downstream from the Ledges, easy class I–II riffles alternate with fastwater stretches for about 3.0 miles until the river turns left, leaving Route 7, which has been following on the right shore. When the river bends back to the right again, a stone boat ramp appears on the right bank; this is the takeout. A longer trip can be made by continuing downstream and taking out either at Swift's Bridge or as far down as Kent (about 25.0 miles total if you take out above the dam at Bulls Bridge).

Release information for the next twenty-four hours can be obtained by calling Northeast Utilities' river-information number at 860-824-7861. This number reaches a recorded message that tells you when and how much the station plans to release. The information is usually given in terms of the number of generators they'll be running and the total cfs the station will be putting out. Each generator can handle between 400 and 600 cfs. Water-release information is updated only during the spring, summer, and fall.

Housatonic River–Bulls Bridge Section (Conn.)

Bulls Bridge to Route 7
Trip B

DISTANCE (MILES)	2.5		**TOO LOW**	
SHUTTLE (MILES)	2.5		**LOW**	1
AVG. DROP (FEET/MILE)	45		**MED.**	3
MAX. DROP (FEET/MILE)	100		**HIGH**	6/7
DIFFICULTY	IV (V)		**TOO HIGH**	
SCENERY	Good		**GAUGE LOCATION**	Bulls Bridge
DATE LAST CHECKED	1997			Gaylordsville
RUNOFF PATTERN	n/d/l		**WATER LEVEL INFO.**	Waterline

Bulls Bridge is a local test piece for advanced paddlers. The drops below the covered bridge—the Flume, S-Turn, and Pencil Sharpener—are class IV, while those upstream of the bridge—Stairway to Hell and Threshhold—are solid class V. For the ultra-insane, Dead Horse Falls, on a side channel, is a dangerous class VI with only a few runs logged to date (one paddler broke several bones). The ledgy riverbed causes powerful holes to form at most water levels, and several of the drops are large, with Threshhold leading the group at 30 feet plus, followed by Stairway to Hell at about 20 feet overall; the Flume falls 7 feet in a single plunge.

The scenery is nothing to sneeze at either. Small cliffs appear from time to time next to the river, and the run takes you through the closest thing Connecticut has to wilderness, with pine forests, low rolling hills, and, of course, a covered bridge at the put-in.

Strong intermediate paddlers should be able to handle everything from the covered bridge down at gauge readings of 5 feet and under on

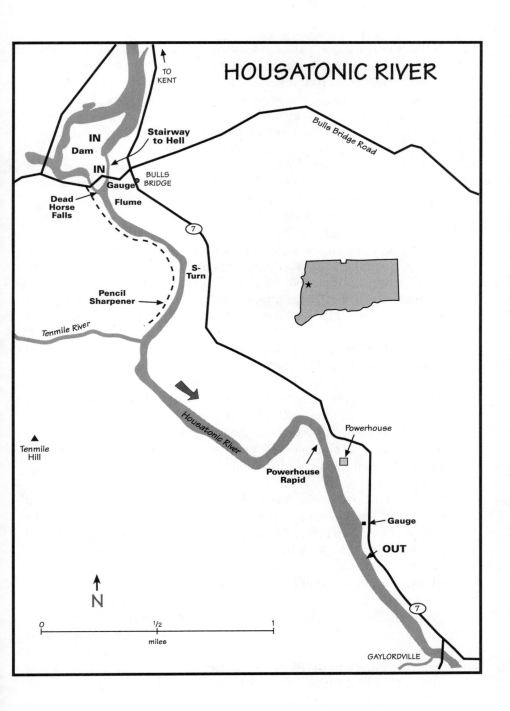

HOUSATONIC RIVER

TO KENT

Bulls Bridge Road

IN
Dam

Stairway
to Hell

IN

Gauge

BULLS
BRIDGE

Dead
Horse
Falls

Flume

7

S-
Turn

Pencil
Sharpener

Tenmile River

Housatonic River

Tenmile
Hill

Powerhouse

Powerhouse
Rapid

Gauge

OUT

7

N

0   1/2   1
miles

GAYLORDVILLE

the Bulls Bridge gauge, although some may choose to walk the Flume due to the high intimidation factor. Above 6 feet the Flume, S-Turn, and Pencil Sharpener verge on class V, as the holes become much beefier. At these levels the entire run is for experts only. Everything above the covered bridge is for experts only at any level.

Threshhold and Stairway to Hell are very serious drops that harshly punish errors in judgment. Threshhold is a 30+-foot, sigmoid-shaped dam. The landing is soft as long as you're still upright at the bottom. Don't even consider going upside down. Stairway to Hell is a complex double drop. The upper drop can be approached from the right or left channel, but either way you must immediately move right as you crest the 7-foot ledge to avoid Mushroom Rock, which lurks 20 feet below and is undercut. If you've caught the eddy on river right above Mushroom, you're in good position for the next move, which involves driving hard left over the second ledge. The seemingly innocent first wave in this drop hides a rock that has munched many an unwary boater. You reach both Stairway and Threshhold via a trail that heads upstream from the parking area nearest the covered bridge.

To get to the put-in, follow Route 7 south from the light in the center of Kent for about 3.75 miles to the next light at Bulls Bridge Road. Go right on Bulls Bridge Road; you will soon cross the covered bridge and see the parking area on the right. The parking area has been the site of some unsavory activity in the past, so lock your car well and hide any valuables. To find the takeout, go back to the intersection of Route 7 and Bulls Bridge Road and continue south on 7 for another 2.25 miles. The pull-off will be on your right about 0.5 mile below the power station in Gaylordsville.

For most people the run starts at the covered bridge. A short trail leads to the river on the upstream side of the bridge. From here there is a very brief warm-up before the entrance to the Flume. This entrance rapid is a short but playful wave train with an interesting pop-up hole at the top. Be sure to roll quickly, since the Flume is not far below. At the bottom of this wave train, the outflow from Dead Horse Falls creates a powerful crosscurrent that pushes hard to the left and causes major turbulence. Cross this aggressively and head for an eddy at river right (easiest) or river left (hairy) above the Flume so you can get your bearings before taking the plunge.

The Flume is most reliably run by aiming for the crest of the drop just left of center while driving from right to left. At the bottom, catch the first eddy you can. They are plentiful on both sides. A couple of interesting variations on the basic line are: catching the eddy on river left directly below the Flume by boofing hard (this has caused at least one shoulder dislocation); or eddying out on river left just above the drop and making the quick turn out of the eddy before shooting over the drop.

Below the Flume there are some challenging surfing waves, then a short flurry of waves and rocks with a large boulder on river left as the river enters a large recovery pool. A cliff now appears on river left with an improbable-looking ladder bolted to it. Soon the right bank becomes rock as well as you approach S-Turn.

The thing that makes S-Turn interesting is a 5-foot ledge at the bottom that extends from river right about three-quarters of the way across the river. The rapid is fairly short—less than 100 yards in all—but landing in the hole at the bottom would make it a very long 100 yards. There are a couple of tongues through the hole that are best left for a second or subsequent run, when you've had a chance to note landmarks on the approach very carefully.

S-Turn is clean on the left side, where a fairly straightforward drive left, then back right, lands you in the pool below. Failing to jog back to the right takes you into a boulder sieve. The eddies on the left shore and in the middle at the top can serve as helpful boat-scouting spots, although these middle eddies are not large and missing them can produce dire consequences.

Shortly below S-Turn is Pencil Sharpener Rapid, which is much longer and more complex. It is composed of several ledges that form interesting holes, diagonal waves, and eddies—a sort of whitewater maze to be navigated by the intrepid boater. At normal water levels the holes are mostly manageable, with the exception of the Pencil Sharpener hole itself, which is grabby at any level.

The easiest line through Pencil Sharpener starts on the right, moves toward the center of the river as you approach the "sharpener," and then moves back right toward the end of the rapid. Along the way there are several holes and diagonals that can either mess up your line or help put you where you want to be, depending on how in control you are. The Pencil Sharpener hole is about 100 feet down the rapid and is formed by a 4-foot ledge extending from the right bank.

The river-left side of Pencil Sharpener Rapid is runnable, but it is somewhat shallow at low water and becomes a labyrinth of grabby hydraulics at high flows. Below Pencil Sharpener a trail leads back to the Flume on river right. This is handy for evacuations or for boaters who prefer a shuttleless three-quarter-mile run that takes in the most difficult drops.

Below the Pencil Sharpener is the confluence with the Ten Mile River and a class III rapid that leads to an easier section for the next three-quarters of a mile. As the river turns left at the bottom of this easy section, another class III rapid leads to the pool above Powerhouse.

While simple to run, Powerhouse (class III) is known mostly for the excellent playing opportunities it offers. The hole that guards the large eddy on river left is grabby, bouncy, and a bit intimidating, with an easy outrun and an eddy right next to it—the perfect play spot for advanced paddlers.

The powerhouse is visible just downstream of the rapid and shortly below is the final rapid, a class III+ with a couple of subtle, but interesting, on-the-fly surfing waves for boaters who are not yet exhausted. The USGS gauge is located just upstream of this last rapid in Gaylordsville. There is a hand-painted gauge on river right under the covered bridge at the put-in (known as the Flintstone Gauge, since a local artist's rendition of Fred is on the same bridge abutment). This gauge is more frequently used by boaters.

Probably the most reliable way to tell if Bulls is running is to call the river-level information number for Falls Village Hydro (860-824-7861). When Falls Village is releasing a high three gates (1,600 cfs+), Bulls starts to run (the Bulls Bridge hydro has a lower capacity than Falls Village).

Hubbard Brook (Mass.-Conn.)

Granville State Forest to Barkhamsted Reservoir

DISTANCE (MILES)	2.75		TOO LOW	
SHUTTLE (MILES)	6		LOW	3.9
AVG. DROP (FEET/MILE)	153		MED.	4.5
MAX. DROP (FEET/MILE)	160		HIGH	
DIFFICULTY	IV–V		TOO HIGH	
SCENERY	Excellent		GAUGE LOCATION	Barkhamsted Res.
DATE LAST CHECKED	1997		WATER LEVEL INFO.	
RUNOFF PATTERN	n/f			

Hubbard Brook is a small, steep stream that runs through Granville State Forest in Massachusetts just north of the border with Connecticut. It is naturally flowing, so you must catch it immediately after a rainstorm, heavy snowmelt, or both. The river is isolated—it runs through a state forest for its entire length—and many of the drops are big. The hairiest ones are easily portaged, and they should at least be scouted before each run. Because of its isolation the scenery is exceptional, with dense forests on each side and only one power-line cut to disturb the otherwise pristine setting.

The Hubbard is narrow, so downed trees often determine which rapids are runnable. At this writing several rapids are blocked by trees, due to a major windstorm in 1997 that also clogged the Sandy and other area rivers.

There is a hand-painted gauge on the bridge abutment at the put-in, although construction of a new bridge may wipe out this gauge. The USGS gauge at the bottom of the run is used to report canoeability ratings for this section. At the start the river is only about 15 feet wide where it plunges over a steep ledge into a pool below the put-in bridge. This short, class IV warm-up drop hints at what lies downstream, although subse-

HUBBARD BROOK

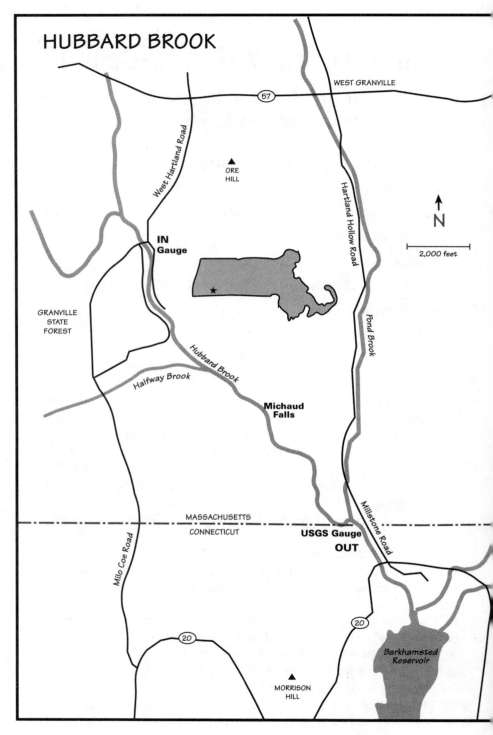

WEST GRANVILLE

57

West Hartland Road

Hartland Hollow Road

▲
ORE
HILL

↑
N

2,000 feet

**IN
Gauge**

GRANVILLE
STATE
FOREST

Hubbard Brook

Halfway Brook

Pond Brook

**Michaud
Falls**

MASSACHUSETTS
CONNECTICUT

Millstone Road

**USGS Gauge
OUT**

Milo Coe Road

20

20

Barkhamsted
Reservoir

▲
MORRISON
HILL

quent rapids are larger and more complex. A short pool leads to a busy class III+ boulder garden until a horizon line appears ahead and a large boulder near the river-left shore signals the first big one.

This 7-foot plunge into a large, deep pool is relatively harmless and is easy to run repeatedly by carrying back up the ledge on river right. It has been run forward, backward, and while twirling a paddle. Any more ideas?

Next is another short boulder garden that leads to a slide. The slide drops a total of about 15 feet over 75 feet and is fairly clean straight down the middle, although pointy boats with bows that are not sufficiently upturned may piton one of the upstream-facing foliations that cause the water to spray up in irregular rooster tails.

More boulder gardens take you under a high-voltage power line to the entrance to a sort of minigorge. The three drops in this gorge increase in size from the 4-foot entrance rapid to the 20-foot Michaud Falls. All three warrant scouting and can be carried on river left by bushwhacking and climbing over and around rocks and small cliffs.

The first drop is a fairly straightforward right-to-left move over a ledge. The next one involves paddling hard off a 5-foot vertical boof, and the last one, Michaud Falls, is a must-scout for any boater.

Michaud Falls (class V) starts with a very narrow slot (about 4 feet wide), where much of the water falls about 15 feet onto a shallow, downstream-sloping ledge. The alternative to this approach is to run it on river right where the water follows a shelf for about 10 feet downstream before cascading over a couple of steep stair steps back toward midstream. Either alternative is hairy, and this is no rapid in which to scout for trout. Below this initial section the water is chaotic, with holes and seam lines running both perpendicular and parallel to the current and shallow ledges with occasional boulders rearing their ugly heads.

Below Michaud Falls the gorge continues for a short distance with another interesting but straightforward drop. A short stretch of easier water follows before a very technical class IV rapid that doglegs right at the bottom. This is followed by a ledgy rapid that, at this writing, had a tree at the bottom completely blocking the channel. Be very cautious here, and scout this one carefully before running or walking. The tree is not easily seen from above.

Following this drop, a long section of class IV boulder gardens takes you to a pool formed by a small dam where the gauge is located. The dam has been run, but it has a very strong hydraulic at its base. The drops below the dam are still class IV. You must take out before the rapid that leads into a large culvert ahead, since from here down the river is protected as a public-drinking-water supply and you are subject to arrest if you are caught on it. Carry through the woods on the left bank to the road just above the river.

The put-in is found off Route 57 between Tolland and West Granby, Massachusetts. Turn south onto West Hartland Road and park where it crosses Hubbard Brook about 1.0 mile south of Route 57. To get to the takeout, continue south on West Hartland Road until it intersects with Route 20 just over the line into Connecticut. Turn left onto Route 20 (east) and follow it until it crosses Hubbard Brook. Take the next left immediately after the river crossing. Follow this access road about 0.25 mile to a parking area next to the gauging station.

There is a staff gauge on the gauging station at the takeout.

Millers River (Mass.)

South Royalston to Athol
Trip A

DISTANCE (MILES)	7		**TOO LOW**	4.4
SHUTTLE (MILES)	n/a		**LOW**	6
AVG. DROP (FEET/MILE)	32		**MED.**	7
MAX. DROP (FEET/MILE)	60		**HIGH**	
DIFFICULTY	II–III		**TOO HIGH**	
SCENERY	Fair		**GAUGE LOCATION**	South Royalston
DATE LAST CHECKED	1997		**WATER LEVEL INFO.**	
RUNOFF PATTERN	d/r/l			

The Millers River has two sections that are commonly canoed. Both offer exciting paddling if the water is up. The river passes through several towns where it picks up the offal of local industry, although recent cleanup efforts have made it much less offensive than in the past. The Millers is an easy winner in the river-most-likely-to-see-fewest-swimmers contest. (It is certainly not as bad as the Cuyahoga River, which runs through Cleveland and which caught on fire in the early seventies, burning several bridges in the process.) At higher water levels, the water is not so obviously objectionable. A wastewater treatment plant in Erving does improve the lower part, although nobody is bottling and selling water yet.

The Upper Millers (trip A) run starts in South Royalston, just a mile below the Birch Hill Dam, which completely controls the discharge. The river offers a pleasant trip in medium water, with no major difficulties. It should require no scouting. In South Royalston there are two bridge crossings; the usual starting spot is below the lower one. Those who wish to start above the first bridge will get to run some fast rapids that slice through town—class II at most levels. Just upstream from the lower bridge is a small dam that should be runnable at a gauge of 6.0. At a gauge

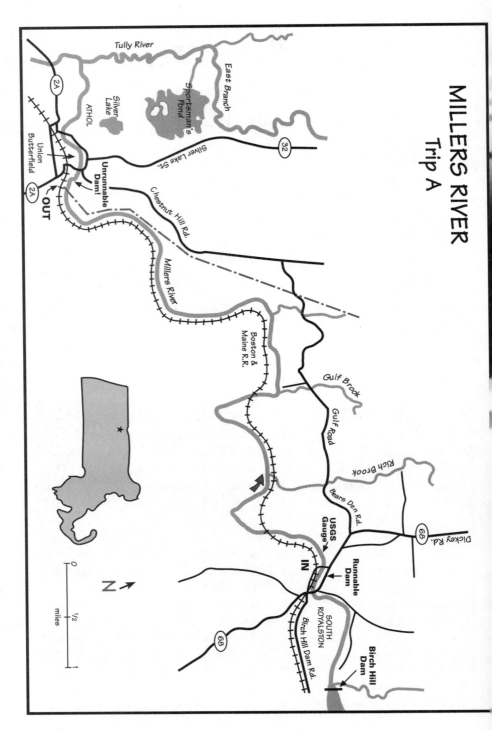

reading of 7.0 the dam is still runnable, but there's a bigger hydraulic. Total drop is 1 to 2 feet. Downstream from the second bridge on both banks are the remains of an old factory. The current in this section is strong at a gauge of 7.0; a few rocks show at 6.0. Shortly downstream from the starting point, islands divide the river into several channels, all of which are passable but possibly very rocky if the gauge isn't 6.0 or above. Class II boaters probably will be challenged by this section. There are also some small (1 to 1.5 feet) drops here.

After some calm water comes an extended rapid that lasts until the railroad bridge in the distance. At a gauge reading of 6.0 this section is scratchy, but at 7.0 it has a strong current with many little hydraulics and rock surfaces showing, calling for moderate rock dodging. The approach to the railroad bridge is rocky, with some nice haystacks just before it where the main stream sprints to the right. These waves are suitable for playing, and they are probably the heaviest of the trip. There is a big eddy on the left, downstream side of the bridge. At a gauge of 7.0, the run from the start to the railroad bridge is class II–III.

Fife Brook Section of the Deerfield. Kayakers approaching Zoar Gap. Photo by Zoar Outdoor

The pace slackens after the railroad bridge, and the river swings gently right in the distance. A left turn downstream begins a quarter-mile to a half-mile of continuous rapids rated class III at 6.0. Many rocks and hydraulics create ample opportunities for play and practice. Smooth water then predominates until the next bridge is passed. As the river approaches the railroad on the left, there are standing-wave rapids in the right turn, a pause, then more rapids. Both channels around the next island are usually clear. After that, the going is easy. As the Millers approaches the railroad again—it's on your left—there are a few easy class II rapids, then, before long, some class III rapids of just about equal difficulty with the long rapids already paddled, though not as continuous. Rocks and angled hydraulics prevail. The takeout, just above the first dam and bridge in Athol, is a short distance from these rapids.

When you see houses, stay close to the right bank and get out near several dirt piles. A factory (Union Butterfield) is farther downstream on the left bank, below the dam and the bridge. The takeout, fairly long and steep, leads to a road in a residential area. To reach this road by car from Route 2A, cross the bridge on the upstream side of the Union Butterfield factory, turn right (Route 32), continue for a short way, then take the first right (Crescent Street) until it becomes a dirt road where cars may be parked. For a shuttle, it is best to stick to hard-surfaced roads and avoid the shorter Gulf Road, which lies north of the river.

The Upper Millers run is much more fluid when the gauge reads 7.0 rather than 6.0. At 7.0 most rocks are underwater, the current is uninterrupted, and the rapids are class III instead of class II. People with no experience beyond class II will find the water challenging, and the rescues even more so.

The gauge for this section is located in South Royalston, on the right bank 500 feet downstream from the second bridge and 1.7 miles downstream from Birch Hill Dam. The Corps of Engineers may be of use for obtaining information about the discharge.

For another river of similar difficulty, try the Chickley or one of the trips on the Westfield.

Millers River (Mass.)

Erving to Millers Falls
Trip B

DISTANCE (MILES)	6.5		TOO LOW	2.9
SHUTTLE (MILES)	6		LOW	3.5
AVG. DROP (FEET/MILE)	29		MED.	4.8
MAX. DROP (FEET/MILE)	64		HIGH	5.5
DIFFICULTY	III		TOO HIGH	
SCENERY	Fair		GAUGE LOCATION	Farley
DATE LAST CHECKED	1997		WATER LEVEL INFO.	
RUNOFF PATTERN	d/r/l			

The Lower Millers, as this section is known, has some of the same drawbacks as the Upper Millers, although it offers better whitewater sport. The run begins near one paper company, ends near another, and passes by a landfill along the way. How's that for scenery? Route 2 follows the river for the first half of the trip, and there is a short picturesque valley near the end. Running the rapids consists mostly of riding up and down haystacks, with little or no vigorous maneuvering. Some stretches of rapids are long, and one in particular (the Funnel) is very heavy and tricky. Parts of the run are excellent for practicing surfing techniques or for instruction. This section is also known for holding enough water to be canoeable when other rivers are not. The Erving Paper Company waste-water treatment plant has improved water quality in the river, but not to the point of potability. Beware of man-made debris around the several abandoned millworks and broken dams that you pass on the trip.

There are several starting points for this trip. The one farthest upstream is by a bridge near the general offices of the Erving Paper Company. Turn off Route 2 at the sign for these offices in the center of Erving, pass under a railroad bridge, and in several hundred feet you will find the

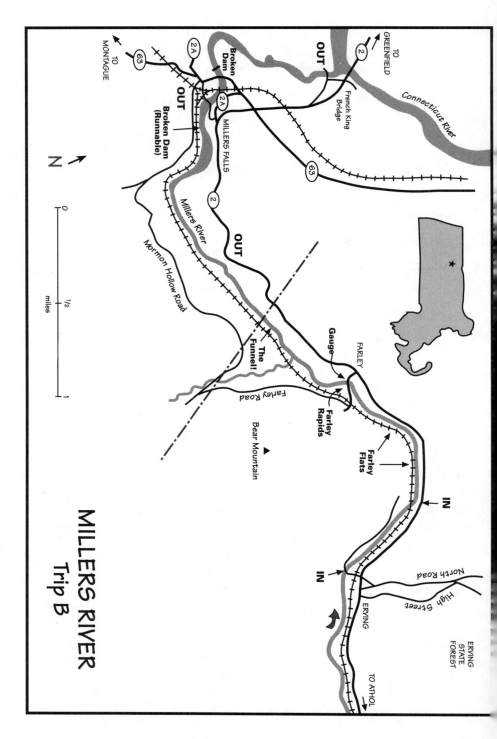

MILLERS RIVER
Trip B

bridge in question. From this spot to the first railroad bridge (1.0 mile) are some easy class II rapids, then smoothly flowing water. This stretch is good to limber up cold muscles, and it lasts just long enough for your legs to go to sleep.

The railroad bridge is an alternate put-in, and the roadside turnoff there is handy for parking and changing—best done on the off-road side of your car lest you cause some commotion on Route 2. A sweeping left turn below holds a long standing-wave rapid, with the largest haystacks toward the end. These waves are good for playing, surfing, and teaching. There's a pause, then another set of rapids follows. These rapids and the one following are collectively known as Farley Flats. An island on the left divides the channel downstream, with most of the water rushing to the right side. The road is close at this point, and on a clear day you can see chain-reaction collisions as motorists dream of shooting the rapids themselves. Near here on Route 2 was a sign stating that in the flood of September 1938, the Millers crested 5.5 feet above the highway. According to the USGS, this crest corresponds to a discharge of some 29,000 cfs.

Farley Rapids are just below the Farley Bridge. The gauge also is located here, on river right just downstream of the bridge. The approach to Farley Rapids is a sharp left turn: the Millers is pushed to the left below the bridge in a fast chute that's mostly choppy haystacks and holes, and is a bit trickier than it looks (class III at medium water). The easy route is right of center.

Downstream of these rapids a low ledge forms an excellent beginner surfing wave at levels above about 4.5. Glassy smooth and fed by a medium-sized eddy on river left, this wave is great for teaching due to its forgiving nature.

After passing the Farley landfill on the right bank, you'll see an abandoned gauging station on the right a bit downstream. This area has been used as a training site for slalom racers, so beware of low wires. After a brief flatwater stretch where a small side creek joins the main river from the left, the first of three closely spaced sets of rapids appears. The first is the easiest—about 50 yards long and mainly waves. A pool follows. The second has somewhat bigger water and stronger crosscurrents than the first. It follows after a right turn, lasts for about 75 yards, and is easiest to run down the middle. At top left in this rapid at high water (above 5 feet) are several large pourovers that can cause a long, nasty swim. After a short length of calmer water, the Millers broadens into a shallow, rocky rapid that leads to the Funnel.

The distance from the end of the second drop to the beginning of the Funnel is only several hundred feet, so don't get too close, lest the accelerating current invite you in like a smiling cannibal. This drop is definitely the hardest of the trip—class IV at most levels. It is most easily scouted from river right, where a narrow path leads from the last eddy in the pool above the Funnel to several good vantage points.

Narrowing quickly, the Millers drops about 15 feet rather spectacularly in the next 100 yards. In medium and high water, it's a straight shot down a fast, turbulent, violent set of haystacks, holes, reaction waves, and boiling eddies. As is typical with this sort of rapid, rocks line the edges, creating abrupt drops, nasty holes, and eddies. The center has the heaviest water but is the cleanest run. Three-quarters of the way down, there's a sloping, 3-foot drop followed by a large wave. The drop is more abrupt on the right than on the left or in the center. Just above this drop on the right is Piton Rock, which rears its ugly head at levels below about 5 feet. Stay away from this rock, since it can cause nasty pinnings and is not always obvious to the boater approaching from upstream.

Twenty yards below is a slight left bend and another drop into a large wave with a powerful eddy on river right. Paddling into this wave from the eddy results in a spectacular jet ferry that can peel your eyelids back with the force of the wave in your face.

The Funnel takes ten seconds to run (or swim). Kick out at the top and you'll have a vicious swim, especially at high water, since the outrun is long and powerful. Below the Funnel a set of power lines crosses the river. Do not attempt to use them to locate this rapid. They are too hard to spot; you'll be in the Funnel before you're ready. Downstream of the Funnel are several class II–III rapids and an island.

Route 2 appears on the right bank as the Millers veers left into class III rapids with haystacks and rocks. Take out on the right just below the rapid and a sharp right turn unless you want to continue through the town of Millers Falls. Climb the hill to a rest area on Route 2.

Below this point comes a long stretch of calmer water that becomes continuous waves (class III-) in high water (4.7 and up). This section is especially pretty, with conifer-lined banks and a small waterfall pouring from the right shore partway down.

The Strathmore Paper (formerly Millers Falls Paper) dam is broken, and you can run it almost anywhere. The water is squirrelly, though, and although Strathmore removed much of the debris several years ago, the bottom is bound to hold some unwanted man-made surprises still. Power lines overhead mark the spot. Below this, you will pass under the Newton Street bridge, where you can take out on river left.

If you decide to continue on, shortly downstream you will float under a railroad bridge. The next bridge, in the center of Millers Falls, marks a former dam site that should be approached with caution. This rapid is short and steep, with large, irregular waves and unknown amounts of re-bar, steel, and concrete. Below this dam on river left is a huge eddy that feeds an exciting surfing wave at medium and high flows.

The takeout in the center of Millers Falls has been closed due to vandalism, so if you run below the Newton Street bridge you must continue to the confluence with the Connecticut. The 1.75 miles are class II, with several meanders, interesting scenery, excellent hawk habitat, and an abundance of strainers where debris has piled up on several midriver islands. Be especially careful of the final rapid, as the river drops over a ledge on river right and then slams into an island that forces it sharply right. Left is usually clear, but if you try to play with these ledges, keep an eye out for trees.

Take out on river right under a decaying steel bridge in sight of the impressive French King Bridge and the French King Gorge of the Connecticut. To reach this takeout from Route 2, proceed half a mile west of the French King Bowling Alley to Dorsey Road (the only left turn after the DPW facility on the right and before the French King Bridge). Follow this road 0.3 mile to the old steel bridge. To reach the gauge in Farley from Route 2, go east from the takeout past a small (former) store in Farley and turn right on the next road—it's a very sharp turn just after the store (Bridge Street). Proceed a short distance to the river. The U.S. Army Corps of Engineers schedules a couple of releases on the Millers each spring in early April. Of course, these releases often just supplement already high natural flows.

Beware of vandalism and theft at all access points on the Millers. This has become more of a problem as river use has increased in the past several years. For a river of similar difficulty to the Millers, try the Quaboag or the West Branch of the Westfield, both reasonably close.

North River (Mass.)

Veratec Dam to Deerfield River

Trip B

DISTANCE (MILES)	3		TOO LOW	
SHUTTLE (MILES)	3		LOW	3.6
AVG. DROP (FEET/MILE)	32		MED.	
MAX. DROP (FEET/MILE)	50		HIGH	
DIFFICULTY	II		TOO HIGH	
SCENERY	Good		GAUGE LOCATION	Shattuckville
DATE LAST CHECKED	1997		WATER LEVEL INFO.	
RUNOFF PATTERN	n/f		http://water.usgs.gov/public/realtime.html	

The lower North is similar in difficulty to the Chickley except that it is larger, gathering inflows from several streams along its path. It is also ledgier, with a few rapids holding interesting hydraulics in medium and high water. The advantage of the North is that it requires minimal runoff to make it runnable, although it is more civilized than the Chickley, making it a bit less scenic.

Start below a wooden dam that diverts water just upstream of the Veratec plant in Colrain. Parking is very limited at the put-in, so plan to unload quickly and leave only one car here. The first half-mile is class I–II, with the heaviest rapid just above the second bridge in a left turn. Beware the outflow from the pipes at the base of the factory. Who knows what microbes lurk therein?

After the second bridge the river becomes flatter as it passes through farm country. Trees are a major hazard here, since the banks are constantly calving into the river. In about three-quarters of a mile the river approaches the road in a left turn with a class II rapid. Be sure to take out just below here on river left, opposite the Shattuckville gauging station.

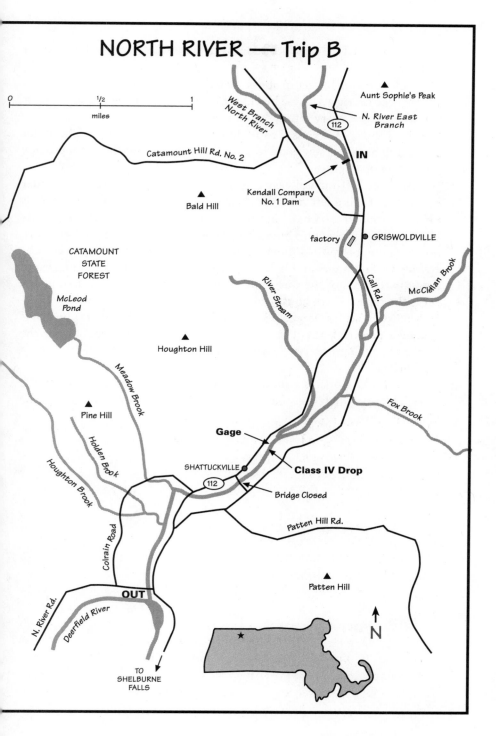

NORTH RIVER — Trip B

0 ½ 1
miles

West Branch North River

Aunt Sophie's Peak

N. River East Branch

112

IN

Catamount Hill Rd. No. 2

Bald Hill

Kendall Company No. 1 Dam

factory

GRISWOLDVILLE

CATAMOUNT STATE FOREST

McLeod Pond

River Stream

Call Rd.

McClellan Brook

Houghton Hill

Meadow Brook

Fox Brook

Pine Hill

Gage

Holden Brook

SHATTUCKVILLE

112

Class IV Drop

Houghton Brook

Bridge Closed

Colrain Road

Patten Hill Rd.

Patten Hill

N. River Rd.

OUT

Deerfield River

N

TO SHELBURNE FALLS

The next rapid deserves a scout and probably will be portaged by most paddlers.

Falling about 12 feet in about 40 feet, this drop is class IV and holds a large hole on river right. The easiest portage is over the ledges on river left, where a seal entry into the pool below is possible.

After the pool, a class II rapid follows as the river curves right under a decaying bridge. A few good ledge holes at the base of this drop provide interesting play spots.

Another half-mile of easy class II follows, until the river runs under Route 112. Here a left turn with a landslide on the outside of it begins three-quarters of a mile of continuous class II, until the North meets the Deerfield at the takeout. Though this final section is the most continuous, no single rapid is more difficult than what has come before. There are several interesting waves and holes for surfing in this section, and one rapid about two-thirds of the way down is not only interesting to run, but has rocks the size of small houses and a gorgelike quality to it.

Take out at the Deerfield just below a popular swimming spot that is usually a powerful class II rapid when the water is high enough for the North to run. Park on North River Road just after crossing the river on a steel bridge.

The lower North is a good choice when the Fife Brook section of the Deerfield is too high. Another creek of similar difficulty in the area is the Chickley River.

Pelham Brook (Mass.)

Rowe Center to Deerfield River

DISTANCE (MILES)	3.25		TOO LOW	
SHUTTLE (MILES)	3.25		LOW	
AVG. DROP (FEET/MILE)	188		MED.	
MAX. DROP (FEET/MILE)	315		HIGH	
DIFFICULTY	V		TOO HIGH	
SCENERY	Good		GAUGE LOCATION	None
DATE LAST CHECKED	1996		WATER LEVEL INFO.	
RUNOFF PATTERN	n/f			

This small stream follows a country road through Rowe, Massachusetts, and is fed by Pelham Pond and a smaller millpond in the center of Rowe. The run itself is only 3.25 miles long from the put-in just downstream of the center of Rowe to the takeout at the Deerfield River. Because of the size of the river (very small) and the severity of the rapids (very severe), you should carefully scout the drivable sections for downed trees and be extremely cautious on the difficult drops that are away from the road, since one strainer can ruin your whole run.

The most difficult rapids are visible from the road just after it crosses Pelham Brook for the second time, coming from Charlemont. Use these drops to judge the water level (there is no gauge) and the suitability of the run to your paddling abilities. Be aware too that the watershed of this creek is so small that its level can vary significantly over a period of an hour or two.

As of this writing, the author does not know of any complete descents of this brook. One run started below the second bridge upstream of the village of Zoar, and the other started in the center of Rowe and was forced to take out at the flowerpot just upstream of the bridge where the first descent started. To date, two rapids remain unrun, though they are both certainly runnable without strainers.

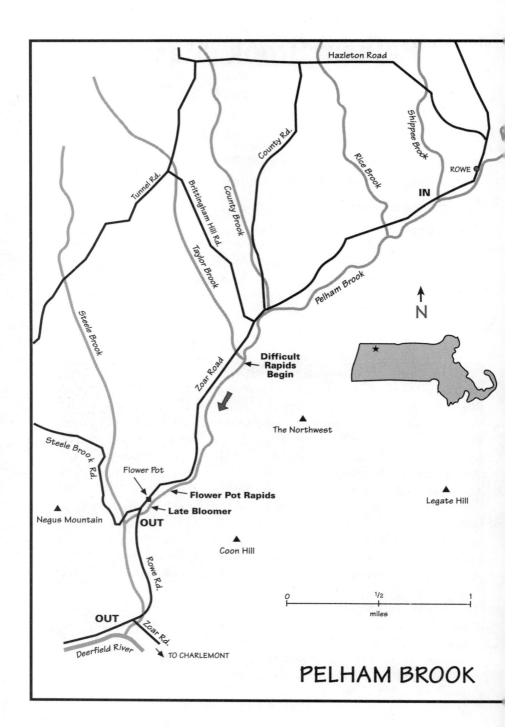

Hazleton Road

Shippee Brook

ROWE

IN

Tunnel Rd.

County Rd.

Rice Brook

Brittingham Hill Rd.

County Brook

County Road

Taylor Brook

Pelham Brook

Steele Brook

Zoar Road

Difficult Rapids Begin

N

▲
The Northwest

Steele Brook Rd.

Flower Pot

▲
Legate Hill

▲
Negus Mountain

Flower Pot Rapids

Late Bloomer

OUT

▲
Coon Hill

Rowe Rd.

0   ½   1
miles

OUT

Zoar Rd.

Deerfield River

→ TO CHARLEMONT

PELHAM BROOK

Start the run downstream of a steep and narrow cascade just below the millpond in Rowe center. After the river flattens somewhat, a low footbridge crosses it opposite a white church. From here the first mile and a half is a pleasant class II–III warm-up as the river winds away from the road through pine forests and passes a house or two. Strainers are frequent.

After the river passes under a power-line cut it heads away from the road and soon becomes more interesting. The drops grow in height until the first of the large drops appears in a right turn. This one is steep, but not unmanageably so, and has frequent eddies. The stair steps are about 3 or 4 feet each and spaced 10 to 15 feet apart. A couple of the holes are grabby at medium water.

The next rapid, Crash Pad, definitely deserves scouting, as a tricky chute leads to a 5-foot plunge that can mess up your line for the technical water below. In 1996, this rapid ended in a channel-wide log that was avoidable only by making a difficult move into the smaller right channel.

West Branch of the Deerfield below the Wall. Photo by Karen Blom

After passing a house on the right, another steep rapid with portageable trees leads to a short, easier section as the river approaches the road again. What follows is the most difficult section.

A narrow, 100-yard straightaway ends in a sharp, steep S-turn drop that feeds a large hole at its base. This is the beginning of the Flowerpot section. The pillow in the right turn is so large at medium water that it could really mess up your line as you head for the trashy hole below. This one has few eddies above it, so be very careful as you approach it for scouting. After a very short pool, a stair-step rapid that is often complicated by trees leads to a right turn that is followed by a couple of hundred yards of extremely steep, intricate water, ending at a large green flowerpot by the side of the road. A single mistake here could result in a very painful, if not terminal swim. This whole section, from the S-turn to the flowerpot is difficult class V; it should be scouted carefully and run by only the most experienced boaters with adequate safety in place.

A short class III–IV section follows Flowerpot as the river comes very close to the road. Soon it leaves the road again and enters Late Bloomer, another serious class V. Late Bloomer is a series of 4- to 6-foot drops with a very messy ending. Be careful to catch the eddy on river left just above, and scout from either or both shores. The line is fairly straightforward, since the river is narrow and there are few options. The trick is putting it all together. There is a large undercut boulder on river left about a third of the way down that probably presents the most immediate hazard, but the prospect of flipping or, heaven forbid, swimming, anywhere in this rapid is a grave one.

After Late Bloomer, the river crosses under the road and a long section of difficult, continuous class IV with few eddies and the potential for many strainers leads to the next bridge. Just below this bridge a sharp right turn with a landslide on the outside of it presents the final difficult drop (class IV) before a short section of class III–IV water leads under two more bridges to the Deerfield.

Quaboag River (Mass.)

Warren to Route 67

DISTANCE (MILES)	5.5		TOO LOW	
SHUTTLE (MILES)	6		LOW	3.9
AVG. DROP (FEET/MILE)	31		MED.	4.4
MAX. DROP (FEET/MILE)	85		HIGH	5.5
DIFFICULTY	II–IV		TOO HIGH	6
SCENERY	Poor		GAUGE LOCATION	West Brimfield
DATE LAST CHECKED	1997		WATER LEVEL INFO.	
RUNOFF PATTERN	n/l		http://water.usgs.gov/public/realtime.html	

The Quaboag is full of variety—from abrupt drops to long rapids with wave trains to a minigorge. Medium-sized, with rapids of sufficient power to demand great respect, the Quaboag holds its water well and is canoeable in the fall during the rainy season. There are many rapids on the Quaboag, and water level will determine the kind of run to expect. In high water less maneuvering is involved, although keeping an open boat from swamping in the many standing waves and souse holes is tough. This level offers the most challenge. Medium water exposes more rocks and makes several rapids more technical. The rapids in general are spaced by calmer water, giving the paddler ample time to rest. This trip on the Quaboag flows through several towns, so the scenery isn't great.

Put in at the Lucy Stone Park, which is about 0.5 mile north of Warren on River Road. Directly in front of the park is an island with a small chute on its left side that can be run by starting above the bridge there. Below the put-in, the water is class I–II until a group of boulders announces the bridge at Warren. Directly below the bridge is a 6-inch drop (low water) starting a standing-wave rapid (class II). One hundred yards below a railroad bridge is another 6-inch drop, starting some short rapids in a right turn. Another railroad bridge follows. From this point to

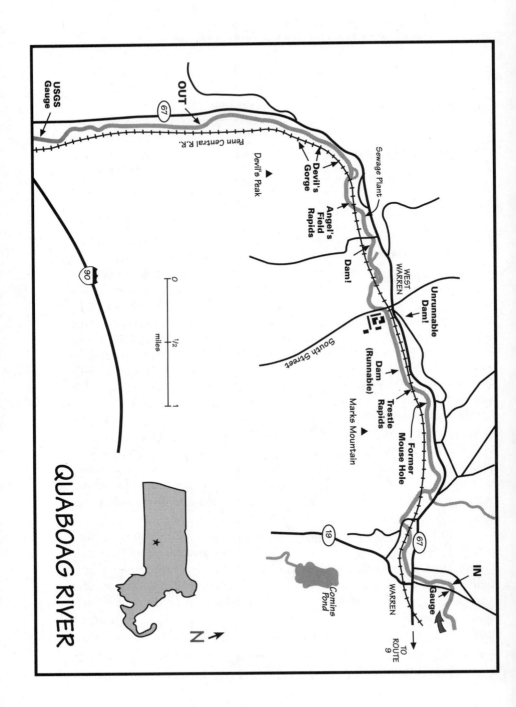

QUABOAG RIVER

N →

USGS Gauge

OUT

Penn Central R.R.

Devil's Peak ▲

Devil's Gorge

Angel's Field Rapids

Dam!

Sewage Plant

WEST WARREN

Unrunnable Dam!

South Street

Dam (Runnable)

Trestle Rapids

Marks Mountain ▲

Former Mouse Hole

Comins Pond

WARREN

Gauge

IN

TO ROUTE 9

0   ½   1
miles

the first portage around an old dam, the river moves swiftly, with intermittent haystacks but no rapids of consequence.

The dam has an outflow on the left through several large tubes, and this area should be avoided at all costs. On the extreme right, the former mouse hole has collapsed and the rapid now can be run just left of the rock jumble formed by the extinct mouse hole.

The next major rapid, Trestle, appears beyond a railroad bridge in a slight left turn. You should scout Trestle if you haven't seen it previously, especially if the water is high, but be very careful when walking on the railroad bridge; two paddlers were hit by a train here while scouting the river for an upcoming trip. There are two main routes you can follow. Both are, in some respects, easier at high than at medium levels. For the less thrilling (though still exciting) route, hug the right bank under the bridge and pass along the concrete foundation, making a sharp right turn into a narrow channel to the right side of an island in the right side of the riverbed. The turn is quite a trick, and, if you make it, the rest of the way is straightforward. If you don't make it, the rest of the way is still straightforward; you just have a harder time of it. As the water level goes down, rocks guarding the approach to this path (and the turn itself) make things more difficult. For the more exciting route, pass either to the right or the left of the bridge support and immediately move to a position left of center in the main channel. Follow the flow through standing waves and rocks and, in high water, be careful of a series of holes near the end of the rapid. In low water, these holes are filled with rocks; you can go around either way.

Shortly downstream is a broken dam that's easy to run on the right side. The current angles first right, then left. This route has haystacks at first, then a small island divides the river into rocky class II–III rapids on either side. Farther downstream the next dam appears. Portage on the right. This is not an easy carry, but it's easier than running the 15- to-20-foot drop. Calm water upstream signals the approaching dam. The water below the dam is class II, then class I, past several bridges and a factory.

Below a railroad bridge there is a fairly sharp left turn, and then comes a large island with rapids on either side. The left side is slightly easier. The next big obstacle is another broken dam (3 feet high). This dam can be run to the left of two stone columns on the extreme left, since it is completely broken there. Going over the dam itself is also possible, but it involves a somewhat greater risk. Downstream past a green bridge, the river veers left away from the road, passes under another railroad bridge, and enters a 75-yard chute with haystacks that will swamp most doubly paddled open boats at high levels. This rapid is known as Angel's Field. In low water, small rocks stick their heads up, with the greatest density being near the bottom of the drop. In general, they are not a problem. A large pool below is handy for recovery. Before this drop, there is also a sewage treatment plant that sometimes adds to the discharge of the river.

Below the pool the river turns right, passes under yet another railroad bridge, flows around an island, and then enters the first of three good sets of rapids. At higher levels these three stretches merge into one long stretch, with only brief lulls in between. This is the Devil's Gorge section. The first rapid has many small rocks that show up at low levels, choppy waves in medium water, and an abrupt drop (Quaboag Drop) at the end at any level. You can't see this drop from above, and it could be a big surprise if you don't know it's there. It is sharpest in the center, so run it on either extreme. The drop is not so sharp in high water as in low water. In high water it is followed immediately by a 3- to 4-foot haystack. The long approach to this drop can be fast and sassy. A short stretch of quickly flowing but relatively calm water follows, and then the next of the three rapids begins. This one is about 100 yards long, class III in medium water, and similar to the previous rapid. Another breather, then the last of the trio appears with nothing new to be encountered.

Because of its length, this stretch is difficult to scout. In addition, it is not at all easy to see from Route 67, which is fairly close. At a gauge reading of 5.5, this section contains many large waves and holes. At this level the entire section is rated class IV. Take out at one of the several roadside turnoffs that follow.

The West Brimfield gauge is in Hampden County, on the right bank 10 feet upstream from an abandoned highway bridge site, 0.9 mile upstream from Blodget Mill Brook and 3.5 miles northeast of Palmer. It can be reached via the last roadside turnoff before the turnpike (about 0.8 mile from the turnpike). Don't be too surprised if the external gauge isn't of much help. Some enterprising person has sawed off the bottom portion. A new gauge has been painted on the left, upstream side of the Lucy Stone Bridge at the put-in. Readings from the West Brimfield gauge are reported on the USGS web site at http://water.usgs.gov/public/realtime.html.

For another run similar in difficulty to the Quaboag, try the West Branch of the Westfield or the Millers.

Salmon River (Conn.)

Jeremy River to Route 16

DISTANCE (MILES)	3		**TOO LOW**	
SHUTTLE (MILES)			**LOW**	1.4
AVG. DROP (FEET/MILE)	27		**MED.**	
MAX. DROP (FEET/MILE)	50		**HIGH**	3
DIFFICULTY	II		**TOO HIGH**	
SCENERY	Good		**GAUGE LOCATION**	Comstock Bridge
DATE LAST CHECKED	1981		**WATER LEVEL INFO.**	
RUNOFF PATTERN	n			

When winter skies blow away and the ice is transformed to a more pliable medium, the traditional season opener is the Salmon. Located southeast of Hartford, the Salmon is usually run early in March and can provide a course for training beginners at the start of the spring season. Usually entered via either the Blackledge or the Jeremy River, the Salmon and its smaller associates can provide an easy class II–III run in medium and high water, or a somewhat uninteresting trip in low. In any case, a rusty paddler has ample opportunity to recall skills left behind in the fall without being severely challenged. Since the Jeremy usually has more water and is slightly more interesting than the Blackledge, it is generally the preferred route and will be discussed at length here.

The trip on the Jeremy, and then the Salmon, may be started where old Route 2 crosses the river, south of Marlborough and north of North Westchester. Here the Jeremy varies between one and three boat lengths wide and flows gently around meanders arched with trees leaning toward the river as if saluting a passing procession. The river continues in this way until it passes under the new Route 2 bridge, about 0.33 mile below the start. Here the river turns 90° to the right, and Meadow Brook adds its water from the left as the Jeremy widens and deepens; the going is still easy. Downstream, note several large rocks in the middle and left as the

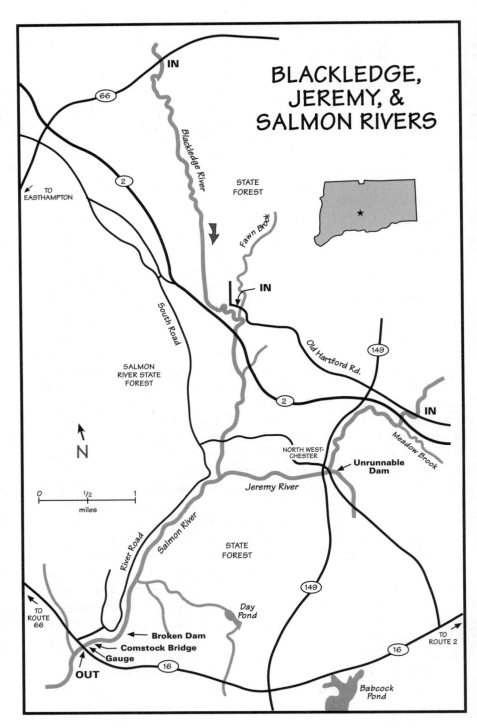

BLACKLEDGE, JEREMY, & SALMON RIVERS

IN

66

2

TO EASTHAMPTON

Blackledge River

STATE FOREST

Fawn Brook

IN

South Road

SALMON RIVER STATE FOREST

Old Hartford Rd.

149

2

IN

Meadow Brook

N

NORTH WEST-CHESTER

Unrunnable Dam

Jeremy River

0   1/2   1
miles

River Road

Salmon River

STATE FOREST

Day Pond

149

TO ROUTE 66

TO ROUTE 2

16

Broken Dam
Comstock Bridge
Gauge
OUT

16

Babcock Pond

340   *Massachusetts, Connecticut, and Rhode Island*

Jeremy approaches the highway on the right bank. Then the river turns left and the rapids begin. They are fairly easy and consist of rock-picking for several meanders, with a short pause and then more rapids in a slight left turn. A row of dilapidated houses high on the right bank watch over shallow rapids that last about 50 yards. This whole section is rated II–II+. Next an iron bridge is passed; the current slows to a stop and the river turns right and a dam in North Westchester must be portaged, best done on the left. Shortly below the dam come more easy rapids, then the river enters a hemlock-shrouded valley housing some rock-dodging rapids. After a right turn, there is a 1- to 1.5-foot ledge extending from the left bank to midstream. It can be avoided on the right. If the water is high enough the ledge can be run almost anywhere, since it slopes gently downward. This section ends in a river-wide ripple followed by a quiet pool; then come easy rapids that drop into a conifer-lined pool. Except for the possibility of fallen trees, there are no substantial difficulties from here to the Blackledge.

The confluence of the Blackledge from the north and the Jeremy from the east forms the Salmon, which is wider than both of its tributaries. The Salmon begins gently, and the first rapid occurs several hundred yards downstream. Probably the most technically difficult rapid normally run, this set has rocks on either side of its entrance, so choose an initial center route. After passing these rocks, ease a bit to the left. This rapid ends with several rock portals on the right, where there is also a nice eddy. A competent paddler should have no trouble here. (If the water is up he may want to play.) The Salmon then continues to flow easily with rocks interspersed, passing under a bridge where there is a small waterfall on the right. The takeout spot is along Bull Hill Road (River Road) by a brick fireplace. If the venturesome want a little more excitement, they can continue for another couple of hundred yards and run an old broken dam.

The dam is upstream from a high dirt cliff on the left and downstream from a small stream that enters right. There is a broad, shallow approach over a rock shelf, then the dam itself—three distinct ledges that can be run in various spots depending on the water level. The first and third ledges are fairly uniform in their 1-foot drop, but the second drops more abruptly (1.5 to 2 feet in several places). In low water, the easiest run is a chute on the extreme right. In any case, stop and look this one over beforehand. Continue on and take out by a covered bridge, just upstream from the Route 16 crossing.

Sandy Brook (Conn.)
Sandy Brook Road to Route 8 Bridge

DISTANCE (MILES)	3.3		TOO LOW	2.1
SHUTTLE (MILES)	3.3		LOW	2.6
AVG. DROP (FEET/MILE)	80		MED.	3.3
MAX. DROP (FEET/MILE)	100		HIGH	
DIFFICULTY	III–IV		TOO HIGH	
SCENERY	Good		GAUGE LOCATION	Route 8 Bridge
DATE LAST CHECKED	1997		WATER LEVEL INFO.	
RUNOFF PATTERN	n/f			

Sandy Brook is a small but extremely interesting stream that runs into the Still River just above Riverton, Connecticut. It has more rocks than even the upper Farmington and it's just as technical—maybe more so. A continuous current; several narrow, intricate chutes; and a plethora of rocks force the canoeist to make split-second decisions time after time. In many cases, a hesitation or wrong choice will result in a very unpleasant situation. Although it's only about 3.0 miles, the trip will seem much longer, especially in low water. Sandy Brook Road follows alongside almost all the way, so a weary rock gardener can take out any time after exhaustion overwhelms her. Again, as with the upper Farmington, water level is critical.

In the winter of 1997, a major windstorm blocked this and other area rivers with trees. At this writing, trees remain a major hazard on this section, although many have been cleared away by helpful paddlers. In addition, an impassable logjam blocks the river below the first bridge. You must take out above this bridge until the logjam is cleared.

A trip may be started anywhere along the stream, but the suggested put-in is near a bridge some 3.0 miles upriver from the gauge. At the put-in, the Sandy is very narrow and flows swiftly, with the first rocky rapids found shortly downstream where a smaller stream enters from the right. About 0.3 mile below the start, in a left turn, is a 3- to 4-foot drop that, in lower water, must be approached on the extreme right of the chute. Just in

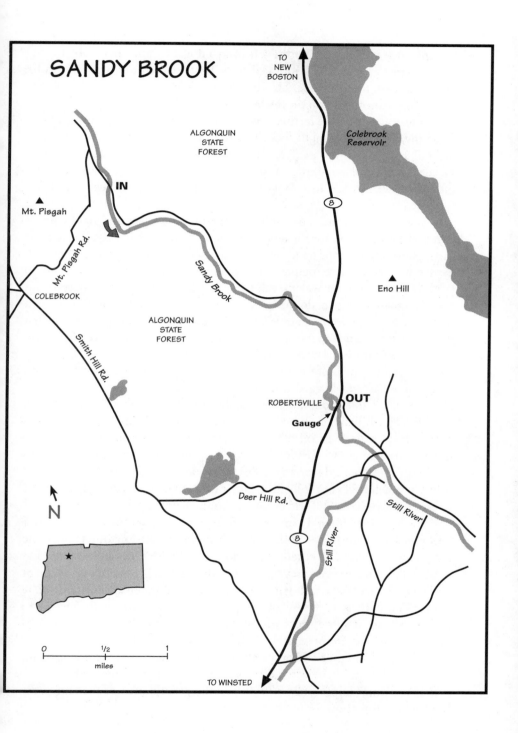

SANDY BROOK

TO
NEW
BOSTON

ALGONQUIN
STATE
FOREST

Colebrook
Reservoir

IN

Mt. Pisgah

Mt. Pisgah Rd.

Sandy Brook

8

COLEBROOK

Eno Hill

ALGONQUIN
STATE
FOREST

Smith Hill Rd.

ROBERTSVILLE

OUT

Gauge

Deer Hill Rd.

Still River

Still River

N

8

miles

0   1/2   1

TO WINSTED

the entrance pull sharply to the left to avoid a rock and then...down. The drop is tight and should be looked over. Portage if in doubt; it would be foolish to ruin the trip here. The drop can be seen from the road. Below is a pool, then another drop on the left.

One-third of a mile farther down, a mass of low boulders in the center splits the channel in a right turn. The right course is clearer, but ends in a drop of 1 to 2 feet over a ledge; it is too dry to run in low water. The chute on the left is intricate—little rocks make a nuisance of themselves. It starts off with an abrupt 1.5- to 2-foot drop and ends in a fast, clear channel. Look this one over also.

The Sandy continues on with an assortment of rocks and tight courses that make it necessary for the boater continually to move his boat. In one left turn, there is what appears to be a broken rock dam with a substantial rock garden below it, where the passage is quite intricate. This rapid is about 50 yards long, and proper water level is important. After the left turn, start out left of center and then do your best. This rapid leads to the first of two bridges, about a quarter of a mile apart. You must take out just before the first bridge to avoid an impassable logjam until it is cleared. Between the two bridges are more small drops requiring a little maneuvering. The first drop comes just after the first right turn. Below the second bridge are more rocks; this section was still clogged with strainers at this writing.

About 2.2 miles from the start, just above a lumberyard and in a right turn with a steep left bank, is another tricky chute requiring a good approach and several crisp turns. Start on the extreme left and p roceed to the center. Near the bottom, a large rock divides the river; go around it. A pool awaits below, as do more rapids in a left turn in the distance. The rest of the way to the Route 8 bridge is much easier but still quick. Either take out there or continue down the class II section to the Still and eventually to the Farmington.

As with the upper Farmington from Otis to New Boston, this river becomes hellish in high water. Although there are shallow quiet spots, the rapids tend to blend together. The rocks are so close that even the water has to plan ahead for the best way to navigate the course. Precise boat placement is absolutely necessary, and you have to know well in advance where you're going. The pace is very fast and requires constant work, with few or no breathers, and in some spots you will even find a touch of good old-fashioned turbulence. Unfortunately, the Sandy has a very short season.

The gauge on the Sandy is on the left bank, attached to the downstream side of the Route 8 bridge, which crosses the stream at Robertsville.

If you want another class IV run in the general area of the Sandy, try the Farmington above New Boston.

Shepaug River (Conn.)
Route 341 to Route 47

DISTANCE (MILES)	7		**TOO LOW**	
SHUTTLE (MILES)	7		**LOW**	0.5
AVG. DROP (FEET/MILE)	40		**MED.**	1
MAX. DROP (FEET/MILE)	50		**HIGH**	2
DIFFICULTY	II–III		**TOO HIGH**	
SCENERY	Good		**GAUGE LOCATION**	Route 47 Bridge
DATE LAST CHECKED	1997		**WATER LEVEL INFO.**	
RUNOFF PATTERN	d			

The Shepaug, along with the Bantam, is one of the earliest rivers to free itself of ice and snow, so it is usually canoed during the middle or the end of March. The upper portions of the Shepaug are sportier than the lower, and in high water they can be very exciting. The stream starts quite narrow and remains so until the confluence with the Bantam. The Shepaug has many islands. Water flow depends on the dam situated at the start: since the upper riverbed is small, when there is a water release many trees suddenly seem to grow in several feet of water, something to concern canoeists because eddying out becomes trickier when you have to fight your way through the brush. Even though most of the trip is quick moving, there are no rapids that require scouting, although fallen trees can be a real hazard anywhere. The Shepaug is usually most challenging for open boats. A road follows the upper half, but it is usually not in view.

To reach the put-in, turn north on Route 341 near the Route 202 bridge that crosses the Shepaug at Woodville. After a short distance on Route 341, take the first right, which is somewhat obscure, and continue until you reach a stone bridge. Just upstream from this bridge is a small dam that can be run in the center. For the larger dam upstream, you'll need a parachute. Below the bridge, the central canoeable channel is about one boat length wide and the rapids quite typical of the whole run—for

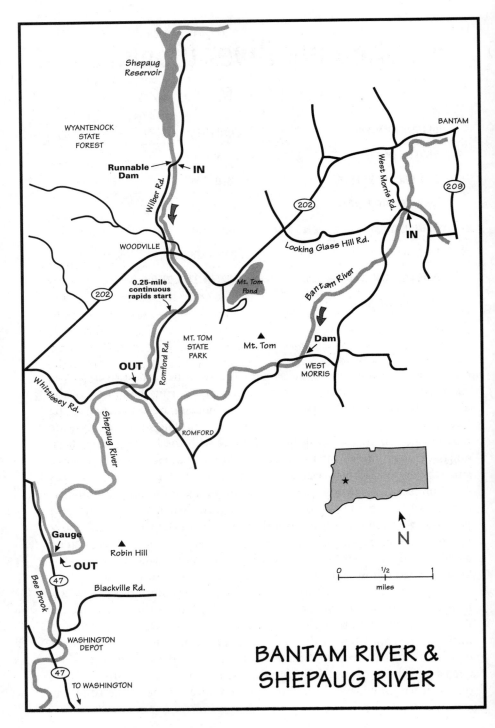

Shepaug
Reservoir

WYANTENOCK
STATE
FOREST

**Runnable
Dam** → **IN**

Wilber Rd.

WOODVILLE

**0.25-mile
continuous
rapids start**

(202)

Mt. Tom
Pond

MT. TOM
STATE
PARK

Romford Rd.

▲
Mt. Tom

OUT

Whittlesey Rd.

Shepaug River

ROMFORD

BANTAM

West Morris Rd.

(202)

Looking Glass Hill Rd.

(209)

IN

Bantam River

Dam

WEST
MORRIS

Gauge

▲
Robin Hill

OUT

(47)

Bee Brook

Blackville Rd.

WASHINGTON
DEPOT

(47)

TO WASHINGTON

★

N

0   ½   1
miles

BANTAM RIVER &
SHEPAUG RIVER

75 to 100 yards, standing waves rush over small rocks and ledges. At a gauge of 0.5, waves measure about 1 foot. The current is a bit pushy and disorienting. An island downstream divides the channel, and there's an abrupt drop of 0.5 to 1 foot over a small rock ledge on the right side. The river then turns right and straddles another island. Later there's a series of haystacks. Past the Route 202 bridge is a small pool. On the left, the exit from the pool leads to a fast, twisty passage.

When you see Romford Road close on the right bank, watch for an island full of brush, which can sometimes block the way. Pass on whichever side looks best. Beyond, in a right turn, you'll find nice, rocky rapids even if you're not looking for them. After the next bridge (Romford Road), the Shepaug turns right into a quarter- to a half-mile of continuous standing-wave rapids that should be good sport for competent boaters and challenging for others. At the end is a brief stretch of quieter water as the river approaches Romford Road (about 25 feet up the left bank); the river then turns right, leading into an interesting rapid that lasts about 25 yards. Usually you can run this rapid in the center or right center. The last two sets of rapids are the hardest on the trip, rated class III at a gauge reading of 0.5. One possibility for taking out is at the next bridge, which is just above the confluence with the Bantam. Since the drive in is not particularly easy, most people will choose to stay with the river and take out at the Route 47 bridge, 3.0 miles farther along.

When the Bantam adds its water from the left, volume increases noticeably and the water is pushier, especially if the level is high. A short distance downstream, a rock cliff on the right marks a good class III rapid. Just after a left turn with several rocks in the center comes another spicy entanglement with water and rocks, followed by another good rapid in a left turn. Next look for a drainpipe about 2 feet in diameter on the left bank—choppy water is ahead. This last rapid is in a right turn with flat, slablike rocks on the left bank and dome-shaped rocks in the water; this is just before the takeout at the Route 47 bridge, where Bee Brook enters from the right side. If the gauge reads 2.0 or more, there will be few rocks evident in this last section, or anywhere on the trip for that matter.

There is a hand-painted gauge on the left, upstream wing of the Route 47 bridge.

For other similarly rated trips in the area try the Salmon.

Middle Branch of the Westfield River (Mass.)

River Road to Littleville Dam

DISTANCE (MILES)	7		TOO LOW	0
SHUTTLE (MILES)	7		LOW	2.2/6.7
AVG. DROP (FEET/MILE)	43		MED.	3
MAX. DROP (FEET/MILE)	50		HIGH	
DIFFICULTY	II–III		TOO HIGH	
SCENERY	Good		GAUGE LOCATION	N. Chester/ Huntington
DATE LAST CHECKED	1997		WATER LEVEL INFO.	
RUNOFF PATTERN	n		http://water.usgs.gov/public/realtime.html	

When the water is up, the Middle Branch offers a fast, sassy romp that'll challenge open boaters and even give closed boats a good time. Continuous rapids with rocks and haystacks, a good gradient, and backwoods scenery are typical. No rapids need be scouted, although the pace is almost nonstop. A road parallels the river, even though it isn't always seen. The last half-mile before Littleville Dam is a little harder than the rest; here the Middle Branch rushes madly through a narrow section, twisting and churning over the many rock patterns.

The easiest way to reach the Middle Branch is to meet in Huntington, Massachusetts, cross the Route 112 bridge over the West Branch, make a 170° left turn on Basket Road, then follow the signs to Dayville Recreation Area. It may also be reached from the north by turning south off Route 143 in West Worthington onto River Road, which parallels the Middle Branch. This turn is not obvious. From River Road, turn on Kinne Brook Road to reach the takeout in a parking lot just upstream of Littleville Dam. This road parallels the lower, harder section and is usually snow covered early in the spring.

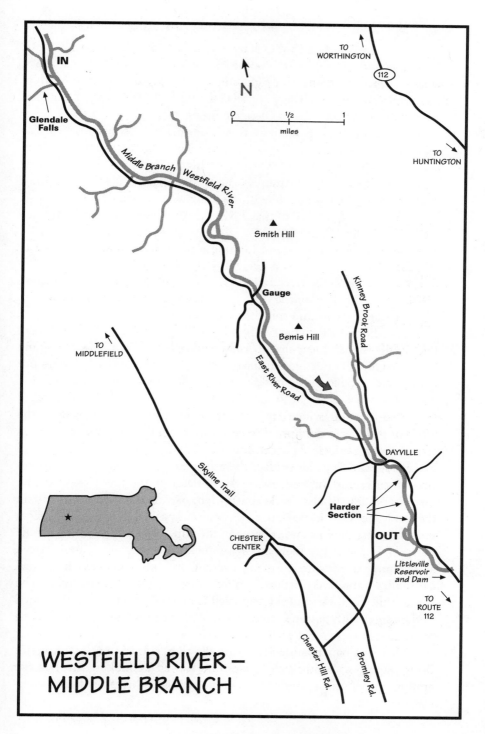

TO
WORTHINGTON

112

TO
HUNTINGTON

IN

**Glendale
Falls**

N

| 0 | 1/2 | 1 |

miles

Middle Branch Westfield River

▲
Smith Hill

Kinney Brook Road

Gauge

▲
Bemis Hill

TO
MIDDLEFIELD

East River Road

Skyline Trail

DAYVILLE

**Harder
Section**

OUT

CHESTER
CENTER

Littleville
Reservoir
and Dam

TO
ROUTE
112

WESTFIELD RIVER –
MIDDLE BRANCH

Chester Hill Rd.

Bromley Rd.

There is no special spot to start a trip, since the road is always close. However, a suggested spot is some 3.2 miles north of North Chester, where there is a field on river right and a rock ledge narrows the width to less than a boat length. There are several houses also. This is just north of a small bridge which crosses Glendale Brook.

It is impractical to detail all rapids on this trip because there are so many and all are quite similar in character. The difficulty is class II–II+ in low water and class III in medium or high. There are countless little ledges, haystacks, and hydraulics, none being particularly dangerous. Almost every turn has a rapid with standing waves and a strong current—none requires a great deal of maneuvering. At higher levels a doubly paddled canoe will take on water.

In a straight section, about 1.0 mile above North Chester, there is a 1- to 2-foot dam that can be run safely anywhere. You can recognize it by the line it forms across the river and the smooth water just upstream. A small pool is located below on the left, closely followed by several fast, narrow, winding channels around some islands.

Just before the thriving metropolitan village of North Chester is seen, the Middle Branch turns sharply right, with a 1- to 2-foot ledge preceding the actual turn. This ledge is usually run on the extreme right or left, since there is a hydraulic in the middle. A short, steep-sided gorge full of fast-water and a few rocks at lower levels follows. In 2.0 to 2.5 miles, you'll reach the Dayville Bridge; the excitement reduces in intensity along the way. For those who don't want to continue down the harder section (class III), Dayville Bridge is a good takeout.

Below the Dayville Bridge, there is a small pool in low water or a smooth current in medium water. The outlet from the pool is on the right, then the Middle Branch loops sharply left. As you enter this turn, stay on the inside, because several large rocks prevent passage on the outside. This section is very narrow and faster than the trip above. This first turn is the sharpest. In low water there are many rocks to avoid, which are replaced at medium levels with a strong current, lots of haystacks, and small hydraulics. Low levels definitely offer more interesting maneuvers. The end of this section and of the trip itself is marked by a low boulder patch in the center with passages on either side; it is covered at a gauge reading of 2.5 to 3.0.

There is a hand-painted gauge on the right side of the North Chester Bridge support (Smith Road). It can be viewed by looking through the grating of the bridge floor or by walking across to the east side and looking down.

North Branch of the Westfield River (Mass.)

Cummington to Chesterfield Gorge
Trip A

DISTANCE (MILES)	7.2		TOO LOW	0/4.9
SHUTTLE (MILES)	5.4		LOW	1
AVG. DROP (FEET/MILE)	36		MED.	2/6.9
MAX. DROP (FEET/MILE)	60		HIGH	
DIFFICULTY	III		TOO HIGH	
SCENERY	Good		GAUGE LOCATION	Rte 9 Bridge/Huntington
DATE LAST CHECKED	1997		WATER LEVEL INFO.	
RUNOFF PATTERN	n			http://water.usgs.gov/public/realtime.html

This trip on the North Branch is probably one of the most pleasant to be experienced. Moderate rapids, delightful scenery, and an isolated stretch of river all greet the paddler on a crisp spring morning. And, if your friends show up on time, you have the start of a good day.

This trip is ideally suited for open boats, since the water is seldom overwhelmingly high. The rapids are mostly straightforward, yet it takes a fair amount of finesse to negotiate them with grace. Once Route 9 leaves the river, the boater enters a section that is isolated from all roads, and this part contains the main rapids. If the water is low, the run will be highly annoying, as you'll be scraping over one rock after another.

One good starting point for this trip is at an old iron bridge on Route 9 that is south and east of Cummington. There are also other spots on Route 9 downstream from this bridge in the form of roadside turnoffs. At the bridge, the Westfield is about 75 feet wide and smooth flowing. From the iron bridge to the entrance of the Swift River (2.2

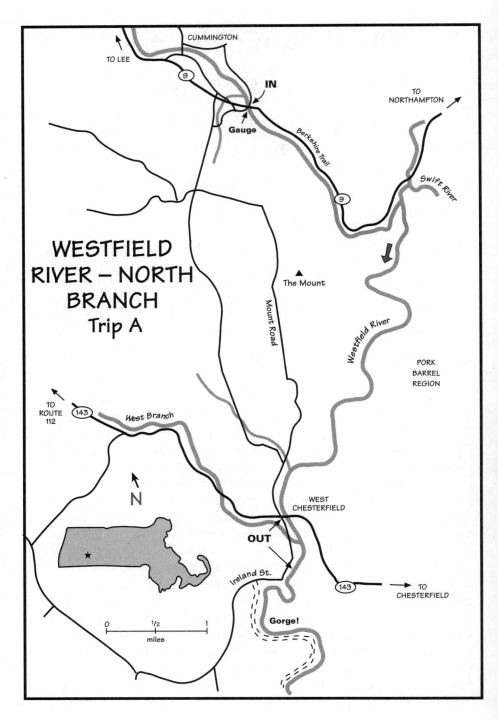

WESTFIELD
RIVER – NORTH
BRANCH
Trip A

CUMMINGTON

TO LEE

9

IN

Gauge

Berkshire Trail

9

TO
NORTHAMPTON

Swift River

The Mount

Westfield River

PORK
BARREL
REGION

Mount Road

TO
ROUTE
112

143

West Branch

N

WEST
CHESTERFIELD

OUT

143

TO
CHESTERFIELD

Ireland St.

Gorge!

0   1/2   1
miles

miles), the canoeing will depend on the water level. If the level is low, irritating rock-dodging is in order, whereas medium or high water covers these obstacles with easily run haystacks. There should be nothing dangerous or complicated here.

Entering from the left side, the Swift River adds its volume to the Westfield, which makes a 120° turn to the right into a section known locally as the Pork Barrel, which drops an average of 40 feet per mile. In low water, a small standing wave appears slightly downstream from the mouth of the Swift, but it disappears at medium levels. At this point, Route 9 leaves the scene regardless of water level. The Westfield then meanders through a relatively inaccessible valley until a road comes close on the right side. This road signals the end of the Pork Barrel region, which has rapids containing 2- and 3-foot haystacks in medium water. Most of the heavier waves can be avoided by careful maneuvering. There are no "interesting" rapids or ones that need to be scouted in the Pork Barrel, unless a tree is trying to get into the act. There are several sharp turns, though, and the current can be strong. This section is rated class III in medium water, class II in low water. It should present little challenge to the experienced; however, be aware that you are relatively isolated from civilization during this portion of the trip, which can be a problem if you need help.

Past the Route 143 bridge, the river is rather shallow. Between here and the Chesterfield Gorge, there are several standing-wave rapids, the last in a right turn ending in a long pool with a beach area on the right. Take out here, since there are no more convenient places before the Chesterfield Gorge. The gorge itself is sometimes runnable, depending on water level, type of boat, strength of party, etc. The most difficult spot requires negotiating a sharp 3- to 4-foot drop followed almost immediately by a complicated maneuver through some rocks. Although the gorge is not very long, the walls are precipitous, and it is well worth a visit. The entrance to the gorge is in a very sharp left turn.

To shuttle for this trip, proceed north from the iron bridge on Route 9 for several hundred yards, turn left onto Fairgrounds Road, take the left fork at the fairgrounds, and continue past the Route 143 bridge to an old graveyard, shaded by a large tree, on the left side of the road. There is a private road leading to the river here. Ask permission before using this road for a takeout, though. If for some reason you can't use this road, take out at the Route 143 bridge. In any case, be sure that you know where the gorge is, so you don't venture in unknowingly.

There is a hand-painted gauge on the right downstream side of the Route 9 bridge at the start. The Huntington gauge reading is on the West Branch. It is given for cross-reference and because its readings are reported on the USGS web page at http://water.usgs.gov/public/realtime.html. This page also gives readings for the Knightville Dam on the North Branch just below the Chesterfield Gorge. However, the reservoir above the dam is able to hold a fair amount of water, so what's going out is not always a good indicator of what's coming in.

For another river in the area that is similar in difficulty to this trip, try the Middle Branch or the lower part of the West Branch of the Westfield.

North Branch of the Westfield River (Mass.)

Chesterfield Gorge to Knightville Dam

Trip B

DISTANCE (MILES)	9.2		TOO LOW	0
SHUTTLE (MILES)	16		LOW	1
AVG. DROP (FEET/MILE)	12		MED.	2/6.9
MAX. DROP (FEET/MILE)	40		HIGH	
DIFFICULTY	I–III		TOO HIGH	
SCENERY	Good		GAUGE LOCATION	Rte 9 Bridge/Huntington
DATE LAST CHECKED	1997		WATER LEVEL INFO.	
RUNOFF PATTERN	n		http://water.usgs.gov/public/realtime.html	

This section of the North Branch shows both white- and flatwater. The rapids are mostly straightforward, and none should require any scouting. However, as the trip progresses and nears the Knightville Dam, the current slows to a stop, so the boater must provide some locomotion. This trip is away from main roads, although there is a dirt road that follows the river almost the whole way.

If you are looking for a class II trip, put in below the Chesterfield Gorge—start above it and you'll go up a notch or two in difficulty. A small dirt road off the main road leads to the gorge and beyond (see map for details). This dirt road is class IV, extremely tough going, especially in wet weather when the road offers more of a challenge than the river.

The rapids below the gorge are similar in character to those above. There are several noteworthy stretches: the first two merely involve haystacks in turns, whereas the next requires maneuvering through a short section of large boulders. These will be in the class II–III range depending

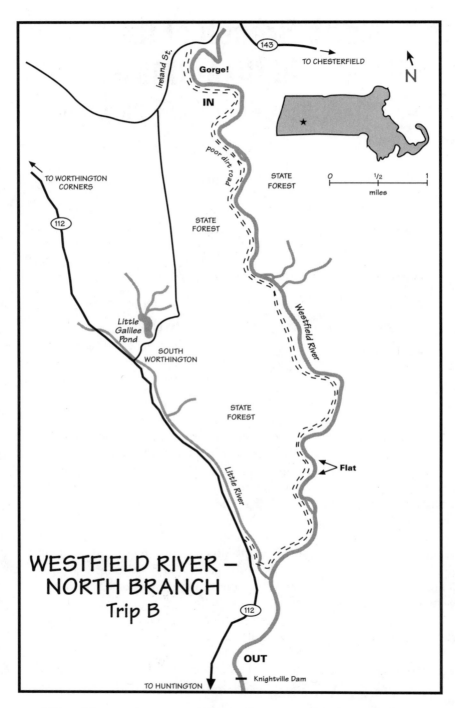

143

TO CHESTERFIELD

Ireland St.

Gorge!

IN

N

poor dirt road

STATE
FOREST

TO WORTHINGTON
CORNERS

112

STATE
FOREST

Westfield River

Little
Galilee
Pond

SOUTH
WORTHINGTON

STATE
FOREST

Flat

Little River

0   ½   1
miles

**WESTFIELD RIVER –
NORTH BRANCH
Trip B**

112

OUT

TO HUNTINGTON   Knightville Dam

356   *Massachusetts, Connecticut, and Rhode Island*

on water level. The last rapid is easy to recognize because the rocks seem to extend across the river. Passageways exist on both right and left. The right channel requires a slight left turn, then a slight right turn. The left channel requires a slightly sharper right turn. Downstream, an overhead cable signals the end of the interesting water, although one more set of rapids remains. As you approach Knightville Dam the current slackens, the scenery becomes flatter, and the canoeing is lakelike.

One of the more difficult things about this trip is the shuttle. Proceed back to Chesterfield and take Route 143 north to Worthington Corners, and then take Route 112 south to just above the dam. A shoddy-looking road leads to the river. Alternatively, cars can be left at the dam itself. It is also possible to proceed south on the main road from West Chesterfield, pass the gorge and Little Galilee Pond, and finally connect with Route 112.

The gauge for this section is on the right downstream side of the Route 9 iron bridge near Cummington. The Huntington gauge is on the West Branch, and is given as a reference because it reports readings to the USGS web site.

North Branch of the Westfield River (Mass.)
Knightville Dam to Huntington
Trip C

DISTANCE (MILES)	5.2		**TOO LOW**	n/a
SHUTTLE (MILES)	5.5		**LOW**	4.5
AVG. DROP (FEET/MILE)	17		**MED.**	5
MAX. DROP (FEET/MILE)	45		**HIGH**	n/a
DIFFICULTY	III		**TOO HIGH**	n/a
SCENERY	Fair		**GAUGE LOCATION**	Knightville Dam
DATE LAST CHECKED	1997		**WATER LEVEL INFO.**	
RUNOFF PATTERN	d/r		http://water.usgs.gov/public/realtime.html	

This trip on the Westfield covers much of the course where an annual downriver race takes place during the first weekend in April. The race lasts for about 10.0 miles; it demands endurance, strength, the ability to maneuver a boat around rocks, and a little something to keep you warm after a cold swim. Water on this run is supplied by the outflow of Knightville Dam, which is always a factor when this trip is under consideration. Usually the outflow is an advantage, because you can find out ahead of time if there will be a water release and how much. This part of the North Branch is by far the biggest of the three trips described. It is also significantly larger than any other river section of the Westfield system discussed in this book. The rapids offer varied difficulties, ranging from heavy water to intricate rock-picking. Bear in mind also that rescues will be difficult because of the large size of the riverbed and a possible strong current. Discharges in the spring of several thousand cfs are not unusual.

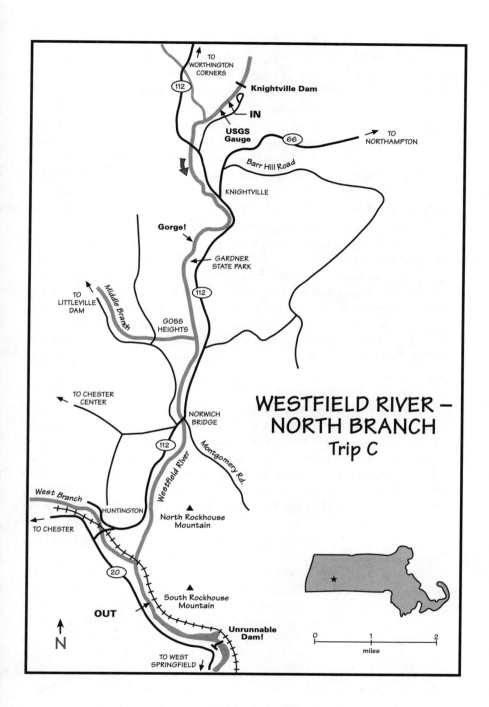

TO
WORTHINGTON
CORNERS

112

Knightville Dam

IN

TO
NORTHAMPTON

66

USGS
Gauge

Barr Hill Road

KNIGHTVILLE

Gorge!

GARDNER
STATE PARK

112

TO
LITTLEVILLE
DAM

Middle Branch

GOSS
HEIGHTS

TO CHESTER
CENTER

NORWICH
BRIDGE

112

Montgomery Rd.

WESTFIELD RIVER –
NORTH BRANCH
Trip C

Westfield River

West Branch

HUNTINGTON

TO CHESTER

North Rockhouse
Mountain

20

South Rockhouse
Mountain

OUT

N

Unrunnable
Dam!

TO WEST
SPRINGFIELD

0   1   2
miles

Westfield River, North Branch   359

Start this trip near a picnic area downstream from Knightville Dam, where the river has plenty of rocks and a fast current. A class II warm-up leads to an easy ripple just before a right turn. After the first left turn, there is a set of haystacks measuring 1 to 2 feet in height at a gauge reading of 4.8. Past a bridge and a flat stretch, watch out for strainers on river right. Soon another wavy rapid in a left turn awaits the eager paddler. Some houses on the left mark a drop through a long rapid, rather straightforward in medium water but rocky in low water, requiring a zigzag course. The river is very wide here, so there's plenty of room for maneuvering. A large boulder on the right marks the end, while a similar one in the middle of the river marks the beginning of still another rapid.

A left turn uncovers a large, picturesque pool with a camping area on the left and a precipitous rock cliff on the right. Downstream, a short gorge section forms. There are two well-defined sets of rapids here, both of which have easy and hard routes. The first rapid is about 25 yards long and is most straightforwardly run on the right, where there is fast water. The extreme left has a narrow chute between the bank and a rock. In the middle, the riverbed drops a little more abruptly, creating standing waves of 2 to 3 feet at a gauge reading of 4.8. The center outflow is turbulent, and there are strong eddies on either side.

After a slight hesitation, the river moves on to the second drop. A shallow island divides the river here into a channel at either extreme. The left side, known as the Bypass, is easier and safer, with a small series of tricky haystacks starting a narrow passage. The current is fast, and the eddies are shifty. The right side of the riverbed is a different story. Subdivided still more by several large boulders, the right channel has most of the water pouring through another narrow channel. Pass just to the right of the large subdividing boulder, then move left to avoid two huge, powerful haystacks that are in the middle of the river, spaced about 25 feet apart. Look this stretch over if you haven't seen it before—it is the heaviest on the trip.

The going then becomes easy. The Middle Branch enters and the next bridge announces the beginning of an easy haystack rapid. After this, and passing what appears to be an old iron bridge or dam support on the right bank, the Westfield starts falling through a boulder patch more rapidly than before. After a brief halt, another boulder patch follows. Both sets of rapids are good class III rock-dodging practice, so they present ample opportunity to pin your canoe around a rock. Both sections can be seen from the road, and during the downriver race in April this area is clogged with spectators. During the course of the day, they usually get some good viewing. The open-canoe route here is to the extreme left in medium to high water, in the middle when the river is low.

Next you pass two bridges, the West Branch joins in from the right, and the Westfield turns left. The takeout normally used is found shortly downstream by a picnic area at a roadside turnoff on the right shore.

The gauge is located on the left bank 0.2 mile downstream from Knightville Dam. The external staffs are scattered about, so keep looking. Information about water releases can be obtained from the USGS web site.

If you would like another trip of similar difficulty (although it is a little smaller), try trip B on the West Branch of the Westfield. (Trip A is a little harder than both trip B and this trip.)

West Branch of the Westfield River (Mass.)

Bancroft to Chester
Trip A

DISTANCE (MILES)	6		**TOO LOW**	5.1
SHUTTLE (MILES)	6.3		**LOW**	5.9
AVG. DROP (FEET/MILE)	50		**MED.**	6.9
MAX. DROP (FEET/MILE)	100		**HIGH**	
DIFFICULTY	III–IV		**TOO HIGH**	
SCENERY	Excellent		**GAUGE LOCATION**	Huntington
DATE LAST CHECKED	1997		**WATER LEVEL INFO.**	
RUNOFF PATTERN	n/f		http://water.usgs.gov/public/realtime.html	

To reach Bancroft, go north on Route 20 about 2.2 miles past Chester to Bancroft Road, which angles off to the right up a steep hill. If the rocks in the river are covered at Bancroft, expect a roller-coaster ride below. However, if they are somewhat bare, a fair amount of maneuvering will be called for in several spots. Most rapids are followed by pools. In several places the channel is quite narrow, so fallen trees could be a real hazard, especially at higher levels. A railroad follows the river, but there are no roads close by until the Middleville Road approaches near the end, so the trip is somewhat isolated. The first 3.0 miles of the trip are definitely the most exciting; thereafter the rapids are more straightforward, although there is still a strong current. This trip is rated class III–IV depending on water level.

For a longer run with more-exciting water, you can put in 3.5 miles upstream of Bancroft in Becket. This class IV section has several technical rapids and one innocuous-looking wooden crib dam that has been

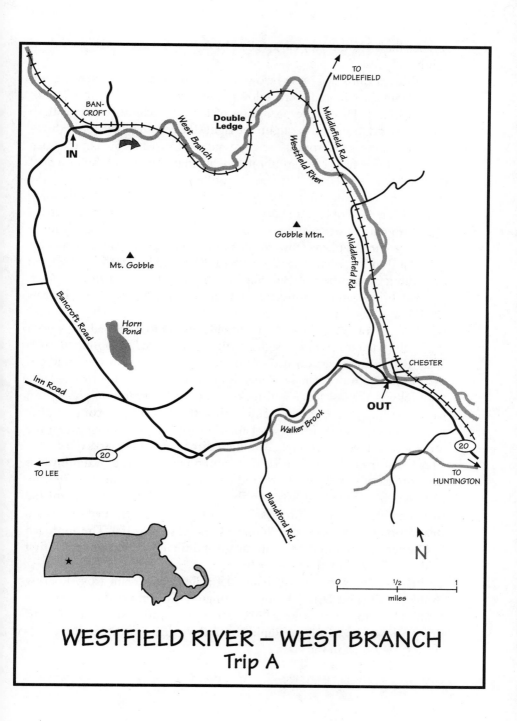

WESTFIELD RIVER – WEST BRANCH
Trip A

responsible for some very close calls. Don't take this seemingly easy drop lightly.

About a third of a mile below the start in Bancroft, a small stream enters from the left, and there follows a fair-sized flat section at the tip of a small island. This is the beginning of a fairly technical section. Both routes around the island are tight; the right side is preferable. About three-quarters of the way around the right side are two narrow chutes, each dropping 1 to 2 feet. They are about a boat length apart and can be a boat width wide in low water. They are a bit of a surprise, as they come at the end of a left turn and cannot be seen very far in advance. Afterwards, there is a very small pool and a short, intense rock garden leading to a sharp right turn with a rock wall on the outside. After a brief section of calmer water, the current pushes toward the right bend and the path narrows for a 100-yard rock garden. The river valley is deep and isolated here, far from everything except the railroad. Shortly, the river turns left under a high railroad bridge and continues to fall around rocks and down narrow channels.

In one straight section, the Westfield appears to be closed in by both banks and then drops out of sight. At this spot two ledges, about 20 yards apart with a total vertical drop of 4 feet, are runnable in the middle if there's enough water. The last ledge is more abrupt than the first. A large pool follows the last ledge and makes an excellent swimming hole. At a gauge reading of 6.9, the hydraulic below this last drop becomes rather mean and ugly, so you may want to scout for the best course when the water level is medium or high. Another railroad crossing marks the downstream exit from the pool. From this point onward, the rapids diminish in intensity except for a few drops and a ledge (low water) shortly after the approach of Middlefield Road on the left. This road comes close for the first time after two more railroad bridges are passed. In medium water, this section is fast moving, with many haystacks (class III). The approach to Chester is straightforward with no great difficulties. Take out at the first bridge in Chester by the Chester Inn.

The gauge is on the left bank, 0.4 mile downstream from Roaring Brook on Skyline Drive. From Huntington Center, go north over the Route 112 bridge and make a 170° degree turn onto Basket Road. Follow this road past Broken Dam Rapids until the gauge is sighted on the outside of a left turn in the river.

West Branch of the Westfield River (Mass.)

Chester to Huntington
Trip B

DISTANCE (MILES)	7.5		TOO LOW	4.9
SHUTTLE (MILES)	7.5		LOW	5.9
AVG. DROP (FEET/MILE)	30		MED.	6.9
MAX. DROP (FEET/MILE)	40		HIGH	
DIFFICULTY	II–III		TOO HIGH	
SCENERY	Fair		GAUGE LOCATION	Huntington
DATE LAST CHECKED	1997		WATER LEVEL INFO.	
RUNOFF PATTERN	n/f		http://water.usgs.gov/public/realtime.html	

This lower section of the West Branch is somewhat wider and has less of a gradient than its upstream counterpart. With well-defined rapids, mostly of the standing-wave variety, and many islands that divide the main channel into fast, narrow chutes, this trip presents a sporty run for advanced beginners. It is also a good place to try out old techniques in a new boat. The rapids are usually followed by patches of quieter water and occasionally by a stretch where little discernible current can be found. If the upper part is too low, this section can still be runnable. At medium levels, it is rated class III. Route 20 parallels this section of the West Branch, and a secondary road also follows along on the north side the last half of the trip.

Put in at the upstream bridge in Chester near the Chester Inn. Here the river is more than 100 feet wide and rather shallow. The main channel is on the right, although you can scrape along a short way on the left until you reach deeper water below. One hundred yards beyond this bridge a 6-

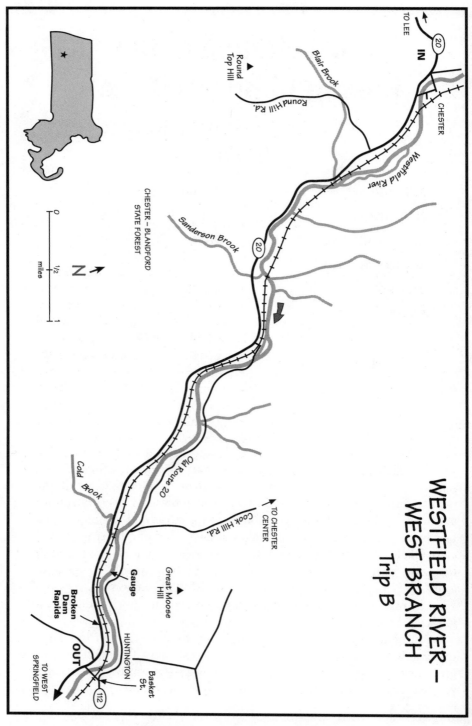

WESTFIELD RIVER —
WEST BRANCH

Trip B

to 12-inch ledge extends from the left bank to center stream. The right side is clear. Walker Brook also enters in this stretch.

After the first railroad bridge there are several hundred yards of standing waves, which are easy to run anywhere; after a brief pause there are more. These are typical of the rapids on this trip, with just a few being heavier (one or two stretches with rocks to avoid). An island then appears; either side is OK, although the right channel is livelier. Islands are a recurring theme.

Downstream somewhat, after a little less-interesting water, a slight right turn serves as an entrance to another long standing-wave rapid. This one is easily run, as there are few obstacles. You'll meet larger waves at the end. Look for a collection of abandoned cars enhancing the scenery on the right bank, then get ready to enter a nice chute in a slight left turn that has 2-foot waves at the bottom in low to medium water. The river then narrows and passes swiftly in a tight S-turn. Another railroad bridge signals still more standing waves, which approach the highway, then turn left. Beyond is a metal bridge, not open to general traffic since both sides are closed. Another island shortly below has a chute on the right side and tricky crosscurrents at the bottom. The left side is straight and fast.

Below the next railroad bridge, which should be run on the left since the right is full of trees and brush, the river turns right and approaches a short rapid that requires a bit of maneuvering around several large rocks. Three boulders, two in the right center and one on the left, force the paddler to the extreme right or to left center. A calm spot below is handy for regrouping. A few standing waves also get into the act here. Moving on, the paddler will pass several more islands and similar rapids.

The next major rapid is Gauging Station Rapid (class III). After a slight left turn, notice a concrete wall 5 feet high and 15 feet long on the left shore just before the next right turn. The river drops abruptly here, 2 feet on the extreme left. There is a chute with strong crosscurrents, a large standing wave in the center, and a small drop on the right side. In low water the approach is shallow, and in medium levels there is a good hydraulic following the drop on the left and center. This is the heaviest rapid yet encountered on the trip, and you may want to look at it beforehand if you are unsure of yourself. After a short stretch of quick but calmer water comes another class III rapid (in medium water).

Upon passing a small overhead bridge, look downstream for a large boulder on the left side of the river. This is a signal for the beginning of Broken Dam Rapid, which is rated class IV at medium levels. If you want to scout, it is best to do so from the left side by the boulder. On the right side, the main channel picks up speed, dodges a few rocks, and then turns sharply right, only to pile headlong into a stone wall. The current then turns abruptly left, pounding over several large, partially submerged rocks to fall finally into a hole and a series of standing waves. Overall, Broken Dam Rapid has water that is powerful and fast, and the whole rapid is tight. If you run it, alignment is critical. Miscalculate just a little, and you'll know what a rag feels like in a washing machine gone mad. At medium levels, only a huge boulder in the left center is visible as a landmark. This rapid is only about 30 yards long. The takeout in Huntington is shortly downstream, by a white church just before the Route 112 bridge.

The gauge is in Hampshire County, on the left bank 0.4 mile downstream from Roaring Brook on Skyline Drive. From Huntington Center take the Route 112 bridge over the river and immediately make a sharp left turn onto Basket Road. Follow this road past Broken Dam Rapid until the gauge is sighted.

For another trip of similar difficulty in the immediate area, try the Middle Branch of the Westfield.

Glossary

Big water—Rapids in which the volume and the water formations, such as holes and waves, are the main obstacles.

Boil—An area of strongly upwelling water, often seen at high levels and on big-water runs.

Boof—A technique used to run a steep drop that may be shallow at the base. By leaning back and running the drop at an angle, the boater can land flat on the hull with a resounding "BOOF!" and avoid pitoning on the rocks at the bottom. Boofing drops higher than about 10 feet can be hazardous to your spine.

Bow—The front of a boat.

Bow pin—To trap the bow of a boat at the base of a steep drop. Often the end of the boat is wedged between two rocks or timbers. Bow pinning can be fatal.

Broach—To pin sideways on a rock or to bridge between two rocks.

C-1—A single canoe with a deck that often looks to the uninitiated like a kayak. The paddler kneels and uses a single-bladed paddle.

C-2—A double canoe with a deck. Both paddlers kneel and use single-bladed paddles.

CFS—Cubic feet per second, the standard unit for measuring the flow in a river.

Channel—An area of a river defined by the banks, a bank and an island, a bank and a rock, or two rocks.

Chute—A steep channel that is often defined by a rock on either side.

Closed boat—A boat with a deck, such as a kayak, C-1, or C-2.

Crest—The high point on top of a wave.

Crosscurrent—A current that enters the main current from the side. Crosscurrents often exist on a small scale.

Discharge—The amount of water being released from a dam or passing a specific cross-sectional area in a given time interval, measured in cubic feet per second (cfs).

Downriver race—A point-to-point race on whitewater in which the only criterion is time from start to finish.

Drop—A section of a rapid, or an entire rapid, depending on the context.

Dryway—A section of river that has been dewatered due to a diversion project that takes water away from the natural riverbed and runs it through a canal or tube dropping at a lower gradient than the riverbed. When it reaches the powerhouse at the base of the dryway, the water from the canal is dropped through the turbines with a greater amount of head (vertical drop) than it had at the dam to generate hydropower. Releases into dryways have been a major focus of whitewater-access groups in recent years.

Eddy—A calm spot formed downstream of a rock or other obstruction in the riverbed. Eddies may be still or may move upstream. In big water, eddies are often turbulent and boily.

Eddy-hop—To scout a rapid by paddling from eddy to eddy, always being sure the next stopping place is within sight.

Eddy line—The shear zone where the current moving downstream meets the eddy water moving upstream. This is usually an area of whirlpools and boils.

Eddy turn—A maneuver that allows a paddler to stop in an eddy to scout, regroup, rest, or play. By using the current differential between the downstream current and the upstream-moving eddy water, a paddler can turn his boat quickly upstream after crossing the eddy line with speed at an appropriate angle.

Ender—An acrobatic maneuver in which a boater sticks one end of the boat into a strong downhill current in a hole or on the edge of a pourover, causing his boat to do a cartwheel end over end.

Eskimo roll / roll—A method of righting a canoe or kayak using the paddle and hips. An important recovery technique for intermediate and advanced boaters.

Falls—A large, abrupt drop. In the Northeast some rapids are known as falls, even though they do not drop abruptly.

Fastwater—Featureless water moving downstream.

Ferry—A maneuver that allows a paddler to get across the river without losing ground. To ferry you point one end of the boat upstream at an angle to the current and paddle against it to neutralize its force.

Flatwater—Water that is not moving, such as a lake or a pond.

Fold—An area where one current flows over another at oblique angles. Folds can be very unstable areas.

Gauge—An instrument used to measure the discharge in a river at a given time. Some gauges can be read from the river, and some must be read remotely.

Gnarl—Hairier than hair. Also known as "gnar" if you're way rad.

Gradient—The steepness of the riverbed, usually stated in feet per mile.

Hair—Whitewater that makes your hair stand on end.

Haystack—A tall, narrow standing wave.

Hole—A formation caused by water flowing over a rock or ledge and reversing back on itself at the base. The surface water flows upstream and is highly aerated (forming the "white" in "whitewater"), while deeper down, the current is flowing downstream and out of the hole. Holes can be friendly or vicious depending on the degree of recirculation, the steepness of the entry, and the volume of water involved.

Hydraulic—Same as a hole, although often used to describe the dangerous hole formed at the base of a dam.

Inflatable—A boat that relies on air pressure to maintain its shape and rigidity. Rafts, inflatable kayaks, and catarafts fit into this category.

Kayak, or K-1—A boat used on whitewater and flatwater that is highly maneuverable and can be rolled upside down and righted again without exiting. Kayak paddlers sit with their legs out in front of them and use double-bladed paddles.

Ledge—A rock shelf that extends most or part of the way across a river. Ledgy rivers often have a large number of holes.

Lining—To avoid running a rapid by guiding a boat (usually an open canoe or an inflatable) around it on the edges holding the bow and stern lines.

Low-head dam—A dam between 1 and 10 feet high that may look innocuous, but can often be a killer. Low-head dams often have very dangerous hydraulics at their bases.

Meander—What a river does naturally when it hits flatter terrain. Meanders eventually become oxbows.

Moving water—Same as fastwater.

OC-1 / OC-2—An open canoe for a single (OC-1) or double (OC-2) paddler.

Open boat—A boat without a deck, such as an open canoe.

Oxbow—A meander that has been cut off from the main river.

Pancake—Same as a boof, but more tasty.

Peel out—The opposite of an eddy turn, a peel out allows a paddler to leave an eddy and continue downstream.

Pillow—The water that piles up upstream of a rock or other obstruction, creating an area of boils and folds that tends to keep boaters off the rock. Not all rocks form pillows.

Pirouette—An ender in which, at the height of the cartwheel, the boater quickly spins the boat on its long axis, causing it to land upright.

Piton—To hit a rock dead on with the end of a boat, causing sudden deceleration and hardly ever causing any damage to the rock.

Play-boating—A paddling style that emphasizes surfing holes and waves, enders, and eddy-hopping.

Pool—A calm spot at the top or the bottom of a rapid. Also a good place to learn to roll in the winter.

Pop-up—An ender that doesn't go all the way over.

Portage—To carry a boat around a rapid or other obstruction. Always an honorable option.

Pourover—Water flowing in a fairly shallow sheet over a rock and creating a hole on the downstream side with a flat and often very powerful recirculation.

Put-in—The location from which a trip is started.

Rapid—A distinct stretch of whitewater that may last for as little as 50 feet or as much as a mile or more.

Rating table—A table showing the relationship between discharge in cfs and gauge reading in feet for a particular river.

Reactionary wave—A wave formed by water hitting an obstacle and rebounding off it. Often a sign that closer inspection is needed.

Retendo—An ender that keeps a boat and boater in a hole so they can repeat the maneuver posthaste.

Reversal—Same as a hole.

River left—The left side of the river, looking downstream.

River right—The right side of the river, looking downstream.

Rock garden—A rapid with numerous rocks.

Rodeo—A style of boating in which enders, retendos, cartwheels, and other acrobatic moves in a hole or other feature are done in very short, specially designed boats. Rodeo competitions are held from the local to the world-class level.

Rooster tail—A steep, irregular wave usually formed by water hitting an obstacle and spraying straight up in the air.

Run—A section of river done as a single trip.

S-Turn—A channel that bends first one way, then the other.

Scout—To look at a rapid from the shore in order to decide both if and where to run.

Seam line—An area where two currents meet at an acute angle.

Self-rescue—Any of a number of techniques that allow a boater to help himself after a capsize.

Shuttle—To drive vehicles to the takeout or put-in in preparation for running a river. Often the most complicated, time-consuming, and frustrating part of a river trip.

Slalom race—A whitewater race in which the object is to paddle between wooden poles, known as "gates," suspended above a rapid. The competition is judged based on speed and accuracy. Penalties are given for hitting or missing a gate and add time to a competitor's final score .

Souse hole—Same as a hole.

Splat—A squirt move in which the paddler does a bow or stern squirt on the pillow formed by a rock or a wall. This can result in a dangerous pin if the rock is not chosen carefully or the paddler is not skillful enough.

Squirting—A subculture of paddling in which very small boats with very sharp edges are used to perform such underwater and acrobatic moves as blasts, splats, screw-ups, and mystery moves.

Standing wave—A wave formed by one of three conditions: a narrowing of the riverbed, a steepening of the riverbed, or an increase in the volume of water. In contrast to ocean waves, standing waves don't generally move much upstream or downstream.

Stern—The back of a boat.

Stopper wave—A wave with a significant foam pile on top that can stop a boat and may, if powerful enough, back-ender it or cause it to surf for an indefinite period of time.

Strainer—Anything that allows water to pass through but keeps solid objects, such as boats and paddlers, from doing so. Especially common types of strainers are trees (especially on the outsides of bends), timber-crib dams, trash racks on dams, and, on the more urban rivers, shopping carts.

Surfing—A method of riding a wave or a hole in which a boat is made to stay in one place by careful placement on the river feature in question.

Can also be done unintentionally when a boater fails to punch through a hole with sufficient speed.

Swamp—To take on water in an open boat.

Takeout—The location at which a trip ends.

Technical—Used to describe rapids where rocks are the main obstacles.

Tidal rip—A rapid formed by a tidal current being squeezed into a narrow opening. Often a great place to paddle when nothing else is running.

Trough—The low point between two waves.

Undercut rock—A rock with an upstream face that overhangs the oncoming current and can trap debris and paddlers. Undercuts aren't always obvious, since the part of the rock exposed at the surface may not give any indication that the underwater part of the rock is undercut. Undercut rocks can be very dangerous.

Water reading—A skill that allows a boater to know what's downstream by picking up subtle hints from water formations ahead.

Watershed—The area drained by a river. Rivers with larger watersheds tend to have higher volumes and longer seasons.

Wave train—A series of standing waves in which the first wave is usually the largest, the second is usually the steepest, and the rest get smaller moving downstream.

Whitewater—Water moving downstream with rocks and other obstructions that form such features such as waves, holes, eddies, and drops.

Wildwater race—See *downriver race.*

Whitewater Clubs
in the Northeast

Adirondack Mountain Club, P.O. Box 867, Lake Placid, NY 12946

Appalachian Mountain Club, 5 Joy Street, Boston, MA 02108

Club Adventure, P. O. Box 184, Woodstock, VT 05091

Cornell Outdoor Education Program, Ithaca, NY 14850

Hampshire College Outdoor Program, Amherst, MA 01002

Housatonic Area Canoe and Kayak Squad, c/o Clarke Outdoors, Route 7, Cornwall, CT 06753

Kayak and Canoe Club of Boston, Boston, MA 02109

Kayak and Canoe Club of New York, New York, NY 10001

Ledyard Canoe Club, P. O. Box 9, Hanover, NH 03755

Marlboro College Outdoor Program, Marlboro, VT 05344

Merrimack Valley Paddlers, P. O. Box 233, Hollis, NH 03049

Metropolitan Canoe and Kayak, Brooklyn, NY 11201

Mount Washington Valley Paddlers, Franconia, NH 03580

Moxie Gore Paddling Club, South Paris, ME 04281

Penobscot Paddle and Chowder Society, Stillwater, ME 04489

Rhode Island Canoe Association, Providence, RI 02904

University of Massachusetts Outing Club, Amherst, MA 01002

Vermont Paddlers Club, 11 Discovery Road, Essex Junction, VT 05452

About the Author

Bruce Lessels started paddling at the age of 15 with the Boston AMC. He has run rivers in many states as well as Europe, South America, and Asia. Bruce was a member of the U.S. Whitewater Team from 1984 to 1988 and won an individual bronze and a team gold medal in C-1 in the 1987 World Whitewater Championships in Bourg St. Maurice, France.

He has written articles for *Canoe and Kayak, River Runner, Paddler, US Air, Hour Detroit, AMC Outdoors,* and *Snow Country* magazines. He is the author of the *Whitewater Handbook*, published by the AMC, and the *Deerfield River Guidebook*, which is now out of print.

He and his wife, Karen, started Zoar Outdoor, an outdoor center on the Deerfield River in Charlemont, Massachusetts, in 1989, which they now run when they are not running after their two young daughters. Bruce has a B.A. in Geology from Amherst College.

About the AMC

Since 1876, the Appalachian Mountain Club has promoted the protection, enjoyment, and wise use of the mountains, rivers, and trails of the Northeast. The AMC believes that successful, long-term conservation depends on first-hand experience and enjoyment of the outdoors. The AMC is a nonprofit organization whose membership of more than 76,000 members enjoy hiking, canoeing, skiing, walking, rock climbing, bicycling, camping, kayaking, and backpacking, while safeguarding the environment. All AMC programs and facilities are open to the public.

AMC Huts & Lodges
AMC offers unique lodging throughout the Northeast. Spend a night at one of eight huts, each a day's hike apart, in the White Mountains of New Hampshire, or drive to Bascom Lodge atop Mt. Greylock in western Massachusetts. Also accessible by car are Pinkham Notch Lodge and Crawford Hostel in New Hampshire, and Mohican Outdoor Center in the Delaware Water Gap of western New Jersey.

AMC Outdoor Adventures
Whether you're new to the outdoors or an old hand, the AMC offers workshops and guided trips that will teach you new skills, refine your expertise, or just get you outside in good company. Choose from more than 100 workshops and adventures offered in New Hampshire, Massachusetts, New York, and New Jersey. Whether you're going solo, with your family and kids, or with friends, there is something for everyone.

Each of our 11 chapters—from Maine to Washington, D.C.—offers hundreds of activities close to home. Chapter leaders arrange hiking and bicycling trips and teach the basics of cross-country skiing, whitewater and flatware canoeing, and other outdoor skills.

Volunteering
If you like to hike, discover the lasting satisfaction that comes with volunteering to maintain or build trails. No experience is necessary—we'll teach you what you need to know. The AMC leads volunteer trail building and

maintenance crews throughout the Northeast. Our professional and volunteer crews take great pride in maintaining 1,400 miles of trails throughout the region.

Paddlers can also help clean up a river, monitor water quality, or help negotiate access with private landowners.

Conservation Leadership

Much of the Northeast's outdoor recreation opportunities would not be possible without a commitment to protecting land and keeping trails, rivers, and mountains accessible. Since its founding, the AMC has been at the forefront of the conservation movement. We're working to keep our air clean and healthy, our waterfalls clear, our rivers running free, and recreational activities open.

AMC Membership

Join the Appalachian Mountain Club and share the benefits of membership. Your membership includes a one-year subscription to *AMC Outdoors*, telling you where to go for outdoor recreation and keeping you informed on conservation issues throughout the Northeast. Members also enjoy discounts on AMC books, maps, workshops, and lodgings, as well as free affiliation to one of AMC's eleven chapters.

For more information on AMC, call 617-523-0636. To join, send a check for $40 for an adult, or $65 for a family to AMC Membership, 5 Joy Street, Boston, MA 02108; or call 617-523-0636 for payment by Visa or MasterCard. Find us on the web at www.outdoors.org.

Other Titles by AMC

AMC Books & Maps
The AMC publishes an extensive line of books. Our publications are available at most bookstores and outdoor retailers. To order by phone, call 800-262-4455, or order through the web at www.outdoors.org.

Paddling Skills

River Rescue, 3d edition	Slim Ray & Les Bechdel
AMC Whitewater Handbook, 3d edition	Bruce Lessels

Sea Kayaking Guides

Sea Kayaking along the New England Coast	Tamsin Venn
Sea Kayaking along the Mid-Atlantic Coast	Tamsin Venn

Canoe Guides

Quiet Water Canoe Guide: Maine	Alex Wilson & John Hayes
Quiet Water Canoe Guide: Massachusetts/ Connecticut/Rhode Island	Alex Wilson
Quiet Water Canoe Guide: New York	John Hayes & Alex Wilson
Quiet Water Canoe Guide: New Hampshire/Vermont	Alex Wilson

River Guides
AMC River Guide: Maine
AMC River Guide Massachusetts/Connecticut/Rhode Island
AMC River Guide: New Hampshire/Vermont

Notes